Mc
Graw
Hill

Cover and Title Page: Nathan Love

www.mheonline.com/readingwonders

Send all inquiries to:
McGraw-Hill Education
2 Penn Plaza
New York, NY 10121

ISBN: 978-0-02-132055-4
MHID: 0-02-132055-1

Printed in the United States of America

7 8 9 10 11 12 13 LMN 24 23 22 21 20

D

ELD
Companion Worktext

Program Authors
Diane August
Jana Echevarria
Josefina V. Tinajero

Think it Through

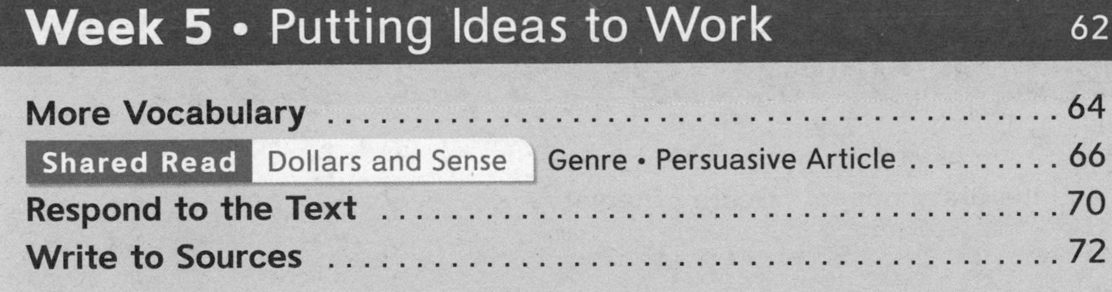

Amazing Animals

Week 3 • Natural Connections 100

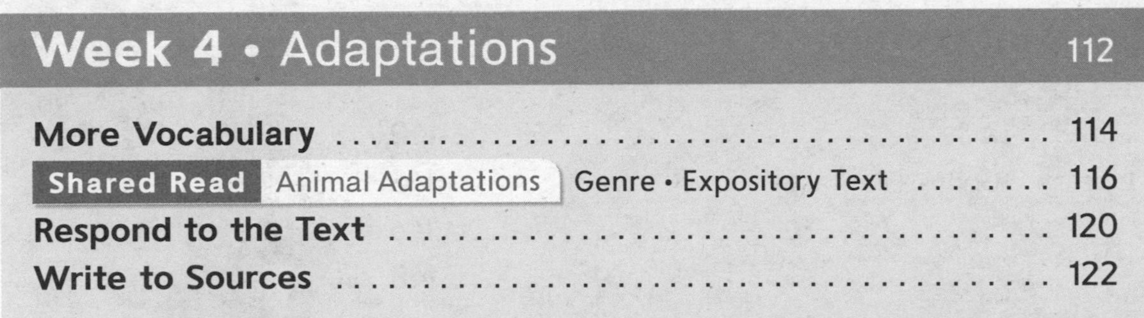

Week 4 • Adaptations 112

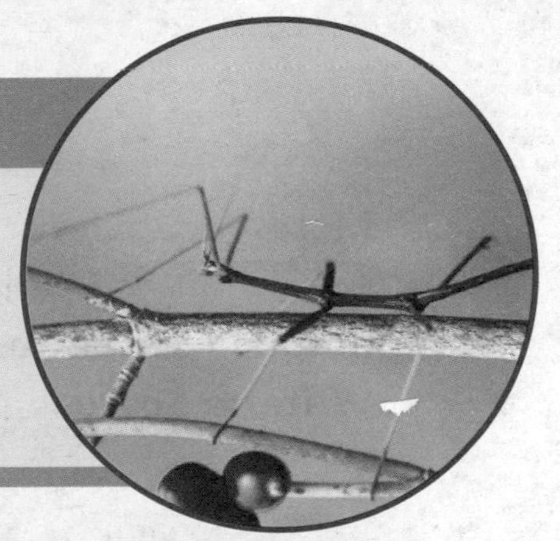

Week 5 • Animals All Around 124

THAT'S THE Spirit!

(t) Richard Johnson; (b) Jim Reed/Digital Vision/Getty Images

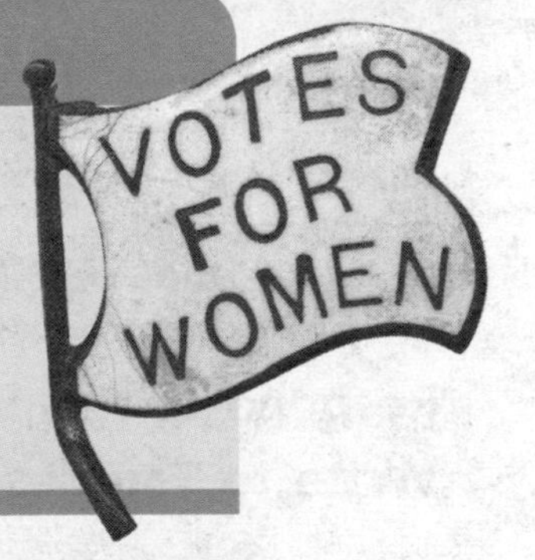
VOTES
FOR
WOMEN

Unit 4

FACT OR FICTION?

(t) R. G. Roth; (b) Chris Boyd

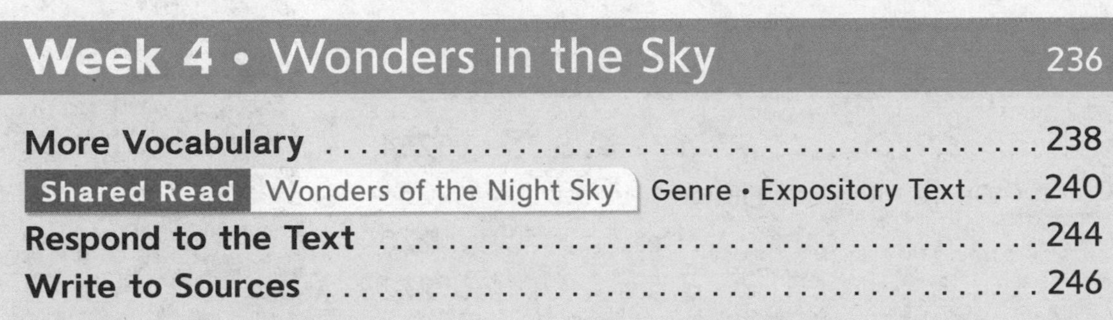

Figure It Out

(t) James Bernardin; (b) Josee Basaillon

Week 3 • Inventions 286

Week 4 • Zoom In 298

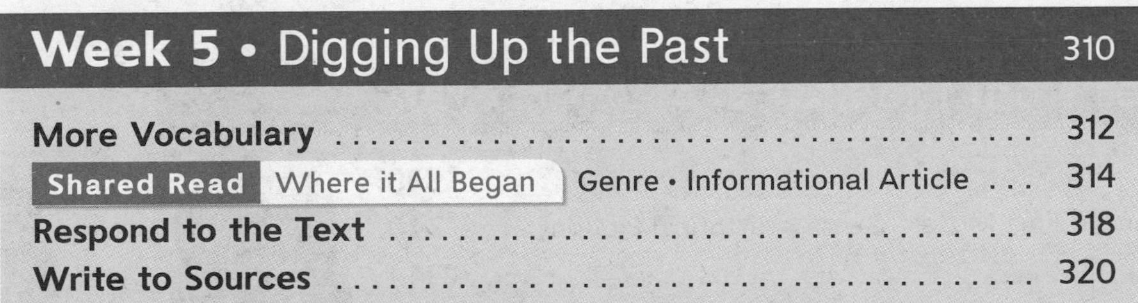

Week 5 • Digging Up the Past 310

Past, Present, and Future

(t) David McCall Johnston; (b) Neil Shigley

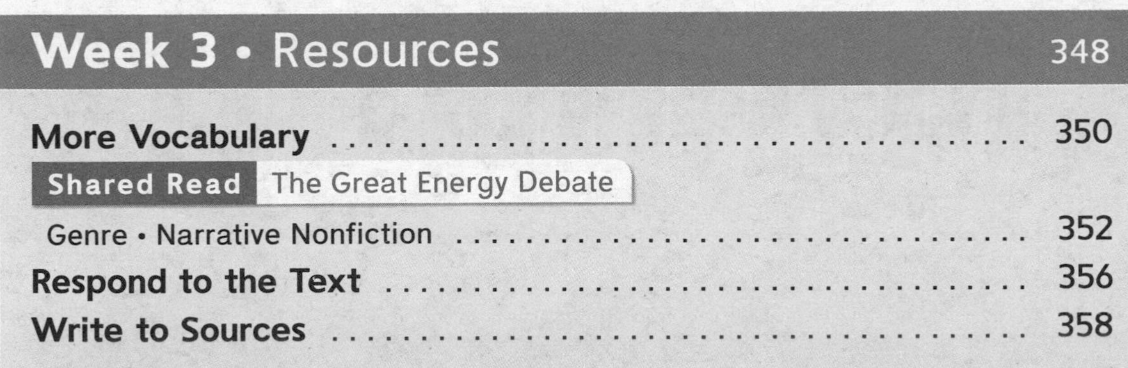

Week 3 • Resources 348

Week 4 • Money Matters 360

Week 5 • Finding My Place 372

Unit 1

Think it Through

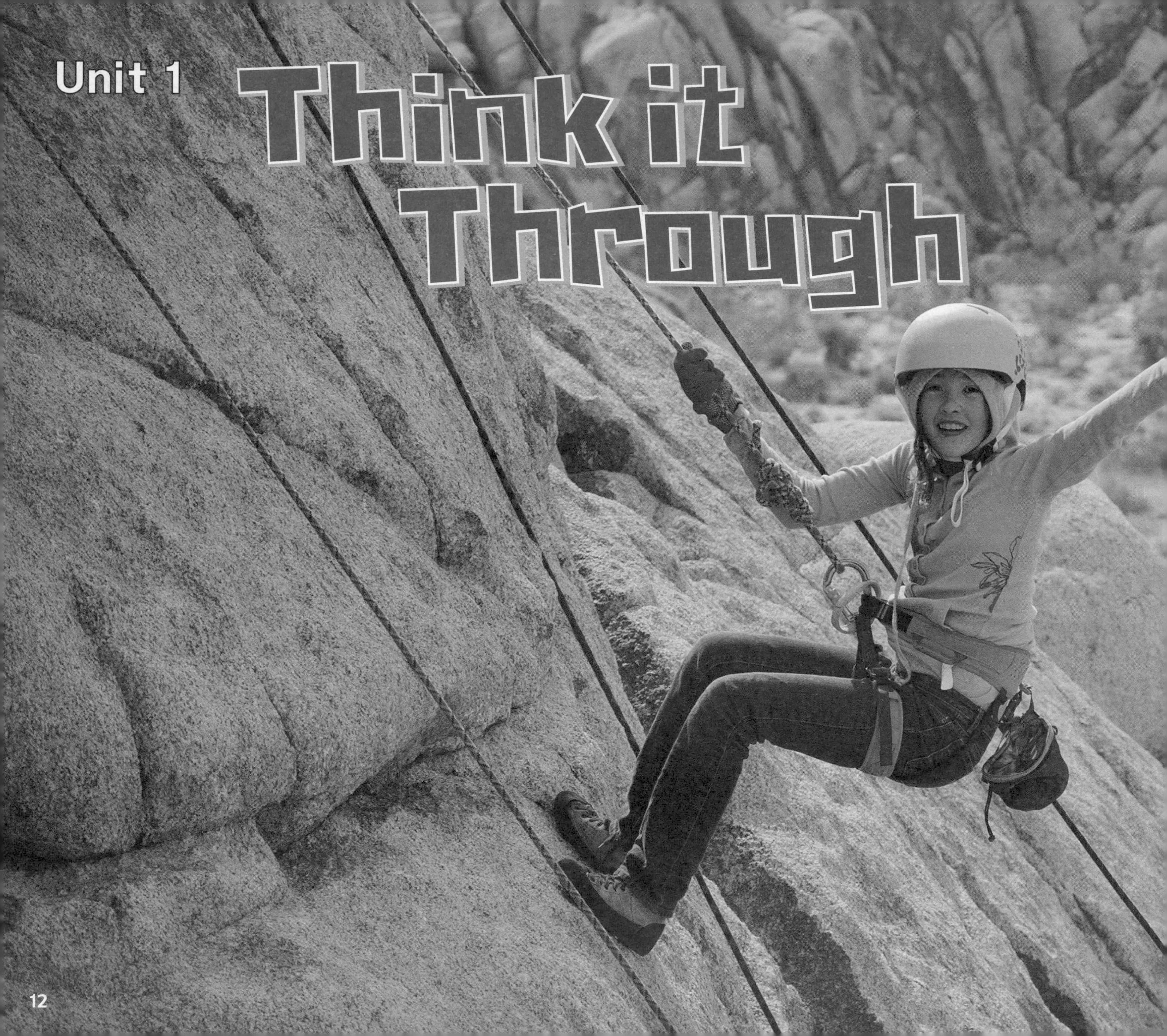

The Big Idea

How can a challenge bring out our best?

Stephen Simpson/Iconica/Getty Images

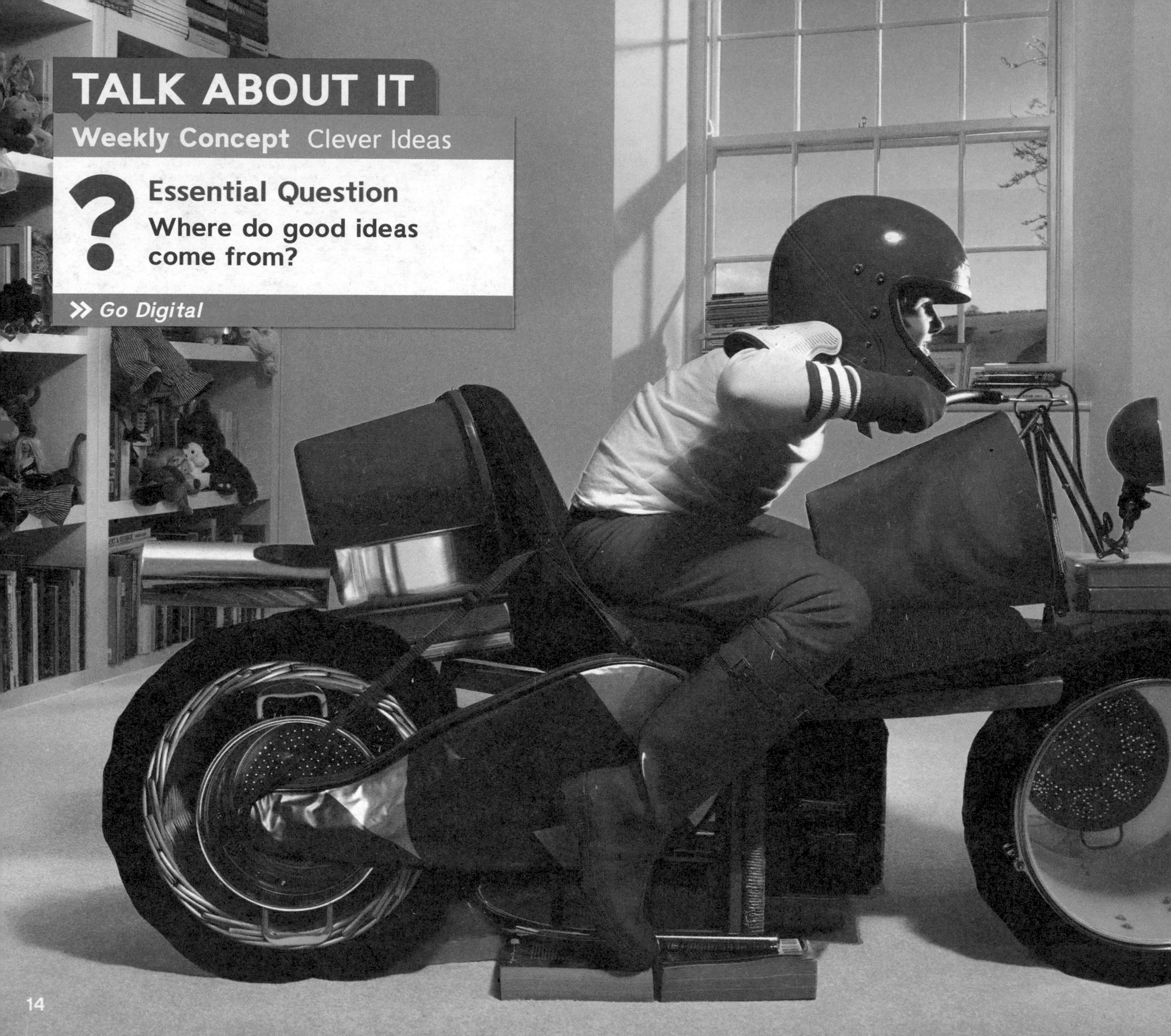

TALK ABOUT IT

Weekly Concept Clever Ideas

Essential Question

Where do good ideas come from?

» Go Digital

What idea does the boy have for a bike? In the idea web, write about the things he uses for a bike. Describe how people get good ideas.

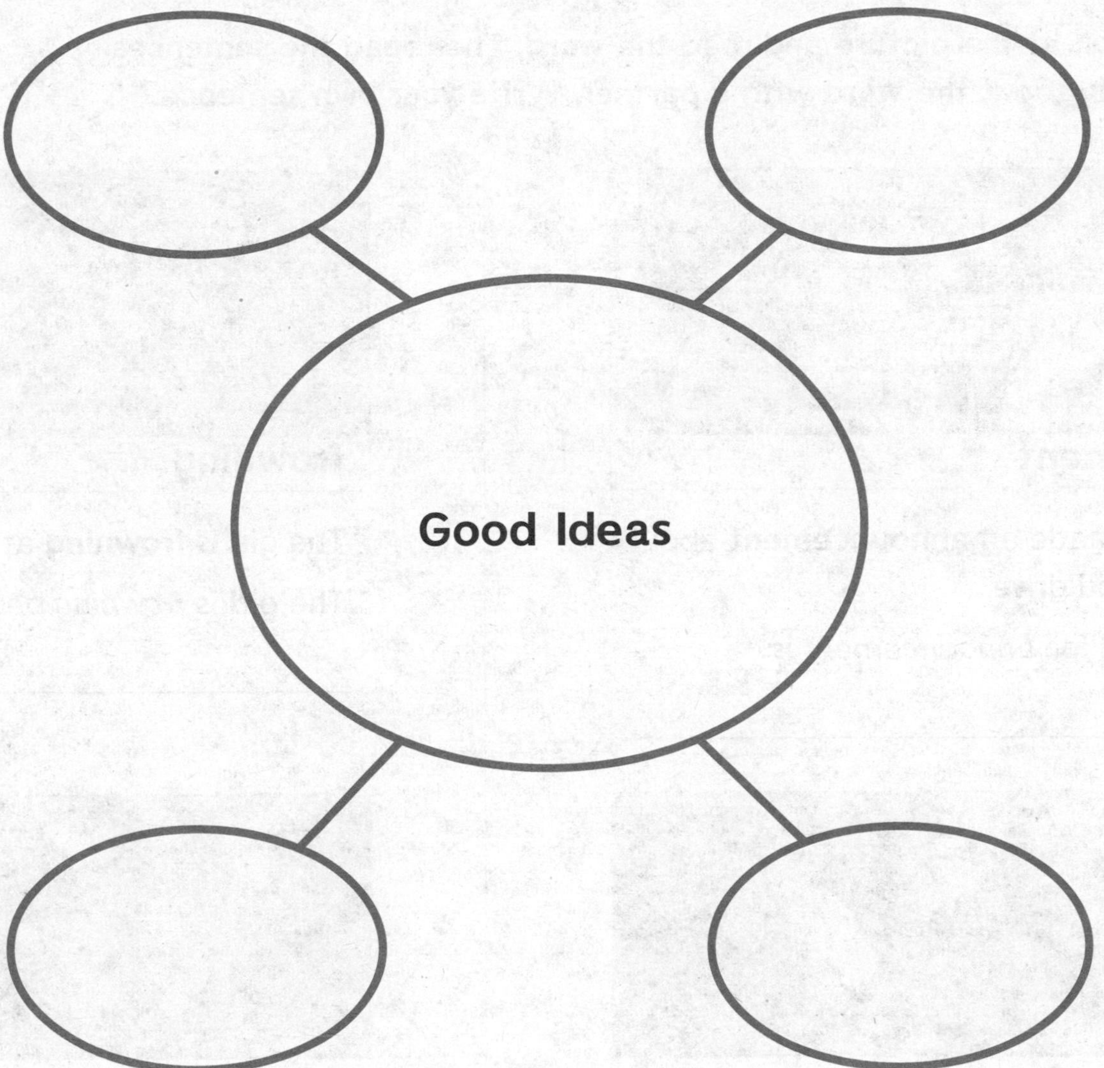

Discuss how the boy may have come up with the idea for the bike. Use the words from the chart. You can say:

The boy got his idea for a bike by ______________________________.

Tim Macpherson/Stone+/Getty Images

ELD.PI.4.1.Ex, ELD.PI.4.1.Br, ELD.PI.4.5.Ex, ELD.PI.4.5.Br, ELD.PI.4.12a.Ex, ELD.PI.4.12a.Br See the California Standards section.

More Vocabulary

Look at the picture and read the word. Then read the sentences. Talk about the word with a partner. Write your own sentence.

announcement

The student made an **announcement** about the school food drive.

Another word for *announcement* is

_______________________________________.

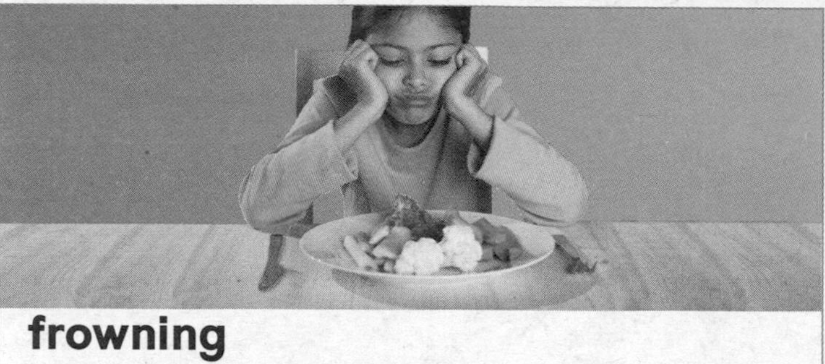

frowning

The girl is **frowning** at her food.

The girl is *frowning* because she __________

_______________________________________.

carved

The man **carved** wood to make a mask.

Other things that can be *carved* are _______

_______________________________________.

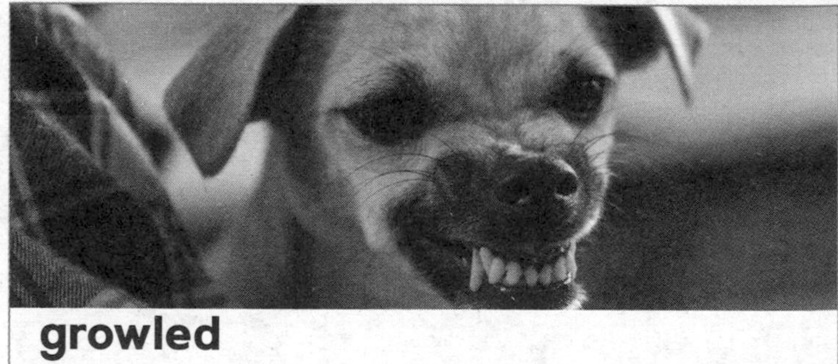

growled

The dog **growled** at the cat.

Another word for *growled* is _______________

_______________________________________.

 ELD.PI.4.1.Ex, ELD.PI.4.1.Br, ELD.PI.4.5.Ex, ELD.PI.4.5.Br, ELD.PI.4.12a.Ex, ELD.PI.4.12a.Br See the California Standards section.

huge

The ship is **huge**.

Some other things that are *huge* are

_______________ and _______________.

serious

The girl is **serious** about studying for a test.

I am *serious* about ____________________

____________________.

Words and Phrases
Phrasal Verbs

take up **= to occupy**
My family will <u>take up</u> residence in town.

sign up **= to join**
I will <u>sign up</u> for the team.

Read the sentences below. Write the phrasal verb that means the same as the underlined words.

We will <u>occupy</u> space on the top floor.

We will ________ space on the top floor.

I will be the first to <u>join</u> the club.

I will be the first to ________ for the club.

» *Go Digital* **Add these phrasal verbs to your New Words notebook. Write a sentence to show the meaning of each.**

Text Evidence

1 Talk About It

Look at the illustration. Read the title. Talk about what you see. Write your ideas.

What does this title tell you?

____

____

What is the dragon doing?

____

____

What kinds of problems does the dragon cause?

____

____

Take notes as you read the text.

Shared Read Genre • Fairy Tale

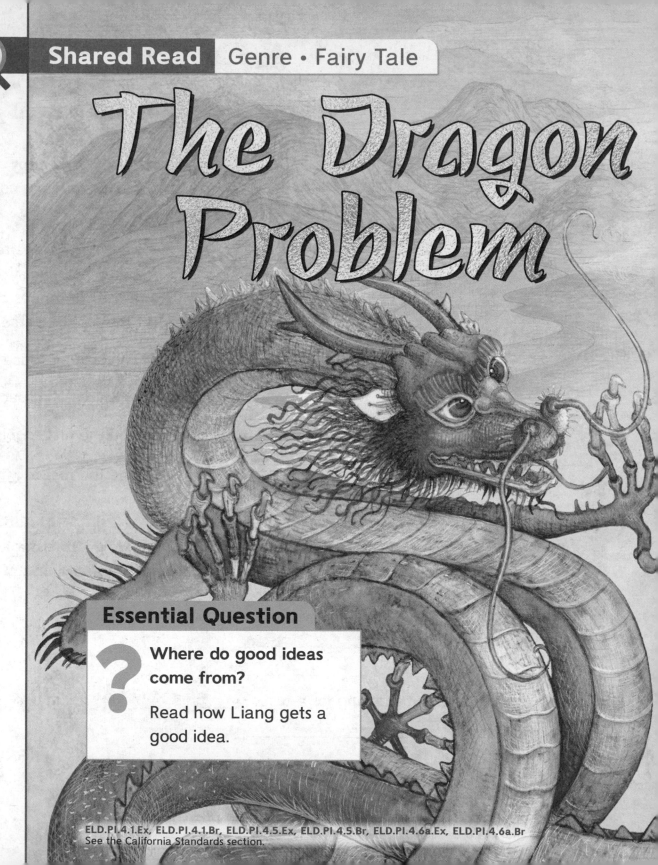

The Dragon Problem

Essential Question

Where do good ideas come from?

Read how Liang gets a good idea.

ELD.PI.4.1.Ex, ELD.PI.4.1.Br, ELD.PI.4.5.Ex, ELD.PI.4.5.Br, ELD.PI.4.6a.Ex, ELD.PI.4.6a.Br
See the California Standards section.

Once upon a time, long before computers, baseball, or pizza, there lived a young man named Liang. During the day, Liang helped his father build furniture. At night, he made unique, original toys for the children in the village. He made birds with flapping wings. He **carved** dragons with rippling, moving scales, sharp claws, and red eyes. Every child in the village had one of Liang's dragons.

Liang knew a lot about dragons because one lived nearby on a mountain. A few times a year, the dragon would swoop down on the village. He ate water buffalo, pigs, and any people unlucky enough to be around. The Emperor had done nothing to get rid of the dragon even though his summer palace was near Liang's village.

One day in May, the Emperor and his family arrived to take up residence at his summer palace. As the **procession** passed through the village, the gracious Princess Peng smiled kindly at Liang. He fell instantly in love.

At dinner that night, Liang told his father that he wanted to marry Princess Peng. His father almost choked on the stale, hard rice ball he was eating.

"You're joking," his father said when he finally could speak.

"I'm **serious**!" insisted Liang.

His father began laughing so hard that the old chair he was sitting on broke. He lay on top of the flattened chair still laughing.

Valerie Sokolova

ELD.PI.4.1.Ex, ELD.PI.4.1.Br, ELD.PI.4.5.Ex, ELD.PI.4.5.Br, ELD.PI.4.6a.Ex, ELD.PI.4.6a.Br, ELD.PI.4.7.Ex, ELD.PI.4.7.Br, ELD.PI.4.12a.Ex, ELD.PI.4.12a.Br, ELD.PII.4.1.Ex, ELD.PII.4.1.Br
See the California Standards section.

Text Evidence

1 Comprehension

Sequence

Reread the second and third sentences in the first paragraph. Circle the words that tell you the sequence of events that Liang follows.

2 Sentence Structure ACT

Reread the third sentence in the second paragraph. Circle the noun that the pronoun *He* refers to.

3 Specific Vocabulary ACT

Look at the second sentence in the third paragraph. The word *procession* means "a group of people walking together." Where is the procession going?

____

______________________________.

Text Evidence

1 Comprehension

Sequence

Reread the fourth paragraph. Draw a box around the words that tell what happens after Liang heard the announcement. Circle the words that tell what Liang did when he could not find Lee.

2 Sentence Structure ACT

Reread the second sentence in the seventh paragraph. Circle the two things that Ling Ling tells Liang to do. Underline the word that connects the two things.

3 Specific Vocabulary ACT

Reread the seventh paragraph. Look at the word *alarm*. Underline a clue in the paragraph that tells what alarm means. What will alarm the real dragon?

____

____

"I'll show him," Liang muttered angrily as he stomped out of the room.

The next morning, the Emperor's messenger made an official **announcement**.

"His Most Noble Emperor proclaims that whoever gets rid of the dragon will marry his daughter, Princess Peng."

When he heard the announcement, Liang raced to the palace to be the first to sign up. Then he looked for his friend Lee to help him brainstorm ideas for getting rid of the dragon. Unfortunately, Lee was away. Liang sat on a bench **frowning**. Nearby, children were playing with the toy dragons he had made them.

"Liang, what's wrong?" the children asked.

"I have to get rid of the dragon on the mountain," he told them.

"I have an idea," said little Ling Ling. "Why don't you carve a giant dragon and leave it by the cave? It will **alarm** the real dragon and scare him into flying away."

Liang stared at her. "Perfect!" he shouted and rushed home. He worked frantically for days making a huge, scary dragon's head. The night he finished, he loaded it onto a cart and went up the mountain. When he got near the cave, Liang put the wooden head on top of a big rock. From the front, it looked like the rest of the dragon's body was behind the rock.

ELD.PI.4.1.Ex, ELD.PI.4.1.Br, ELD.PI.4.5.Ex, ELD.PI.4.5.Br, ELD.PI.4.6a.Ex, ELD.PI.4.6a.Br, ELD.PI.4.7.Ex, ELD.PI.4.7.Br, ELD.PI.4.12a.Ex, ELD.PI.4.12a.Br, ELD.PII.4.1.Ex, ELD.PII.4.1.Br
See the California Standards section.

Liang hid in the bushes and gave a loud roar. "What's that noise?" **growled** the dragon rushing out of his cave. Then he saw the massive dragon head glaring at him. "Go away, or I'll eat you up," he commanded.

The **huge** dragon continued to glare at him. "He must be very strong. He's not afraid of me," thought the dragon, who, like all bullies, was a **coward**. He decided that now was a good time to take a long trip.

"Actually, I'm leaving now. Please make yourself at home in my cave," the dragon called out as he flew away.

A year later, Liang and Princess Peng were married. They opened a toy shop together and lived happily ever after.

Valerie Sokolova

Make Connections

? Talk about where Liang's idea for scaring the dragon came from. ESSENTIAL QUESTION

Tell about a time when a friend helped you think of a good idea. TEXT TO SELF

ELD.PI.4.1.Ex, ELD.PI.4.1.Br, ELD.PI.4.5.Ex, ELD.PI.4.5.Br, ELD.PI.4.6a.Ex, ELD.PI.4.6a.Br, ELD.PI.4.7.Ex, ELD.PI.4.7.Br, ELD.PI.4.11b.Ex, ELD.PI.4.11b.Br, ELD.PI.4.12a.Ex, ELD.PI.4.12a.Br

See the California Standards section.

Text Evidence

1 Sentence Structure ACT

Reread the first sentence in the first paragraph. Underline the subject that tells who the sentence is about. Circle the words that tell two things he is doing.

2 Specific Vocabulary ACT

Reread the second paragraph. The word *coward* means "someone who is not brave." Underline the words that show the dragon is a coward.

3 Talk About It

Do you think the dragon will come back? Justify your answer.

____

____

____

____

Respond to the Text

Partner Discussion **Work with a partner. Describe what you learned about "The Dragon Problem." Write the page numbers where you found text evidence.**

What did you learn about Liang in the story?	**Text Evidence**
I read that during the day Liang ______________________ ______________________.	Page(s): ________
In the text, Liang sees the Emperor and his family and wants to ______________________.	Page(s): ________
Based on the text, Liang hears the Emperor's announcement and ______________________.	Page(s): ________

How did Liang solve the dragon problem?	**Text Evidence**
I learned Liang gets an idea from Ling Ling to ______________.	Page(s): ________
The dragon sees the wood dragon and thinks ______________.	Page(s): ________
The dragon tells the wood dragon ______________.	Page(s): ________

Group Discussion **Present your answers to the group. Cite text evidence to justify your thinking. Listen to and discuss the group's opinions about your answers.**

ELD.PI.4.1.Ex, ELD.PI.4.1.Br, ELD.PI.4.3.Ex, ELD.PI.4.3.Br, ELD.PI.4.5.Ex, ELD.PI.4.5.Br, ELD.PI.4.9.Ex, ELD.PI.4.9.Br, ELD.PI.4.10b.Ex, ELD.PI.4.10b.Br, ELD.PI.4.11a.Ex, ELD.PI.4.11a.Br, ELD.PI.4.12a.Ex, ELD.PI.4.12a.Br See the California Standards section.

Write **Work with a partner. Review your notes about "The Dragon Problem." Then write your answer to the Essential Question. Use text evidence to support your answer. Use vocabulary words from this week's reading in your writing.**

How does Liang get a good idea to get rid of the dragon?

Liang wants to get rid of the dragon because ______________________________

____.

Liang uses Ling Ling's idea of ______________________________________

____.

The dragon flies away because ______________________________________

____.

COLLABORATE

Share Writing **Present your writing to the class. Discuss their opinions. Think about what they have to say. Did they justify their claims? Explain why you agree or disagree with their claims.**

I agree with ____________ because____________.

I disagree with ____________ because ____________.

ELD.PI.4.1.Ex, ELD.PI.4.1.Br, ELD.PI.4.2.Ex, ELD.PI.4.3.Ex, ELD.PI.4.3.Br, ELD.PI.4.5.Ex, ELD.PI.4.5.Br, ELD.PI.4.9.Ex, ELD.PI.4.9.Br, ELD.PI.4.10b.Ex, ELD.PI.4.10b.Br, ELD.PI.4.11a.Ex, ELD.PI.4.11a.Br, ELD.PI.4.12a.Ex, ELD.PI.4.12a.Br See the California Standards section.

Write to Sources

pages 18-21

Take Notes About the Text **I took notes about the story on a sequence chart to help answer the question: *What happens when Liang returns to the village after scaring the dragon away?***

First, Liang falls in love with the Emperor's daughter.

↓

Then the Emperor says the person who gets rid of the dragon can marry his daughter.

↓

Next, Ling Ling gives Liang a great idea.

↓

Soon afterward Liang carves a giant wood dragon. It scares the real dragon away.

 ELD.PI.4.1.Ex, ELD.PI.4.1.Br, ELD.PI.4.5.Ex, ELD.PI.4.5.Br, ELD.PI.4.6a.Ex, ELD.PI.4.6a.Br, ELD.PI.4.12a.Ex, ELD.PI.4.12a.Br, ELD.PII.4.1.Ex, ELD.PII.4.1.Br, ELD.PII.4.2b.Ex, ELD.PII.4.2b.Br See the California Standards section.

Write About the Text I used my notes from my sequence chart to write a paragraph to describe what happens after Liang scares the dragon away.

Student Model: *Narrative Text*

Liang couldn't believe it. The wood dragon scared the real dragon away! He gathers some shiny green scales to show the Emperor. Then he runs back to the village.

"Your idea worked!" Liang said to Ling Ling. Then the children and Liang go to tell the Emperor the great news.

TALK ABOUT IT

Text Evidence

Draw a box around a sentence that comes from the notes. Why did Kyle use this sentence to describe a detail in his story?

Grammar

Circle two words that describe the noun *scales*. Why did Kyle use these words?

Connect Ideas

Underline the two sentences that tell what Liang does after the dragon is gone. How can you combine the sentences to connect the ideas?

Your Turn

Add an event to the story. Tell what happens when Liang tells his father he is marrying the princess. Use details from the story.

>> *Go Digital*
Write your response online. Use your editing checklist.

ELD.PI.4.1.Ex, ELD.PI.4.1.Br, ELD.PI.4.2.Ex, ELD.PI.4.2.Br, ELD.PI.4.5.Ex, ELD.PI.4.5.Br, ELD.PI.4.6a.Ex, ELD.PI.4.6a.Br, ELD.PI.4.10b.Ex, ELD.PI.4.10b.Br, ELD.PI.4.12a.Ex, ELD.PI.4.12a.Br, ELD.PII.4.1.Ex, ELD.PII.4.1.Br, ELD.PII.4.2b.Ex, ELD.PII.4.2b.Br, ELD.PII.4.4.Ex, ELD.PII.4.4.Br See the California Standards section.

TALK ABOUT IT
Weekly Concept Think of Others
Essential Question
How do your actions affect others?
Go Digital

Write in the chart how the girls' actions will affect others. Think about how people's actions affect others.

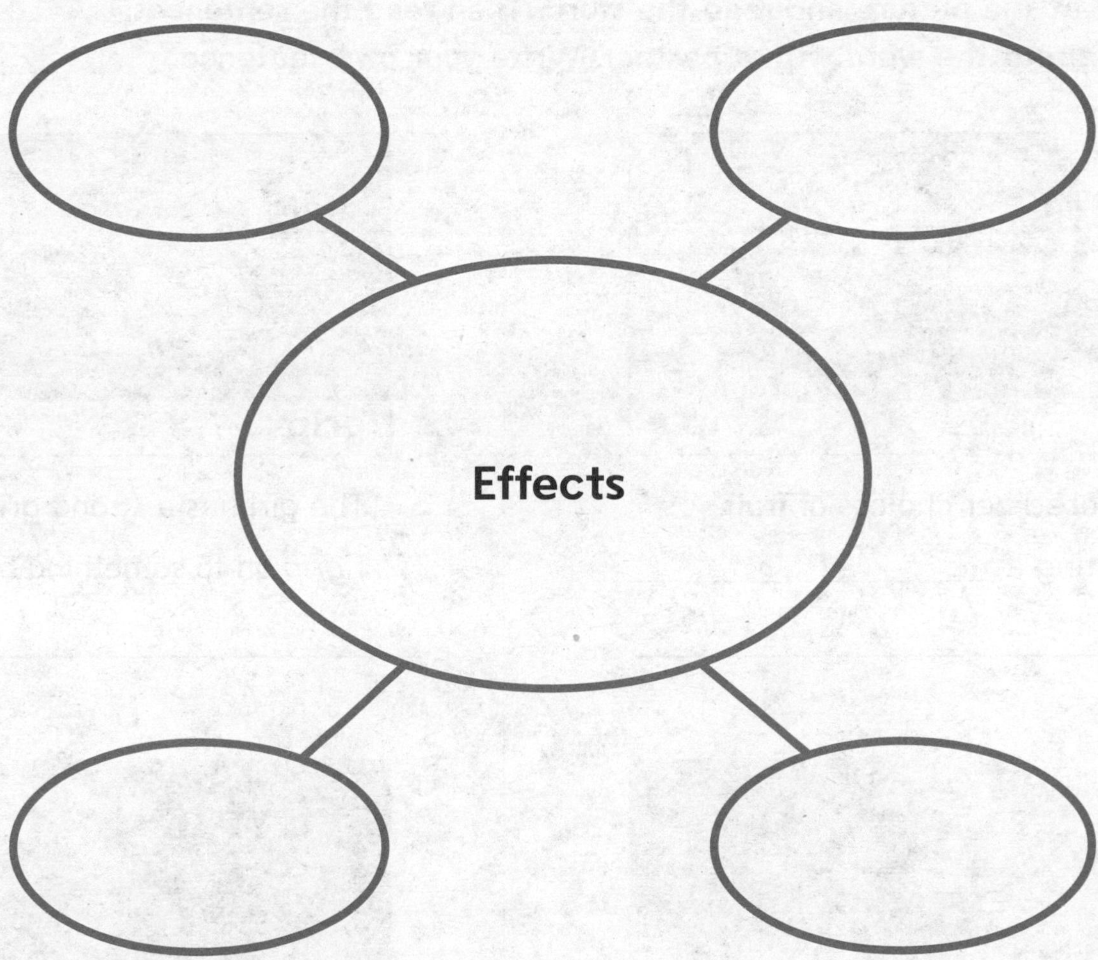

Discuss how the girls' actions may affect others. Use the words from the chart. You can say:

The girls' actions may affect others because ______________________

or ____.

ELD.PI.4.1.Ex, ELD.PI.4.1.Br, ELD.PI.4.5.Ex, ELD.PI.4.5.Br, ELD.PI.4.12a.Ex, ELD.PI.4.12a.Br See the California Standards section.

More Vocabulary

Look at the picture and read the word. Then read the sentences. Talk about the word with a partner. Write your own sentence.

considered

The girl **considered** her choices of fruit.

I *considered* eating a ____________________

or a ______________________________.

continuing

The children are **continuing** to read a book in class.

A story I am *continuing* to read in class is

______________________________.

grip

The girl has a strong **grip** on the leash.

I *grip* on to something because ____________

______________________________.

interrupted

The girl **interrupted** her grandfather's nap.

I *interrupted* someone when I ____________

______________________________.

 ELD.PI.4.1.Ex, ELD.PI.4.1.Br, ELD.PI.4.5.Ex, ELD.PI.4.5.Br, ELD.PI.4.12a.Ex, ELD.PI.4.12a.Br See the California Standards section.

juggling

The people watch a **juggling** act.

The woman is using __________ in the *juggling* act.

resentful

The boy is **resentful** about having to work.

Another word for *resentful* is ____________

____________________________________.

Words and Phrases
Comparative Endings

The ending *-er* is used to compare two things.
My sister is <u>older</u> than me.

The ending *-est* is used to compare three or more things.
I am the <u>youngest</u> student in the class.

Read the sentences below. Write the word that completes the sentence.

I am ________ than my brother.

taller **tallest**

My dog is the ________ dog in town.

louder **loudest**

» Go Digital **Add these comparative endings to your New Words notebook. Write a sentence to show the meaning of each.**

Text Evidence

1 Talk About It

Look at the illustration. Read the title. Talk about what you see. Write your ideas.

What does this title tell you?

____

____

____

____

What is the girl doing?

____

____

____

____

Take notes as you read the text.

Shared Read Genre • Realistic Fiction

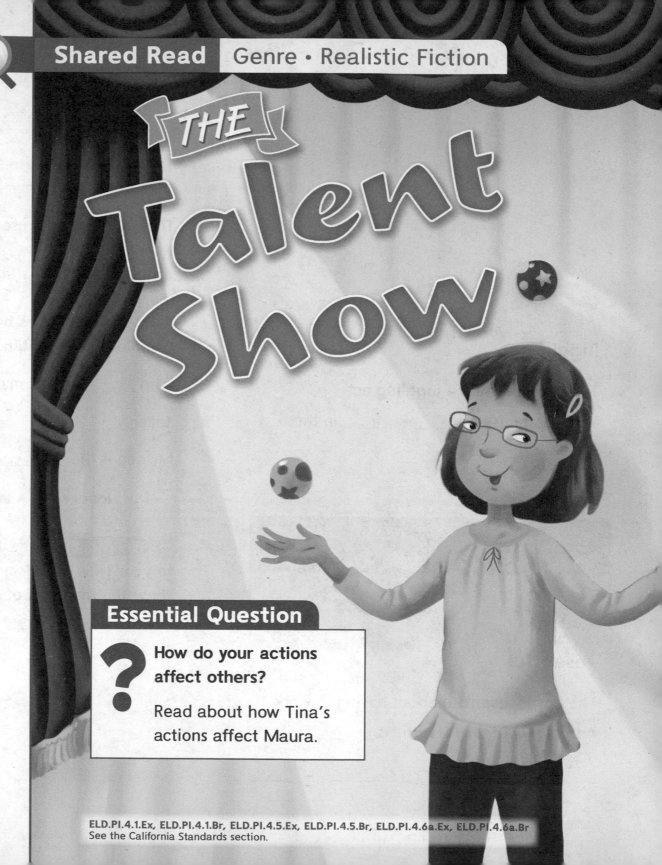

THE Talent Show

Essential Question

How do your actions affect others?

Read about how Tina's actions affect Maura.

ELD.PI.4.1.Ex, ELD.PI.4.1.Br, ELD.PI.4.5.Ex, ELD.PI.4.5.Br, ELD.PI.4.6a.Ex, ELD.PI.4.6a.Br
See the California Standards section.

"Tina, there's a school talent show in three weeks," I shouted to my best friend. My older brother had been teaching me **juggling**, and I knew he'd help me with my act for the show.

Tina ran over to the bulletin board and read the poster. "Maura, what's our act going to be?" Tina asked me.

"Our act?" I said, taking a tighter grip on my books.

Tina grinned, pointed to the poster and said, "It says acts can be individuals, partners, or small groups."

My **grip** on my books became uncomfortably tight. "You want to do an act together?"

"It'll be fun," Tina said.

I hesitated for a second before **continuing**. "I've got an idea and. . . ."

Tina **interrupted** me. "Yeah, me too; let's talk at lunch."

During math, I tried to think of how I would tell Tina that I wanted to do my own act. After all, we are best friends; we should be able to see eye to eye about this. The problem is Tina always takes charge, I don't speak up, and then I end up feeling **resentful** about the whole **situation**.

I desperately wanted to win, but it was more than that. I wanted to win on my own—with an act that was all mine.

Chris Vallo

ELD.PI.4.1.Ex, ELD.PI.4.1.Br, ELD.PI.4.5.Ex, ELD.PI.4.5.Br, ELD.PI.4.6a.Ex, ELD.PI.4.6a.Br, ELD.PI.4.7.Ex, ELD.PI.4.7.Br, ELD.PI.4.12a.Ex, ELD.PI.4.12a.Br See the California Standards section.

Text Evidence

1 Sentence Structure ACT

Reread the second sentence in the ninth paragraph. Circle the punctuation mark that separates the complete sentences.

2 Specific Vocabulary ACT

Look at the word *situation* in the last sentence in the ninth paragraph. The word *situation* means "things that are happening at the same time." What was the situation Maura was feeling resentful about?

____

______________________________.

3 Comprehension
Problem and Solution

Reread the ninth paragraph. Circle the sentence that describes Maura's problem.

Text Evidence

1 Sentence Structure ACT

Reread the fifth paragraph. Circle the noun that the pronoun *she* refers to. Underline two actions *she* is doing.

2 Specific Vocabulary ACT

Look at the word *respectful* in the sixth paragraph. The suffix -*ful* means "full of" and *respect* means "appreciate the value of someone." What does *respectful* mean?

____

____

COLLABORATE

3 Talk About It

According to Maura's grandmother Maura is not respectful of her own ideas. Do you agree? Why or why not? Justify your answer.

____

____

At lunch, Tina started talking as soon as we sat down. "I have it all planned out. My inspiration came from that new TV show, 'You've Got Talent.' We can sing along to a song and do a dance routine, and my mother can make us costumes."

"Yeah, that's good," I said. "But I had another idea." I told her about my juggling act.

Tina **considered** it. "Nah, I don't think I can learn to juggle in three weeks and I'd probably drop the balls," she said. "We don't want to be humiliated, right?"

At recess, I ran around the track a couple of times just to let off steam.

When my grandmother picked me up after school, she drove a few minutes and finally said, "Cat got your tongue?"

I explained about the talent show as she listened carefully. "So, Tina is not being **respectful** of your ideas, but it sounds as if you aren't either."

"What?" I shouted. "I told Tina her idea was good."

"No," said my grandmother, "I said that you weren't respectful of your own ideas, or you would have spoken up. I understand that you're friends, but you're still accountable for your own actions."

ELD.PI.4.1.Ex, ELD.PI.4.1.Br, ELD.PI.4.5.Ex, ELD.PI.4.5.Br, ELD.PI.4.6a.Ex, ELD.PI.4.6a.Br, ELD.PI.4.6b.Ex, ELD.PI.4.6b.Br, ELD.PI.4.11a.Ex, ELD.PI.4.11a.Br, ELD.PI.4.12a.Ex, ELD.PI.4.12a.Br
See the California Standards section.

I thought about this. "So what should I do?" I asked.

"I advise you to tell the truth," she said. "It wouldn't hurt to let Tina know what you want. Besides," my grandmother added, "it will be good for your self-esteem!"

When we got home, I took 12 deep breaths, called Tina, and told her that I was going to do my juggling act. She was curt on the phone, and I spent all night worrying she would be mad at me.

The next day, she described her act and her costume. But the biggest surprise came at recess, when we played a game that I chose, not Tina.

I guess **standing up for** myself did pay off.

Make Connections

Talk about how Maura was affected by Tina's actions. ESSENTIAL QUESTION

Tell about a time when someone wouldn't listen to your ideas. What did you do? TEXT TO SELF

Chris Vallo

Text Evidence

1 Sentence Structure ACT

Reread the second paragraph. Draw a box around the words that tell who is speaking. Circle the punctuation marks that show someone is speaking.

2 Comprehension

Problem and Solution

Reread the last three paragraphs. Underline the sentences that tell the solution to Maura's problem.

3 Specific Vocabulary ACT

Reread the last three paragraphs. In the last sentence the idiom *standing up for* means "to support an idea or how you feel about something." How does Maura feel about standing up for herself?

____

____

____

ELD.PI.4.1.Ex, ELD.PI.4.1.Br, ELD.PI.4.5.Ex, ELD.PI.4.5.Br, ELD.PI.4.6a.Ex, ELD.PI.4.6a.Br, ELD.PI.4.8.Ex, ELD.PI.4.8.Br, ELD.PI.4.12a.Ex, ELD.PI.4.12a.Br See the California Standards section.

Respond to the Text

Partner Discussion **Work with a partner. Answer the questions. Discuss what you learned about "The Talent Show." Write the page numbers where you found text evidence.**

What did you learn about Tina and Maura in the story?	**Text Evidence**
I read that for the talent show Maura wants to ________________.	Page(s): ________
For the talent show, Tina wants to ________________ ________________________.	Page(s): ________
Maura feels bad because ________________ ________________________.	Page(s): ________

What did you learn about Maura in the story?	**Text Evidence**
I learned that Maura feels that Tina ________________.	Page(s): ________
Maura's grandmother advises Maura to ________________.	Page(s): ________
In the end, Maura feels ________________.	Page(s): ________

Group Discussion **Present your answers to the group. Cite text evidence to justify your thinking. Listen to and discuss the group's opinions about your answers.**

ELD.PI.4.1.Ex, ELD.PI.4.1.Br, ELD.PI.4.3.Ex, ELD.PI.4.3.Br, ELD.PI.4.5.Ex, ELD.PI.4.5.Br, ELD.PI.4.9.Ex, ELD.PI.4.9.Br, ELD.PI.4.10b.Ex, ELD.PI.4.10b.Br, ELD.PI.4.11a.Ex, ELD.PI.4.11a.Br, ELD.PI.4.12a.Ex, ELD.PI.4.12a.Br See the California Standards section.

Write **Work with a partner. Review your notes about "The Talent Show." Then write your answer to the essential question. Use text evidence to support your answer. Use vocabulary words from this week's reading in your writing.**

How do Tina's actions affect Maura?

Maura thinks that Tina ______________________________

____

______________________________.

Tina's actions make Maura feel ______________________________.

Maura realizes that she must ______________________________

____

______________________________.

COLLABORATE

Share Writing **Present your writing to the class. Discuss their opinions. Think about what the class has to say. Did they justify their claims? Explain why you agree or disagree with their claims.**

I agree with ____________ because ____________.

I disagree with ____________ because ____________.

ELD.PI.4.1.Ex, ELD.PI.4.1.Br, ELD.PI.4.3.Ex, ELD.PI.4.3.Br, ELD.PI.4.5.Ex, ELD.PI.4.5.Br, ELD.PI.4.9.Ex, ELD.PI.4.9.Br, ELD.PI.4.10b.Ex, ELD.PI.4.10b.Br, ELD.PI.4.11a.Ex, ELD.PI.4.11a.Br, ELD.PI.4.12a.Ex, ELD.PI.4.12a.Br See the California Standards section.

Write to Sources

pages 30-33

Take Notes About the Text **I took notes on the chart about the story to help answer the question:** ***What was the phone conversation between Maura and Tina at the end of the story? Include details.***

Maura	Tina
Maura tells Tina about the talent show.	Tina is excited. She wants to do an act with Maura.
Maura wants to do her own act and juggle.	Tina wants to sing and dance. Her mom will make costumes.
Maura calls Tina. She tells Tina that she wants to do her own act.	Tina is not friendly.

Rick Gomez/Blend Images/Getty Images

 ELD.PI.4.1.Ex, ELD.PI.4.1.Br, ELD.PI.4.5.Ex, ELD.PI.4.5.Br, ELD.PI.4.6a.Ex, ELD.PI.4.6a.Br See the California Standards section.

Write About the Text **I used my notes from the chart to write dialogue for the phone conversation between Maura and Tina at the end of the story.**

Student Model: *Narrative Text*

"Hi, Tina. It's Maura. Can we talk about the talent show?"

"Sure!" Tina said. "I picked out our song. I started making up a dance. Can you come over and practice?"

"I'm sorry. I can't," I said nervously. "I'm going to do my own act. I'm going to juggle."

"What about our song and dance act?" asked Tina.

I said, "You can do the act on your own."

"Oh, okay. I'll see you in school tomorrow," Tina said.

TALK ABOUT IT

Text Evidence

Draw a box around a detail that comes from the notes. Why did Petra use this detail in the dialogue?

Grammar

Circle the people the pronoun *our* refers to in the sentence: "I picked out our song."

Connect Ideas

Underline the sentences in the second paragraph that tells what Tina says about the act. How can you combine the sentences to connect the ideas?

Your Turn

Write a dialogue between Maura and Tina when Maura chooses a game to play at recess. Use details from the story.

>> *Go Digital*
Write your response online. Use your editing checklist.

ELD.PI.4.1.Ex, ELD.PI.4.1.Br, ELD.PI.4.2.Ex, ELD.PI.4.2.Br, ELD.PI.4.5.Ex, ELD.PI.4.5.Br, ELD.PI.4.6a.Ex, ELD.PI.4.6a.Br, ELD.PI.4.10b.Ex, ELD.PI.4.10b.Br, ELD.PI.4.12a.Ex, ELD.PI.4.12a.Br, ELD.PII.4.2a.Ex, ELD.PII.4.2a.Br, ELD.PII.4.6.Ex; ELD.PII.4.6.Br See the California Standards section.

TALK ABOUT IT

Weekly Concept Take Action

Essential Question

How do people respond to natural disasters?

Go Digital

How are the people in the helicopter helping? Write details in the chart. Describe how people help others in emergencies.

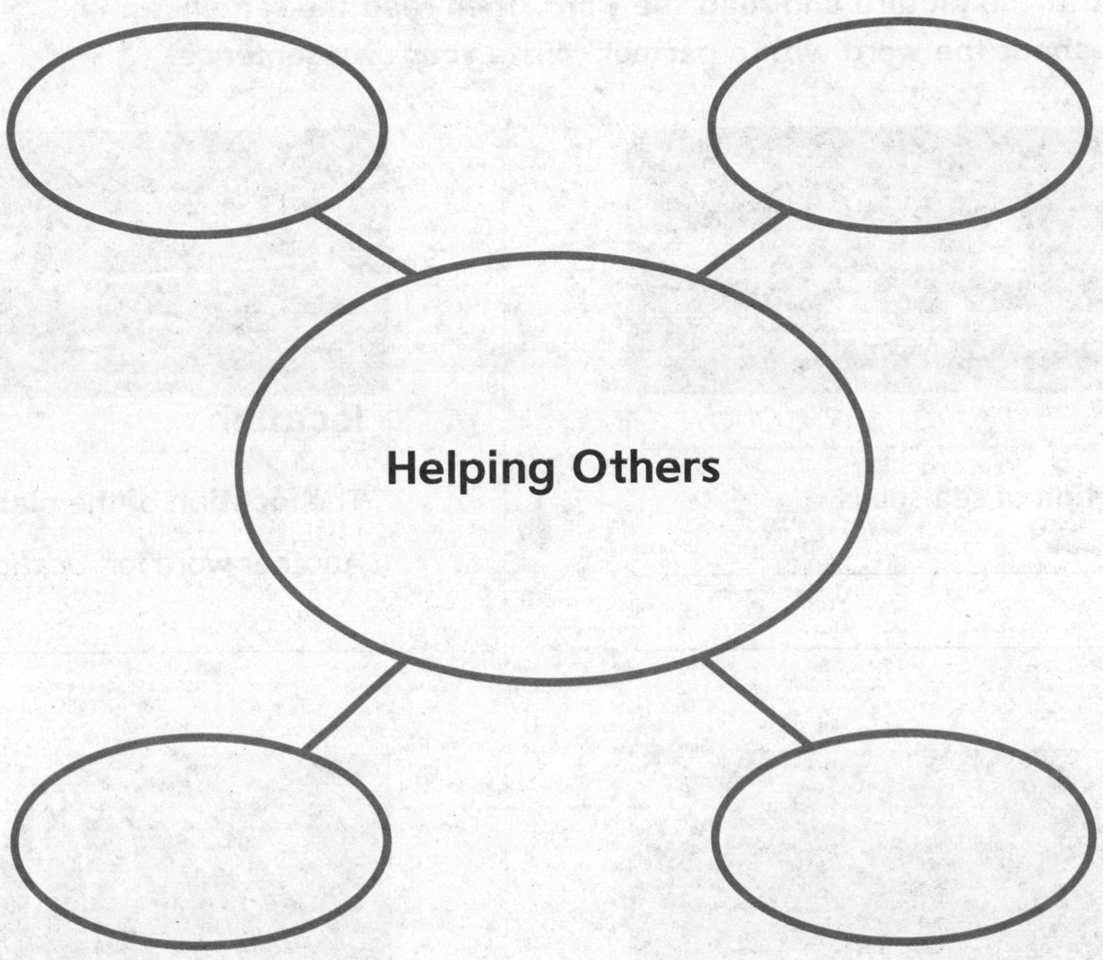

Discuss how people respond to natural disasters. Use the words from the chart. You can say:

During a natural disaster, rescue workers ______________________,

______________________, and ______________________.

More Vocabulary

Look at the picture and read the word. Then read the sentences. Talk about the word with a partner. Write your own sentence.

collection

This is a **collection** of sea shells.

A *collection* is ______________________________

______________________________.

location

The **location** of the plane is in the sky.

Another word for *location* is ______________________________

______________________________.

damage

The tree has **damage**.

There is *damage* to the tree because

______________________________.

occurs

Ice melting **occurs** in the sunlight.

Melting *occurs* when ______________________________

______________________________.

(tl)Adrian Weston/Alamy; (tr)imageshop/zefa visual media uk ltd/Alamy ; (bl)Danielrao/iStock/360/Getty Images; (br)Frank Krahmer/Photographer's Choice RF/Getty Images

 ELD.PI.4.1.Ex, ELD.PI.4.1.Br, ELD.PI.4.5.Ex, ELD.PI.4.5.Br, ELD.PI.4.12a.Ex, ELD.PI.4.12a.Br See the California Standards section.

Words and Phrases
Subordinate Conjunctions

surface

We set our lunch down on the **surface** of the picnic table.

Another word for *surface* is ________________.

warn

The weatherman can **warn** us about dangerous storms.

It is important to *warn* people about storms because ______________________________.

The subordinate conjunctions *because* and *when* connect two ideas.

The word *when* tells the time that something happens.
I sleep <u>when</u> it is bedtime.

The word *because* tells why something happens.
The man fell <u>because</u> he was tired.

Read the sentences below. Underline the conjunction in each sentence.

The girls are late because there is a storm.

I look at the stars when it is dark outside.

» *Go Digital* **Add the conjunctions *when* and *because* to your New Words notebook. Write a sentence to show the meaning of each.**

(l)John Thoeming/McGraw-Hill Education; (r)Image Source/Getty Images

Text Evidence 

1 Talk About It

Look at the photograph. Talk about what you see. Write your ideas.

What does this title tell you?

____

____

What evidence shows that the Grand Canyon was affected by erosion?

I can see that the Grand Canyon was effected by erosion because

____

____

Take notes as you read the text.

Shared Read Genre • Expository

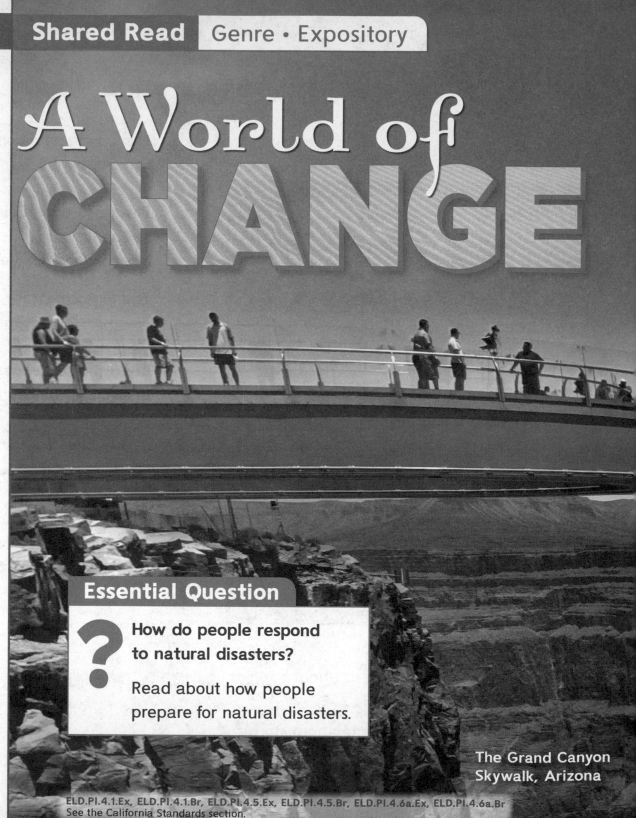

A World of CHANGE

Essential Question

How do people respond to natural disasters?

Read about how people prepare for natural disasters.

The Grand Canyon Skywalk, Arizona

ELD.PI.4.1.Ex, ELD.PI.4.1.Br, ELD.PI.4.5.Ex, ELD.PI.4.5.Br, ELD.PI.4.6a.Ex, ELD.PI.4.6a.Br
See the California Standards section.

Earth may seem as if it is a large rock that never changes. Actually, our planet is in a constant state of change. Natural changes take place every day. These activities alter the **surface** of Earth. Some of these changes take place slowly over many years. Others happen in just minutes. Whether they are slow or fast, both kinds of changes have a great effect on our planet.

Slow and Steady

Some of Earth's biggest changes can't be seen. That is because they are happening very slowly. Weathering, erosion, and deposition are three natural processes that change the surface of the world. They do it one grain of sand at a time.

Weathering **occurs** when rain, snow, sun, and wind break down rocks into smaller pieces. These tiny pieces of rock turn into soil, but they are not carried away from the landform.

Erosion occurs when weathered pieces of rock are carried away by a natural force such as a river. This causes landforms on Earth to get smaller. They may even completely collapse over time. The Grand Canyon is an example of the effect of erosion. It was carved over thousands of years by the Colorado River.

After the process of erosion, dirt and rocks are then dropped in a new **location**. This process is called deposition. Over time, a large **collection** of deposits may occur in one place. Deposition by water can build up a beach. Deposition by wind can create a substantial landform, such as a sand dune.

ELD.PI.4.1.Ex, ELD.PI.4.1.Br, ELD.PI.4.5.Ex, ELD.PI.4.5.Br, ELD.PI.4.6a.Ex, ELD.PI.4.6a.Br, ELD.PI.4.7.Ex, ELD.PI.4.7.Br, ELD.PI.4.12a.Ex, ELD.PI.4.12a.Br, See the California Standards section

Text Evidence

1 Comprehension

Compare and Contrast

Reread the first paragraph. How are Earth's natural changes alike? Circle the words that tell you. How are the natural changes different? Underline the words that tell you.

2 Sentence Structure ACT

Reread the first sentence in the third paragraph. Circle the commas. Underline the words that tell what rain, snow, sun, and wind do.

3 Specific Vocabulary ACT

Reread the fourth paragraph. The word *erosion* means "the process that gradually reduces or destroys something." What does *erosion* do to landforms?

Erosion causes landforms to ______

____

______________________________.

Text Evidence

1 Sentence Structure 

Reread the first sentence in the fourth paragraph. Circle the commas in the sentence. What do the words inside the commas compare?

____

____

COLLABORATE

2 Talk About It

Reread the second paragraph. Describe the ways people try to stop beach erosion. Write about it.

____

_______________.

3 Specific Vocabulary

Reread the fifth paragraph. The word *potential* means "something that is possible." Underline what volcanic eruptions have the potential to do.

Although erosion is a slow process, it still creates problems for people. Some types of erosion are dangerous. They can be seen as a hazard to communities.

To help protect against beach erosion, people build structures that block ocean waves from the shore. They may also use heavy rocks to keep the land from eroding. Others grow plants along the shore. The roots of the plants help hold the soil and make it less likely to erode.

Unfortunately, people cannot protect the land when fast natural processes occur.

Fast and Powerful

Fast natural processes, like slow processes, change the surface of Earth. But fast processes are much more powerful. They are often called natural disasters because of the destruction they cause. Volcanic eruptions and landslides are just two examples.

Volcanoes form around openings in Earth's crust. When pressure builds under Earth's surface, hot melted rock called magma is forced upwards. It flows up through the volcano and out through the opening. Eruptions can occur without warning. They have the **potential** to cause a crisis in a community.

ELD.PI.4.1.Ex, ELD.PI.4.1.Br, ELD.PI.4.5.Ex, ELD.PI.4.5.Br, ELD.PI.4.6a.Ex, ELD.PI.4.6a.Br, ELD.PI.4.8.Ex, ELD.PI.4.8.Br See the California Standards section.

(bkgd) Westend61/Getty Images; (r) Neil Stewart

Like volcanic eruptions, landslides can happen without warning. They occur when rocks and dirt, loosened by heavy rains, slide down a hill or mountain. Some landslides are small. Others can be quite large and cause severe **damage**.

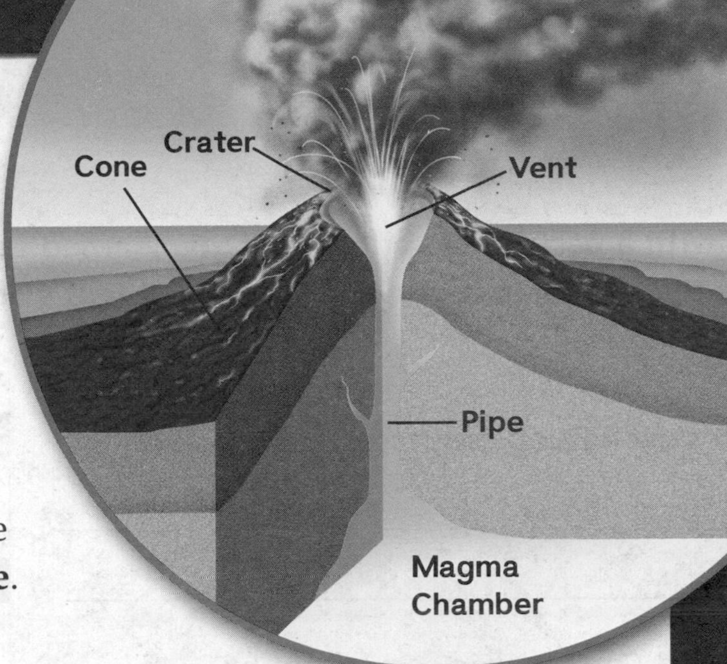

This diagram shows a volcano erupting.

Be Prepared

In contrast to slow-moving processes, people cannot prevent the effects of fast-moving natural disasters. Instead, scientists try to predict when these events will occur so that they can **warn** people. Still, some disasters are unpredictable and strike without warning. It is important for communities to have an emergency plan in place so that they can be evacuated quickly.

The surface of Earth constantly changes through natural processes. These processes can be gradual or swift. They help to make Earth the amazing planet that it is!

Make Connections

Talk about different ways that people prepare for natural disasters. ESSENTIAL QUESTION

How can you help others who have been in a natural disaster? TEXT TO SELF

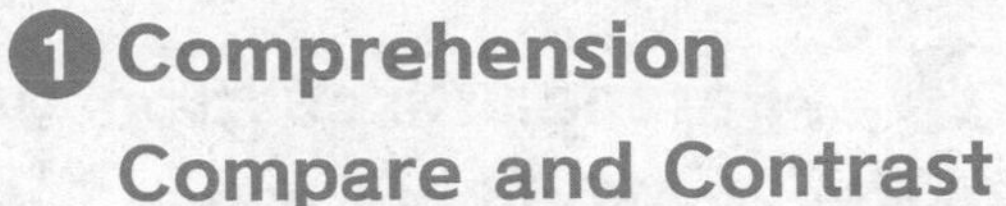

Text Evidence

1 Comprehension Compare and Contrast

Reread the first paragraph. How are volcanic eruptions and landslides similar? Circle the words that tell you. Underline the word that shows a comparison.

2 Sentence Structure ACT

Reread the last sentence in the second paragraph. Draw a box around the noun that the pronoun *they* refers to. Circle why an emergency plan is important.

3 Talk About It

Discuss how a fast-moving disaster is different than a slow-moving disaster. Then write about it.

____

____

ELD.PI.4.1.Ex, ELD.PI.4.1.Br, ELD.PI.4.5.Ex, ELD.PI.4.5.Br, ELD.PI.4.6a.Ex, ELD.PI.4.6a.Br, ELD.PI.4.12a.Ex, ELD.PI.4.12a.Br, ELD.PII.4.2a.Ex, ELD.PII.4.2a.Br See the California Standards section.

Respond to the Text

Partner Discussion **Work with a partner. Describe what you learned about "A World of Change." Write the page numbers where you found text evidence.**

What did you learn about slow natural processes?	Text Evidence
Weathering occurs when ____________________ ____________________.	Page(s): ________
Based on the text, the Grand Canyon was carved out by ________ ____________________.	Page(s): ________
People try to stop beach erosion by ____________________ ____________________.	Page(s): ________

What did you learn about fast natural processes?	Text Evidence
Volcanic eruptions can ____________________.	Page(s): ________
I learned that landslides often happen when ________ ____________________.	Page(s): ________
Emergency plans are important because ____________________.	Page(s): ________

Group Discussion **Present your answers to the group. Cite text evidence to justify your thinking. Listen to and discuss the group's opinions about your answers.**

ELD.PI.4.1.Ex, ELD.PI.4.1.Br, ELD.PI.4.3.Ex, ELD.PI.4.3.Br, ELD.PI.4.5.Ex, ELD.PI.4.5.Br, ELD.PI.4.9.Ex, ELD.PI.4.9.Br, ELD.PI.4.10b.Ex, ELD.PI.4.10b.Br, ELD.PI.4.11a.Ex, ELD.PI.4.11a.Br, ELD.PI.4.12a.Ex, ELD.PI.4.12a.Br See the California Standards section.

Write Review your notes about "A World of Change." Then write your answer to the essential question. Use text evidence to support your answer. Use vocabulary words from this week's reading in your writing.

How do people prepare for natural disasters?

People try to prevent beach erosion by ______________________________

____.

People can't prevent fast natural processes, so scientists try to __________

____.

It is important to have an emergency plan because ____________________

____.

COLLABORATE

Share Writing Present your writing to the class. Discuss their opinions. Think about what they have to say. Did they justify their claims? Explain why you agree or disagree with their claims.

I agree with ______________ because ______________.

I disagree with ______________ because ______________.

ELD.PI.4.1.Ex, ELD.PI.4.1.Br, ELD.PI.4.3.Ex, ELD.PI.4.3.Br, ELD.PI.4.5.Ex, ELD.PI.4.5.Br, ELD.PI.4.9.Ex, ELD.PI.4.9.Br, ELD.PI.4.10b.Ex, ELD.PI.4.10b.Br, ELD.PI.4.11a.Ex, ELD.PI.4.11a.Br, ELD.PI.4.12a.Ex, ELD.PI.4.12a.Br See the California Standards section.

Write to Sources

Take Notes About the Text I took notes on this Venn diagram to answer the question: ***How does the author compare fast and slow natural processes? Use text evidence.***

pages 42-45

Different: Slow Changes	Alike: Slow and Fast Changes	Different: Fast Changes
Changes happen over a long period of time. People try to protect the land.	Changes the surface of Earth.	Changes happen suddenly. People cannot prevent these changes.

Thinkstock Images/Stockbyte/Getty Images

 ELD.PI.4.1.Ex, ELD.PI.4.1.Br, ELD.PI.4.5.Ex, ELD.PI.4.5.Br, ELD.PI.4.6a.Ex, ELD.PI.4.6a.Br, ELD.PII.4.1.Ex, ELD.PII.4.1.Br See the California Standards section.

Write About the Text **I used notes from my Venn diagram to write a paragraph to compare slow and fast natural processes.**

Student Model: *Informational Text*

The author describes slow and fast natural processes in "A World of Change." Both kinds of natural processes can change the surface of Earth. Slow changes are changes like erosion and weathering. They happen over a long time, so people can protect the land from these changes. But fast changes are changes like landslides and volcanoes. They happen very fast. People cannot protect the land from these changes. These are ways slow and fast changes are alike and different.

TALK ABOUT IT

Text Evidence

Draw a box around a sentence that tells how fast and slow processes are alike. Why is this an important detail?

Grammar

Circle a present-tense verb. Why did Sara use the present tense?

Condense Ideas

Underline the sentences that describe fast changes. How can you condense these sentences into one detailed sentence?

Your Turn

Which kind of change seems more dangerous? Use text evidence.

>> *Go Digital*
Write your response online. Use your editing checklist.

ELD.PI.4.1.Ex, ELD.PI.4.1.Br, ELD.PI.4.2.Ex, ELD.PI.4.2.Br, ELD.PI.4.5.Ex, ELD.PI.4.5.Br, ELD.PI.4.6a.Ex, ELD.PI.4.6a.Br, ELD.PI.4.12a.Ex, ELD.PI.4.12a.Br, ELD.PII.4.1.Ex, ELD.PII.4.1.Br, ELD.PII.4.7.Ex, ELD.PII.4.7.Br See the California Standards section.

TALK ABOUT IT

Weekly Concept Ideas in Motion

Essential Question

How can science help you understand how things work?

» Go Digital

What are the ways a roller coaster can move? Write the ways a roller coaster can move in the chart.

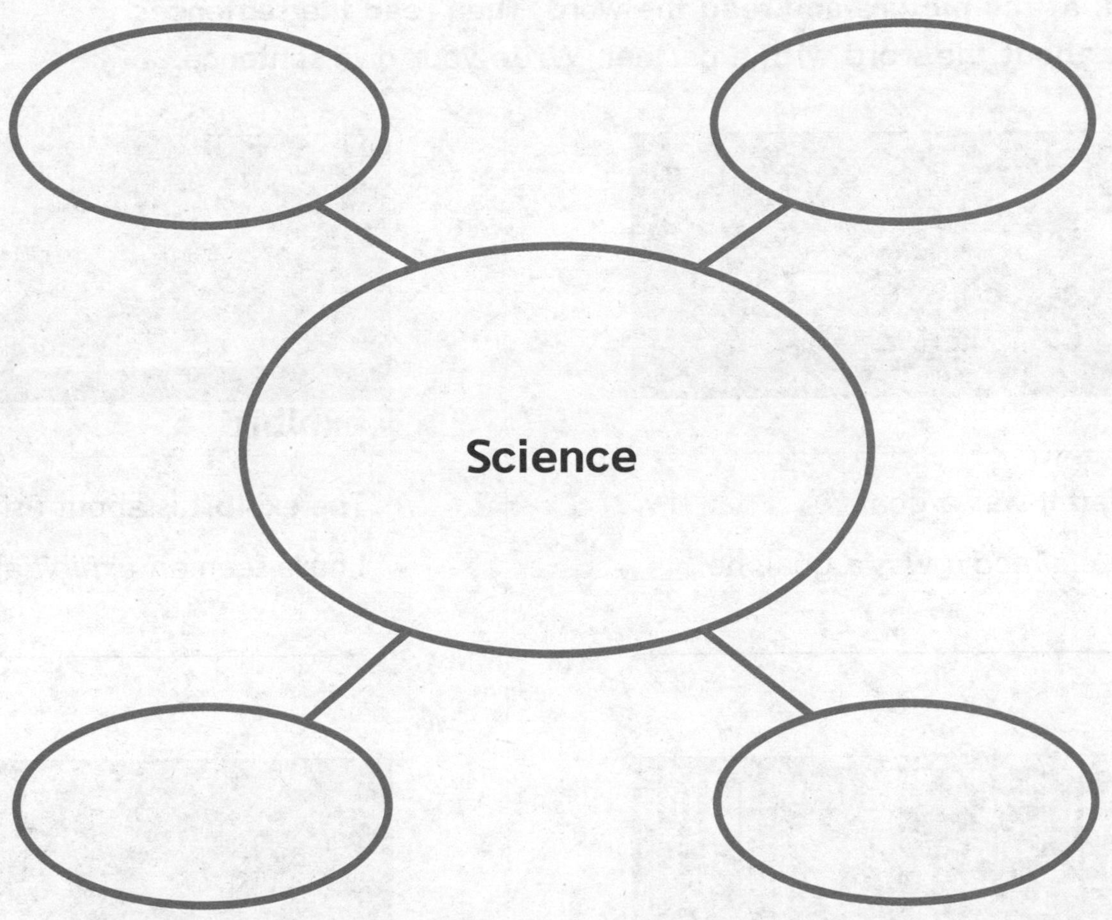

Discuss how science can help you understand how a roller coaster works. Use the words from the chart. You can say:

A roller coaster can move ________________ and ________________.

A roller coaster goes fast because ________________.

Gunter Marx/Alamy Stock Photo

ELD.PI.4.1.Ex, ELD.PI.4.1.Br, ELD.PI.4.5.Ex, ELD.PI.4.5.Br, ELD.PI.4.12a.Ex, ELD.PI.4.12a.Br See the California Standards section.

More Vocabulary

Look at the picture and read the word. Then read the sentences. Talk about the word with a partner. Write your own sentence.

claimed

The boy **claimed** it was a goal.

When the boy *claimed* it was a goal, he ____

______________________________________.

distance

The playground is a short **distance** from the school.

The *distance* I live from school is __________

______________________________________.

exhibit

The **exhibit** is about fish.

I have seen an *exhibit* about __________

______________________________________.

increase

Runners **increase** their speed at the end of a race.

Another word for *increase* is __________

______________________________________.

(tl)Image Source/SuperStock; (tr)veronka & cia/Monument Open/Getty Images; (bl)Evgesh/iStock/360/Getty Images; (br)Ingram Publishing

 ELD.PI.4.1.Ex, ELD.PI.4.1.Br, ELD.PI.4.5.Ex, ELD.PI.4.5.Br, ELD.PI.4.12a.Ex, ELD.PI.4.12a.Br See the California Standards section.

responded

The boy **responded** to the question.

Another word for *responded* is ____________.

whispered

The girl **whispered** to her friend.

I *whispered* at the library because ________

________________________________.

Words and Phrases

Contractions: Pronoun + Verb

A contraction is a short form of two words. An apostrophe stands for the missing letter.

I'm **= I am**
I'm in the car.

it's **= it is**
It's a red car.

Read the sentences below. Write the contraction for the underlined words.

I am in a play at school.

________ in a play at school.

It is a play that I read last year.

________ a play that I read last year.

» *Go Digital* **Add these contractions to your New Words notebook. Write a sentence to show the meaning of each.**

ELD.PI.4.1.Ex, ELD.PI.4.1.Br, ELD.PI.4.5.Ex, ELD.PI.4.5.Br, ELD.PI.4.12a.Ex, ELD.PI.4.12a.Br See the California Standards section.

Text Evidence

1 Talk About It

Look at the picture. Read the title. Talk about what you see. Write your ideas.

What does this title tell you?

____

____

Who are the characters in the story?

____

____

What are the boys planning to do?

____

____

Take notes as you read the story.

Shared Read Genre • Narrative Nonfiction

THE BIG Race

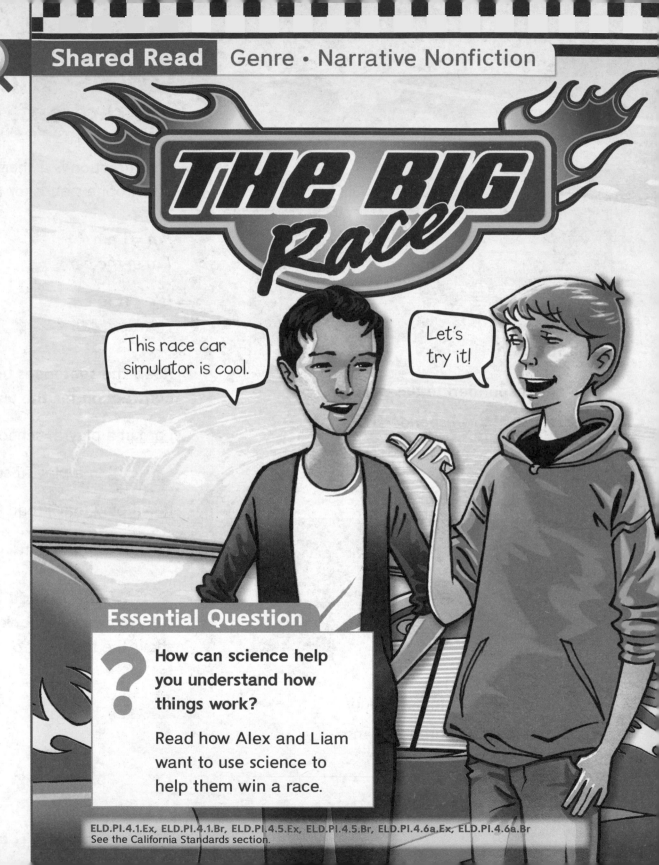

This race car simulator is cool.

Let's try it!

Essential Question

How can science help you understand how things work?

Read how Alex and Liam want to use science to help them win a race.

ELD.PI.4.1.Ex, ELD.PI.4.1.Br, ELD.PI.4.5.Ex, ELD.PI.4.5.Br, ELD.PI.4.6a.Ex, ELD.PI.4.6a.Br
See the California Standards section.

Alex and Liam planned to build a car for the soap box derby. As a result of their inquiry into how to build a fast car, they had come to the science museum today for answers. Last week, Alex's mother had called one of the museum's scientists. When they walked into the museum, a woman in a lab coat and inline skates zoomed up and greeted them.

"Hi, I'm Clara. Are you the boys who want to know what will make a car go fast?"

"Yes, I'm Alex, and that's Liam," Alex **responded**.

"Why are you wearing inline skates, Clara?" Liam asked.

"I'm a champion skater!" Clara **claimed**, doing a spin. Then she **whispered**, "That's not my true identity. I'm a scientist. Skates make it easier to get around. Follow me!"

IT'S ABOUT SPEED

"Welcome to our On the Move **exhibit**," Clara announced as they entered a large room. "So, tell me about the race."

"There will be 20 cars in the race. We'll be going down the steepest hill in town!" Alex said.

"Sounds thrilling! It must be exciting to go fast!" Clara answered as she pressed buttons on a machine. "This is a **virtual** race car, and this screen shows you the virtual race course and your speed. Speed is the **distance** an object moves in a certain amount of time."

Craig Phillips

ELD.PI.4.1.Ex, ELD.PI.4.1.Br, ELD.PI.4.5.Ex, ELD.PI.4.5.Br, ELD.PI.4.6a.Ex, ELD.PI.4.6a.Br, ELD.PI.4.7.Ex, ELD.PI.4.7.Br, ELD.PI.4.12a.Ex, ELD.PI.4.12a.Br
See the California Standards section.

Text Evidence

1 Comprehension

Cause and Effect

Reread the first paragraph. Why did the boys go to the science museum? Underline the words that tell you.

They went to the science museum

because ______________________

______________________.

2 Sentence Structure ACT

Reread the second sentence in the first paragraph. Underline the nouns in the first sentence that the possessive pronoun *their* refers to. Circle what their inquiry was.

3 Specific Vocabulary ACT

Reread the last paragraph. The word *virtual* means "something that is created on a computer or on the Internet." Underline the words that tell what the virtual machine does.

Text Evidence

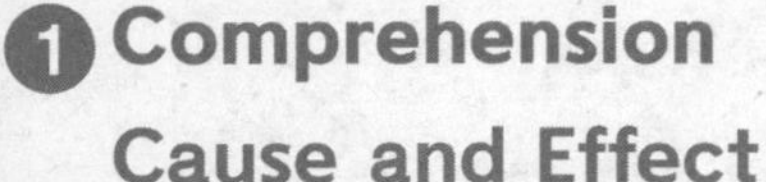

1 Comprehension

Cause and Effect

Reread the fourth paragraph. Why is it important that the boys learn about forces?

Forces cause things to ____________

____

2 Sentence Structure ACT

Reread the fourth sentence in the fourth paragraph. Circle the commas. Underline the part of the sentence that tells what causes an object to increase its speed.

COLLABORATE

3 Talk About It

Discuss why Alex and Liam need to know about forces to build a fast car. Then write about it.

____

____

____

FORCES AT WORK

A force is a push or a pull.

Alex and Liam climbed into the machine. Each seat had a steering wheel and a screen in front of it.

Clara said, "Since you want to build a fast car, you need to know about forces and how they affect motion."

"What's a force?" asked Liam.

Clara continued, "A force is a push or a pull. Forces cause things to move or cause a change in motion. When I apply a big enough force on an object, like this stool, it moves. If two objects are exactly the same, the object that receives a bigger force will accelerate, or **increase** its speed," Clara said, pushing two stools at the same time.

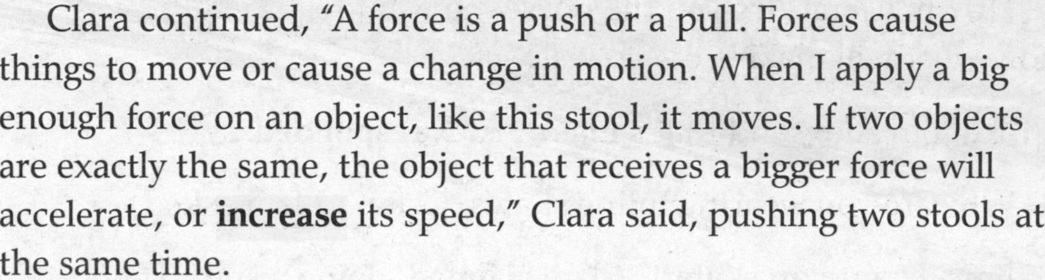

"Which stool received a bigger force?" Clara asked.

"The one on the right. It went farther," said Liam.

"So, giving our car a big push at the top of the hill will cause it to accelerate and go faster," Alex summarized.

There's a sharp curve coming up!
I'm going to accelerate now!

ELD.PI.4.1.Ex, ELD.PI.4.1.Br, ELD.PI.4.5.Ex, ELD.PI.4.5.Br, ELD.PI.4.6a.Ex, ELD.PI.4.6a.Br, ELD.PI.4.12a.Ex, ELD.PI.4.12a.Br See the California Standards section.

GRAVITY AND FRICTION

Clara smiled, "Right! Another force acting on your car is gravity. Gravity is a pulling force between two objects." Clara took a tennis ball out of her pocket. "When I drop this ball, gravity pulls it towards the floor. It's the same force that pulls your car down the hill."

"So, a big push gives us an advantage over other cars, and gravity will keep us going. How do we stop?" Liam asked.

"You'll need friction. Friction is a force between two surfaces that slows objects down or stops them from moving. For example, I lean back on my skates, and the friction between the rubber stoppers and the floor slows me down," said Clara.

"Thanks, Clara! The virtual race car was cool! I knew we had the skills and capabilities to win the race, but now we have science on our side, too," Liam grinned.

Craig Phillips

Make Connections

Talk about ways that science can help you understand how objects move. ESSENTIAL QUESTION

How can science help you understand your favorite activities? TEXT TO SELF

Text Evidence

1 Comprehension
Cause and Effect

Reread the third paragraph. Underline the force that causes an object to slow down. Circle the words that tell how it slows down an object.

2 Sentence Structure ACT

Reread the third sentence in the third paragraph. Underline the independent clauses, or the sentences that can stand on their own. Circle the word that connects the two clauses together.

COLLABORATE

3 Talk About It

Discuss why Liam says they have science on their side. Then write about it.

____

____

____

ELD.PI.4.1.Ex, ELD.PI.4.1.Br, ELD.PI.4.5.Ex, ELD.PI.4.5.Br, ELD.PI.4.6a.Ex, ELD.PI.4.6a.Br, ELD.PI.4.12a.Ex, ELD.PI.4.12a.Br See the California Standards section.

Respond to the Text

Partner Discussion **Work with a partner. Describe what you learned about "The Big Race." Write the page numbers where you found text evidence.**

What did Alex and Liam learn about forces?	**Text Evidence**
Alex and Liam discovered that a force can be a ______________ ______________________________.	Page(s): ________
If two objects are the same, the object that gets a bigger force will ______________________________ ______________________________.	Page(s): ________
Gravity is a pulling force between ______________________.	Page(s): ________

How will Alex and Liam use what they learned to build their car?	**Text Evidence**
They can make their car go faster by ______________________.	Page(s): ________
Gravity will keep the car ______________________.	Page(s): ________
Friction is a force that ______________________ ______________________________.	Page(s): ________

Group Discussion **Present your answers to the class. Cite text evidence to justify your thinking. Listen to and discuss the group's opinions about your answers.**

ELD.PI.4.1.Ex, ELD.PI.4.1.Br, ELD.PI.4.3.Ex, ELD.PI.4.3.Br, ELD.PI.4.5.Ex, ELD.PI.4.5.Br, ELD.PI.4.9.Ex, ELD.PI.4.9.Br, ELD.PI.4.10b.Ex, ELD.PI.4.10b.Br, ELD.PI.4.11a.Ex, ELD.PI.4.11a.Br, ELD.PI.4.12a.Ex, ELD.PI.4.12a.Br See the California Standards section.

COLLABORATE

Write **Work with a partner. Review your notes about "The Big Race." Then write your answer to the essential question. Use text evidence to support your answer. Use vocabulary words from this week's reading in your writing.**

How can science help Alex and Liam win a soap box derby race?

Based on the text, if all the cars are exactly the same, the car that will go the fastest will be the car that ______________________________

______________________________.

Gravity helps because ______________________________

______________________________.

Friction is a force that slows down or stops an object by ______________________________

______________________________.

COLLABORATE

Share Writing **Present your writing to the class. Discuss their opinions. Think about what they have to say. Did they justify their claims? Explain why you agree or disagree with their claims.**

I agree with ____________ because ____________.

I disagree with ____________ because ____________.

ELD.PI.4.1.Ex, ELD.PI.4.1.Br, ELD.PI.4.3.Ex, ELD.PI.4.3.Br, ELD.PI.4.5.Ex, ELD.PI.4.5.Br, ELD.PI.4.9.Ex, ELD.PI.4.9.Br, ELD.PI.4.10b.Ex, ELD.PI.4.10b.Br, ELD.PI.4.11a.Ex, ELD.PI.4.11a.Br, ELD.PI.4.12a.Ex, ELD.PI.4.12a.Br See the California Standards section.

Write to Sources

Take Notes About the Text **I took notes on this idea web to answer the question:** ***What information does the author in "The Big Race" tell about how forces affect motion?***

pages 54-57

The author tells about how forces affect motion.

Pushes and pulls are forces that move objects.

Gravity pulls objects down. It is a pulling force.

Friction is a force that slows down an object or stops it from moving.

Comstock/Stockbyte/Getty Images

 ELD.PI.4.1.Ex, ELD.PI.4.1.Br, ELD.PI.4.5.Ex, ELD.PI.4.5.Br, ELD.PI.4.6a.Ex, ELD.PI.4.6a.Br See the California Standards section.

Write About the Text **I used notes from my idea web to write a paragraph about how the author describes how forces affect motion.**

Student Model: *Informational Text*

The author describes different forces in "The Big Race." Pushes and pulls are forces that move objects. Gravity is a pulling force. It will pull objects downward. Friction is a force that will slow an object down or stop it. The author shows how forces affect motion.

TALK ABOUT IT

Text Evidence

Draw a box around a detail that tells what happens when you pull or push objects. Why did Henry include this detail?

Grammar

Circle the words that describe *gravity*. Which word best describes the kind of force gravity is?

Condense Ideas

Underline the sentences that tell about gravity. How can you combine these sentences into one detailed sentence?

Your Turn

Why does the author tell about gravity and friction? Use text evidence in your writing.

>> *Go Digital*
Write your response online. Use your editing checklist.

ELD.PI.4.1.Ex, ELD.PI.4.1.Br, ELD.PI.4.2.Ex, ELD.PI.4.2.Br, ELD.PI.4.5.Ex, ELD.PI.4.5.Br, ELD.PI.4.6a.Ex, ELD.PI.4.6a.Br, ELD.PI.4.10a.Ex, ELD.PI.4.10a.Br, ELD.PI.4.12a.Ex, ELD.PI.4.12a.Br, ELD.PII.4.1.Ex, ELD.PII.4.1.Br, ELD.4.PII.7.Ex, ELD.PII.4.7.Br See the California Standards section.

TALK ABOUT IT
Weekly Concept Putting Ideas to Work
?
Essential Question
How can starting a business help others?
» Go Digital

What kind of business does the woman have? Write how a business can help others in the chart. Discuss how a business like the one in the photograph can help people.

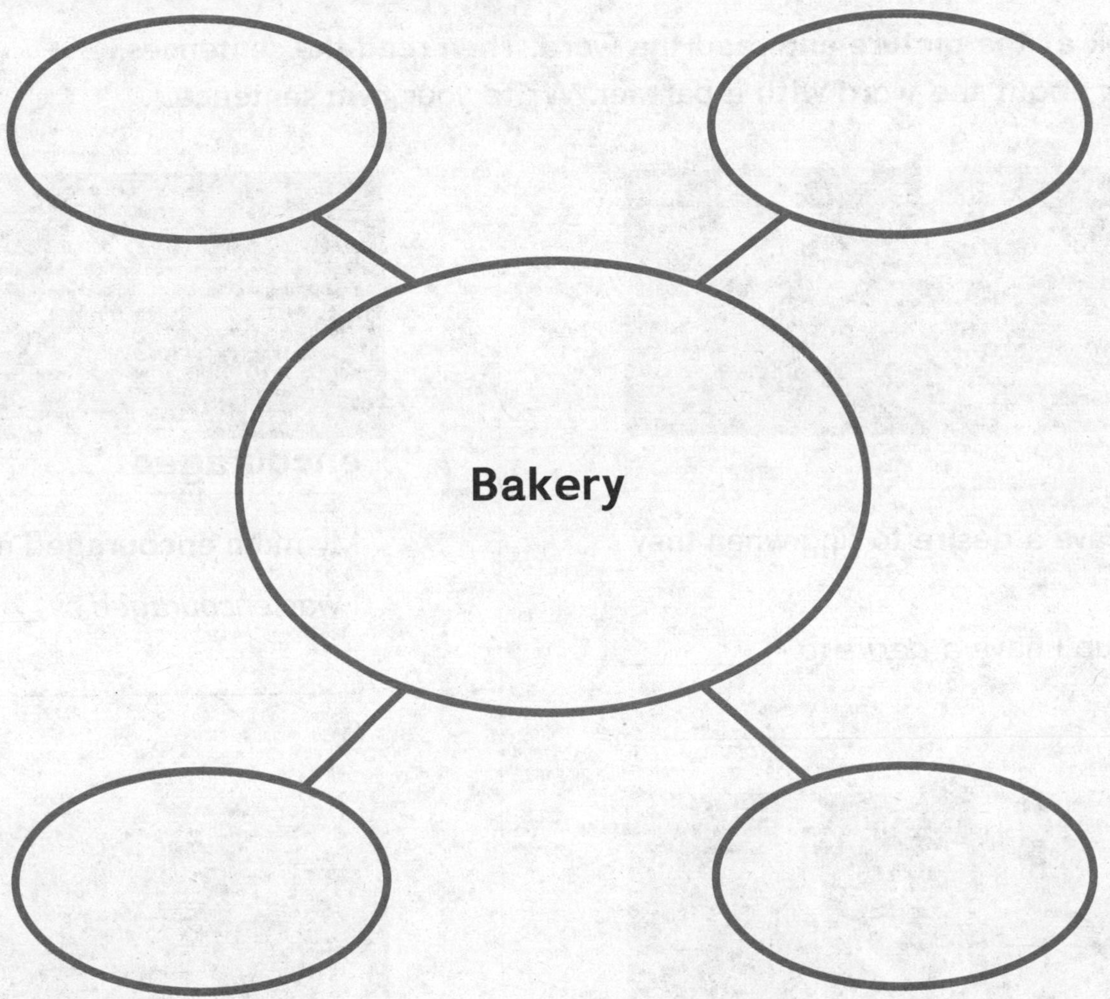

Discuss the things a business can do to help others. Use the words from the chart. You can say:

A business can help others because ________________________________

____.

ELD.PI.4.1.Ex, ELD.PI.4.1.Br, ELD.PI.4.5.Ex, ELD.PI.4.5.Br, ELD.PI.4.12a.Ex, ELD.PI.4.12a.Br See the California Standards section.

More Vocabulary

COLLABORATE

Look at the picture and read the word. Then read the sentences. Talk about the word with a partner. Write your own sentence.

desire

The children have a **desire** to sing when they grow up.

When I grow up I have a *desire* to ________

________________________________.

encouraged

My mom **encouraged** me to ride a bike.

I was *encouraged* by ________________

________________________________.

donated

Students **donated** food to the school food drive.

Another word for *donated* is ____________

________________________________.

expanded

The city is being **expanded** to build more housing.

Another word for *expanded* is ____________

________________________________.

 ELD.PI.4.1.Ex, ELD.PI.4.1.Br, ELD.PI.4.5.Ex, ELD.PI.4.5.Br, ELD.PI.4.12a.Ex, ELD.PI.4.12a.Br See the California Standards section.

immediately

The students will go **immediately** to their next class.

Another word for *immediately* is ___________.

purchased

Many tickets were **purchased** at the station.

I *purchased* ________ from ___________.

Words and Phrases
Multiple-Meaning Words

company **= a business**
The company sells shoes.

company **= visitors**
We have company tonight.

Read the sentences below. Circle the word that tells the meaning of the underlined word.

My mom works for a company.

business visitors

We had company after dinner.

business visitors

» Go Digital **Add these multiple-meaning words to your New Words notebook. Write a sentence to show the meaning of each.**

(l)Vstock LLC/Getty Images; (r)Danita Delimont/Getty Images

COLLABORATE

1 Talk About It

Look at the photograph. Read the title. Talk about what you see. Write your ideas.

What does this title tell you?

____

____

How is the man helping the children?

____

____

Take notes as you read.

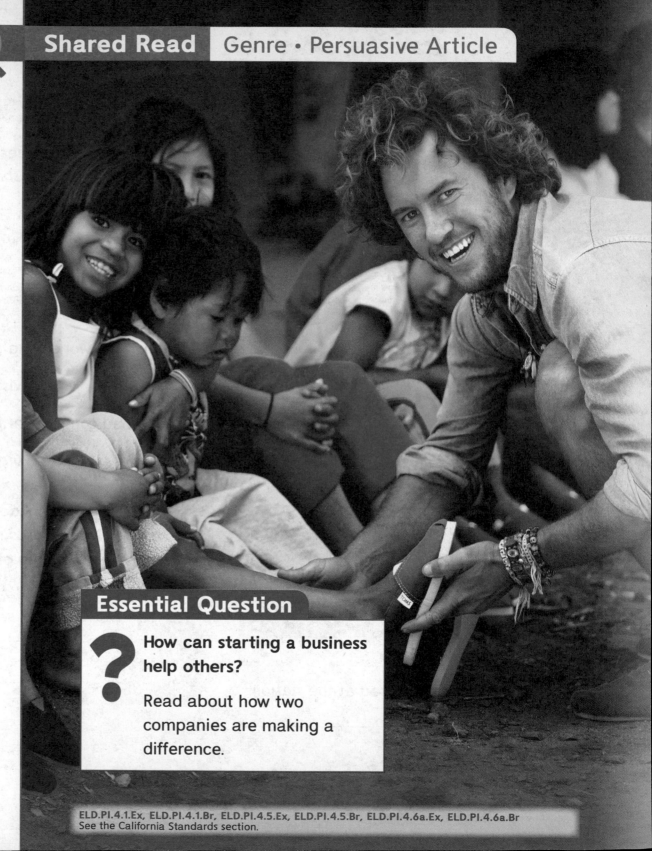

Essential Question

How can starting a business help others?

Read about how two companies are making a difference.

ELD.PI.4.1.Ex, ELD.PI.4.1.Br, ELD.PI.4.5.Ex, ELD.PI.4.5.Br, ELD.PI.4.6a.Ex, ELD.PI.4.6a.Br
See the California Standards section.

Dollars and $ENSE

Behind the success of these big businesses is a desire to help others.

Good business is not always about the **bottom line**. A compassionate company knows that making money is not the only way to measure success. Many large businesses in the United States and all over the world are finding unusual ways to help people in need.

Hearts and Soles

After starting and running four businesses, Blake Mycoskie wanted a break from his usual routine. In 2006, he traveled to Argentina, in South America, and while he was there he learned to sail and dance. He also visited poor villages where very few of the children had shoes. Mycoskie decided he had to do something. "I'm going to start a shoe company, and for every pair I sell, I'm going to give one pair to a kid in need."

For this new undertaking, Mycoskie started the business using his own money. He named it TOMS: Shoes for Tomorrow. The slip-on shoes are modeled on shoes that are traditionally worn by Argentine workers.

Mycoskie **immediately** set up his innovative one-for-one program. TOMS gives away one pair of shoes for every pair that is **purchased**. Later that year, Mycoskie returned to Argentina and gave away 10,000 pairs of shoes. By 2011, TOMS had **donated** over one million pairs.

Text Evidence

1 Specific Vocabulary ACT

Reread the first paragraph. The idiom *bottom line* is a business phrase that means "the amount of money a business has made or lost." Underline what the author says is as important as the bottom line.

2 Comprehension

Main Idea and Key Details

Reread the second paragraph. Circle one detail that supports the main idea in the paragraph.

What is the main idea?

____

____

____

3 Sentence Structure ACT

Reread the third sentence in the last paragraph. Circle the word that connects Mycoskie's two actions. Underline his two actions.

ELD.PI.4.1.Ex, ELD.PI.4.1.Br, ELD.PI.4.5.Ex, ELD.PI.4.5.Br, ELD.PI.4.6a.Ex, ELD.PI.4.6a.Br, ELD.PI.4.8.Ex, ELD.PI.4.8.Br, ELD.PI.4.12a.Ex, ELD.PI.4.12a.Br See the California Standards section.

Text Evidence

1 Talk About It

Reread the first paragraph. Discuss how TOMS affects the communities it works with.

2 Specific Vocabulary

Reread the third sentence in the third paragraph. The word *launch* means "to start something that is usually very important." What did the company launch?

Why was it important?

3 Sentence Structure

Reread the fourth sentence in the third paragraph. Underline the independent clause, or the part of the sentence that can stand on its own.

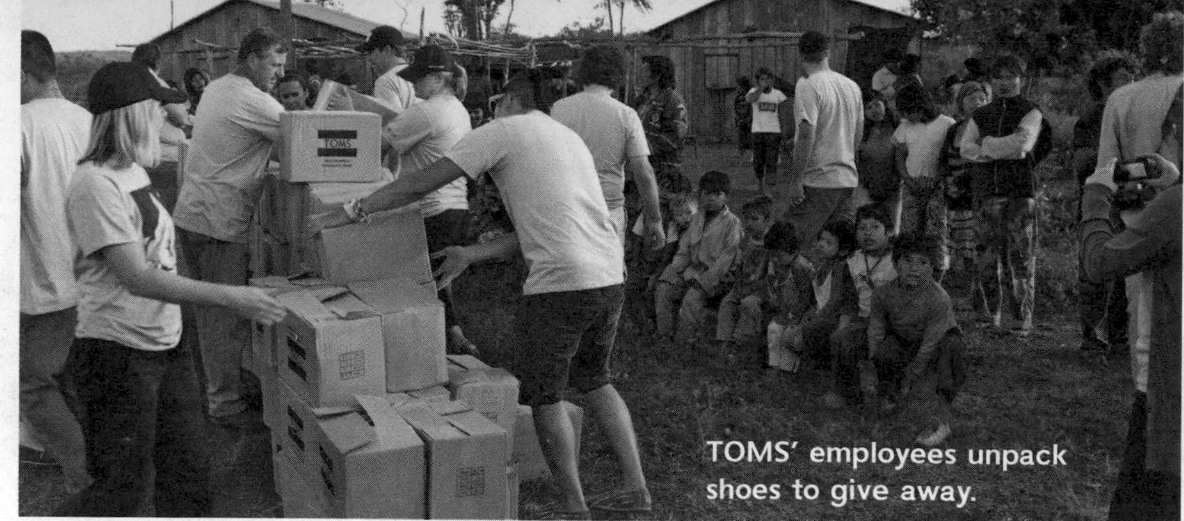

TOMS' employees unpack shoes to give away.

The company has **expanded** to sell eyeglasses. In a similar program, one pair of eyeglasses is donated for every pair that is bought.

Mycoskie is pleased and surprised. "I always thought I would spend the first half of my life making money and the second half giving it away," Mycoskie says. "I never thought I could do both at the same time."

Giving Back Rocks!

Have you ever seen a Hard Rock Cafe? The company runs restaurants and hotels. In 1990, the company **launched** a new enterprise: charity. Since then, it has given away millions of dollars to different causes. Its motto is Love All, Serve All.

One way the company raises funds for charity is by selling a line of T-shirts. The process starts with rock stars designing the art that goes on the shirts. Then the shirts are sold on the Internet. Part of the money that is raised from the sales of the shirts is given to charity.

Employees at Hard Rock Cafe locations are **encouraged** to raise money for their community. Every store does it differently.

The Hard Rock Cafes are successful and give back to the community.

ELD.PI.4.1.Ex, ELD.PI.4.1.Br, ELD.PI.4.5.Ex, ELD.PI.4.5.Br, ELD.PI.4.6a.Ex, ELD.PI.4.6a.Br, ELD.PI.4.7.Ex, ELD.PI.4.7.Br, ELD.PI.4.12a.Ex, ELD.PI.4.12a.Br See the California Standards section.

Top Five Biggest Charities

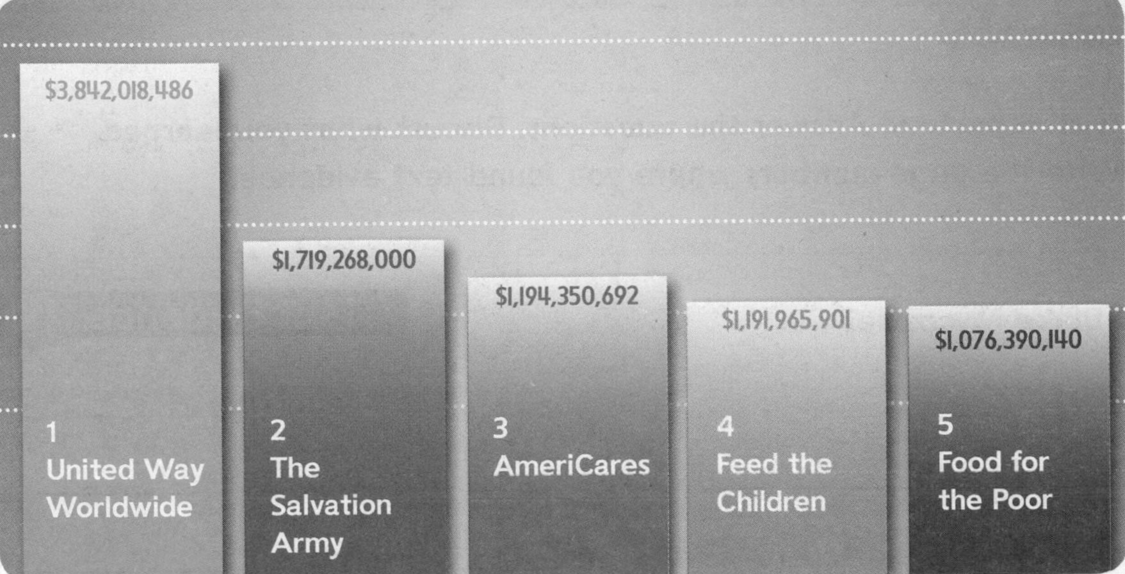

Source: The Chronicle Of Philanthropy

Individuals as well as businesses are committed to helping people in need. This graph shows the American charities that got the most donations in one recent year and how much money they raised.

The restaurant in Hollywood, Florida, worked with some exceptional students from two Florida high schools. Together, they put on an event to raise money for the Make-A-Wish Foundation. The foundation grants wishes to children with serious medical problems.

The Bottom Line

Every day companies are thinking of innovative ways to give back to their community. If you own a business, making a profit is important. However, helping others is just as important as the bottom line. Helping others is good business!

Make Connections

How do the two companies profiled in this article help others? ESSENTIAL QUESTION

If you owned a business, how would you use some of your profits to help others? TEXT TO SELF

Text Evidence

1 Sentence Structure ACT

Reread the second sentence in the first paragraph. Circle the nouns in the first sentence that the pronoun *they* refers to. Underline the actions *they* do.

2 Comprehension

Main Idea and Key Details

Look at the chart. How does it connect with the main idea of the selection?

____

____

3 Talk About It

The author's purpose for writing "Dollars and Sense" is to persuade the reader. Do you think the author succeeded? Justify your answer.

____

______________________________.

ELD.PI.4.1.Ex, ELD.PI.4.1.Br, ELD.PI.4.3.Ex, ELD.PI.4.3.Br, ELD.PI.4.5.Ex, ELD.PI.4.5.Br, ELD.PI.4.6a.Ex, ELD.PI.4.6a.Br, ELD.PII.4.2a.Ex, ELD.PII.4.2a.Br See the California Standards section.

Respond to the Text

Partner Discussion **Work with a partner. Answer the questions. Discuss what you learned about "Dollars and Sense." Write the page numbers where you found text evidence.**

What did you learn about Blake Mycoskie?	**Text Evidence**
I read he started TOMS so that ______________________.	Page(s): __________
TOMS also gives away ______________________.	Page(s): __________
According to the author Blake Mycoskie started TOMS after he ______ ______________________.	Page(s): __________

What did you learn about the Hard Rock Cafe?	**Text Evidence**
Based on the text, it raises money by ______________________.	Page(s): __________
The company encourages its workers to ______________________.	Page(s): __________
One restaurant in Florida raised money for ______________________.	Page(s): __________

Group Discussion **Present your answers to the group. Cite text evidence to justify your thinking. Listen to and discuss the group's opinions about your answers.**

ELD.PI.4.1.Ex, ELD.PI.4.1.Br, ELD.PI.4.3.Ex, ELD.PI.4.3.Br, ELD.PI.4.5.Ex, ELD.PI.4.5.Br, ELD.PI.4.9.Ex, ELD.PI.4.9.Br, ELD.PI.4.10b.Ex, ELD.PI.4.10b.Br, ELD.PI.4.11a.Ex, ELD.PI.4.11a.Br, ELD.PI.4.12a.Ex, ELD.PI.4.12a.Br See the California Standards section.

Write Review your notes about "Dollars and Sense." Then write your answer to the essential question. Use text evidence to support your answer. Use vocabulary words from this week's reading in your writing.

How can a business help others?

Many large businesses think that being successful is ______________________

____.

Based on the text, companies help others by ______________________

____.

According to the author, companies are always looking for new ways to ________

____.

COLLABORATE

Share Writing Present your writing to the class. Discuss their opinions. Think about what they have to say. Did they justify their claims? Explain why you agree or disagree with their claims.

I agree with ____________ because ____________.

I disagree with ____________ because ____________.

ELD.PI.4.1.Ex, ELD.PI.4.1.Br, ELD.PI.4.3.Ex, ELD.PI.4.3.Br, ELD.PI.4.5.Ex, ELD.PI.4.5.Br, ELD.PI.4.9.Ex, ELD.PI.4.9.Br, ELD.PI.4.10b.Ex, ELD.PI.4.10b.Br, ELD.PI.4.11a.Ex, ELD.PI.4.11a.Br, ELD.PI.4.12a.Ex, ELD.PI.4.12a.Br See the California Standards section.

Write to Sources

pages 66-69

Take Notes About the Text **I took notes on this idea web to answer this question:** ***Do you think TOMS does a good job of helping people?***

Opinion
TOMS does a good job of helping people.

- TOMS gives away shoes to kids who need them.
- They donate one pair of shoes for every pair they sell.
- Now they donate eyeglasses, too.
- TOMS makes money and gives it away at the same time.

Stockbyte/Getty Images

 ELD.PI.4.1.Ex, ELD.PI.4.1.Br, ELD.PI.4.5.Ex, ELD.PI.4.5.Br, ELD.PI.4.6a.Ex, ELD.PI.4.6a.Br, ELD.PI.4.11a.Ex, ELD.PI.4.11a.Br See the California Standards section.

Write About the Text **I used notes from my idea web to write an opinion about whether TOMS does a good job of helping people.**

Student Model: *Opinion*

I think TOMS does a good job of helping people. TOMS gives away shoes to kids who need them. They donate one pair of shoes for every pair they sell. They give away glasses. TOMS makes money and donates things. Everyone wins!

TALK ABOUT IT

Text Evidence

Draw a box around a detail that comes from the notes. Does the sentence provide a supporting detail?

Grammar

Underline a phrase that describes the kids. Why does the writer add this phrase?

Connect Ideas

Circle the sentences that tell what TOMS gives away. How can you combine the sentences into one sentence?

Your Turn

Do you think other companies are as good as TOMS in helping people? Use text evidence in your writing.

>> *Go Digital*
Write your response online. Use your editing checklist.

ELD.PI.4.1.Ex, ELD.PI.4.1.Br, ELD.PI.4.2.Ex, ELD.PI.4.2.Br, ELD.PI.4.5.Ex, ELD.PI.4.5.Br, ELD.PI.4.6a.Ex, ELD.PI.4.6a.Br, ELD.PI.4.10a.Ex, ELD.PI.4.10a.Br, ELD.PI.4.11a.Ex, ELD.PI.4.11a.Br, ELD.PI.4.12a.Ex, ELD.PJ.4.12a.Br, ELD.PII.4.6.Ex, ELD.PII.4.6.Br See the California Standards section.

Unit 2

Amazing Animals

The Big Idea

What can animals teach us?

Gary Vestal/Photographer's Choice/Getty Images

TALK ABOUT IT

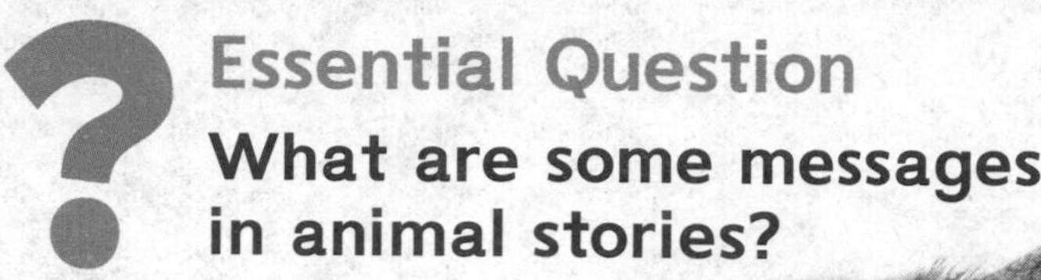

Weekly Concept Literary Lessons

Essential Question

What are some messages in animal stories?

» *Go Digital*

What is the squirrel doing? Describe what you see in the chart. What kind of message does the picture tell you?

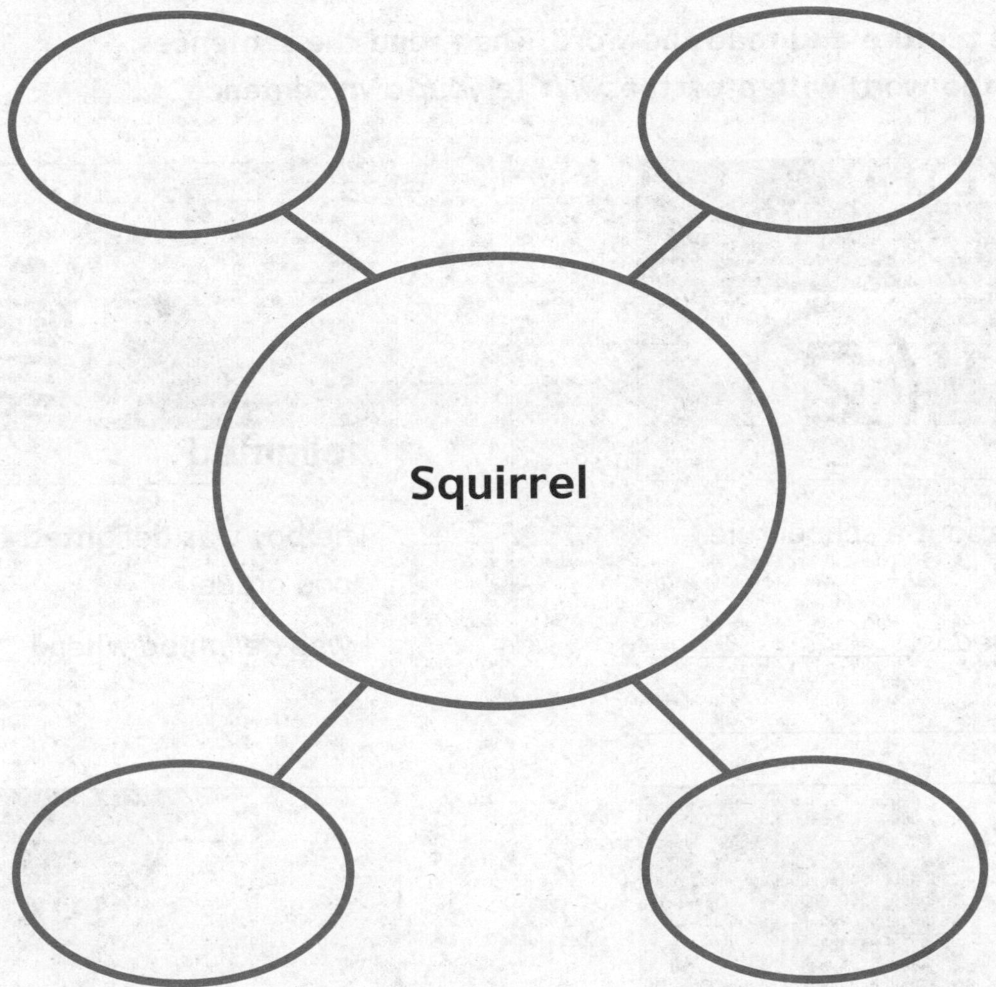

Look at the photo of the squirrel. Discuss the kind of message this photo tells. Use the words from the chart. You can say:

The squirrel is________________.

The message is _______________.

ELD.PI.4.1.Ex, ELD.PI.4.1.Br, ELD.PI.4.5.Ex, ELD.PI.4.5.Br, ELD.PI.4.12a.Ex, ELD.PI.4.12a.Br See the California Standards section.

More Vocabulary

COLLABORATE

Look at the picture and read the word. Then read the sentences. Talk about the word with a partner. Write your own sentence.

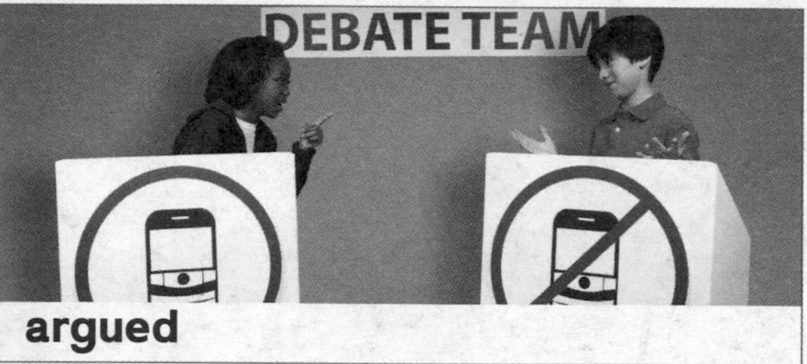

argued

The students **argued** about a school rule in a debate.

Another word for *argued* is ______________

______________________________.

assistance

To get on the train, the woman needs the **assistance** of the dog.

Another word for *assistance* is ____________

______________________________.

delighted

The boy was **delighted** to receive a good grade.

I was *delighted* when I ________________.

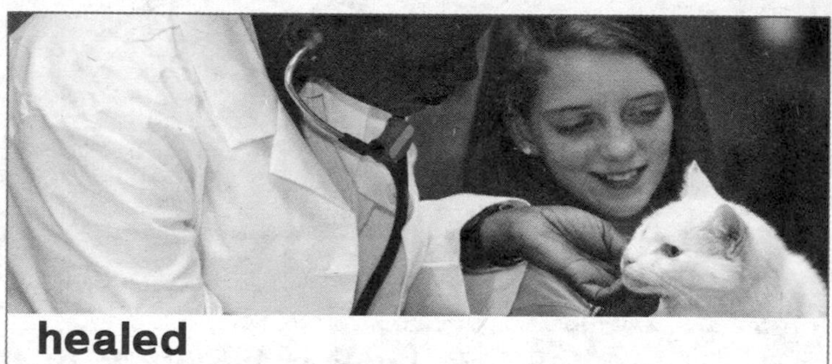

healed

The cat **healed** after visiting the veterinarian.

Another definition for *healed* is ____________

______________________________.

(tl)Eclipse Studios/McGraw-Hill Education; (tr) Westend61/Glow Images; (bl)Altrendo images/Altrendo/Getty Images; (br)Kali Nine LLC/iStock/360/Getty Images

 ELD.PI.4.1.Ex, ELD.PI.4.1.Br, ELD.PI.4.5.Ex, ELD.PI.4.5.Br, ELD.PI.4.12a.Ex, ELD.PI.4.12a.Br See the California Standards section.

magnificent

The woman stared at the **magnificent** tree.

Another word for *magnificent* is ____________

____.

reward

The **reward** for the girl's hard work was a blue ribbon.

My parents gave me a *reward* when I ______

____.

Words and Phrases
Suffixes: *-ly* and *-er*

The suffix *-ly* tells the way something is done.

The dog suddenly started to bark.

The suffix *-er* can be added to a word to tell what a person does.

The crier shouted out news to the people.

Read the sentences below. Write the word that means the same as the underlined words.

The window slammed shut in a sudden way.

____

The person who took the photograph made a copy of the photograph.

____

» Go Digital **Add the suffixes to your New Words notebook. Write a sentence to show the meaning of each.**

Text Evidence

1 Talk About It

Look at the illustration. Read the title. Talk about what you see. Write your ideas.

What does this title tell you?

____

____

____

______________________________.

What is the bird doing?

____

____

____

______________________________.

Take notes as you read the story.

Shared Read Genre • Folktale

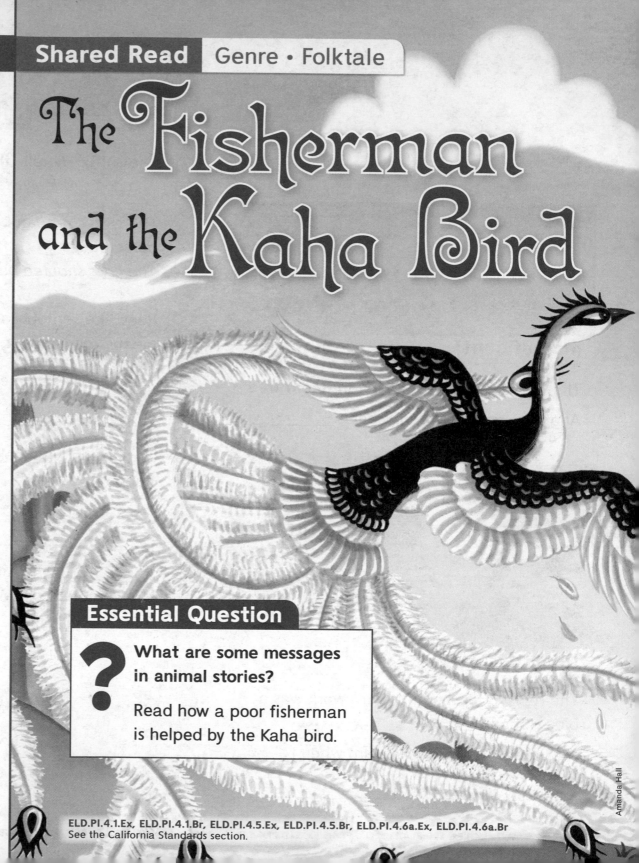

The Fisherman and the Kaha Bird

Essential Question

What are some messages in animal stories?

Read how a poor fisherman is helped by the Kaha bird.

Amanda Hall

ELD.PI.4.1.Ex, ELD.PI.4.1.Br, ELD.PI.4.5.Ex, ELD.PI.4.5.Br, ELD.PI.4.6a.Ex, ELD.PI.4.6a.Br
See the California Standards section.

Long ago there lived an old fisherman who made his pitiful living catching fish. All day the old man sat on the riverbank waiting for the fish to bite. But he never had more than one or two small fish to sell at the market. He and his wife were always hungry.

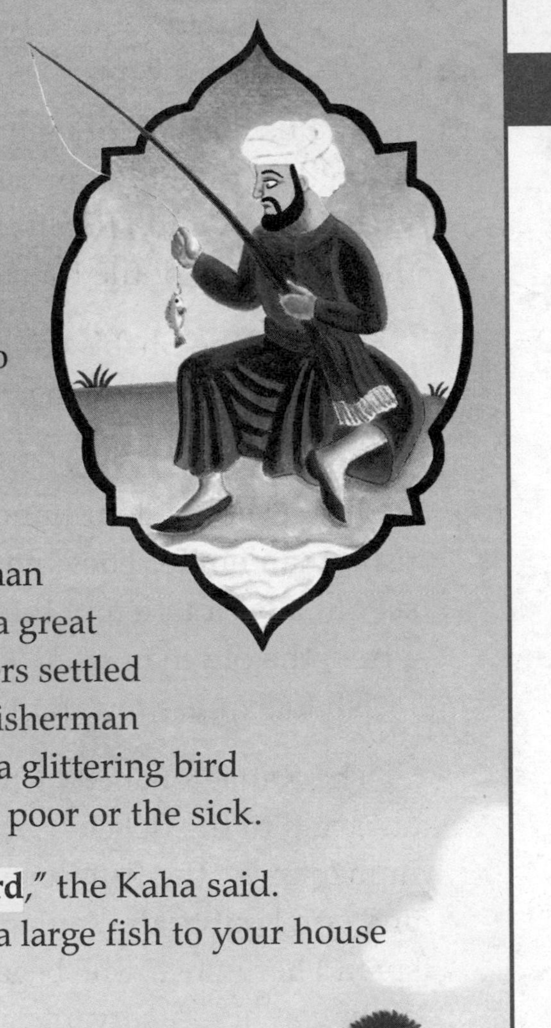

One morning, the tired old fisherman trudged slowly to the river. Suddenly a great bird with bright, dazzling silver feathers settled in the tree above him. The **delighted** fisherman knew this was the **magnificent** Kaha, a glittering bird that occasionally appeared to help the poor or the sick.

"I see you work for very little **reward**," the Kaha said. "I wish to help. Every day I will bring a large fish to your house that you can sell at the market."

The old man couldn't believe his luck. As the days passed, the honest Kaha kept her promise. The fisherman sold the fish and came home with plenty of food. Soon he was bringing home clothing made from brightly colored silk fabric for his wife.

At the market one day, the Shah's crier made an announcement: "Find the great Kaha for our **eminent** Shah and receive a reward of fifty bags of gold!"

Amanda Hall

ELD.PI.4.1.Ex, ELD.PI.4.1.Br, ELD.PI.4.5.Ex, ELD.PI.4.5.Br, ELD.PI.4.6a.Ex, ELD.PI.4.6a.Br, ELD.PI.4.7.Ex, ELD.PI.4.7.Br, ELD.PI.4.12a.Ex, ELD.PI.4.12a.Br See the California Standards section.

Text Evidence

1 Sentence Structure ACT

Reread the third sentence in the second paragraph. Circle the comma that separates the sentence into two parts. Draw a box around the part that tells what the Kaha is.

2 Comprehension

Reread the fourth paragraph. How did the old man's luck change after he met the Kaha bird? Underline the sentences that tell you.

3 Specific Vocabulary ACT

Look at the last sentence in the last paragraph. The word *eminent* means "well known and important." Why is the *eminent* Shah offering a reward?

The eminent Shah is offering a reward for ______________________

______________________________.

Text Evidence

1 Comprehension

Reread the first paragraph. Why was the fisherman arguing with himself?

2 Sentence Structure ACT

Reread the second sentence in the third paragraph. Who does the pronoun *they* refer to? Underline the nouns in the first sentence that refer to the pronoun *they*.

COLLABORATE

3 Talk About It

Reread the last paragraph. Discuss what happened to the Kaha bird. Then write about it.

The fisherman thought, "If I had fifty bags of gold, I would be rich! But how can I betray the bird?" He **argued** with himself until, finally, his greed for gold blinded him to the generosity of the Kaha bird.

He told the Shah's crier about the Kaha and requested **assistance** in catching her. He asked for four hundred men to help him.

That evening, four hundred servants followed the fisherman home. They hid among the trees as the fisherman set out a feast to tempt the bird. When the Kaha landed in a tree, the old man said, "Come dine with me, dear friend. I wish to express my gratitude."

The Kaha, touched by the fisherman's kindness and attracted to the delicious meal, flew down to join him. Immediately, the fisherman grabbed the Kaha by the feet and cried out to the servants to help him. The startled Kaha spread her wings. She began to fly up with the fisherman pulling at her. A servant caught the fisherman by the feet, but the bird rose higher. A second and third servant grabbed onto the first until soon four hundred servants hung by one another's feet as the Kaha soared upward.

ELD.PI.4.1.Ex, ELD.PI.4.1.Br, ELD.PI.4.5.Ex, ELD.PI.4.5.Br, ELD.PI.4.6a.Ex, ELD.PI.4.6a.Br, ELD.PI.4.12a.Ex, ELD.PI.4.12a.Br, ELD.PII.4.2a.Ex, ELD.PII.4.2a.Br See the California Standards section.

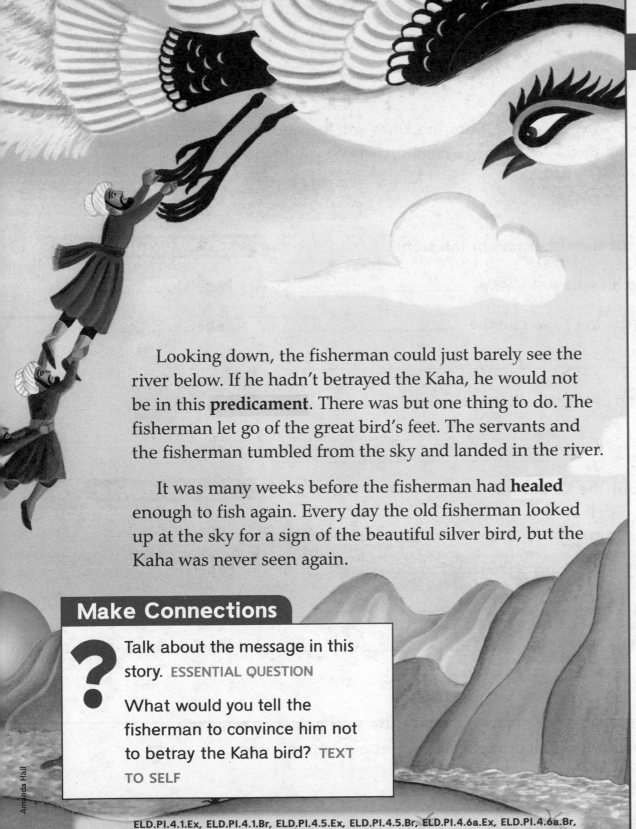

Looking down, the fisherman could just barely see the river below. If he hadn't betrayed the Kaha, he would not be in this **predicament**. There was but one thing to do. The fisherman let go of the great bird's feet. The servants and the fisherman tumbled from the sky and landed in the river.

It was many weeks before the fisherman had **healed** enough to fish again. Every day the old fisherman looked up at the sky for a sign of the beautiful silver bird, but the Kaha was never seen again.

Make Connections

? Talk about the message in this story. ESSENTIAL QUESTION

What would you tell the fisherman to convince him not to betray the Kaha bird? TEXT TO SELF

Amanda Hall

ELD.PI.4.1.Ex, ELD.PI.4.1.Br, ELD.PI.4.5.Ex, ELD.PI.4.5.Br, ELD.PI.4.6a.Ex, ELD.PI.4.6a.Br, ELD.PI.4.7.Ex, ELD.PI.4.7.Br, ELD.PI.4.12a.Ex, ELD.PI.4.12a.Br See the California Standards section.

Text Evidence

1 Specific Vocabulary ACT

Reread the second sentence in the first paragraph. A *predicament* is "a difficult situation." Why is the fisherman in a predicament?

The fisherman is in a predicament because he ____________________

____________________.

2 Sentence Structure ACT

Reread the last sentence in the first paragraph. Circle the subjects that tell who the sentence is about. Underline the words that tell two things they did.

3 Talk About It

Discuss how the Kaha bird probably felt about how the fisherman treated her. Then write about it.

____

____________________.

Respond to the Text

Partner Discussion **Work with a partner. Describe what you learned about "The Fisherman and the Kaha Bird." Write page numbers where you found text evidence.**

What did you learn about the fisherman in the story?	**Text Evidence**
I read the fisherman and his wife are always ______________.	Page(s): ______
When the fisherman meets the Kaha bird, he ______________ ______________.	Page(s): ______
In the story, the fisherman betrays the Kaha because ______________.	Page(s): ______

What did you learn about the Kaha bird?	**Text Evidence**
I learned that the Kaha is ______________.	Page(s): ______
The Kaha brings the fisherman ______________ ______________.	Page(s): ______
In the story, the fisherman tricks Kaha by ______________.	Page(s): ______

Group Discussion **Present your answers to the class. Cite text evidence to justify your thinking. Listen to and discuss the group's opinions about your answers.**

ELD.PI.4.1.Ex, ELD.PI.4.1.Br, ELD.PI.4.3.Ex, ELD.PI.4.3.Br, ELD.PI.4.5.Ex, ELD.PI.4.5.Br, ELD.PI.4.9.Ex, ELD.PI.4.9.Br, ELD.PI.4.10b.Ex, ELD.PI.4.10b.Br, ELD.PI.4.12a.Ex, ELD.PI.4.12a.Br See the California Standards section.

Write **Work with a partner. Review your notes about "The Fisherman and the Kaha Bird." Then write your answer to the essential question. Use text evidence to support your answer. Use vocabulary words from this week's reading in your writing.**

How does the Kaha help the fisherman?

The Kaha helps the fisherman by ______________________________

______________________________.

The fisherman forgets about the Kaha's kindness because ______________

______________________________.

In the end of the story, the fisherman ______________________________

______________________________.

COLLABORATE

Share Writing **Present your writing to the class. Discuss their opinions. Think about what they have to say. Did they justify their claims? Explain why you agree or disagree with their claims.**

I agree with ____________ because ____________.

I disagree with ____________ because ____________.

ELD.PI.4.1.Ex, ELD.PI.4.1.Br, ELD.PI.4.5.Ex, ELD.PI.4.5.Br, ELD.PI.4.9.Ex, ELD.PI.4.9.Br, ELD.PI.4.10b.Ex, ELD.PI.4.10b.Br, ELD.PI.4.11a.Ex, ELD.PI.4.11a.Br, ELD.PI.4.12a.Ex, ELD.PI.4.12a.Br See the California Standards section.

Write to Sources

pages 80–83

Take Notes About the Text **I took notes about the story on this sequence chart to help write this letter:** ***Write a letter from the Kaha bird to the fisherman. Tell him why he will never see you again.***

The Kaha bird helps the poor fisherman by bringing him fish.

↓

The Shah offers a reward for the Kaha bird.

↓

The fisherman tricks the Kaha bird. He invites the Kaha to dinner and tries to trap her.

↓

The Kaha bird gets away and is never seen again.

Write About the Text **I used notes from my sequence chart to write a letter that tells why the fisherman will never see the Kaha bird again.**

Student Model: *Narrative Text*

Dear Fisherman,

You tricked me! I helped you by bringing you fish. Then the Shah offered a reward for finding me. You invited me to dinner. You were really trying to trap me for the reward. You will never see me again. I don't help greedy people.

Sincerely,

The Kaha Bird

TALK ABOUT IT

Text Evidence

Draw a box around the detail from the sequence chart that begins the letter. Why is this a strong opening?

Grammar

Circle a past-tense verb. Why is the letter written in the past tense?

Connect Ideas

Underline the sentences about the fisherman's dinner. How can you combine the sentences to connect the ideas?

Your Turn

Write a letter from the fisherman to the Kaha bird. Tell the Kaha bird why you are sorry. Use text evidence.

>> *Go Digital*
Write your response online. Use your editing checklist.

ELD.PI.4.1.Ex, ELD.PI.4.1.Br, ELD.PI.4.2.Ex, ELD.PI.4.2.Br, ELD.PI.4.5.Ex, ELD.PI.4.5.Br, ELD.PI.4.6a.Ex, ELD.PI.4.6a.Br, ELD.PI.4.10b.Ex, ELD.PI.4.10b.Br, ELD.PI.4.12a.Ex, ELD.PI.4.12a.Br, ELD.PII.4.1.Ex, ELD.PII.4.1.Br, ELD.PII.4.3.Ex, ELD.PII.4.3.Br, ELD.PII.4.6.Ex, ELD.PII.4.6.Br See the California Standards section.

TALK ABOUT IT

Weekly Concept Animals in Fiction

Essential Question

How do animal characters change in familiar stories?

>> *Go Digital*

Describe the frog in the photo. Write about the kind of character the frog might be in a story in the chart.

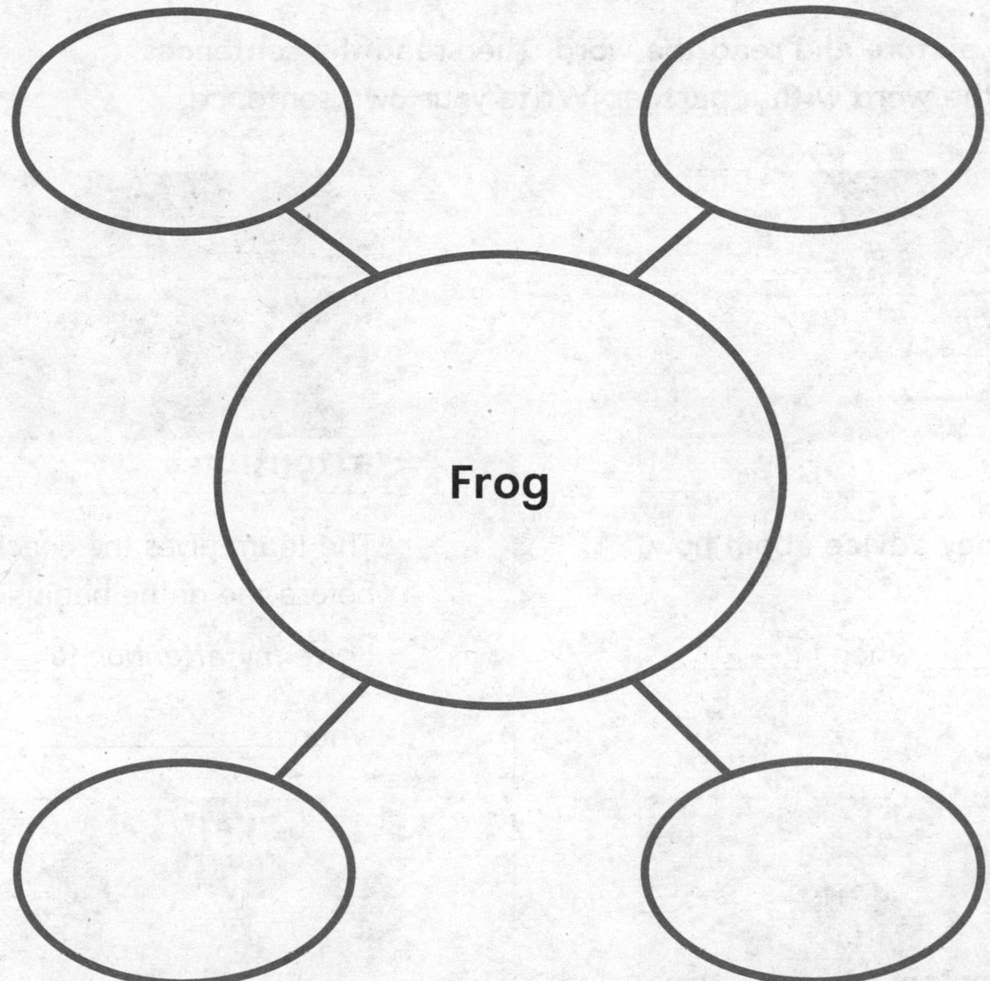

Look at the photo of the frog. What kind of story character might the frog be? Use the words from the chart. You can say:

The frog can be a ________________ because it ____________.

wildpixel/iStock/Getty Images

ELD.PI.4.1.Ex, ELD.PI.4.1.Br, ELD.PI.4.5.Ex, ELD.PI.4.5.Br, ELD.PI.4.12a.Ex, ELD.PI.4.12a.Br See the California Standards section.

More Vocabulary

Look at the picture and read the word. Then read the sentences. Talk about the word with a partner. Write your own sentence.

advice

The teacher gives the boy **advice** about how to solve a problem.

I get *advice* from ________ when I ________.

attention

The team gives the coach their **attention** before the game begins.

I give my *attention* to ____________________

when ________________________________.

approach

The penguins **approach** the water for a swim.

Another meaning for *approach* is __________

________________________________.

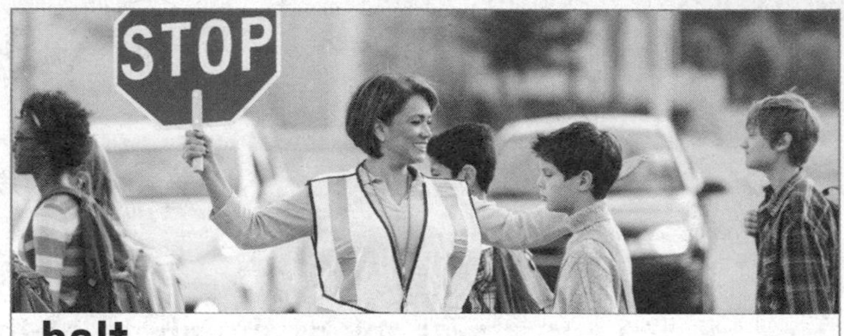

halt

The crossing guard tells the cars to **halt**.

Another word for *halt* is ____________________

________________________________.

nervously

The man **nervously** looks at his watch.

Underline the suffix.

The man is acting in a nervous way because

____.

pause

There was a **pause** between each inning of the game.

Another word for *pause* is _______________

____.

Words and Phrases
Prefixes: *un-* and *dis-*

The prefix *un-* means *not.*

The woman is unsure of the weather.

The prefix *dis-* means *not* or *the opposite of.*

I saw the sun disappear behind a cloud.

Read the sentences below. Write a word with a prefix that means the same as the underlined words.

My friend was not sure if he could play.

My friend was ____________________ if he could play.

The puddle of water will not appear in a few days.

The puddle of water will _______________ in a few days.

» Go Digital **Add these prefixes to your New Words notebook. Write a sentence to show the meaning of each.**

Text Evidence

1 Talk About It

Look at the picture. Read the title. Talk about what you see. Write your ideas.

What does this title tell you?

____

____

Why are the ants carrying water?

____

____

Why is Grasshopper resting?

____

____

Take notes as you read the play.

Shared Read Genre • Drama

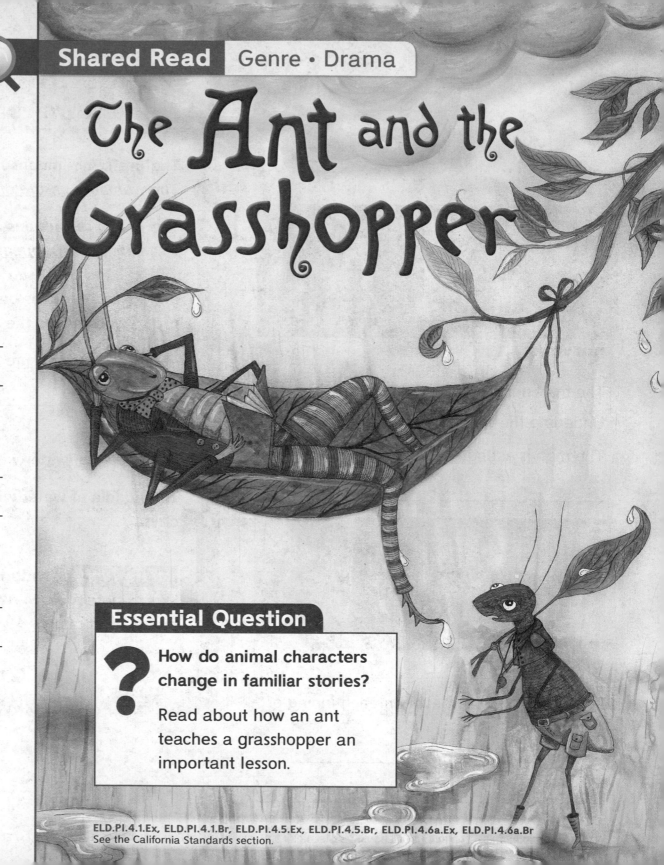

The Ant and the Grasshopper

Essential Question

How do animal characters change in familiar stories?

Read about how an ant teaches a grasshopper an important lesson.

ELD.PI.4.1.Ex, ELD.PI.4.1.Br, ELD.PI.4.5.Ex, ELD.PI.4.5.Br, ELD.PI.4.6a.Ex, ELD.PI.4.6a.Br
See the California Standards section.

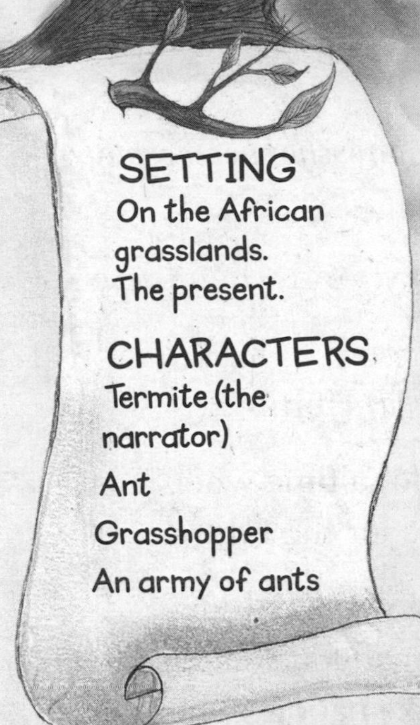

Scene I

(It is raining heavily on the African grasslands. Termite turns and sees the audience.)

TERMITE: *(Happily)* Yipes! I didn't see you. Welcome to the great plains of Africa! We're **soggy** now because it's the rainy season. Sorry. *(She shrugs and smiles.)* Today, we'll visit two very different friends of mine–Ant and Grasshopper. Maybe you have heard of them from other familiar stories. Let's see what my buddies are up to!

(An army of ants march in, carrying leaves filled with water. They ***approach*** *Grasshopper, who lounges lazily under a plant.)*

ANT: *(In a loud voice)* Company, **halt**! *(The ants stop.)*

GRASSHOPPER: *(Stretching and yawning)* Ant, old pal! Good to see you! I was just napping when I heard your feet pounding down the way. What's all the commotion?

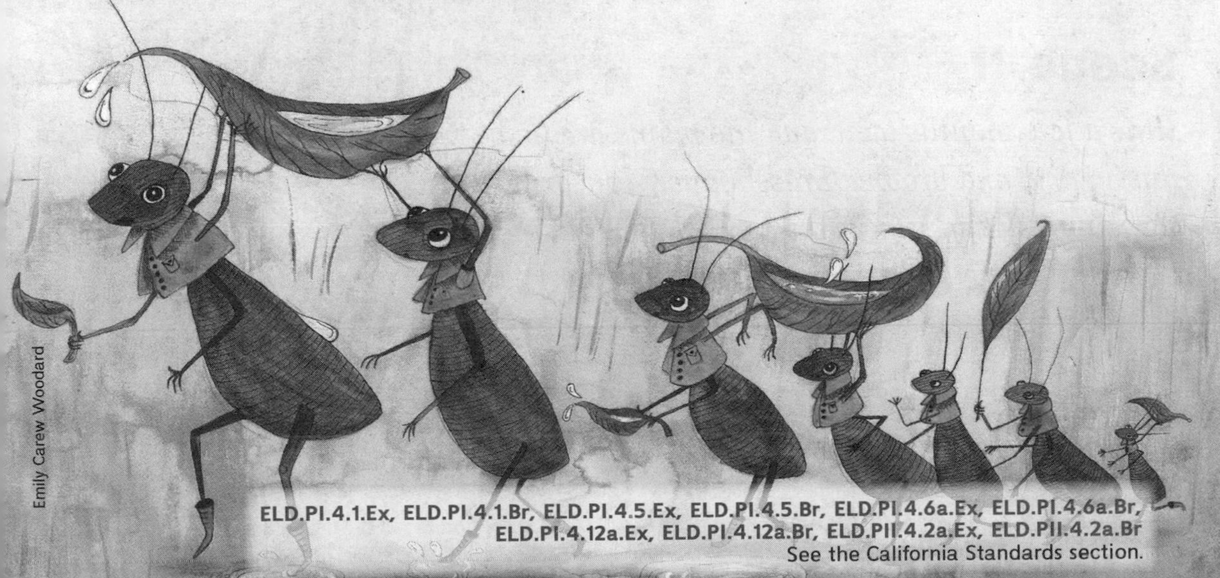

Emily Carew Woodard

ELD.PI.4.1.Ex, ELD.PI.4.1.Br, ELD.PI.4.5.Ex, ELD.PI.4.5.Br, ELD.PI.4.6a.Ex, ELD.PI.4.6a.Br, ELD.PI.4.12a.Ex, ELD.PI.4.12a.Br, ELD.PII.4.2a.Ex, ELD.PII.4.2a.Br
See the California Standards section.

1 Specific Vocabulary

Reread line 3 in the part of Termite. Circle the word *soggy*. Underline a clue in the sentence that tells what soggy means.

The African grasslands is soggy

during ______________.

2 Sentence Structure

Reread the last three lines in the part of Termite. Underline the nouns that the pronoun *them* refers to. What is Termite's relationship to Ant and Grasshopper?

Termite, Ant, and Grasshopper

are ______________.

3 Comprehension

Theme

Reread the second stage direction. Underline the words that tell what the ants are doing while it rains. Circle the words that tell what Grasshopper is doing while it rains.

Text Evidence

1 Sentence Structure ACT

Reread the stage directions in the second paragraph. Underline the subject in the first sentence. Circle the actions of the subject.

2 Specific Vocabulary ACT

Reread Grasshopper's second part. The word *toil* means "very hard work." Underline a clue in the paragraph that tells what *toil* means.

Circle the word in the paragraph that means the opposite of *toil.*

COLLABORATE

3 Talk About It

Ant tells Grasshopper he will regret being lazy. Discuss why Ant thinks this way. Do you agree? Write about it.

____

____

____

____

ANT: *(Looking annoyed)* Grasshopper, have you noticed what falls from the sky above you?

(Ant stands at ***attention*** *and points up at a cloud. Grasshopper sleepily rises and stands next to Ant. He looks at the sky.)*

ANT: Rain, Grasshopper! Rain falls from the sky! And when there is rain, there is work to be done.

GRASSHOPPER: *(Smiling then scratching his head)* Huh?

ANT: *(Sighing)* You should be collecting water for a time when it is unavailable. Instead, you lie here without a care for the future.

GRASSHOPPER: *(Laughing)* Oh, don't be so serious, ol' buddy! There is plenty of water now, and that's all that matters. You need to relax! You're much too tense. Why don't you make napping your new specialty instead of all this silly **toil**? Stop working so hard all the time!

ANT: *(Shaking his head as he grows frustrated)* The rainy season will not last forever, Grasshopper. Your carefree attitude will disappear with the water, and soon you will regret being lazy and wish you had been more energetic.

(The ants march off as Grasshopper continues to laugh.)

Scene II

(It is a few months later, and the plains are now dusty, dry, and brown. Grasshopper, appearing weak and sickly, knocks on Ant's door. Ant, seeming strong and healthy, opens the door.)

ELD.PI.4.1.Ex, ELD.PI.4.1.Br, ELD.PI.4.5.Ex, ELD.PI.4.5.Br, ELD.PI.4.6a.Ex, ELD.PI.4.6a.Br, ELD.PI.4.7.Ex, ELD.PI.4.7.Br, ELD.PI.4.11a.Ex, ELD.PI.4.11a.Br See the California Standards section.

GRASSHOPPER: *(Nervously)* Hi there, pal. . . . I was in the neighborhood. Boy, can you believe how hot it is? So . . . uh . . . I was wondering if maybe . . . by chance . . . you might have some water for your old friend.

(Ant tries to close the door, but Grasshopper quickly grabs it.)

GRASSHOPPER: *(Begging wildly)* PLEASE, Ant! I am so thirsty! There isn't a drop of water anywhere!

ANT: *(After a **pause**)* We ants worked hard to collect this water, but we cannot let you **suffer**. *(Giving Grasshopper a sip of water)* Do not think us selfish, but we can only share a few drops with you. I warned you that this time would come. If you had prepared, you would not be in this situation.

(Grasshopper walks slowly away. Termite watches him go.)

TERMITE: Although Ant has done a good deed, tired, cranky Grasshopper must still search for water. Grasshopper learned an important lesson today. Next time, he will follow Ant's **advice**!

Emily Carew Woodard

Make Connections

? Talk about how Ant and Grasshopper act like real people. ESSENTIAL QUESTION

Explain why you are more like Ant or more like Grasshopper. TEXT TO SELF

ELD.PI.4.1.Ex, ELD.PI.4.1.Br, ELD.PI.4.5.Ex, ELD.PI.4.5.Br, ELD.PI.4.6a.Ex, ELD.PI.4.6a.Br, ELD.PI.4.12a.Ex, ELD.PI.4.12a.Br See the California Standards section.

Text Evidence

1 Sentence Structure ACT

Reread Grasshopper's first dialogue. Circle the punctuation marks that show Grasshopper is talking in a nervous way. Why is Grasshopper nervous?

____

____

2 Specific Vocabulary ACT

Reread the lines for Ant. The word *suffer* means "to feel pain or have a hard time." How did Ant help Grasshopper? Underline the words.

Why doesn't Grasshopper have his own water?

Grasshopper does not have water because ________________.

3 Comprehension

Theme

Reread the ending. Underline the sentences that tell about the theme of the story.

Respond to the Text

Partner Discussion **Work with a partner. Describe what you learned about "The Ant and the Grasshopper." Write page numbers where you found text evidence.**

What do you learn about Ant?	**Text Evidence**
I read Ant works to ______.	Page(s): ______
Ant tells his friend Grasshopper ______.	Page(s): ______
In the end of the story, Ant does a good deed by ______.	Page(s): ______

What do you learn about Grasshopper?	**Text Evidence**
I read Grasshopper does not work because ______.	Page(s): ______
Grasshopper thinks Ant needs to ______.	Page(s): ______
In the end of the story, Grasshopper ______.	Page(s): ______

Group Discussion **Present your answers to the class. Cite text evidence to justify your thinking. Listen to and discuss the group's opinions about your answers.**

ELD.PI.4.1.Ex, ELD.PI.4.1.Br, ELD.PI.4.3.Ex, ELD.PI.4.3.Br, ELD.PI.4.5.Ex, ELD.PI.4.5.Br, ELD.PI.4.9.Ex, ELD.PI.4.9.Br, ELD.PI.4.10b.Ex, ELD.PI.4.10b.Br, ELD.PI.4.12a.Ex, ELD.PI.4.12a.Br See the California Standards section.

Write Work with a partner. Review your notes about "The Ant and the Grasshopper." Then write your answer to the essential question. Use text evidence to support your answer. Use vocabulary words from this week's reading in your writing.

What lesson does Ant teach Grasshopper?

Ant showed Grasshopper that working hard ______________________________

____.

Grasshopper learns that being lazy ______________________________

____.

The lesson Ant teaches Grasshopper is ______________________________

____.

COLLABORATE

Share Writing Present your writing to the class. Discuss their opinions. Think about what they have to say. Did they justify their claims? Explain why you agree or disagree with their claims.

I agree with ______________ because ______________.

I disagree with ______________ because ______________.

ELD.PI.4.1.Ex, ELD.PI.4.1.Br, ELD.PI.4.5.Ex, ELD.PI.4.5.Br, ELD.PI.4.9.Ex, ELD.PI.4.9.Br, ELD.PI.4.10b.Ex, ELD.PI.4.10b.Br, ELD.PI.4.11a.Ex, ELD.PI.4.11a.Br, ELD.PI.4.12a.Ex, ELD.PI.4.12a.Br See the California Standards section.

Write to Sources

Take Notes About the Text **I took notes on this chart to respond to the prompt:** ***Ant sends Grasshopper away. Write what Termite might say to Ant after Grasshopper leaves.***

pages 92–95

ANT	GRASSHOPPER
Ant tells Grasshopper there is work to be done. He should be collecting water.	Grasshopper says there is plenty of water. He tells Ant to relax.
Ant says the rain won't last forever. And he will regret being lazy.	Grasshopper laughs.
Ant answers the door and sees a sickly Grasshopper.	Grasshopper nervously asks Ant for water.
Ant shares a few drops.	Grasshopper leaves slowly.

 ELD.PI.4.1.Ex, ELD.PI.4.1.Br, ELD.PI.4.5.Ex, ELD.PI.4.5.Br, ELD.PI.4.6a.Ex, ELD.PI.4.6a.Br See the California Standards section.

Write About the Text **I used notes from my chart to write what Termite might say to Ant after Grasshopper leaves.**

Student Model: *Narrative Text*

TERMITE: That was nice of you, Ant. Why did you share water with that lazy grasshopper?

ANT: Grasshopper looked sick and thirsty. I had to share a few drops with him.

TERMITE: Do you think he learned his lesson?

ANT: I hope so. Now let's have a nice cool drink.

TALK ABOUT IT

Text Evidence

Draw a box around a detail from the notes. Why did Tori use this supporting detail?

Grammar

Circle a noun phrase that Ant uses to describe Grasshopper. What word describes the noun?

Connect Ideas

Underline the sentences where Ant tells about sharing water with Grasshopper. How can you combine the sentences to connect the ideas?

Your Turn

Grasshopper sees Ant during the rainy season. Write what Grasshopper and Ant say to each other.

>> *Go Digital*
Write your response online. Use your editing checklist.

ELD.PI.4.1.Ex, ELD.PI.4.1.Br, ELD.PI.4.2.Ex, ELD.PI.4.2.Br, ELD.PI.4.5.Ex, ELD.PI.4.5.Br, ELD.PI.4.6a.Ex, ELD.PI.4.6a.Br, ELD.PI.4.10b.Ex, ELD.PI.4.10b.Br, ELD.PII.4.6.Ex, ELD.PII.4.6.Br See the California Standards section.

TALK ABOUT IT

Weekly Concept Natural Connections

Essential Question

How are all living things connected?

» *Go Digital*

Write the living things you see in the photograph in the chart. Describe what the living things in the photograph are doing. What living things are there that you cannot see?

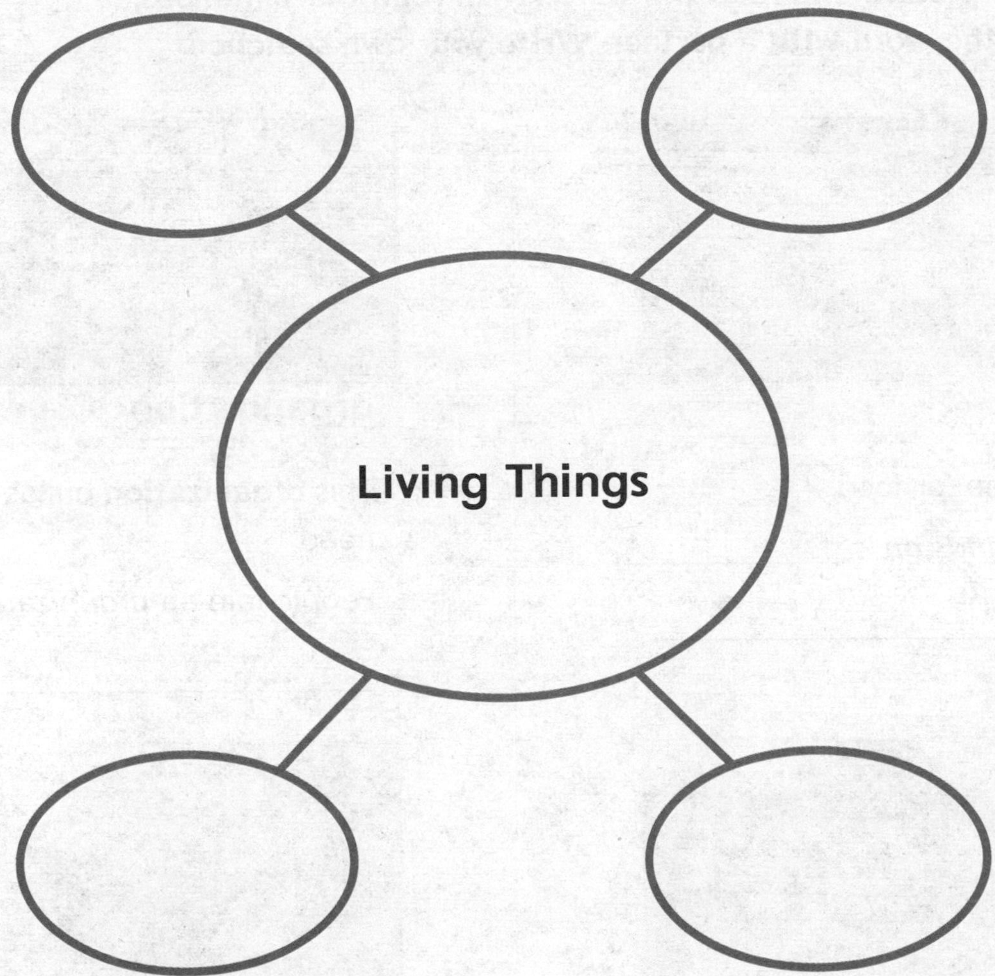

Look at the photo of living things. Discuss how the living things in the picture are connected. Use the words from the chart. You can say:

The __________ and __________ are connected because __________

____.

ELD.PI.4.1.Ex, ELD.PI.4.1.Br, ELD.PI.4.5.Ex, ELD.PI.4.5.Br, ELD.PI.4.12a.Ex, ELD.PI.4.12a.Br See the California Standards section.

More Vocabulary

Look at the picture and read the word. Then read the sentences. Talk about the word with a partner. Write your own sentence.

depends on

My dog **depends on** me for food.

Another word for *depends on* is ____________

____.

ignore

The boy tries to **ignore** his little brother.

I *ignore* ________ when __________________

____.

organization

This **organization** builds homes for people in need.

People join an *organization* because

____.

relationship

A baby elephant has a close **relationship** with its mother.

They have a close relationship because ________

____.

rescue

The helicopter is used to **rescue** people when they are in trouble.

Another word for *rescue* is ____________________

____.

resembles

The boy **resembles** his older brother.

Another word for *resembles* is ________________

____.

Words and Phrases

Phrasal Verbs

breaks down **= to stop working**

Pollution breaks down the relationship between coral and algae.

breaks through **= to move past something that is in your way**

The diver breaks through the water's surface.

Read the sentences below. Write the phrasal verb that means the same as the underlined words.

The old car often stops working.

The old car often ____________________.

The airplane moves past the thick clouds.

The airplane ____________________ the thick clouds.

» *Go Digital* **Add these phrasal verbs to your New Words notebook. Write a sentence to show the meaning of each.**

Text Evidence

COLLABORATE

1 Talk About It

Look at the photograph. Read the title. Talk about what you see. Write your ideas.

What does this title tell you?

____

____

____

____

What is the photographer doing?

____

____

____

____

Take notes as you read the text.

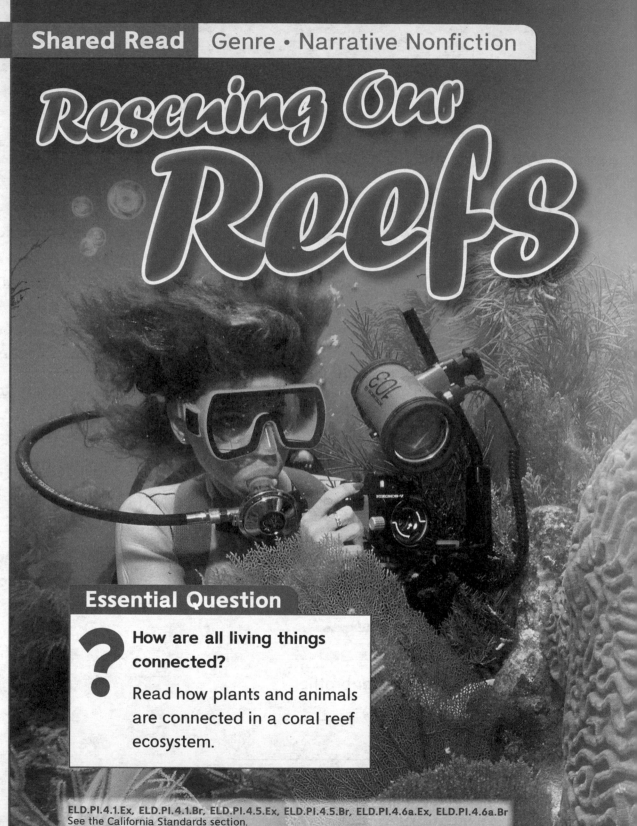

Rescuing Our Reefs

Essential Question

?

How are all living things connected?

Read how plants and animals are connected in a coral reef ecosystem.

ELD.PI.4.1.Ex, ELD.PI.4.1.Br, ELD.PI.4.5.Ex, ELD.PI.4.5.Br, ELD.PI.4.6a.Ex, ELD.PI.4.6a.Br
See the California Standards section.

Sitting on the side of the boat, the photographer fixes her scuba tank and mask. She waves to a man in a fishing boat. Then she dives backwards into the clear waters of the Florida Keys. She swims, breathing through her regulator. A large, colorful coral reef is laid out before her eyes. Sea anemones, red hind fish, gaudy parrotfish, yellow angelfish, and other animals **ignore** her as they go about their business. Life in this reef has flourished and grown.

Connections

The photographer knows the plants and animals in a reef ecosystem need each other to **survive**. Reefs are made up of billions of tiny animals called coral polyps. Plant-like algae live inside the coral. The algae use a process called photosynthesis to turn energy from the sun into food for themselves and the coral. In return, the coral gives the algae a home and the carbon dioxide needed for photosynthesis. Algae are a part of the food chain called producers. Producers make their own energy.

The photographer sees a blue and yellow parrotfish nibbling at the coral. She takes a picture. The parrotfish breaks apart the coral to get to the algae-filled polyps inside. In a food chain, the parrotfish is a consumer. Consumers cannot produce their own energy. As the parrotfish eats the algae, energy is passed through the food chain.

Parrotfish

In the distance, the photographer notices the long silver body of a barracuda lurking. The sea grass ripples in the current, swaying back and forth. It almost hides the hungry predator. She snaps a photo and swims on.

ELD.PI.4.1.Ex, ELD.PI.4.1.Br, ELD.PI.4.5.Ex, ELD.PI.4.5.Br, ELD.PI.4.6a.Ex, ELD.PI.4.6a.Br
See the California Standards section.

Text Evidence

1 Sentence Structure ACT

Reread the first sentence. Underline the subject that tells who the sentence is about. Circle the words that tell two things she is doing.

2 Specific Vocabulary ACT

Look at the first sentence in the second paragraph. The word *survive* means "to be able to stay alive."

In order to survive, coral and algae ______________________

______________________.

3 Comprehension

Main Idea and Details

Reread the third paragraph. What does the parrotfish need to survive? Underline a detail.

Text Evidence

1 Specific Vocabulary ACT

Reread the first paragraph. Look at the word *bleached*. Underline a clue in the sentence that tells what *bleached* means. What word in the next sentence means the opposite of *bleached?*

___

2 Sentence Structure ACT

Reread the first sentence in the third paragraph. Circle the punctuation mark that breaks the sentence into two parts. Underline what happens if pollution gets into the water.

COLLABORATE

3 Talk About It

Describe the relationship between plants and animals in the food chain. Then write about it.

___

___

Coral Bleaching

The photographer shoots more photos as she swims. The reef must have looked like this hundreds of years ago. But then she stops and stares at a big area of **bleached**, white coral. Once colorful, the whitish coral now looks like the broken pieces of a crumbled castle.

Coral **depends on** a natural balance to stay healthy. Climate change and pollution can cause an imbalance. Some areas have dried up from droughts while others have had more rain. Too much sun and warmer ocean temperatures can cause coral bleaching.

If pollution gets into the water or the water gets too warm, the **relationship** between the coral and algae breaks down. The algae stop making food. The coral ejects the algae. The algae are what give the coral its color. The coral loses its color. It starves because it needs the algae to make food for it.

Energy is passed along in a food chain.

Sun gives energy.

Plants use energy to grow.

Animals eat plants.

Animals eat animals.

ELD.PI.4.1.Ex, ELD.PI.4.1.Br, ELD.PI.4.5.Ex, ELD.PI.4.5.Br, ELD.PI.4.6a.Ex, ELD.PI.4.6a.Br, ELD.PI.4.8.Ex, ELD.PI.4.8.Br See the California Standards section.

Many plants and animals depend on the coral for food and shelter. As more and more coral reefs die, many animals and plants that live in these reefs may become extinct. The beautiful reef the photographer had seen earlier would **resemble** the white, crumbling reef before her.

Balancing Act

She turned and swam back to the boat. Later today, she would send her photographs to the Nature Conservancy. It is an **organization** that works to **rescue** our fragile reefs. Scientists there are trying to rebuild the reefs by attaching small pieces of staghorn coral to concrete blocks. Staghorn coral is used to grow new coral. Once the coral grows, the blocks are planted in the reefs.

The photographer hopes her pictures will help **spread the word**. They show the relationship between pollution, climate change, and coral bleaching. She breaks through the water's surface and climbs into the boat.

"I got some good shots of the healthy reef and the sick reef!" she shouts to her partner. Once aboard, she immediately begins putting her photos on her laptop.

Make Connections

Talk about how the plants and animals that live in the coral reef are connected. ESSENTIAL QUESTION

What could you do to help rescue the coral reefs? TEXT TO SELF

ELD.PI.4.1.Ex, ELD.PI.4.1.Br, ELD.PI.4.4Ex, ELD.PI.4.4.Br, ELD.PI.4.5.Ex, ELD.PI.4.5.Br, ELD.PI.4.6a.Ex, ELD.PI.4.6a.Br, ELD.PI.4.8.Ex, ELD.PI.4.8.Br See the California Standards section.

Text Evidence

1 Comprehension
Main Idea and Details

Reread the second paragraph. What does the Nature Conservancy do? Underline two details.

2 Specific Vocabulary ACT

Look at the first sentence in the third paragraph. The idiom *spread the word* means "tells lots of people about something."

What message is the photographer hoping to spread the word about?

____

____

3 Talk About It

What is the author's purpose in "Rescuing Our Coral Reefs?" Does it inform, persuade, or entertain? Justify your answer.

____

____

Respond to the Text

Partner Discussion **Work with a partner. Describe what you learned about "Rescuing Our Reefs." Write the page numbers where you found text evidence.**

What did you learn about plants in the reef?	Text Evidence
I read that algae ______________________________ ______________________________.	Page(s): ________
Based on the text, pollution causes algae to ______________.	Page(s): ________
According to the author, algae depend on coral to ____________ ______________________________.	Page(s): ________

What did you learn about coral in the reef?	Text Evidence
I learned that coral ______________________________.	Page(s): ________
Pollution causes coral to ______________________________.	Page(s): ________
Coral depends on algae to ______________________________.	Page(s): ________

Group Discussion **Present your answers to the group. Cite text evidence to justify your thinking. Listen to and discuss the group's opinions about your answers.**

 ELD.PI.4.1.Ex, ELD.PI.4.1.Br, ELD.PI.4.3.Ex, ELD.PI.4.3.Br, ELD.PI.4.5.Ex, ELD.PI.4.5.Br, ELD.PI.4.9.Ex, ELD.PI.4.9.Br, ELD.PI.4.10b.Ex, ELD.PI.4.10b.Br, ELD.PI.4.12a.Ex, ELD.PI.4.12a.Br See the California Standards section.

Write Work with a partner. Look at your notes about "Rescuing Our Reefs." Then write your answer to the essential question. Use text evidence to support your answer. Use vocabulary words from this week's reading in your writing.

How are the plants and animals in a coral reef connected?

Algae need coral to survive because ______________________________

____

______________________________.

Based on the text, pollution causes algae to ______________________________

____

______________________________.

Therefore, ______________ and ______________ are connected because

______________________________.

COLLABORATE

Share Writing Present your writing to the class. Discuss their opinions. Think about what they have to say. Did they justify their claims? Explain why you agree or disagree with their claims.

I agree with ____________ because ____________.

I disagree with ____________ because ____________.

ELD.PI.4.1.Ex, ELD.P1.4.I.Br, ELD.PI.4.2.Ex, ELD.PI.4.2.Br, ELD.PI.4.5.Ex, ELD.PI.4.5.Br, ELD.PI.4.9.Ex, ELD.PI.4.9.Br, ELD.PI.4.10b.Ex, ELD.PI.4.10b.Br, ELD.PI.4.11a.Ex, ELD.PI.4.11a.Br, ELD.PI.4.12a.Ex, ELD.PI.4.12a.Br See the California Standards section.

Write to Sources

Take Notes About the Text **I took notes on this idea web to answer the question:** ***What information does the author tell about the food chain?***

pages 104–107

Detail
Algae get energy from the sun.

Detail
Algae use energy to make food.

Main Idea
The author tells about the food chain.

Detail
Parrotfish cannot make food.

Detail
Parrotfish eat algae to get energy.

 ELD.PI.4.1.Ex, ELD.PI.4.1.Br, ELD.PI.4.5.Ex, ELD.PI.4.5.Br, ELD.PI.4.6a.Ex, ELD.PI.4.6a.Br See the California Standards section.

Write About the Text **I used my notes from my idea web to write a paragraph about the food chain.**

Student Model: *Informative Text*

The author describes the food chain in "Rescuing Our Reefs." Algae are plants that live inside coral reefs. Algae get energy from the sun. Algae use the energy to make food. Parrotfish cannot make food. Parrotfish eat algae to get energy. The author shows how algae and parrotfish are a part of the food chain.

TALK ABOUT IT

Text Evidence

Draw a box around a sentence that comes from the notes. Why did Zoe use this information as a supporting detail?

Grammar

Underline a present-tense verb. Why did Zoe use the present tense to write about the food chain?

Connect Ideas

Circle the sentences about parrotfish. How can you combine the sentences to connect ideas?

Your Turn

What information does the author tell about the Nature Conservancy? Use text evidence in your writing.

>> *Go Digital*
Write your response online. Use your editing checklist.

ELD.PI.4.1.Ex, ELD.PI.4.1.Br, ELD.PI.4.2.Ex, ELD.PI.4.2.Br, ELD.PI.4.5.Ex, ELD.PI.4.5.Br, ELD.PI.4.6a.Ex, ELD.PI.4.6a.Br, ELD.PI.4.10b.Ex, ELD.PI.4.10b.Br, ELD.PI.4.12a.Ex, ELD.PI.4.12a.Br, ELD.PII.4.6.Ex, ELD.PII.4.6.Br See the California Standards section.

TALK ABOUT IT

Weekly Concept Adaptations

Essential Question

What helps an animal survive?

>> *Go Digital*

Describe how the chameleon in the photograph looks. Write the description in the chart.

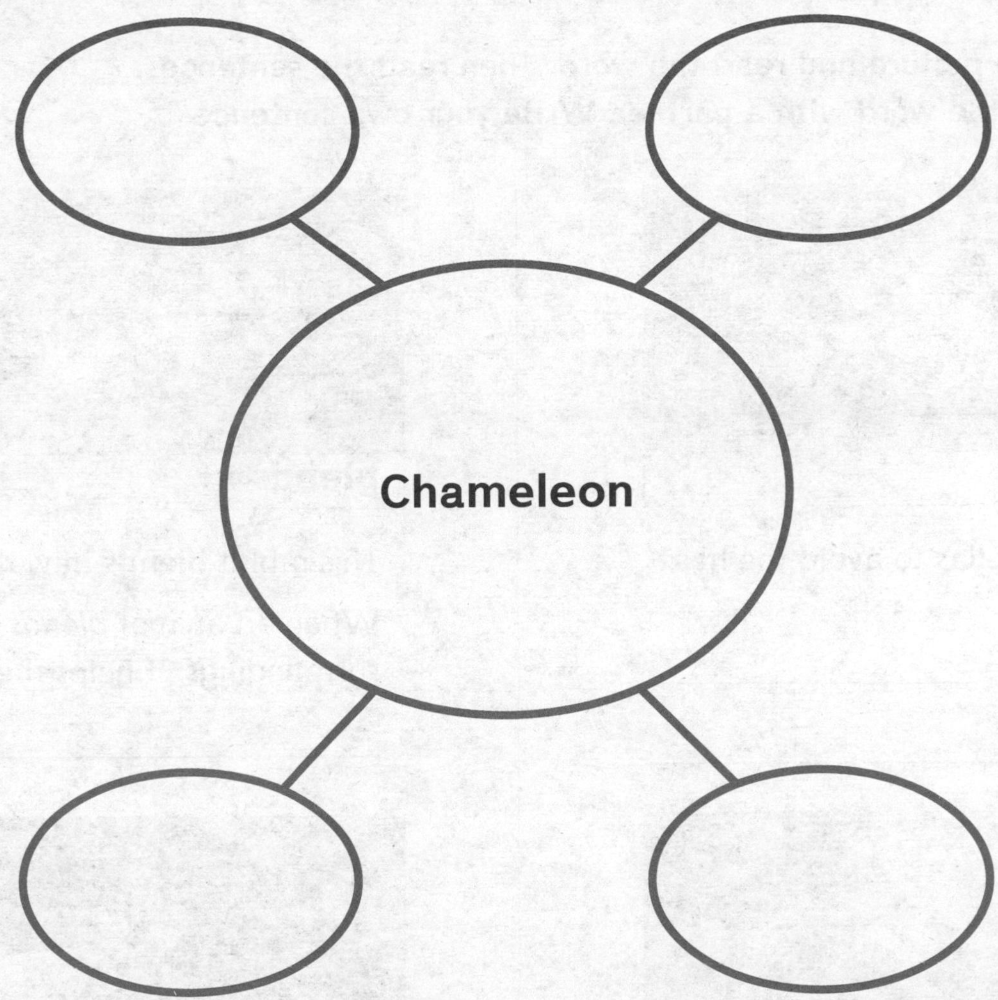

Look at the photograph. Discuss what helps the chameleon to survive. Use the words from the chart. You can say:

The chameleon is able to survive because ____________.

It also has ____________.

ELD.PI.4.1.Ex, ELD.PI.4.1.Br, ELD.PI.4.5.Ex, ELD.PI.4.5.Br, ELD.PI.4.12a.Ex, ELD.PI.4.12a.Br See the California Standards section.

More Vocabulary

Look at the picture and read the word. Then read the sentences. Talk about the word with a partner. Write your own sentence.

avoid

People sit under umbrellas to **avoid** the heat of the sun.

I *avoid* the sun because ______________________

____.

benefit

The plants **benefit** from the sun.

Plants *benefit* from the sun because ________

____.

blends in

This rabbit **blends in** with the snow.

When an animal *blends in* with its surroundings, it helps the animal because

____.

compact

The **compact** car is easier to park.

Another word for *compact* is ______________________.

decline

Crops **decline** during a drought.

Another word for *decline* is ______________

______________________________.

harsh

The girl is dressed for **harsh** weather.

Harsh weather is when ______________

______________________________.

Words and Phrases
Multiple-meaning Words

Multiple-meaning words are spelled and pronounced the same but have different meanings.

The word *spot* can mean "to see."
I <u>*spot*</u> a bird in the tree.

The word *spot* can also mean "a mark or stain."
There is a <u>*spot*</u> on the shirt.

Read the sentences below. Write the meaning of the underlined multiple-meaning word.

I was able to <u>spot</u> the moon last night. ______________

My dog has a white <u>spot</u> on its tail. ______________

» *Go Digital* **Add the multiple-meaning word to your New Words notebook. Write two sentences to show the meaning of each.**

(t)Marcophoto/iStock/360/Getty Images; (b)sdominick/iStock/360/Getty Images

Text Evidence

1 Talk About It

Look at the photograph. Read the title. Talk about what you see. Write your ideas.

What does this title tell you?

____

____

Where are the animals?

____

____

What are the animals doing?

____

____

Take notes as you read the text.

Shared Read Genre • Expository Text

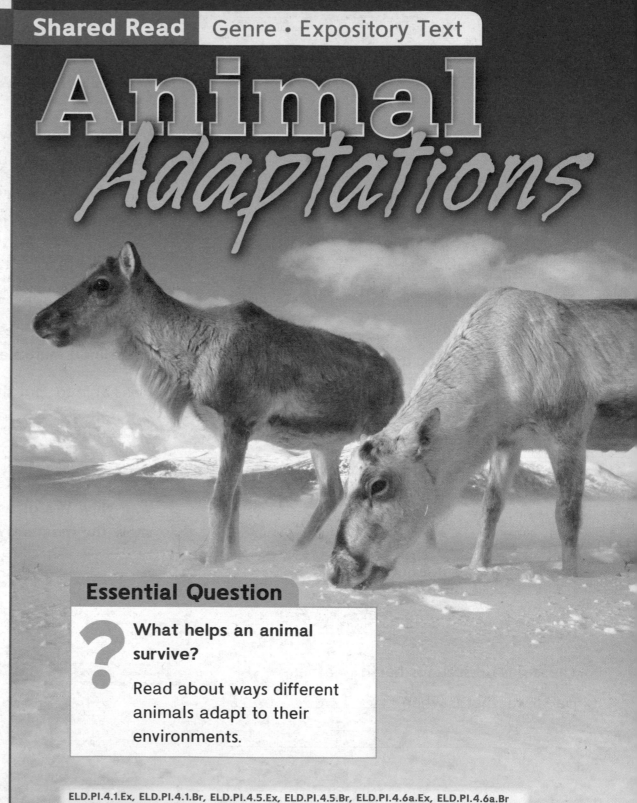

Animal Adaptations

Essential Question

What helps an animal survive?

Read about ways different animals adapt to their environments.

ELD.PI.4.1.Ex, ELD.PI.4.1.Br, ELD.PI.4.5.Ex, ELD.PI.4.5.Br, ELD.PI.4.6a.Ex, ELD.PI.4.6a.Br
See the California Standards section.

What would you do if you saw a skunk raise his tail? If you knew anything about skunks, you would run in the opposite direction! Skunks have a built-in survival system. They can blast a predator with a horrible-smelling spray produced by the glands under their tails.

When a skunk turns and sprays a predator, the foul-smelling mist can travel up to 10 feet.

The special ways that animals have to survive are called adaptations. These include physical **traits** such as the skunk's spray and animals with bright colors and markings that warn predators that they are poisonous. Some animals can sense the smallest vibrations in the ground. Others hear sounds from miles away. An adaptation can also be a behavioral trait. An example of a behavioral trait would be birds that migrate south every winter to **avoid harsh** temperatures.

Staying Warm

Brrrr! Imagine living in a place where the average annual temperature is an extraordinary 10° to 20° F. Welcome to the Arctic tundra of Alaska, Canada, Greenland, and Russia, home of the caribou. To stay warm, caribou have two layers of fur and a thick layer of fat. They also have **compact** bodies. Only 4 or 5 feet long, caribou can weigh over 500 pounds.

The tip of the caribou's nose and mouth is called a muzzle. It is covered in short hair. This hair helps to warm the air before they inhale it into their lungs. It also helps to keep them warm as they push snow aside to find food.

ELD.PI.4.1.Ex, ELD.PI.4.1.Br, ELD.PI.4.5.Ex, ELD.PI.4.5.Br, ELD.PI.4.6a.Ex, ELD.PI.4.6a.Br, ELD.PI.4.12a.Ex, ELD.PI.4.12a.Br See the California Standards section.

Text Evidence

1 Specific Vocabulary ACT

Reread the second paragraph. The word *traits* means "special qualities that something or someone has." Underline an example of a physical trait that helps an animal survive. Circle an example of a behavioral trait that helps an animal survive.

2 Sentence Structure ACT

Reread the second sentence in the third paragraph. Circle the commas. Underline the name of each place. What animal lives in these places? ____________________

3 Comprehension

Main Idea and Details

Reread the last two paragraphs. Why can caribou survive in the harsh Arctic tundra? Write two details.

Caribou can survive because

____

____________________.

Text Evidence

1 Comprehension

Main Idea and Details

Reread the first paragraph. What do caribou eat? Underline the food. Write the reason why caribou can eat this food.

Caribou eat ____________________

because they ____________________.

2 Sentence Structure ACT

Reread the last sentence in the first paragraph. Circle the comma that breaks the sentence into two parts. Underline what happens when the snow melts.

COLLABORATE

3 Talk About It

Discuss the ways phasmids hide from their predators. Then write about it.

____

____

Lichen can grow in extreme temperatures.

Finding Food

Every day, a caribou eats over six pounds of lichen! Caribou have unusual stomachs. The stomach's four chambers are designed to digest lichen. It is one of the few foods they can find in the winter. Even so, caribou still have a tough time in the coldest part of winter when their food sources **decline**. That's why they travel from the tundra to a large forest area, where food is easier to find. When the melting snow dribbles into streams, they know that it is time to return up north.

Insects in Disguise

Look closely at the photo of the tree branch. Can you spot the insect? It is a phasmid. Some phasmids are known as leaf insects, or walking sticks. Phasmids look like leaves or twigs. These insects can change colors to really **blend in** with their surroundings. In this way, they are camouflaged from predators. It's as if they disappear from sight! These insects are nocturnal, which means that they are active at night. This is another adaptation that helps them avoid predators. It's hard to spot these insects in daylight, let alone at night.

This phasmid is called a walking stick because it looks like a stick with legs.

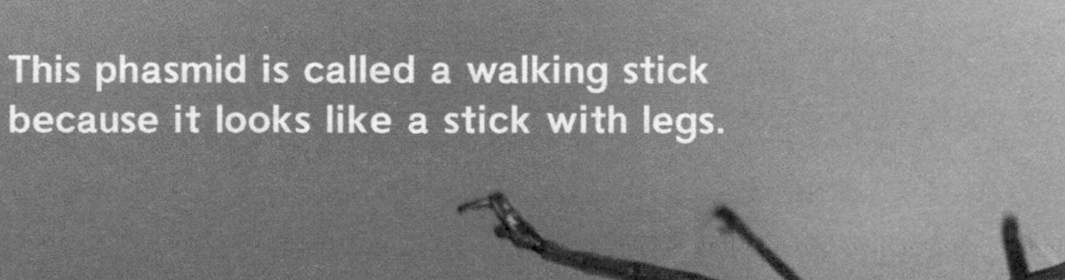

ELD.PI.4.1.Ex, ELD.PI.4.1.Br, ELD.PI.4.5.Ex, ELD.PI.4.5.Br, ELD.PI.4.6a.Ex, ELD.PI.4.6a.Br, ELD.PI.4.12a.Ex, ELD.PI.4.12a.Br See the California Standards section.

The alligator's physical adaptations include its log-shaped body. Other animals have trouble spotting the motionless alligator in the water.

Water, Please!

In Florida's vast Everglades ecosystem, the dry season is brutal for many plants and animals. Alligators have found a way to survive these dry conditions in the freshwater marshes. They use their feet and snouts to clear dirt from holes in the limestone bedrock. When the ground dries up, the alligators can drink from their water holes.

Other species **benefit** from these water holes, too. Plants grow there. Other animals find water to survive the dry season. However, the animals that visit alligator holes become easy prey. The normally motionless alligator may pounce on them without warning. But luckily, alligators eat only a few times each month. Many animals take their chances and **revisit** the alligator hole when they need water. In the end, it's all about survival!

Make Connections

How do adaptations help an animal survive? ESSENTIAL QUESTION

Describe an animal adaptation that you have seen. TEXT TO SELF

ELD.PI.4.1.Ex, ELD.PI.4.1.Br, ELD.PI.4.5.Ex, ELD.PI.4.5.Br, ELD.PI.4.6a.Ex, ELD.PI.4.6a.Br
See the California Standards section.

Text Evidence

1 Comprehension
Main Idea and Details

Reread the first paragraph. Alligators have adaptations that help them to survive in the Everglades. Underline the adaptation that helps alligators to survive.

2 Specific Vocabulary ACT

Reread the second paragraph. The prefix *re-* means "again." The word *revisit* means "to visit again." Why do the animals revisit the alligator hole?

Animals revisit the alligator hole

because ______________________.

3 Sentence Structure ACT

Reread the last sentence in the second paragraph. Underline the punctuation that breaks the sentence into two parts. Circle the prepositional phrase, or the part of the sentence that tells when something happens.

Respond to the Text

Partner Discussion Work with a partner. Describe what you learned about "Animal Adaptations." Write the page numbers where you found text evidence.

What did you learn about caribou?	Text Evidence
I read that caribou can live in the Arctic tundra because they have ________________.	Page(s): ________
The caribou's muzzle helps it stay warm because ________________.	Page(s): ________
Based on the text, lichen is an important food source for caribou because ________________.	Page(s): ________

What did you learn about alligators?	Text Evidence
I read that alligators live in ________________.	Page(s): ________
Alligators can survive very dry conditions by ________________.	Page(s): ________
Based on the text, alligators help other animals to survive because ________________.	Page(s): ________

Group Discussion Present your answers to the group. Cite text evidence to justify your thinking. Listen to and discuss the group's opinions about your answers.

 ELD.PI.4.1.Ex, ELD.PI.4.1.Br, ELD.PI.4.3.Ex, ELD.PI.4.3.Br, ELD.PI.4.5.Ex, ELD.PI.4.5.Br, ELD.PI.4.9.Ex, ELD.PI.4.9.Br, ELD.PI.4.11a.Ex, ELD.PI.4.11a.Br, ELD.PI.4.12a.Ex, ELD.PI.4.12a.Br See the California Standards section.

Write Work with a partner. Review your notes about "Animal Adaptations." Then write your answer to the essential question. Use text evidence to support your answer. Use vocabulary words from this week's reading in your writing.

What helps an animal to survive?

Caribou have adapted to survive in cold places because ______________________

____

____.

Alligators have adapted to survive in the Everglades because ________________

____

____.

Therefore, animals have learned to survive in harsh environments because ______

____.

COLLABORATE

Share Writing Present your writing to the class. Discuss their opinions. Think about what they have to say. Did they justify their claims? Explain why you agree or disagree with their claims.

I agree with ____________ because ____________.

I disagree with ____________ because ____________.

ELD.PI.4.1.Ex, ELD.PI.4.1.Br, ELD.PI.4.3.Ex, ELD.PI.4.3.Br, ELD.PI.4.5.Ex, ELD.PI.4.5.Br, ELD.PI.4.9.Ex, ELD.PI.4.9.Br, ELD.PI.4.10b.Ex, ELD.PI.4.10b.Br, ELD.PI.4.11a.Ex, ELD.PI.4.11a.Br, ELD.PI.4.12a.Ex, ELD.PI.4.12a.Br See the California Standards section.

Write to Sources

pages 116–119

Take Notes About the Text I took notes on the idea web to answer the question: ***How do winter temperatures affect how caribou find food?***

Detail
Caribou eat over six pounds of lichen a day.

Detail
There isn't as much lichen on the tundra in winter.

Main Idea
It is hard for caribou to find food during the coldest time of winter.

Detail
Caribou travel to the forest to find food.

Detail
They return to the tundra when the snow starts melting.

 ELD.PI.4.1.Ex, ELD.PI.4.1.Br, ELD.PI.4.5.Ex, ELD.PI.4.5.Br, ELD.PI.4.6a.Ex, ELD.PI.4.6a.Br See the California Standards section.

Write About the Text **I used my notes from my idea web to write a paragraph about how winter temperatures affect how caribou find food.**

Student Model: *Informative Text*

It is hard for caribou to find food during the coldest time of winter. Caribou eat over six pounds of lichen a day. There isn't as much lichen on the tundra during the winter. Caribou travel to the forest. The forest has more food. The caribou return to the tundra when the snow starts melting.

TALK ABOUT IT

Text Evidence

Draw a box around the first sentence that comes from the notes. What is the main idea of Grant's paragraph?

Grammar

Underline a prepositional phrase in the first sentence. Does the phrase tell where or when?

Connect Ideas

Circle the sentences about the forest. How can you combine the sentences to connect ideas?

Your Turn

How do Florida alligators survive in the dry season? Use text evidence.

>> *Go Digital*
Write your response online. Use your editing checklist.

TALK ABOUT IT

Weekly Concept Animals All Around

Essential Question

How are writers inspired by animals?

» *Go Digital*

Describe what the dolphins are doing. Write in the chart why a writer might be inspired by the dolphins.

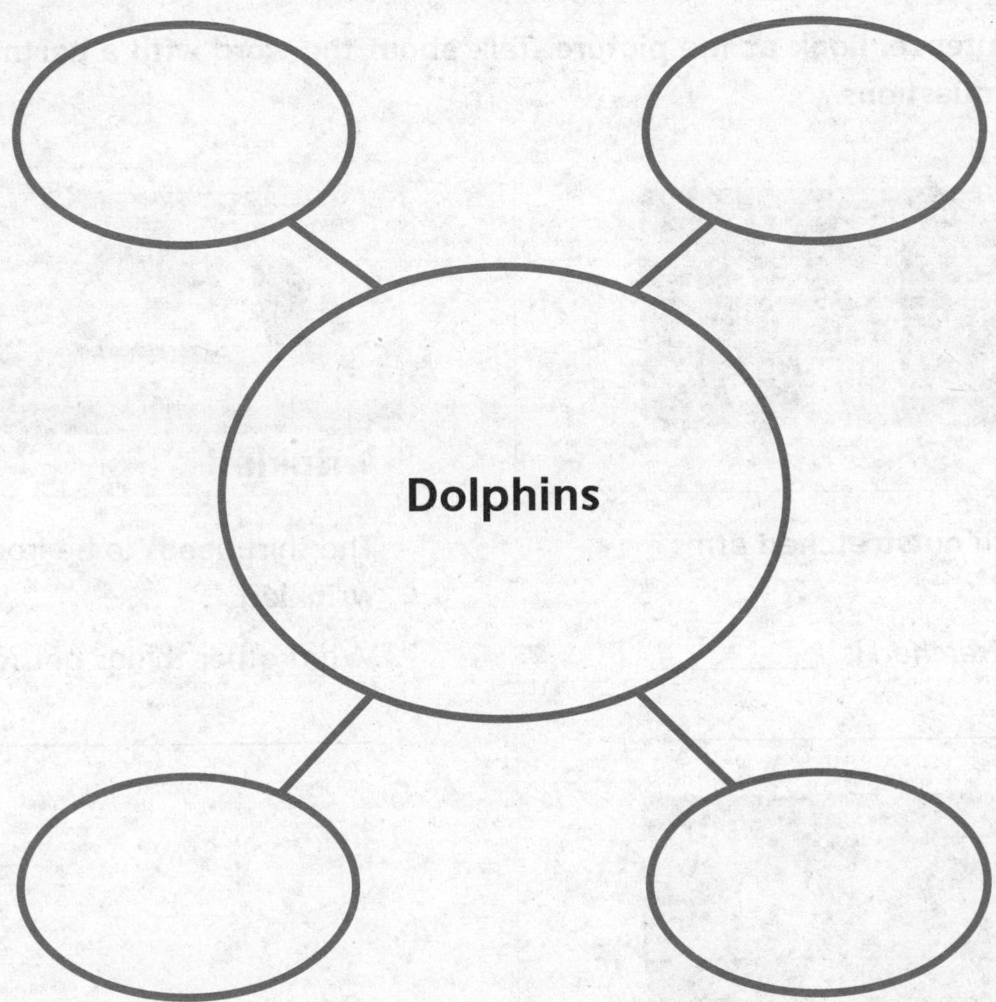

Look at the photo of the dolphins. Discuss why a writer might be inspired to write about dolphins. Use the words from the chart. You can say:

Dolphins are inspiring because they ____________.

ELD.PI.4.1.Ex, ELD.PI.4.1.Br, ELD.PI.4.5.Ex, ELD.PI.4.5.Br, ELD.PI.4.12a.Ex, ELD.PI.4.12a.Br See the California Standards section.

More Vocabulary

Read the sentence. Look at the picture. Talk about the word with a partner. Answer the questions.

outstretched

The children swing with **outstretched** arms at the playground.

Another word for *outstretched* is __________

______________________________.

patiently

The children wait **patiently** for the bus.

When do you have to wait *patiently?*

______________________________.

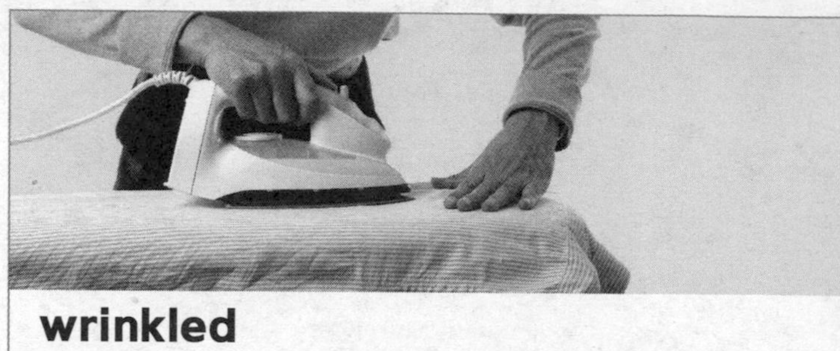

wrinkled

The shirt needs to be ironed because it is **wrinkled**.

What other things get *wrinkled*?

______________________________.

(tl)CEFutcher/iStock/360/Getty Images; (tr)gangliu10/iStock/360/Getty Images; (bl)Purestock/Alamy

 ELD.PI.4.1.Ex, ELD.PI.4.1.Br, ELD.PI.4.5.Ex, ELD.PI.4.5.Br, ELD.PI.4.6b.Ex, ELD.PI.4.6b.Br, ELD.PI.4.12a.Ex, ELD.PI.4.12a.Br See the California Standards section.

Poetry Terms

metaphor

A **metaphor** compares two unlike things.

The jet plane is a big silver bird.

rhyme

The words cat, sat, and mat **rhyme**. They end in the same sound.

We saw a little **cat**.
It sat happily on a **mat**.

simile

A **simile** compares two different things. It uses *like* or *as*.

The wind roars like a lion.
The wind is as loud as a roaring lion.

meter

Meter is the rhythm in a poem. It is a pattern of stressed and unstressed syllables.

Twinkle, twinkle, little star.
How I wonder where you are.

COLLABORATE

Work with a partner. Make up two similes and a metaphor. Use the words below.

snow	**blanket**
sun	**ball**
car	**thunder**

Simile:

The ___ is like a ___.

The ___ is as loud as ___.

Metaphor:

The ___ is a ___.

(tl)Corbis Premium Collection/Alamy; (tlr)Pixtal/age fotostock; (tr)Deirdre Motto/Stockbyte/Getty Images; (bll)George Doyle/Getty Images; (blr)Stephan Rech/Zoonar/age fotostock; (br) Jill Fromer/Getty Images

Text Evidence 

1 Literary Element
Metaphor

Reread the first line of "Dog." What does the poet compare the dog to? Circle the word. Write it.

____

2 Comprehension
Point of View

Look at the second line. Who does the pronoun *my* refer to? Write it on the line.

____

3 Sentence Structure ACT

Reread the second and third lines. What does the dog do first? What does the dog do next? Underline the verbs. Write the words.

____

____

Shared Read Genre • Poetry

DOG

A brown boomerang,
my dog flies off, arcs his way
back into my arms.

— Jeffrey Boyle

Essential Question

How are writers inspired by animals?

Read how poets use creative thinking to write about animals.

ELD.PI.4.1.Ex, ELD.PI.4.1.Br, ELD.PI.4.5.Ex, ELD.PI.4.5.Br, ELD.PI.4.6a.Ex, ELD.PI.4.6a.Br, ELD.PI.4.7.Ex, ELD.PI.4.7.Br, ELD.PII.4.2a.Ex, ELD.PII.4.2a.Br See the California Standards section.

THE EAGLE

He clasps the crag with crooked hands;
Close to the sun in lonely lands,
Ring'd with the azure world, he stands.

The **wrinkled** sea beneath him crawls;
He watches from his mountain walls,
And like a thunderbolt he falls.

— Alfred, Lord Tennyson

Alessandra Cimatoribus

ELD.PI.4.1.Ex, ELD.PI.4.1.Br, ELD.PI.4.5.Ex, ELD.PI.4.5.Br, ELD.PI.4.6a.Ex, ELD.PI.4.6a.Br, ELD.PI.4.7.Ex, ELD.PI.4.7.Br, ELD.PII.4.2a.Ex, ELD.PII.4.2a.Br See the California Standards section.

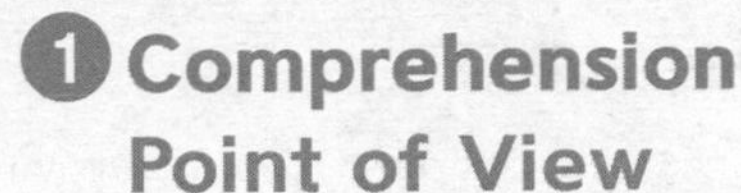

1 Comprehension
Point of View

Reread the first three lines of the poem. Circle the pronouns. Who do the pronouns refer to?

____

2 Literary Element
Rhyme

Reread the first three lines of the poem. Underline the words that rhyme. Write the words.

______________________________.

3 Talk About It

Reread the first line of the poem. Discuss why the poet compares the eagle's claws to crooked hands. Write your reasons.

____

____

Text Evidence

1 Literary Element
Rhyme

Reread the first four lines of the poem. Circle the words that rhyme. Write the words.

____

2 Comprehension
Point of View

From whose point of view is the poem written?

____

Underline the pronouns that tell you.

3 Talk About It

Reread the ninth and tenth lines. Discuss the reasons why the poet compares the skinny branch to a bridge. Underline the words that tell you.

CHIMPANZEE

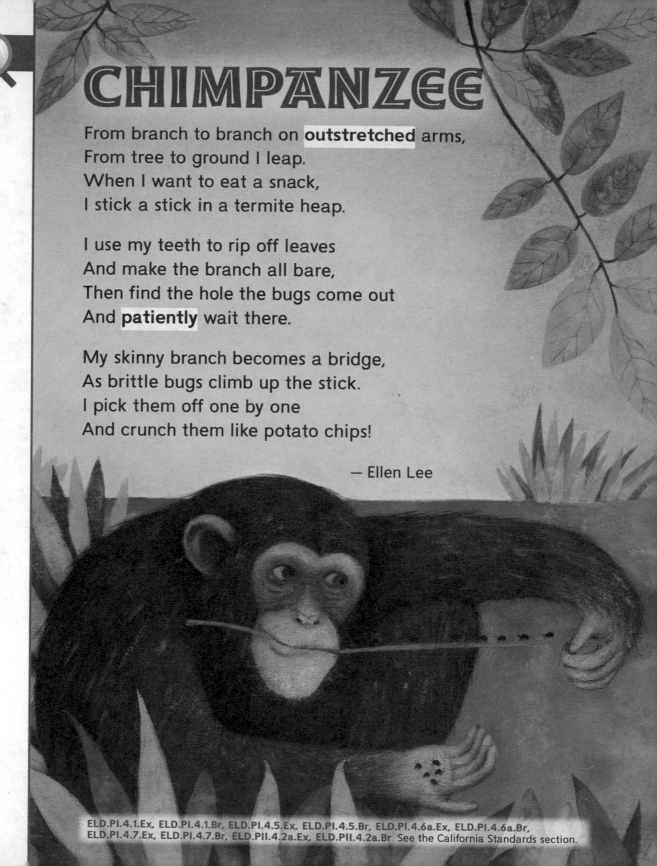

From branch to branch on **outstretched** arms,
From tree to ground I leap.
When I want to eat a snack,
I stick a stick in a termite heap.

I use my teeth to rip off leaves
And make the branch all bare,
Then find the hole the bugs come out
And **patiently** wait there.

My skinny branch becomes a bridge,
As brittle bugs climb up the stick.
I pick them off one by one
And crunch them like potato chips!

— Ellen Lee

ELD.PI.4.1.Ex, ELD.PI.4.1.Br, ELD.PI.4.5.Ex, ELD.PI.4.5.Br, ELD.PI.4.6a.Ex, ELD.PI.4.6a.Br, ELD.PI.4.7.Ex, ELD.PI.4.7.Br, ELD.PII.4.2a.Ex, ELD.PII.4.2a.Br See the California Standards section.

Rat

Teeth like jackhammers,
I chew through concrete **for fun**,
bring the outdoors in!

— Rosa Sandoval

Make Connections

Talk about the creative ways that the poets portray animals. ESSENTIAL QUESTION

What animal would you write a poem about? Why? TEXT TO SELF

ELD.PI.4.1.Ex, ELD.PI.4.1.Br, ELD.PI.4.5.Ex, ELD.PI.4.5.Br, ELD.PI.4.6a.Ex, ELD.PI.4.6a.Br, ELD.PI.4.7.Ex, ELD.PI.4.7.Br, ELD.PII.4.2a.Ex, ELD.PII.4.2a.Br See the California Standards section.

Text Evidence

1 Literary Element
Simile

Reread the first line of the poem. What are the rat's teeth like? Circle the word that tells you. Write the word.

____

2 Comprehension
Point of View

From whose point of view is the poem written?

____

Underline the pronoun that tells you.

3 Specific Vocabulary ACT

The words *for fun* mean "doing something because you like to." What does the rat do for fun? Draw a box around the words. Write a sentence about something you like to do for fun.

____

____

Respond to the Text

Partner Discussion **Work with a partner. Describe what you learned about "Dog" and "Chimpanzee." Write the line numbers where you found text evidence.**

How does the poet write about his dog in "Dog"?	**Text Evidence**
The poet says his dog is like a ________________.	Line(s): ________
In the poem, the actions of the dog are ________ and ________.	Line(s): ________

How does the poet write about a chimpanzee in "Chimpanzee"?	**Text Evidence**
The chimpanzee goes from branch to branch on ________________.	Line(s): ________
The chimpanzee uses a branch as a ________________.	Line(s): ________
In the end, bugs climb up the branch and the chimpanzee ________.	Line(s): ________

Group Discussion **Present your answers to the group. Cite text evidence to justify your thinking. Listen to and discuss the group's opinions about your answers.**

 ELD.PI.4.1.Ex, ELD.PI.4.1.Br, ELD.PI.4.3.Ex, ELD.PI.4.3.Br, ELD.PI.4.5.Ex, ELD.PI.4.5.Br, ELD.PI4.7.Ex, ELD.PI.4.7.Br, ELD.PI.4.9.Ex, ELD.PI.4.9.Br, ELD.PI.4.11a.Ex, ELD.PI.4.11a.Br, ELD.PI.4.12a.Ex, ELD.PI.4.12a.Br See the California Standards section.

Write **Work with a partner. Review your notes about "Dog" and "Chimpanzee." Then write your answer to the essential question. Use text evidence to support your answer. Use vocabulary words from this week's reading in your writing.**

How are writers inspired by animals?

In the poem "Dog," the writer tells about the way his dog ________________________

____

____.

In the poem "Chimpanzee," the writer tells about the way a chimpanzee gets a snack by describing ____

____

____.

A writer can be inspired by an animal because of the way an animal ____________

____

____.

COLLABORATE

Share Writing **Present your writing to the class. Discuss their opinions. Think about what they have to say. Did they justify their claims? Explain why you agree or disagree with their claims.**

I agree with ____________ because ____________.

I disagree with ____________ because ____________.

ELD.PI.4.1.Ex, ELD.PI.4.1.Br, ELD.PI.4.3.Ex, ELD.PI.4.3.Br, ELD.PI.4.5.Ex, ELD.PI.4.5.Br, ELD.PI.4.7.Ex, ELD.PI.4.7.Br, ELD.PI.4.9.Ex, ELD.PI.4.9.Br, ELD.PI.4.10b.Ex, ELD.PI.4.10b.Br, ELD.PI.4.11a.Ex, ELD.PI.4.11a.Br, ELD.PI.4.12a.Ex, ELD.PI.4.12a.Br See the California Standards section.

Write to Sources

Take Notes About the Text **I took notes on the idea web to answer the question:** ***How did the poet of "Chimpanzee" use metaphor?***

pages 128–131

Detail
My skinny branch becomes a bridge.

Detail
The branch is being compared to a bridge.

Metaphor
A metaphor compares two things.

Detail
The brittle bugs climb up the stick.

Detail
The bugs climb toward the chimpanzee.

Todd Warnock/Digital Vision/Getty Images

Write About the Text **I used my notes from my idea web to write about metaphors.**

Student Model: *Informative Text*

A metaphor compares two things. "My skinny branch becomes a bridge" is an example of a metaphor. It says the branch is a bridge. The brittle bugs climb up the branch. They climb to the chimpanzee. I can picture how the chimpanzee gets bugs with his branch to eat.

TALK ABOUT IT

Text Evidence

Draw a box around a sentence about metaphor that comes from the notes. How does the sentence help to describe a metaphor?

Grammar

Underline the modal verb *can* in the last sentence. What is Katia able to do?

Condense Ideas

Circle the sentences about the bugs climbing up the branch. How can you condense the sentences into one detailed sentence?

Your Turn

How does the poet use metaphor in the poem "Dog"? Use text evidence.

>> *Go Digital*
Write your response online. Use your editing checklist.

ELD.PI.4.1.Ex, ELD.PI.4.1.Br, ELD.PI.4.2.Ex, ELD.PI.4.2.Br, ELD.PI.4.5.Ex, ELD.PI.4.5.Br, ELD.PI.4.6a.Ex, ELD.PI.4.6a.Br, ELD.PI.4.10a.Ex, ELD.PI.4.10a.Br, ELD.PI.4.12a.Ex, ELD.PI.4.12a.Br, ELD.PII.4.7.Ex, ELD.PII.4.7.Br See the California Standards section.

UNIT 3

THAT'S THE Spirit!

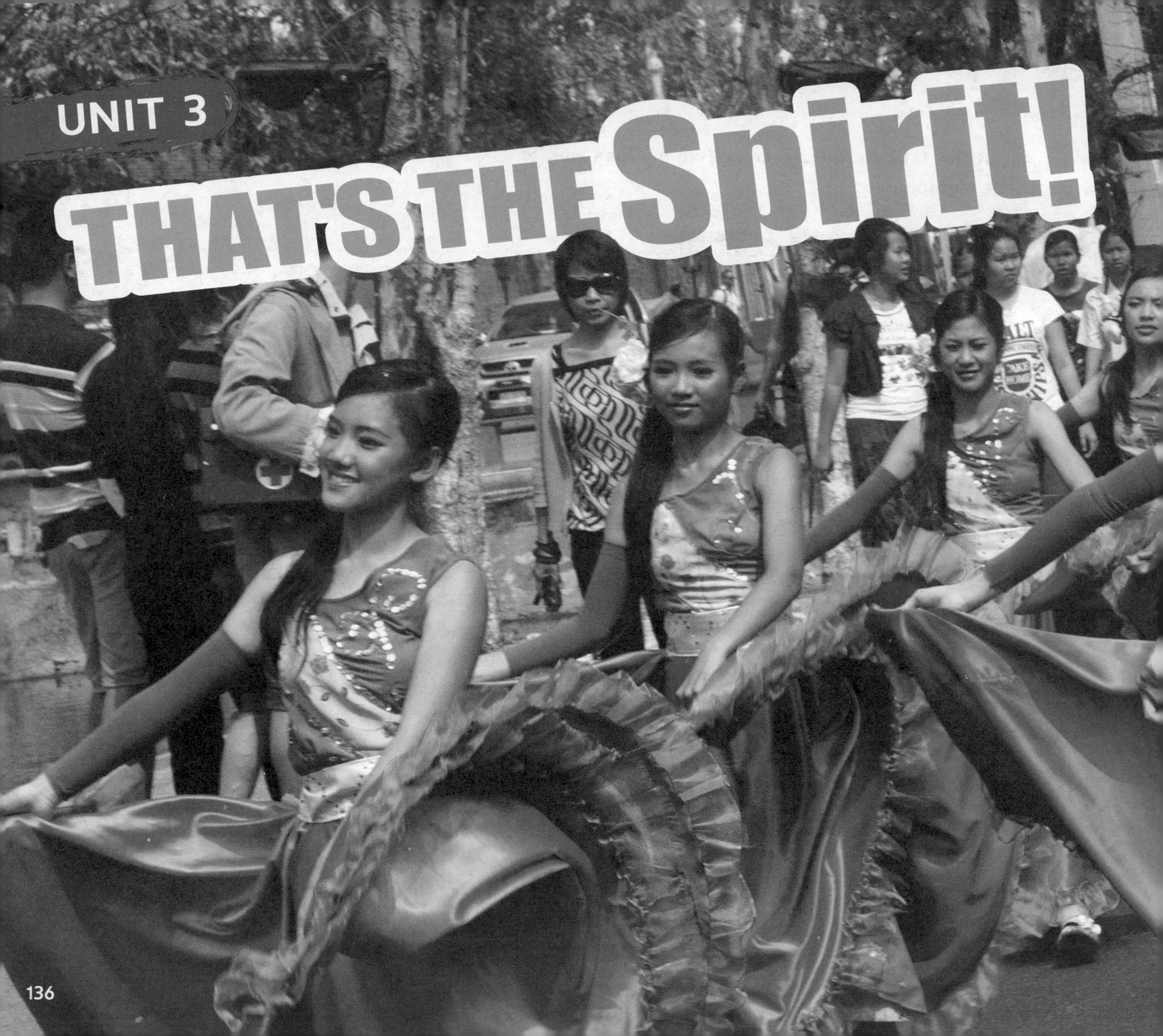

THE Big Idea

How can you show your community spirit?

John Elk/Lonely Planet Images/Getty Images

TALK ABOUT IT
Weekly Concept Friendship
Essential Question
How can you make new friends feel welcome?
Go Digital

What are the boys doing? Write what they are doing in the chart. Describe how people can make new friends.

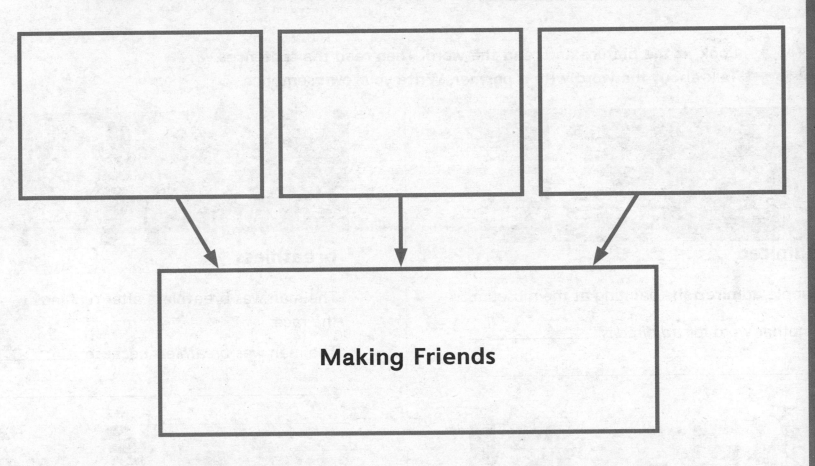

Making Friends

Discuss how you can make new friends feel welcome. Use the words from the chart. You can say:

I can make new friends feel welcome by ____________,

____________, and ____________ with them.

ELD.PI.4.1.Ex, ELD.PI.4.1.Br, ELD.PI.4.5.Ex, ELD.PI.4.5.Br, ELD.PI.4.12a.Ex, ELD.PI.4.12a.Br
See the California Standards section.

More Vocabulary

Look at the picture and read the word. Then read the sentences. Talk about the word with a partner. Write your own sentence.

admired

People **admired** the painting at the museum.

Another word for *admired* is ______________

______________________________________.

arrived

The students **arrived** for class on time.

I *arrived* at school on time for ______________

______________________________________.

breathless

The man was **breathless** after running the race.

The man was *breathless* because ______________

______________________________________.

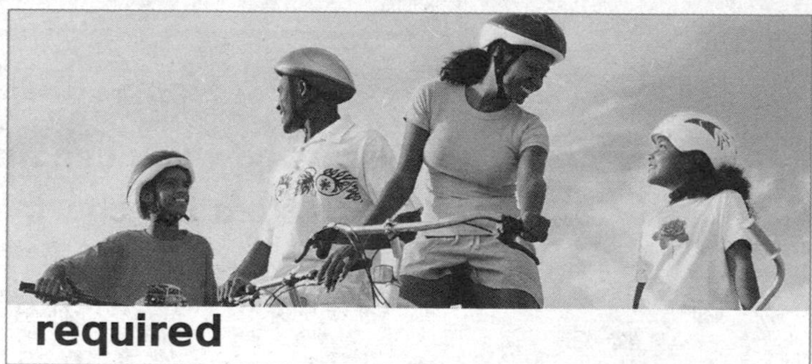

required

People are **required** to wear helmets when they ride bikes.

Another definition for *required* is ______________

______________________________________.

scrambled

Ants **scrambled** on the ground looking for food.

Another word for *scrambled* is ______________

______________________________.

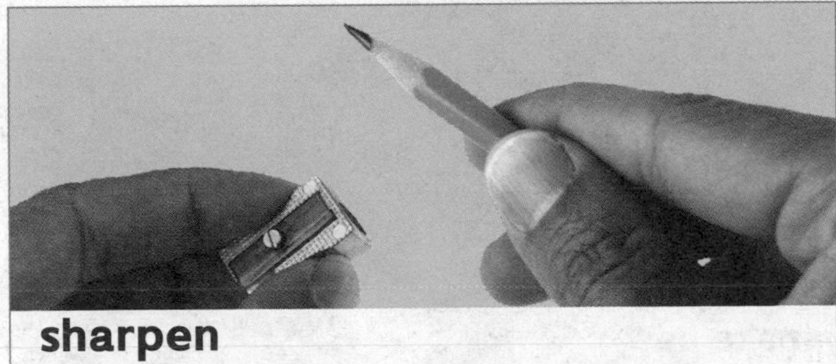

sharpen

It is a good idea to **sharpen** your pencil before doing your homework.

I *sharpen* a pencil because ______________

______________________________.

Words and Phrases

Homophones: *its* and *it's*

A homophone is a word that sounds the same as another word. But it does not have the same spelling and meaning.

The possessive pronoun *its* tells who owns something.

The dog chewed on <u>its</u> bone.

The contraction *it's* stands for "it is."

***It's* is a pronoun plus a verb.**

<u>It's</u> time to eat lunch.

Read the sentences below. Write the homophone that can replace the underlined words.

The tiger licked <u>the tiger's</u> paws. ______________

<u>It is</u> hot outside today. ______________

» Go Digital **Add the homophones to your New Words notebook. Write a sentence to show the meaning of each.**

Text Evidence

1 Talk About It

Look at the illustration. Read the title. Talk about what you see. Write your ideas.

What does this title tell you?

____

____

____

______________________________.

Describe the people in the illustration. What are they doing?

____

____

____

______________________________.

Take notes as you read the story.

Shared Read Genre • Fantasy

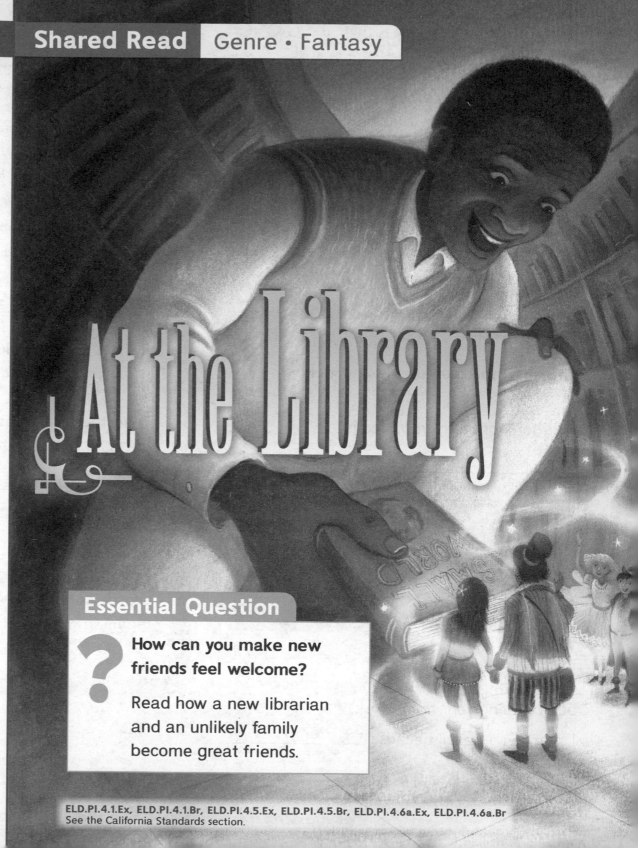

At the Library

WORLD SMALL

Essential Question

How can you make new friends feel welcome?

Read how a new librarian and an unlikely family become great friends.

ELD.PI.4.1.Ex, ELD.PI.4.1.Br, ELD.PI.4.5.Ex, ELD.PI.4.5.Br, ELD.PI.4.6a.Ex, ELD.PI.4.6a.Br
See the California Standards section.

Rick Dodson **admired** the pink and orange sky as he waved good-bye to Mrs. Rio and locked the library door. As the sun began its **descent** behind the Blue Ridge Mountains, Rick started walking to his office to collect his jacket. Seeing a jumble of books on a reading table, he sighed and began to gather them into a neat pile.

"No," he stated firmly, and returned the books to the table. "Not tonight."

The librarian never left any books out, but today was his birthday, which meant a brisk walk to the Cupcake Café for a birthday treat before it closed at 5:30 P.M.

That evening, as he sat at home in his book-filled living room, Rick thought about the old friends who had called to wish him a happy birthday. If only this job had not **required** him to move halfway across the country . . . After six months here, he had made more than one new acquaintance but no real friends yet.

"Books are my friends," he thought, which reminded him of the books sitting on the table at the library. "I might as well go back tonight and shelve them," he decided.

He entered the library and flicked on the lights. Immediately, he noticed a book, *Small World,* face down on the floor. "What's going on?" he muttered as he bent down and cautiously lifted up the book. "Ahhh," he yelled and dropped the book.

Four miniature figures **scrambled** out of the way as the book landed on the floor with a thud.

"Mr. Dodson," exclaimed a **breathless** voice, "we are enchanted to make your acquaintance."

"What . . . who . . . " Rick stammered.

Richard Johnson

ELD.PI.4.1.Ex, ELD.PI.4.1.Br, ELD.PI.4.6a.Ex, ELD.PI.4.6a.Br, ELD.PI.4.7.Ex, ELD.PI.4.7.Br, ELD.PI.4.12a.Ex, ELD.PI.4.12a.Br See the California Standards section.

Text Evidence

1 Specific Vocabulary A C T

Reread the second sentence in the first paragraph. The word *descent* means "the process of going down." Underline what was in its descent. Circle the words that tell where the descent took place.

2 Sentence Structure A C T

Reread the third paragraph. Circle the punctuation marks. This sentence can be made into two sentences. Underline the two sentences.

3 Comprehension

Reread the fourth paragraph. How does Rick feel about moving across the country for the library job?

Rick feels ______________________

____

____

______________________.

Text Evidence

COLLABORATE

1 Talk About It

Reread the third paragraph. Explain why the Bookers read Rick's file.

2 Specific Vocabulary ACT

Reread the second sentence in the fourth paragraph. The word *expectantly* means "in a way that is looking forward to something happening." Why were the Bookers looking at Rick expectantly?

____

______________________________.

3 Sentence Structure ACT

Reread the second sentence in the eleventh paragraph. Circle the word that connects Rick's thoughts. Underline the independent clauses, or the words that make up complete sentences.

"We're the Bookers! I'm William. This is Emily and our children, Harry and Clementine. By the way, happy birthday!"

"You know it's my birthday?"

"Naturally, we read your file when you **arrived** six months ago. It's only logical that we would want to learn about the new librarian."

"You were scrounging through my files?" Rick said, collapsing into a nearby chair. He rubbed his eyes, but the tiny figures were still there—looking up at him **expectantly**.

Suddenly, the nimble Bookers began shimmying up the table. "We're absolutely trustworthy," Emily assured him.

"Haven't you heard of Bookers?" William asked. "Every library has Bookers!"

"We ensure everything runs smoothly," said Emily. "Seen any mice around? They love to gnaw on everything."

Rick slowly shook his head.

"I do nightly rodent patrols," Harry stated proudly. "Those mice run at the sight of me," he added scornfully.

"Do your chairs ever squeak?" inquired Clementine. "No! That's because we oil them!"

Rick considered the past six months. He hadn't seen one mouse, his chairs never squeaked, and his pencils were never dull.

"The pencils?" he asked.

"We **sharpen** them nightly," William replied.

"But why?" asked Rick.

ELD.PI.4.1.Ex, ELD.PI.4.1.Br, ELD.PI.4.5.Ex, ELD.PI.4.5.Br, ELD.PI.4.6a.Ex, ELD.PI.4.6a.Br, ELD.PI.4.7.Ex, ELD.PI.4.7.Br, ELD.PI.4.12a.Ex, ELD.PI.4.12a.Br See the California Standards section.

"Look around!" exclaimed William. "We work and read. Bookers and libraries are complementary. We belong together."

"To be honest, Mr. Dodson," said Emily, "we wanted to meet you because we thought that we could be friends."

Rick Dodson grinned. "Call me, Rick. And I'd love to be friends," he said.

Rick eventually made other new friends, but he still spent many evenings with the Bookers. He bought a toy car for Harry's rodent patrol, and he read scary stories aloud to Clementine. Every year on his birthday, he brought cupcakes for his friends to share with him.

Make Connections

Talk about how the Bookers made Rick Dodson feel welcome. ESSENTIAL QUESTION

How do you make new students in your school feel welcome? TEXT TO SELF

Richard Johnson

ELD.PI.4.1.Ex, ELD.PI.4.1.Br, ELD.PI.4.6a.Ex, ELD.PI.4.6a.Br, ELD.PI.4.12a.Ex, ELD.PI.4.12a.Br
See the California Standards section.

Text Evidence

1 Talk About It

Discuss why the Bookers belong in libraries. Describe the things Bookers do in libraries.

2 Sentence Structure

Reread the second paragraph. Underline the person speaking. Circle the person she is speaking to.

3 Comprehension

Point of View

Reread the last paragraph. What does the narrator think about Rick's friendship with the Bookers?

____

____

____

______________________________.

Respond to the Text

Partner Discussion Work with a partner. Describe what you learned about "At the Library." Write the page numbers where you found text evidence.

What did you learn about Rick at the beginning of the story?	Text Evidence
I read that Rick likes ________________.	Page(s): ________
Rick can't be with his old friends because ________________.	Page(s): ________
At the end of the story, Rick feels ________________ ________________.	Page(s): ________

What did you learn about the Bookers?	Text Evidence
The Bookers take care of ________________.	Page(s): ________
At the end of the story, the Bookers tell Rick they ________________ ________________.	Page(s): ________

Group Discussion Present your answers to the group. Cite text evidence to justify your thinking. Listen to and discuss the group's opinions about your answers.

 ELD.PI.4.1.Ex, ELD.PI.4.1.Br, ELD.PI.4.3.Ex, ELD.PI.4.3.Br, ELD.PI.4.5.Ex, ELD.PI.4.5.Br, ELD.PI.4.9.Ex, ELD.PI.4.9.Br, ELD.PI.4.11a.Ex, ELD.PI.4.11a.Br, ELD.PI.4.12a.Ex, ELD.PI.4.12a.Br See the California Standards section.

Write **Work with a partner. Review your notes about "At the Library." Then write your answer to the essential question. Use text evidence to support your answer. Use vocabulary words from this week's reading in your writing.**

How did the Bookers make Rick feel welcome?

The Bookers and libraries go together because ______________________

____.

The Bookers help Rick in the library by ______________________

____.

At the end of the story, the Bookers make Rick feel welcome by ____________

____.

COLLABORATE

Share Writing **Present your writing to the class. Discuss their opinions. Think about what they have to say. Did they justify their claims? Explain why you agree or disagree with their claims.**

I agree with ______________ because ______________.

I disagree with ______________ because ______________.

ELD.PI.4.1.Ex, ELD.PI.4.1.Br, ELD.PI.4.3.Ex, ELD.PI.4.3.Br, ELD.PI.4.5.Ex, ELD.PI.4.5.Br, ELD.PI.4.9.Ex, ELD.PI.4.9.Br, ELD.PI.4.10b.Ex, ELD.PI.4.10b.Br, ELD.PI.4.11a.Ex, ELD.PI.4.11a.Br, ELD.PI.4.12a.Ex, ELD.PI.4.12a.Br See the California Standards section.

Write to Sources

Take Notes About the Text I took notes on an idea web about the story. It will help me respond to the prompt: ***Have William write a letter to other Bookers at another library. Tell them about Rick Dodson. Use details from the story.***

pages 142–145

Detail
When he met us, he was surprised.

Detail
He was very happy when we asked him to be our friend.

Main Idea
Rick Dodson is the new librarian.

Detail
He spends a lot of evenings with us at the library.

Detail
He shares cupcakes with us on his birthday.

 ELD.PI.4.1.Ex, ELD.PI.4.1.Br, ELD.PI.4.5.Ex, ELD.PI.4.5.Br, ELD.PI.4.6a.Ex, ELD.PI.4.6a.Br See the California Standards section.

Write About the Text **I used my notes from my idea web to write a letter from William to other Bookers. The letter tells them about Rick Dodson.**

Student Model: *Narrative Text*

Dear Lake Vista Library Bookers,

We have a new librarian named Rick Dodson. When he met us, he was surprised. He was happy that we wanted to be friends. Now, we spend many evenings at the library with Rick.

Best of all, he shares cupcakes with us on his birthday. We like our librarian.

Your friend,

William

TALK ABOUT IT

Text Evidence

Draw a box around a sentence from the notes that tells how Rick felt when the Bookers asked to be his friend. Does the sentence provide a supporting detail?

Grammar

Circle an action verb. Why did Shaun use action verbs?

Connect Ideas

Underline the last two sentences in the first paragraph. Use a connecting word to combine the sentences into one sentence.

Your Turn

Pretend you are Rick Dodson. Write a letter to a friend telling about meeting the Bookers. Use details from the story.

>> *Go Digital*
Write your response online. Use your editing checklist.

TALK ABOUT IT

Weekly Concept Helping the Community

Essential Question

In what ways can you help your community?

>> *Go Digital*

What are the girls doing in their community? Write how the girls are helping their community in the chart. Discuss the ways people can help their community.

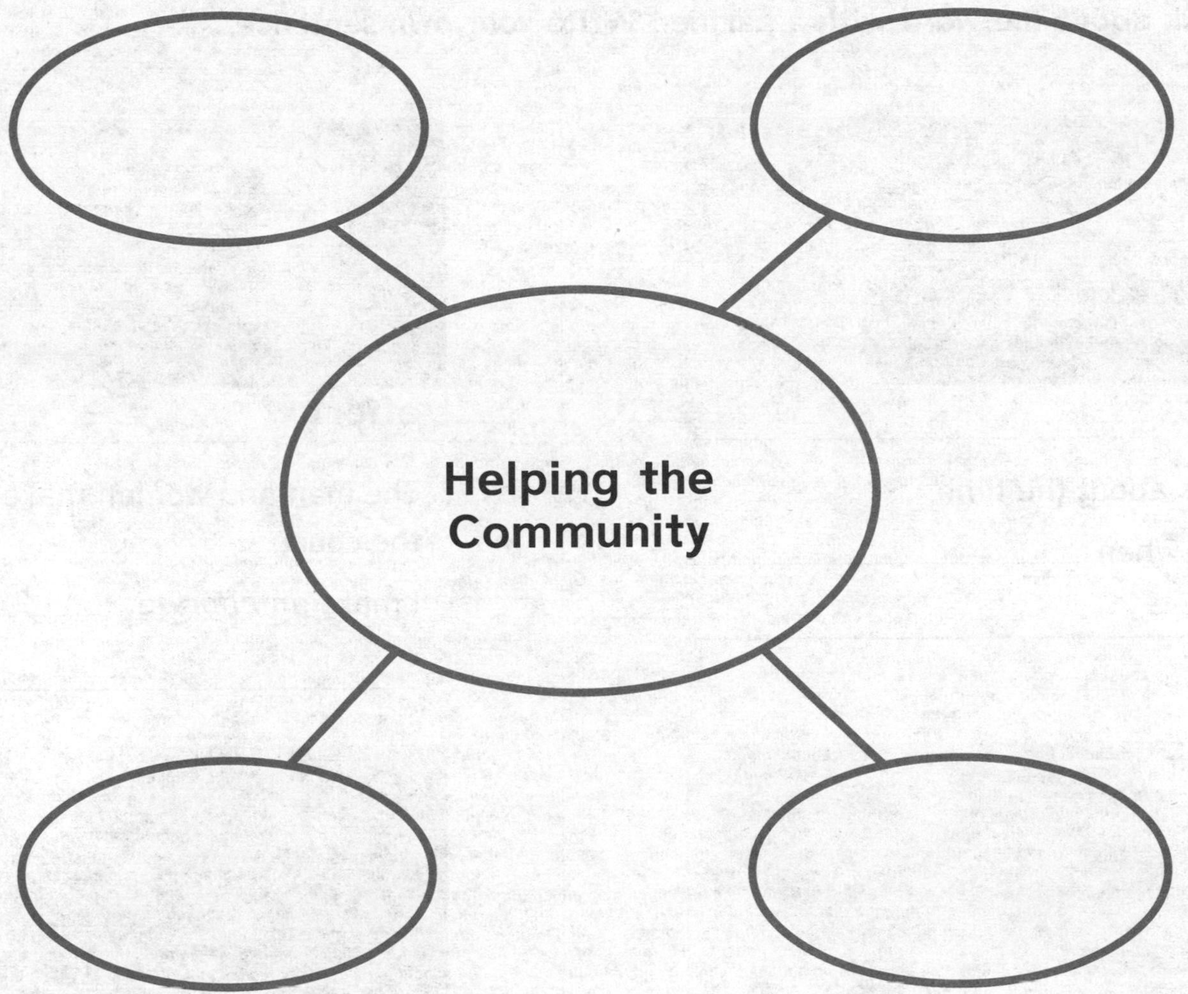

Discuss how you can help your community. Use the words from the chart. You can say:

I can help my community by ____________, ______________,

and ____________.

ELD.PI.4.1.Ex, ELD.PI.4.1.Br, ELD.PI.4.5.Ex, ELD.PI.4.5.Br, ELD.PI.4.12a.Ex, ELD.PI.4.12a.Br
See the California Standards section.

More Vocabulary

Look at the picture and read the word. Then read the sentences. Talk about the word with a partner. Write your own sentence.

anxious

He is **anxious** about the time.

I am *anxious* when ______________________

______________________________________.

delayed

People will be **delayed** getting to work because of the snow.

Another word for *delayed* is ______________

______________________________________.

effort

The man and woman make an **effort** to lift the couch.

I make an *effort* to ______________________

______________________________________.

ferocious

The **ferocious** wind bends the trees.

Another word for *ferocious* is ______________

______________________________________.

(ul)JumpStock/iStock/360/Getty Images; (ur)Terry Vine/Blend Images; (bl)Peter Spiro/iStock/360/Getty Images; (br)George Doyle/Getty Images

 ELD.PI.4.1.Ex, ELD.PI.4.1.Br, ELD.PI.4.5.Ex, ELD.PI.4.5.Br, ELD.PI.4.12a.Ex, ELD.PI.4.12a.Br See the California Standards section.

improved

The plant **improved** with more sun and water.

The word *improved* means ______________

______________________________________.

possessions

The girl keeps her **possessions** in a locker.

I keep my *possessions* ______________

______________________________________.

Words and Phrases

Suffixes: *-ness* and *-ion*

A suffix is a letter or letters added to the end of a word. It changes the meaning of the word.

darkness **= in a state of being dark**
I cannot see in the darkness.

discussion **= the act of discussing something**
We will have a discussion about rocks in class.

Read the sentences below. Add a suffix to the underlined word to complete the sentence.

I was sad when summer ended.

I felt ______________ at the end of summer.

We will discuss the book in class.

We will have a ______________ about the book.

» *Go Digital* **Add these suffixes to your New Words notebook. Write a sentence to show the meaning of each.**

(t)David Cook/blueshiftstudios/Alamy; (b)Wealan Pollard/age fotostock

COLLABORATE

1 Talk About It

Look at the photograph. Read the title. Talk about what you see. Write your ideas.

What does this title tell you?

____

____

____

______________________________.

Who is driving?

____

______________________________.

What are the people outside doing?

____

______________________________.

Take notes as you read the story.

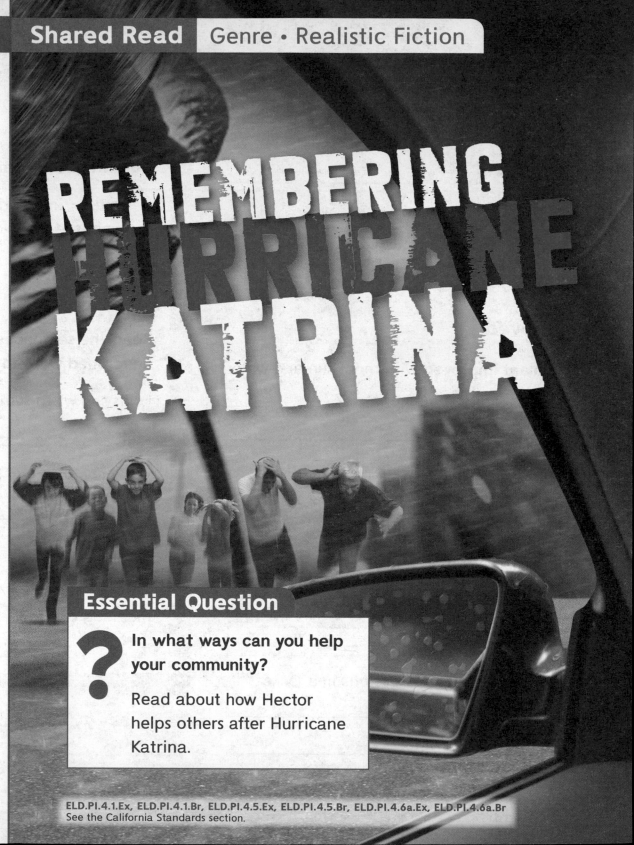

REMEMBERING HURRICANE KATRINA

Essential Question

In what ways can you help your community?

Read about how Hector helps others after Hurricane Katrina.

ELD.PI.4.1.Ex, ELD.PI.4.1.Br, ELD.PI.4.5.Ex, ELD.PI.4.5.Br, ELD.PI.4.6a.Ex, ELD.PI.4.6a.Br
See the California Standards section.

Leaning over my steering wheel, I watched the heavy clouds roll in. The sky became a darker shade of gray, and raindrops were soon scattered across my windshield. A storm was coming. Glancing at the boxes of clothes stacked in the backseat, I smiled to myself.

A torrential downpour of rain began beating against my windshield as lightning flickered across the sky. I pulled the car off the road until my driving visibility **improved**. People on the sidewalk held purses and briefcases over their heads in a futile **effort** to keep from getting wet. Children screamed and danced around in the downpour. The rain reminded me of another storm ten years earlier.

Hurricane Katrina slammed into the Gulf Coast of the United States when I was nine years old. The **ferocious** storm caused untold amounts of damage.

One of my strongest memories from that time was watching the evening news with my aunt. A reporter stood inside the Houston Astrodome, surrounded by thousands of people. They all shared the same **weary** expression. Many wore torn and dirty clothes, and some had no shoes on their feet. They slowly shuffled along, their faces full of sadness.

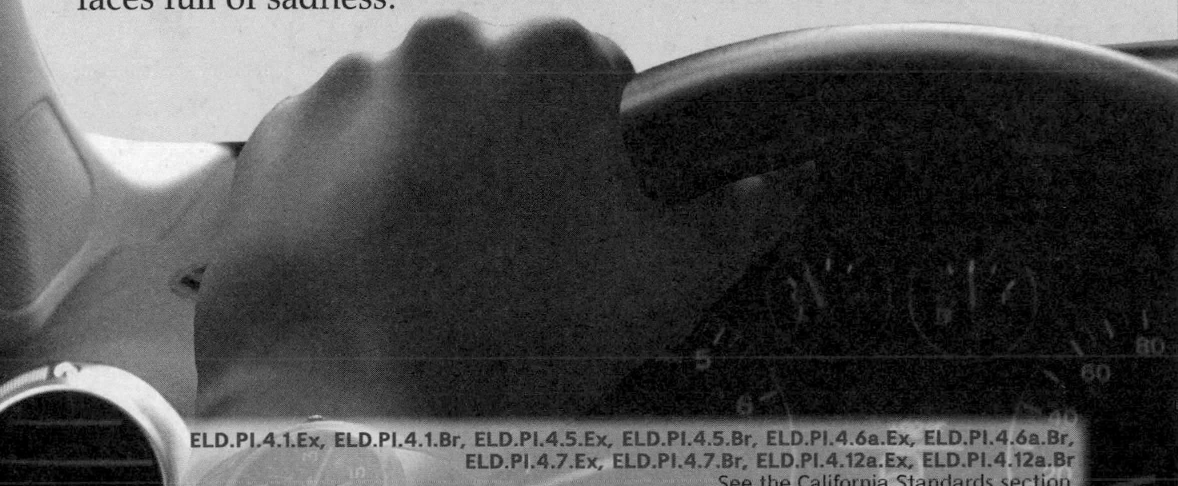

ELD.PI.4.1.Ex, ELD.PI.4.1.Br, ELD.PI.4.5.Ex, ELD.PI.4.5.Br, ELD.PI.4.6a.Ex, ELD.PI.4.6a.Br, ELD.PI.4.7.Ex, ELD.PI.4.7.Br, ELD.PI.4.12a.Ex, ELD.PI.4.12a.Br
See the California Standards section.

Text Evidence

1 Sentence Structure ACT

Reread the first sentence in the second paragraph. Circle the word that connects the two parts of the sentence. Underline the two parts of the sentence.

2 Specific Vocabulary ACT

Reread the third sentence in the last paragraph. The word *weary* means "very tired." In this sentence it describes the expression on people's faces. Why did the people have weary expressions?

____

_______________________________________.

3 Comprehension

Point of View

Reread the last paragraph. Underline the sentences that tell you why Hector had strong memories about Hurricane Katrina.

Text Evidence

1 Comprehension

Point of View

Reread the fourth paragraph. How did Hector feel about the people in the Astrodome?

____

______________________________.

2 Sentence Structure ACT

Reread the third sentence in the fourth paragraph. Underline the part of the sentence that can stand on its own, or the independent clause. Circle the two things the boy was doing.

3 Specific Vocabulary ACT

Reread the first sentence in the fifth paragraph. The word *devised* means "came up with a way to do something." Circle what the devised plan was. Underline the sentence that tells why they wanted to do this.

"Are they here because of the hurricane?" I asked softly.

Aunt Lucia nodded. "*Sí,* Hector. These people are from New Orleans, Louisiana. Just a few days ago, Hurricane Katrina destroyed their homes and **possessions**, and they lost everything they owned, so now they are temporary residents of the Astrodome. It's a place for them to stay until it's safe to go home."

I knew a lot about Katrina. The storm had formed in hot and humid tropical weather and then traveled north. It had come so close to Texas that I worried it would strike us in Houston. It missed us, but other cities were not so lucky.

The TV news reporter looked around. People tried to speak to her, but she was being selective about whom she wanted to interview. I noticed a little boy sitting behind her on a cot, hugging an old teddy bear. Watching him, I knew I had to do something.

The next day, my friends joined me at our volunteer club–the Houston Helpers–and together we **devised** a plan. We wanted to collect toys and give them to the kids at the Astrodome because donating the toys would help bring some happiness into the lives of these families.

Anxious to get started, we made lists of what we needed to do. Then every one of us was assigned a specific task.

ELD.PI.4.1.Ex, ELD.PI.4.1.Br, ELD.PI.4.5.Ex, ELD.PI.4.5.Br, ELD.PI.4.6a.Ex, ELD.PI.4.6a.Br, ELD.PI.4.7.Ex, ELD.PI.4.7.Br, ELD.PI.4.12a.Ex, ELD.PI.4.12a.Br See the California Standards section.

We agreed to spread the word to our schools and other organizations. Three days later, after a Herculean effort on our part, the donation bins were overflowing with new toys!

I'll never forget the day when we entered the Astrodome with our gifts. Children flew toward us from all directions. Smiles lit up their faces as we pulled toys from our bags. Grateful parents thanked us for our generosity and complimented our group leaders on how thoughtful and mature we all were.

BZZZZ. My cell phone jolted me back to the present, and I noticed that the storm had passed.

"Hector?"

"*Sí*, yes, hi, Jeannie."

"Do you have the donations? A few more families have arrived, more victims of yesterday's tornado."

"Yes, I have the clothing donations. The storm **delayed** me, but I'll be there soon!"

I gingerly eased my car into the suddenly busy traffic. It felt good to know that I was making a difference again.

Make Connections

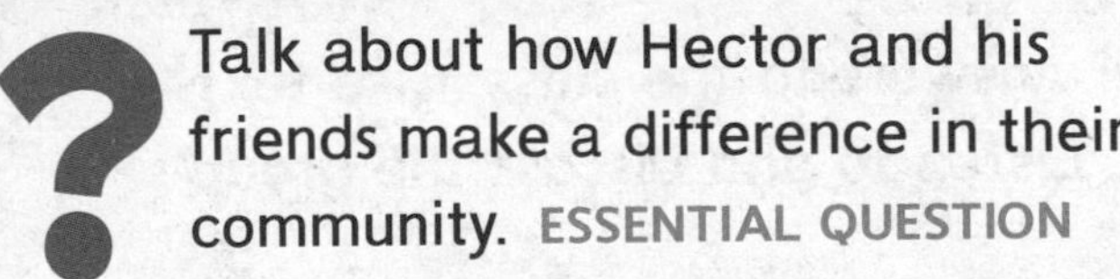

Talk about how Hector and his friends make a difference in their community. ESSENTIAL QUESTION

What are some things that you have done to help your school or community? TEXT TO SELF

ELD.PI.4.1.Ex, ELD.PI.4.1.Br, ELD.PI.4.5.Ex, ELD.PI.4.5.Br, ELD.PI.4.6a.Ex, ELD.PI.4.6a.Br, ELD.PI.4.12a.Ex, ELD.PI.4.12a.Br See the California Standards section.

Text Evidence

1 Comprehension Point of View

Reread the second paragraph. How did Hector feel when he and his friends delivered the toys?

____

______________________________.

2 Sentence Structure ACT

Reread the third paragraph. Circle the punctuation mark that breaks the sentence into two parts. Underline the subject of each part of the sentence.

3 Talk About It

Reread the last three paragraphs. Describe how Hector is continuing to help his community.

____

______________________________.

Respond to the Text

Partner Discussion **Work with a partner. Describe what you learned about "Remembering Hurricane Katrina." Write the page numbers where you found text evidence.**

What does Hector remember about Hurricane Katrina?	**Text Evidence**
Hector remembers watching the news and ______.	Page(s): ______
Hector decided to do something because ______.	Page(s): ______
Hector and his friends decided to ______.	Page(s): ______

What does Hector do to help people after a tornado?	**Text Evidence**
Hector is driving to ______.	Page(s): ______
The clothes donations will help because ______.	Page(s): ______
Hector feels good that ______.	Page(s): ______

Group Discussion **Present your answers to the class. Cite text evidence to justify your thinking. Listen to and discuss the group's opinions about your answers.**

ELD.PI.4.1.Ex, ELD.PI.4.1.Br, ELD.PI.4.3.Ex, ELD.PI.4.3.Br, ELD.PI.4.5.Ex, ELD.PI.4.5.Br, ELD.PI.4.9.Ex, ELD.PI.4.9.Br., ELD.PI.4.11a.Ex, ELD.PI.4.11a.Br, ELD.PI.4.12a.Ex, ELD.PI.4.12a.Br See the California Standards section.

Write Work with a partner. Review your notes about "Remembering Hurricane Katrina." Then write your answer to the essential question. Use text evidence to support your answer. Use vocabulary words from this week's reading in your writing.

How do Hector and his friends help their community?

Hector and his friends helped the people in the Astrodome affected by Hurricane Katrina by ______________________________

______________________________.

Hector and his friends help people after a tornado by ______________________________

______________________________.

At the end of the story, Hector says he feels ______________________________

______________________________.

COLLABORATE

Share Writing Present your writing to the class. Discuss their opinions. Think about what they have to say. Did they justify their claims? Explain why you agree or disagree with their claims.

I agree with ______________ because ______________.

I disagree with ______________ because ______________.

ELD.PI.4.1.Ex, ELD.PI.4.1.Br, ELD.PI.4.3.Ex, ELD.PI.4.3.Br, ELD.PI.4.5.Ex, ELD.PI.4.5.Br, ELD.PI.4.9.Ex, ELD.PI.4.9.Br, ELD.PI.4.10b.Ex, ELD.PI.4.10b.Br, ELD.PI.4.11a.Ex, ELD.PI.4.11a.Br, ELD.PI.4.12a.Ex, ELD.PI.4.12a.Br See the California Standards section.

Write to Sources

Take Notes About the Text **I took notes on this chart to tell about the selection. It will help me respond to the prompt:** ***Pretend you are Hector. Describe what it was like to give out toys at the Astrodome.***

pages 154–157

Hector saw on the news many people at the Astrodome because of Hurricane Katrina.

The hurricane destroyed their homes. They lost everything. People were tired and sad.

Hector and his friends volunteered to collect toys for the kids.

The kids were happy to see Hector and his friends. The parents thanked them for their generosity.

Christa Paustenbaugh Photography/Moment/Getty Images

 ELD.PI.4.1.Ex, ELD.PI.4.1.Br, ELD.PI.4.5.Ex, ELD.PI.4.5.Br, ELD.PI.4.6a.Ex, ELD.PI.4.6a.Br See the California Standards section.

Write About the Text **I used my notes from the chart to write a descriptive paragraph about what it was like for Hector to give out toys.**

Student Model: *Narrative Text*

There were thousands of people at the Astrodome when we arrived. Hurricane Katrina had destroyed their homes. They lost everything. We carried bags of toys we collected. The kids flew toward us from all directions. Soon we started pulling toys from our bags. The kids were so happy. Their smiling faces made me happy, too. The parents were glad we were there. They thanked us. It felt good to help.

TALK ABOUT IT

Text Evidence

Draw a box around a detail from the notes that tells why the people were at the Astrodome. What caused them to be there?

Grammar

Circle a past-tense verb. Why did Ava use the past tense?

Connect Ideas

Underline the two sentences that tell about what the parents did. How can you connect the two sentences into one sentence?

Your Turn

Pretend you were a kid at the Astrodome. Write details about how you felt when the Houston Helpers got there. Use details from the story.

>> *Go Digital*
Write your response online. Use your editing checklist.

ELD.PI.4.1.Ex, ELD.PI.4.1.Br, ELD.PI.4.2.Ex, ELD.PI.4.2.Br, ELD.PI.4.5.Ex, ELD.PI.4.5.Br, ELD.PI.4.6a.Ex, ELD.PI.4.6a.Br, ELD.PI.4.10b.Ex, ELD.PI.4.10b. Br, ELD.PI.4.12a.Ex, ELD.PI.4.12a.Br, ELD.PII.4.6.Ex, ELD. PII.4.6.Br See the California Standards section.

TALK ABOUT IT

Weekly Concept Liberty and Justice

Essential Question

How can one person make a difference?

>> *Go Digital*

Why do you think the boy in the photo wants to be a superhero? In the chart, write the ways that superheroes make a difference. Describe how people can be like superheroes.

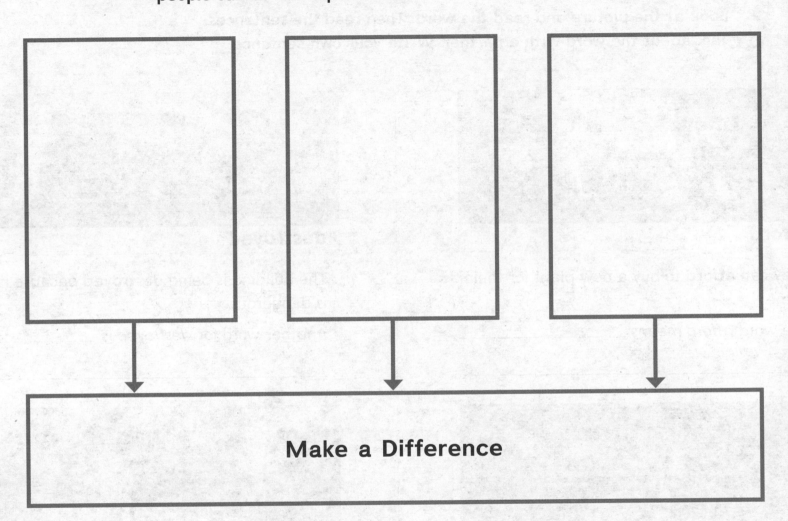

Make a Difference

Discuss how you can make a difference. Use the words from the chart. You can say:

I can make a difference by ______________, ______________, and ____________.

Andrew Rich/Vetta/Getty Images

ELD.PI.4.1.Ex, ELD.PI.4.1.Br, ELD.PI.4.5.Ex, ELD.PI.4.5.Br, ELD.PI.4.12a.Ex, ELD.PI.4.12a.Br
See the California Standards section.

More Vocabulary

Look at the picture and read the word. Then read the sentences. Talk about the word with a partner. Write your own sentence.

afford

They can **afford** to buy a new plant for their home.

The word *afford* means ______________

______________________________.

awarded

The boy was **awarded** first place in the contest.

The boy was *awarded* because ______________

______________________________.

destroyed

The building is being **destroyed** because it is dangerous.

Another word for *destroyed* is ______________

______________________________.

generations

Different **generations** of the family cook together.

The different *generations* of a family include

______________________________.

 ELD.PI.4.1.Ex, ELD.PI.4.1.Br, ELD.PI.4.5.Ex, ELD.PI.4.5.Br, ELD.PI.4.12a.Ex, ELD.PI.4.12a.Br See the California Standards section.

preserve

The ranger is explaining why it is important to **preserve** the park.

It is important to *preserve* a park because

____________________________________.

supported

The fans **supported** their team.

I *supported* ________________________

____________________________________.

Words and Phrases

Compound Words

A compound word is made up of two words put together.

Worms dig tunnels underground.

I can see the mountaintop from my window.

Read the sentences below. Underline the compound word in each sentence. Then write the two words that make up the compound word.

My bedtime is nine o'clock. ________ ________

I cross the street at a crosswalk. ________ ________

Write a sentence using each of the compound words.

____

____

____

» ***Go Digital*** **Add the compound words to your New Words notebook. Write a sentence to show the meaning of each.**

Text Evidence

Shared Read Genre • Biography

COLLABORATE

1 Talk About It

Look at the photograph. Read the title. Talk about what you see. Write your ideas.

What does this title tell you?

____

____

____

____

______________________________.

What is happening to the mountain in the photograph?

____

____

______________________________.

Take notes as you read the text.

Judy's Appalachia

Essential Question

How can one person make a difference?

Read about how one person decided to take a stand.

A mountaintop is leveled to mine for coal in Appalachia.

ELD.PI.4.1.Ex, ELD.PI.4.1.Br, ELD.PI.4.5.Ex, ELD.PI.4.5.Br, ELD.PI.4.6a.Ex, ELD.PI.4.6a.Br
See the California Standards section.

Judy Bonds's six-year-old grandson stood in a creek in West Virginia. He held up a handful of dead fish and asked, "What's wrong with these fish?" All around him dead fish floated belly up in the water. That day became a **turning point** for Judy Bonds. She decided to fight back against the coal mining companies that were poisoning her home.

Marfork, West Virginia

The daughter of a coal miner, Julia "Judy" Bonds was born in Marfork, West Virginia, in 1952. The people of Marfork had been coal miners for **generations** because coal mining provided people with jobs. Coal gave people the energy they needed to light and warm their homes.

But Marfork wasn't just a place where coal miners lived. Marfork was home to a leafy green valley, or holler, surrounded by the Appalachian Mountains on every side. Judy's family had lived in Marfork for generations. Judy grew up there swimming and fishing in the river. She raised a daughter there.

Mountaintop Removal Mining

An energy company came to Marfork in the 1990s. It began a process called mountaintop removal mining. Using dynamite, the company blew off the tops of mountains to get at the large amounts of coal underneath. The process was quicker than the old method of digging for coal underground, but it caused many problems. Whole forests were **destroyed**.

Judy Bonds spoke out against mountaintop removal mining.

ELD.PI.4.1.Ex, ELD.PI.4.1.Br, ELD.PI.4.5.Ex, ELD.PI.4.5.Br, ELD.PI.4.6a.Ex, ELD.PI.4.6a.Br, ELD.PI.4.8.Ex, ELD.PI.4.8.Br, ELD.PI.4.12a.Ex, ELD.PI.4.12a.Br See the California Standards section.

1 Specific Vocabulary ACT

Reread the fourth sentence in the first paragraph. The phrase *turning point* means "a time when an important change begins." Underline the sentence that tells what caused the turning point in Judy's life. Circle the sentence that tells what Judy started to do.

2 Sentence Structure ACT

Reread the fourth sentence in the last paragraph. Circle the connecting word. Underline the independent clauses, or the parts of the sentence that can stand on their own.

3 Talk About It

Reread the last paragraph. Describe the effect mountaintop removal mining had on the surrounding area.

Text Evidence 

1 Specific Vocabulary ACT

Reread the last paragraph. The word *demand* means "to order or insist." Underline the words that tell what Judy demanded. Circle the sentences that tell why Judy demanded this.

2 Sentence Structure ACT

Reread the fourth sentence in the last paragraph. Underline the independent clause, or the part of the sentence that can stand on its own. Then circle the dependent clause, the part of the sentence that cannot stand on its own.

3 Talk About It

Discuss the dates and events on the timeline. What event tells you that Judy Bonds was successful in her work? Then write about it.

____

______________________________.

Dust from the explosions filled the air and settled over the towns. Coal sludge, a mixture of mud, chemicals, and coal dust, got into the creeks and rivers.

Pollution from the mountaintop removal mining began making people living in the towns below the mountains sick. In the area where Judy lived, coal sludge flowed into the rivers and streams. People packed up and left. Judy was heartbroken. The land she loved was being mistreated. She realized that the valley that had always been her home had been poisoned. No longer a safe place to live, it had become dangerous. Judy, her daughter, and her grandson had to leave.

Working for Change

Something had to be done about the pollution. Judy decided it was important to protest against strip mining and **demand** that it be stopped. She felt that she must try to keep the area safe for people. She felt qualified to talk to groups about the injustice of whole towns being forced to move and mountains and forests being destroyed, all because of strip mining. After all, she had grown up in a mining family.

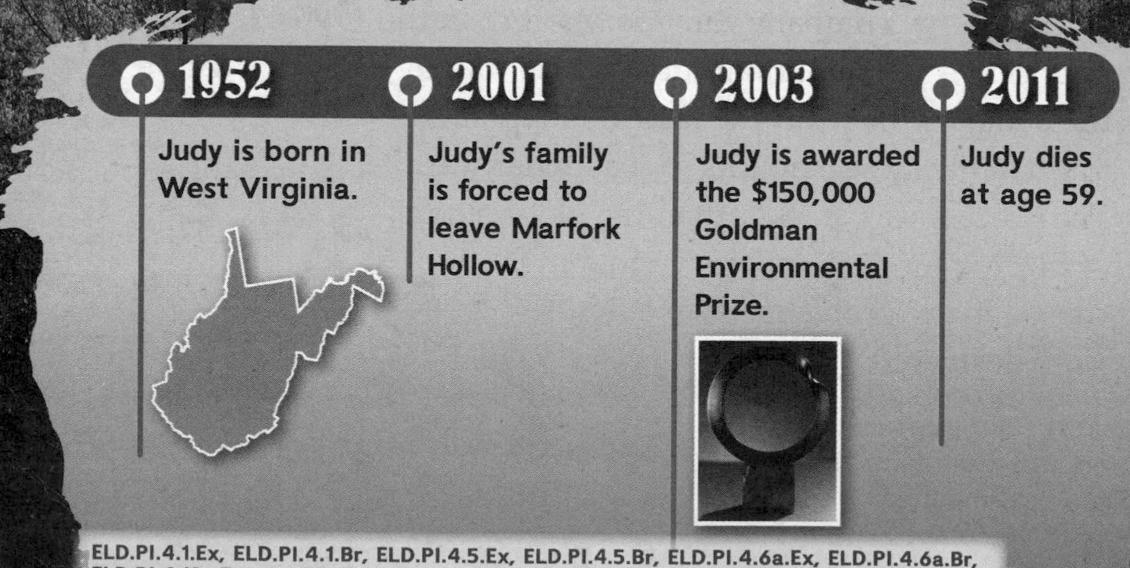

1952
Judy is born in West Virginia.
2001
Judy's family is forced to leave Marfork Hollow.
2003
Judy is awarded the $150,000 Goldman Environmental Prize.
2011
Judy dies at age 59.

ELD.PI.4.1.Ex, ELD.PI.4.1.Br, ELD.PI.4.5.Ex, ELD.PI.4.5.Br, ELD.PI.4.6a.Ex, ELD.PI.4.6a.Br, ELD.PI.4.12a.Ex, ELD.PI.4.12a.Br See the California Standards section.

Judy worked as a volunteer for the Coal River Mountain Watch, a group that fought against mountaintop removal mining. Eventually, she became its executive director. She registered to take part in protests against mining companies. At the protests, Judy faced a lot of anger and insults. Many coal miners were not **opposed** to mountaintop removal mining. They **supported** it because they needed the jobs to provide for their families. Judy knew it would be impossible to boycott the mining companies. The coal miners could not **afford** to leave their jobs. Instead, she pushed for changes to be made to the mining process. Slowly, small changes were made to protect communities in mining areas. In 2003, Judy was **awarded** the Goldman Environmental Prize for her efforts as an activist.

Judy Bonds spoke at protests.

Remembering Judy

Sadly, Judy could not fulfill all of her goals. She was diagnosed with cancer and died in January 2011. But her success has provided encouragement to other activists. Judy may not have been able to stay in her home, but her work will help **preserve** and protect the Appalachian Mountains and help others remain in their homes.

Make Connections

? How did Judy Bonds make a difference? ESSENTIAL QUESTION

What causes do you feel strongly about? TEXT TO SELF

The Monongahela National Forest in West Virginia.

Text Evidence

1 Sentence Structure ACT

Reread the second sentence in the first paragraph. Circle the proper noun in the paragraph that the pronoun *she* refers to.

2 Specific Vocabulary ACT

Reread the fifth sentence in the first paragraph. The word *opposed* means "did not agree with an idea or plan." Why were many of the coal miners not opposed to the mountaintop removal mining?

____

______________________________.

3 Comprehension

Author's Point of View

Reread the last paragraph. Underline two details that tell why the author thinks Judy Bonds made a difference. Then write about it.

____

______________________________.

ELD.PI.4.1.Ex, ELD.PI.4.1.Br, ELD.PI.4.5.Ex, ELD.PI.4.5.Br, ELD.PI.4.6a.Ex, ELD.PI.4.6a.Br, ELD.PI.4.12a.Ex, ELD.PI.4.12a.Br, ELD.PII.4.2a.Ex, ELD.PII.4.2a.Br See the California Standards section.

Respond to the Text

Partner Discussion **Work with a partner. Describe what you learned about "Judy's Appalachia." Write the page numbers where you found text evidence.**

What did you learn about mountaintop removal mining?	**Text Evidence**
Mountaintop removal mining destroyed ______.	Page(s): ______
Pollution from the mining began to ______.	Page(s): ______
According to the text, Judy and her family had to move because ______.	Page(s): ______

What did Judy do about mountaintop removal mining?	**Text Evidence**
Judy Bonds decided to ______.	Page(s): ______
Judy felt qualified to talk to groups because ______.	Page(s): ______
According to the text, instead of boycotting the mining companies, Judy ______.	Page(s): ______

Group Discussion **Present your answers to the group. Cite text evidence to justify your thinking. Listen to and discuss the group's opinions about your answers.**

 ELD.PI.4.1.Ex, ELD.PI.4.1.Br, ELD.PI.4.3.Ex, ELD.PI.4.3.Br, ELD.PI.4.5.Ex, ELD.PI.4.5.Br, ELD.PI.4.9.Ex, ELD.PI.4.9.Br, ELD.PI.4.11a.Ex, ELD.PI.4.11a.Br, ELD.PI.4.12a.Ex, ELD.PI.4.12a.Br See the California Standards section.

Write Work with a partner. Look at your notes about "Judy's Appalachia." Then write your answer to the essential question. Use text evidence to support your answer. Use vocabulary words from this week's reading in your writing.

How did Judy Bonds make a difference for mining communities?

Although it was unpopular, Judy ______________________________

______________________________.

Eventually, small changes ______________________________

____

______________________________.

Judy's work has encouraged ______________________________

____

______________________________.

COLLABORATE

Share Writing Present your writing to the class. Discuss their opinions. Think about what they have to say. Did they justify their claims? Explain why you agree or disagree with their claims.

I agree with ____________ because ____________.

I disagree with ____________ because ____________.

ELD.PI.4.1.Ex, ELD.PI.4.1.Br, ELD.PI.4.3.Ex, ELD.PI.4.3.Br, ELD.PI.4.5.Ex, ELD.PI.4.5.Br, ELD.PI.4.9.Ex, ELD.PI.4.9.Br, ELD.PI.4.10b.Ex, ELD.PI.4.10b.Br, ELD.PI.4.11a.Ex, ELD.PI.4.11a.Br, ELD.PI.4.12a.Ex, ELD.PI.4.12a.Br See the California Standards section.

Write to Sources

Take Notes About the Text I took notes on the idea web about the selection. It will help me answer the question: ***Was Judy's plan to change the mining process a good one?***

pages 166–169

Detail
Judy did not boycott the mining companies.

Detail
She knew miners needed jobs to provide for their families.

Topic
Judy's plan to change the mining process.

Detail
Instead she pushed for changes to mining.

Detail
Small changes were made to protect communities in mining areas.

 ELD.PI.4.1.Ex, ELD.PI.4.1.Br, ELD.PI.4.5.Ex, ELD.PI.4.5.Br, ELD.PI.4.6a.Ex, ELD.PI.4.6a.Br See the California Standards section.

Write About the Text **I used my notes from my idea web to write an opinion about whether Judy's plan was a good one.**

Student Model: *Opinion*

Judy's plan to change the mining process was a good one. Judy did not boycott the mining companies. She knew miners needed jobs to provide for their families. Instead she pushed for changes to mining. As a result, small changes were made to protect communities. Judy's plan worked.

TALK ABOUT IT

Text Evidence

Draw a box around a supporting detail that comes from the notes. Why did Sebastian use this detail as evidence?

Grammar

Circle the prepositional phrase in the third sentence. What does the phrase describe?

Connect Ideas

Underline the second and third sentences. How could you combine these sentences into one sentence?

Your Turn

Were the miners right to be angry with Judy? Use text evidence.

>> *Go Digital*
Write your response online. Use your editing checklist.

ELD.PI.4.1.Ex, ELD.PI.4.1.Br, ELD.PI.4.2.Ex, ELD.PI.4.2.Br, ELD.PI.4.5.Ex, ELD.PI.4.5.Br, ELD.PI.4.6a.Ex, ELD.PI.4.6a.Br, ELD.PI.4.10b.Ex, ELD.PI.4.10b.Br, ELD.PI.4.11a.Ex, ELD.PI.4.11a.Br, ELD.PI.4.12a.Ex, ELD.PI.4.12a.Br, ELD.PII.4.1.Ex, ELD.PII.4.1.Br, ELD.PII.4.6.Ex, ELD. PII.4.6.Br See the California Standards section.

TALK ABOUT IT

Weekly Concept Powerful Words

Essential Question
How can words lead to change?

» *Go Digital*

"Education is the most powerful weapon which you can use to change the world."

–NELSON MANDELA

Describe what the man in the photo is doing. In the chart, write about how his words led to change.

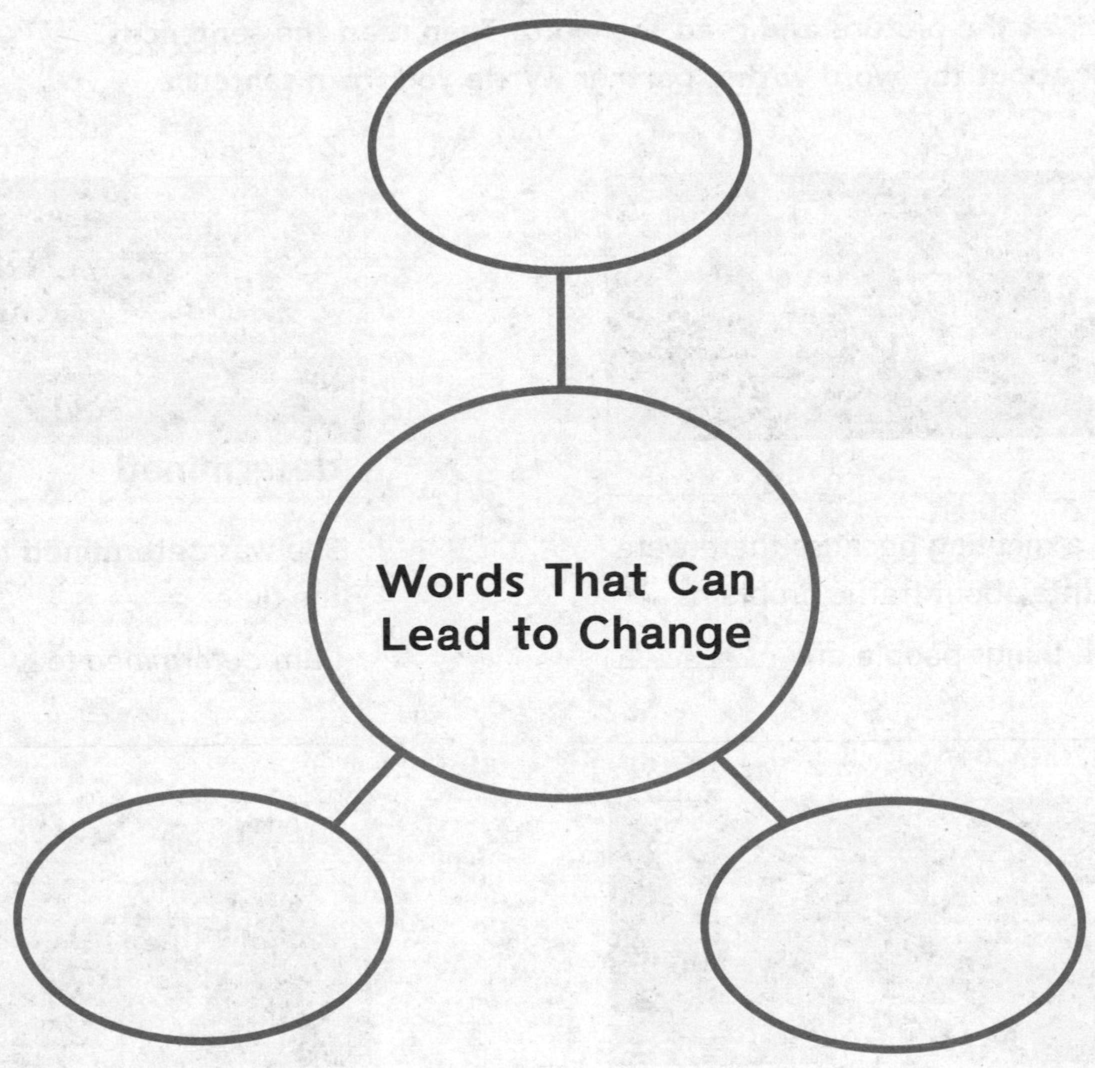

Discuss how words can lead to change. Use the words from the chart. You can say:

Words can lead to change because ______________________.

SZ Photo/The Bridgeman Art Library

ELD.PI.4.1.Ex, ELD.PI.4.1.Br, ELD.PI.4.5.Ex, ELD.PI.4.5.Br, ELD.PI.4.12a.Ex, ELD.PI.4.12a.Br
See the California Standards section.

More Vocabulary

Look at the picture and read the word. Then read the sentences. Talk about the word with a partner. Write your own sentence.

complaints

The town had a meeting because there were many **complaints** about traffic problems.

Complaints are things people are ______________

______________________________________.

determined

She was **determined** to learn the song on the flute.

I am *determined* to ______________________

______________________________________.

deserve

The children **deserve** the applause for their performance.

Another word for *deserve* is ______________

______________________________________.

judge

The **judge** listens to both sides.

A *judge* is a person who ____________________

______________________________________.

(ul)Cade Martin/CDC; (ur)IT Stock Free/Alamy; (bl)Purestock/Alamy; (br)Rich Legg/E+/Getty Images

 ELD.PI.4.1.Ex, ELD.PI.4.1.Br, ELD.PI.4.5.Ex, ELD.PI.4.5.Br, ELD.PI.4.12a.Ex, ELD.PI.4.12a.Br See the California Standards section.

passionate

The group is **passionate** about playing music.

Another word for *passionate* is ______________

____.

refused

The dog **refused** to give up the rope to the boy.

I have *refused* to __________________ because

____.

Words and Phrases

Figurative Language: Idioms

An idiom is a group of words that means something different than the words alone.

touched my heart **= felt strongly toward**

The kindness of the volunteers touched my heart.

paved the way **= led the way**

Sally Ride paved the way for women astronauts.

Read the sentences below. Write the idiom that means the same as the underlined words.

I felt strongly toward my students.

My students ____.

The guide led the way through the crowds.

The guide ______________________ through the crowds.

» Go Digital **Add these idioms to your New Words notebook. Write a sentence to show the meaning of each.**

Text Evidence

1 Talk About It

Look at the photograph. Read the title. Talk about what you see. Write your ideas.

What does this title tell you?

____

____

____

____

______________________________.

What are the women in the photograph doing?

____

____

____

______________________________.

Take notes as you read the text.

Shared Read Genre • Biography

Words for Change

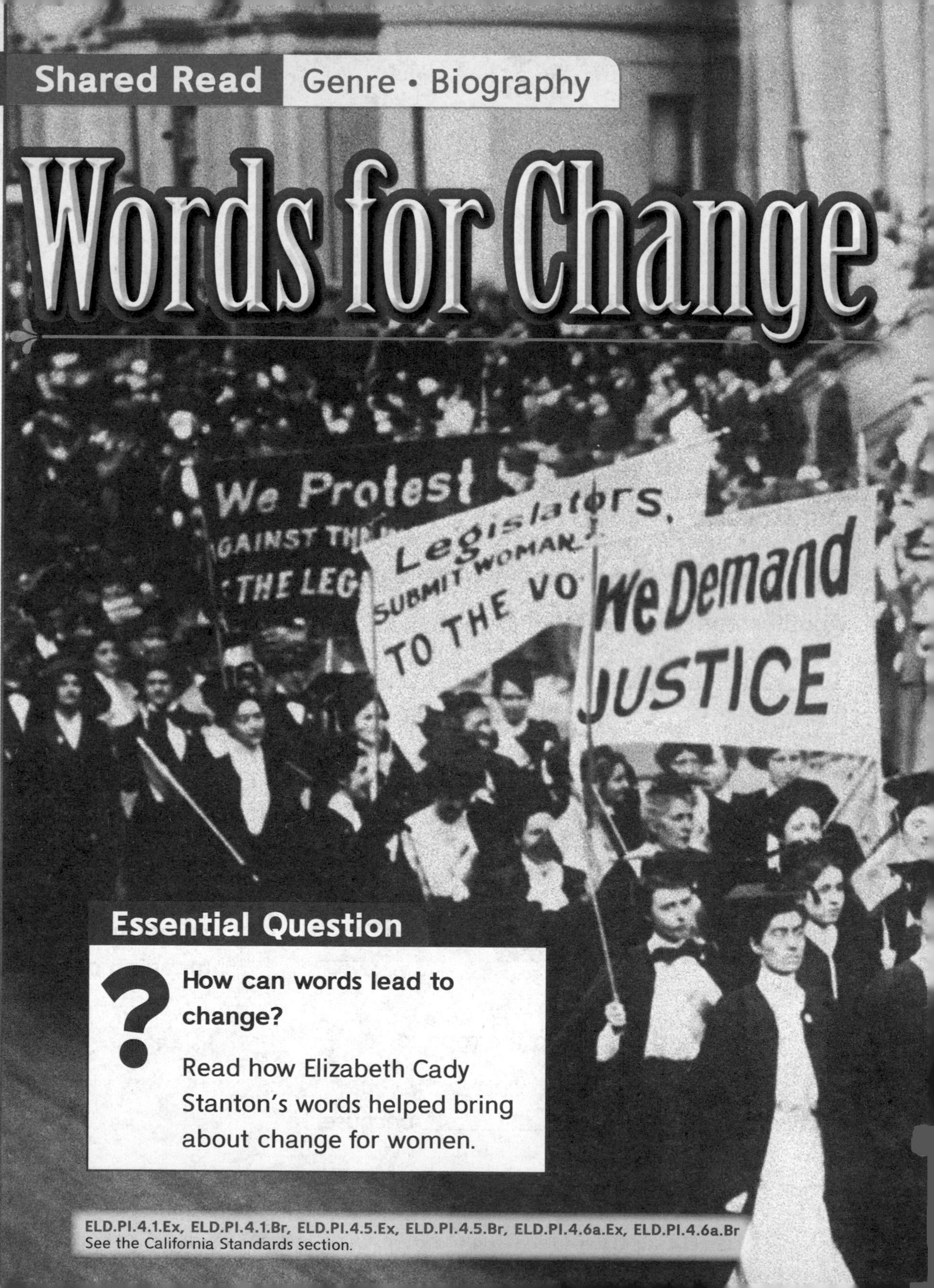

Essential Question

How can words lead to change?

Read how Elizabeth Cady Stanton's words helped bring about change for women.

ELD.PI.4.1.Ex, ELD.PI.4.1.Br, ELD.PI.4.5.Ex, ELD.PI.4.5.Br, ELD.PI.4.6a.Ex, ELD.PI.4.6a.Br
See the California Standards section.

Elizabeth Cady Stanton and her daughter

The Early Years

In 1827, when Elizabeth Cady Stanton was eleven, her father said: "Oh, my daughter, I wish you were a boy." Elizabeth was shattered. From that time on, she became **determined** to prove to her father and the whole world that women—and all people—**deserve** equal treatment.

Elizabeth's father was a lawyer, **judge**, and congressman. She would listen **eagerly** when a woman would come see him for legal advice. But she was often disappointed. Her father could not help them because women did not have the same rights as men did under the law. Married women could not own property or vote. Elizabeth said: "The tears and **complaints** of the women who came to my father for legal advice touched my heart and early drew my attention to the injustice and cruelty of the laws."

Elizabeth began drawing lines through all the laws she opposed in her father's law books. She planned to take a pair of scissors and cut these pages out. Her father had a better idea. He told her that when she was grown up, she must get lawmakers to pass new laws. Then the unfair laws would perish and disappear. Women's lives would be changed.

Suffragettes march in a parade in New York City.

Text Evidence

1 Specific Vocabulary ACT

Reread the second sentence in the second paragraph. Look at the word *eagerly*. *Eager* means "excited about." The suffix *-ly* means "done in the way of." What is the meaning of *eagerly*?

____

______________________________.

2 Comprehension

Author's Point of View

Reread the last paragraph. Underline why Elizabeth drew lines through her father's law books. What was her father's advice?

____

______________________________.

3 Sentence Structure ACT

Reread the second sentence in the last paragraph. Underline the subject. Then circle the two actions the subject wanted to do.

ELD.PI.4.1.Ex, ELD.PI.4.1.Br, ELD.PI.4.5.Ex, ELD.PI.4.5.Br, ELD.PI.4.6a.Ex, ELD.PI.4.6a.Br, ELD.PI.4.6b.Ex, ELD.PI.4.6b.Br, ELD.PI.4.12a.Ex, ELD.PI.4.12a.Br See the California Standards section.

Text Evidence

1 Talk About It

Reread the first paragraph. Discuss how Elizabeth was passionate about rights for African Americans. Explain what was happening to African Americans at that time in history.

2 Specific Vocabulary ACT

Reread the second paragraph. Find the word *activist*. Underline the root word. An *activist* is a person who works hard for social change. What kind of activist was Elizabeth?

____

______________________________.

3 Sentence Structure ACT

Reread the second sentence in the third paragraph. Circle the subjects of the sentence. Underline what they did.

Working for Change

Elizabeth was as **passionate** about the rights of African Americans as she was about those of women. At that time, the country was divided in two by the issue of slavery. While working for reform, she met her husband, the abolitionist Henry Stanton. They were married in 1840. Elizabeth **refused** to use the traditional words "promise to obey" in her wedding vows.

The Seneca Falls Convention

Elizabeth tried to settle into the role of wife and mother. But she wanted to be an **activist** and work for change. She took her father's advice and wrote a proclamation. It was called the "Declaration of Rights and Sentiments." Modeled after the Declaration of Independence, it stated that women should be able to vote and have the same rights as men.

She presented this document in 1848 at America's first women's rights convention in Seneca Falls, New York. Elizabeth and her friend Lucretia Mott organized this important event. In her address at the convention, Elizabeth said,

Because women do feel themselves ... deprived of their most sacred rights, we insist that they have immediate admission to all the rights and privileges which belong to them as citizens of the United States.

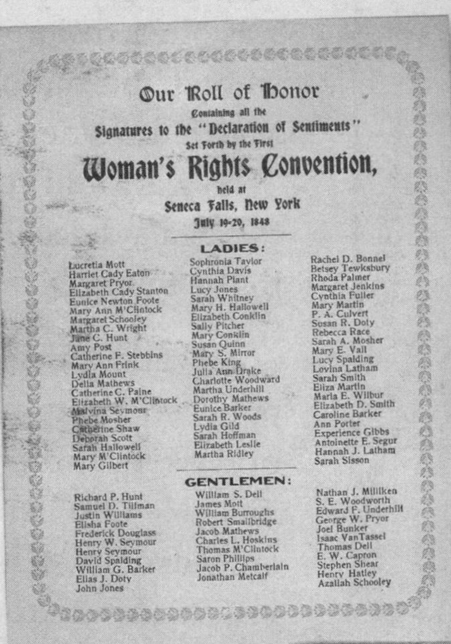

Our Roll of Honor
Containing all the
Signatures to the "Declaration of Sentiments"
Set Forth by the First
Woman's Rights Convention,
held at
Seneca Falls, New York
July 19-20, 1848

LADIES:

Lucretia Mott
Harriet Cady Eaton
Margaret Pryor
Elizabeth Cady Stanton
Eunice Newton Foote
Mary Ann M'Clintock
Margaret Schooley
Martha C. Wright
Jane C. Hunt
Amy Post
Catherine F. Stebbins
Mary Ann Frink
Lydia Mount
Delia Mathews
Catherine C. Paine
Elizabeth W. M'Clintock
Malvina Seymour
Phebe Mosher
Catherine Shaw
Deborah Scott
Sarah Hallowell
Mary M'Clintock
Mary Gilbert
Sophronia Taylor
Cynthia Davis
Hannah Plant
Lucy Jones
Sarah Whitney
Mary H. Hallowell
Elizabeth Conklin
Sally Pitcher
Mary Conklin
Susan Quinn
Mary S. Mirror
Phebe King
Julia Ann Drake
Charlotte Woodward
Martha Underhill
Dorothy Mathews
Eunice Barker
Sarah R. Woods
Lydia Gild
Sarah Hoffman
Elizabeth Leslie
Martha Ridley
Rachel D. Bonnel
Betsey Tewksbury
Rhoda Palmer
Margaret Jenkins
Cynthia Fuller
Mary Martin
P. A. Culvert
Susan R. Doty
Rebecca Race
Sarah A. Mosher
Mary E. Vail
Lucy Spalding
Lovina Latham
Sarah Smith
Eliza Martin
Maria E. Wilbur
Elizabeth D. Smith
Caroline Barker
Ann Porter
Experience Gibbs
Antoinette E. Segur
Hannah J. Latham
Sarah Sisson

GENTLEMEN:

Richard P. Hunt
Samuel D. Tillman
Justin Williams
Elisha Foote
Frederick Douglass
Henry W. Seymour
Henry Seymour
David Spalding
William G. Barker
Elias J. Doty
John Jones
William S. Dell
James Mott
William Burroughs
Robert Smallbridge
Jacob Mathews
Charles L. Hoskins
Thomas M'Clintock
Saron Phillips
Jacob P. Chamberlain
Jonathan Metcalf
Nathan J. Milliken
S. E. Woodworth
Edward F. Underhill
George W. Pryor
Joel Bunker
Isaac VanTassel
Thomas Dell
E. W. Capron
Stephen Shear
Henry Hatley
Azaliah Schooley

List of attendees at the convention

ELD.PI.4.1.Ex, ELD.PI.4.1.Br, ELD.PI.4.5.Ex, ELD.PI.4.5.Br, ELD.PI.4.6a.Ex, ELD.PI.4.6a.Br, ELD.PI.4.7.Ex, ELD.PI.4.7.Br, ELD.PI.4.12a.Ex, ELD.PI.4.12a.Br See the California Standards section.

A Winning Team

Three years later, Elizabeth met Susan B. Anthony. Together, the two made an unstoppable team. Elizabeth was a passionate speaker and writer. Anthony was a gifted leader and organizer. In 1869, they formed the National Woman Suffrage Association. This group was dedicated to helping women gain the right to vote. Congress showed no haste, or hurry, to change the law. Elizabeth toured the country. She spoke about reforms for women and a woman's right to vote. She did not care if her speeches caused tension and made some people angry. She believed in her cause.

Susan B. Anthony and Elizabeth Cady Stanton

Victory At Last

Elizabeth Cady Stanton never got to cast a vote before she died on October 26, 1902. Yet her bold words had a lasting impact. Women finally gained the right to vote on August 18, 1920 when the 19th amendment was **ratified**. Elizabeth Cady Stanton's passion for equal rights paved the way for future women's lives to be changed forever.

Make Connections

Talk about how Elizabeth Cady Stanton helped women gain the right to vote. ESSENTIAL QUESTION

Think about a time when you disagreed with something or wanted to change something. What did you say to try to change it? TEXT TO SELF

ELD.PI.4.1.Ex, ELD.PI.4.1.Br, ELD.PI.4.5.Ex, ELD.PI.4.5.Br, ELD.PI.4.6a.Ex, ELD.PI.4.6a.Br, ELD.PI.4.12a.Ex, ELD.PI.4.12a.Br, ELD.PII.4.2a.Ex, ELD.PII.4.2a.Br
See the California Standards section.

(bkgd) Hulton-Deutsch Collection/Corbis; (tc) Chicago History Museum/Archive Photos/Getty Images (b) The Library of Congress, Manuscript Division; (tr) Courtesy: CSU Archive/Everett Collection/age fotostock

Text Evidence

1 Sentence Structure

Reread the first paragraph. In the second sentence, who are the people the word *together* refers to? Draw a circle around the names of the people. Underline the things that made them unstoppable.

2 Specific Vocabulary

Reread the last paragraph. The word *ratified* means "approved." Underline what was ratified. Describe how it changed women's lives.

____

_______________________________________.

3 Comprehension

Author's Point of View

Reread the last paragraph. Underline two details that tell you the author has great respect for Elizabeth Cady Stanton.

Respond to the Text

Partner Discussion **Work with a partner. Describe what you learned about "Words for Change." Write the page numbers where you found text evidence.**

What did you learn about Elizabeth Cady Stanton's childhood?	**Text Evidence**
I read she was shattered that her father ________________.	Page(s): ________
Elizabeth was determined to prove to her father that ________.	Page(s): ________
Elizabeth's father told Elizabeth that women's lives would be changed if she ________________.	Page(s): ________

What kind of work did Elizabeth do as an adult?	**Text Evidence**
I read Elizabeth worked for women's rights as well as ________.	Page(s): ________
Elizabeth and Lucretia Mott organized a convention. At the convention Elizabeth ________________.	Page(s): ________
Elizabeth and Susan B. Anthony founded the National Woman Suffrage Association, which was dedicated to ________.	Page(s): ________

Group Discussion **Present your answers to the class. Cite text evidence to justify your thinking. Listen to and discuss the group's opinions about your answers.**

 ELD.PI.4.1.Ex, ELD.PI.4.1.Br, ELD.PI.4.3.Ex, ELD.PI.4.3.Br, ELD.PI.4.5.Ex, ELD.PI.4.5.Br, ELD.PI.4.9.Ex; ELD.PI.4.9.Br, ELD.PI.4.11a.Ex, ELD.PI.4.11a.Br, ELD.PI.4.12a.Ex, ELD.PI.4.12a.Br See the California Standards section.

Write Work with a partner. Review your notes about "Words for Change." Then write your answer to the essential question. Use text evidence to support your answer. Use vocabulary words from this week's reading in your writing.

How did Elizabeth Cady Stanton's words bring about change?

From a young age, Stanton had decided to ______________________________

______________________________.

She wrote and spoke about ______________________________

____

______________________________.

Eventually, the work of Stanton and other women led to the ______________

____

______________________________.

COLLABORATE

Share Writing Present your writing to the class. Discuss their opinions. Think about what they have to say. Did they justify their claims? Explain why you agree or disagree with their claims.

I agree with ______________ because ______________.

I disagree with ______________ because ______________.

ELD.PI.4.1.Ex, ELD.PI.4.1.Br, ELD.PI.4.3.Ex, ELD.PI.4.3.Br, ELD.PI.4.5.Ex, ELD.PI.4.5.Br, ELD.PI.4.9.Ex, ELD.PI.4.9.Br, ELD.PI.4.10b.Ex, ELD.PI.4.10b.Br, ELD.PI.4.11a.Ex, ELD.PI.4.11a.Br, ELD.PI.4.12a.Ex, ELD.PI.4.12a.Br See the California Standards section.

Write to Sources

Take Notes About the Text **I took notes on this sequence chart to answer the question:** ***How does the sequence of events help you understand how Elizabeth Cady Stanton helped women gain the right to vote?***

pages 178–181

Elizabeth wrote a proclamation. It said that women should be able to vote.

↓

She presented it in 1848.

↓

Elizabeth and Susan B. Anthony formed the National Woman Suffrage Association in 1869.

↓

Elizabeth died in 1902 without ever voting. Women gained the right to vote in 1920.

Paul Bradbury/OJO Images/Getty Images

 ELD.PI.4.1.Ex, ELD.PI.4.1.Br, ELD.PI.4.5.Ex, ELD.PI.4.5.Br, ELD.PI.4.6a.Ex, ELD.PI.4.6a.Br, ELD.PII.4.1.Ex, ELD.PII.4.1.Br See the California Standards section.

Write About the Text I used my notes from my sequence chart to explain how sequence helped me understand how Elizabeth Cady Stanton helped women gain the right to vote.

Student Model: *Informative Text*

Sequence helped me understand how Elizabeth Cady Stanton helped women gain the right to vote. Elizabeth wrote a proclamation. It said that all women should have the right to vote. She presented it in 1848. In 1869, she formed the National Woman Suffrage Association. She formed it with Susan B. Anthony. Elizabeth died in 1902 without ever voting. At last, women gained the right to vote in 1920. Elizabeth had to fight for women's right to vote for a very long time.

TALK ABOUT IT

Text Evidence

Draw a box around a supporting detail from the notes that tells when women gained the right to vote. How does this detail support the writer's conclusion?

Grammar

Circle a past-tense verb. Why did Drew use the past tense to write about Elizabeth?

Condense Ideas

Underline the two sentences about the National Woman Suffrage Association. How can you make the two sentences into one detailed sentence?

Your Turn

Why did Elizabeth Cady Stanton fight for equal rights? Use text evidence.

>> *Go Digital*
Write your response online. Use your editing checklist.

ELD.PI.4.1.Ex, ELD.PI.4.1.Br, ELD.PI.4.2.Ex, ELD.PI.4.2.Br, ELD.PI.4.5.Ex, ELD.PI.4.5.Br, ELD.PI.4.6a.Ex, ELD.PI.4.6a.Br, ELD.PI.4.10b.Ex, ELD.PI.4.10b.Br, ELD.PI.4.12a.Ex, ELD.PI.4.12a.Br, ELD.PII.4.1.Ex, ELD.PII.4.1.Br, ELD.PII.4.7.Ex, ELD.PII.4.7.Br See the California Standards section.

TALK ABOUT IT

Weekly Concept Feeding the World

Essential Question

In what ways can advances in science be helpful or harmful?

» *Go Digital*

Describe what you see in the photograph. How can science research help or harm people? Write your ideas in the chart.

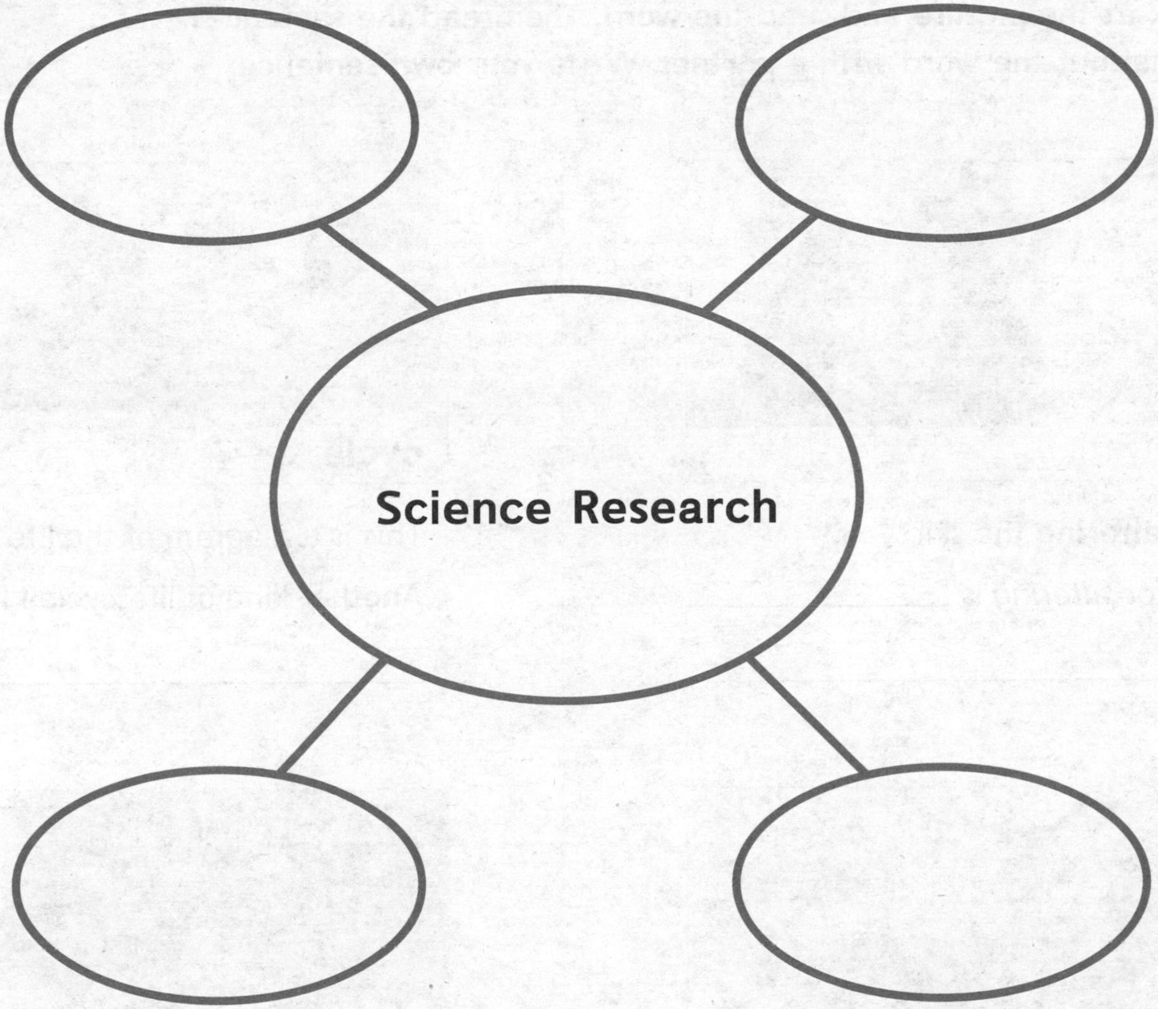

Discuss how science can help or harm people and the environment. Use the words from the chart. You can say:

Science can be helpful when ______________________.

Science can be harmful when ______________________.

ELD.PI.4.1.Ex, ELD.PI.4.1.Br, ELD.PI.4.5.Ex, ELD.PI.4.5.Br, ELD.PI.4.12a.Ex, ELD.PI.4.12a.Br
See the California Standards section.

More Vocabulary

Look at the picture and read the word. Then read the sentences. Talk about the word with a partner. Write your own sentence.

altering

The woman is **altering** the skirt.

Another word for *altering* is ______________

______________________________.

contain

The glass jars **contain** different marbles.

Another word for *contain* is ______________

______________________________.

cycle

This is a diagram of the life **cycle** of a tree.

Another kind of life *cycle* I learned about is

______________________________.

environment

Many living things can be found in a pond **environment**.

I live in an *environment* that has ______________

______________________________.

 ELD.PI.4.1.Ex, ELD.PI.4.1.Br, ELD.PI.4.5.Ex, ELD.PI.4.5.Br, ELD.PI.4.12a.Ex, ELD.PI.4.12a.Br See the California Standards section.

interfere

Talking on the phone will **interfere** with people watching a movie.

Another word for *interfere* is ______________

______________________________.

superior

Whole grain brown breads are **superior** to white bread.

Another word for *superior* is ______________

______________________________.

Words and Phrases

Prepositional Phrases: *from* and *with*

A prepositional phrase is a group of words that begins with a preposition and ends with a noun or a pronoun.

I eat lunch with a friend.

The phrase *with a friend* tells who I eat lunch with.

I got the book from the library.

The phrase *from the library* tells where I got the book.

Read the sentences below. Underline the prepositional phrase in each sentence.

Maya runs from the park.

I like to play catch with my dog.

» *Go Digital* **Add these prepositional phrases to your New Words notebook. Write a sentence to show the meaning of each.**

Text Evidence

1 Talk About It

Look at the photograph. Read the title. Talk about what you see. Write your ideas.

What does this title tell you?

____

____

____

______________________________.

What is the scientist doing?

____

____

____

______________________________.

Take notes as you read the text.

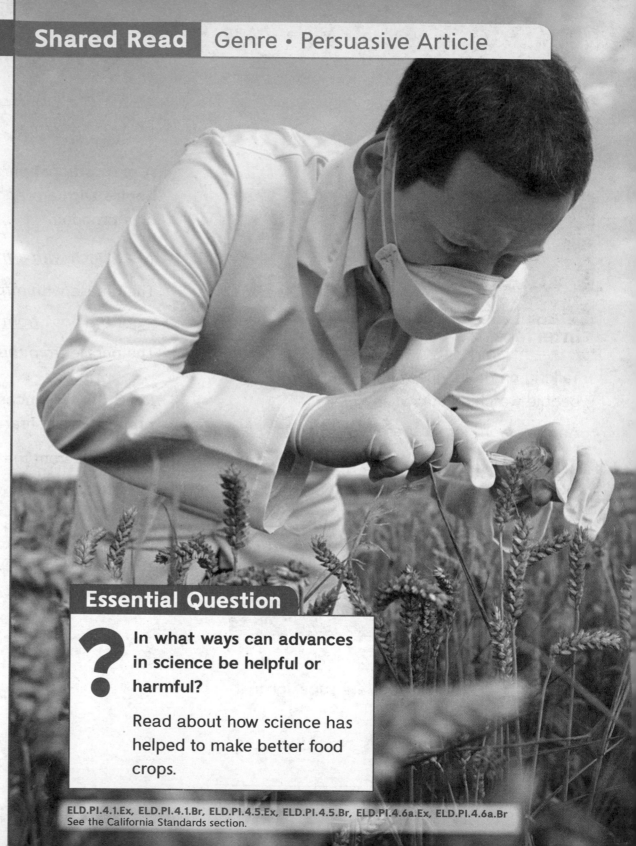

Essential Question

In what ways can advances in science be helpful or harmful?

Read about how science has helped to make better food crops.

ELD.PI.4.1.Ex, ELD.PI.4.1.Br, ELD.PI.4.5.Ex, ELD.PI.4.5.Br, ELD.PI.4.6a.Ex, ELD.PI.4.6a.Br
See the California Standards section.

Food Fight

Is it safe to interfere with Mother Nature?

An incredible thing is happening to our food. Some scientists are using a technique called genetic modification to make **superior** food crops. It involves **altering** a seed's genes. Genes are the "instruction codes" that all living things have inside their cells. A seed's genetic code sets what characteristics it will inherit when it grows into a plant. These could mean how big it will grow and the nutrients it will **contain**.

For thousands of years, farmers made crops better by **crossbreeding** plants. They would add pollen from the sweetest melon plants to the flowers of plants that produced the biggest melons. This would make new plants with big, sweet melons. But this process does not always work. The **cycle** of crossbreeding can take years to get good results.

But advances in gene science have created amazing shortcuts. Using new tools, scientists can put a gene from one living thing into another.

That living thing could be a plant, a bacterium, a virus, or even an animal. These foods are called genetically modified foods, or GM foods. The goal of GM foods is to create foods that can survive insects or harsh conditions or can grow faster. But are these advancements in agriculture good for us?

ELD.PI.4.1.Ex, ELD.PI.4.1.Br, ELD.PI.4.5.Ex, ELD.PI.4.5.Br, ELD.PI.4.6a.Ex, ELD.PI.4.6a.Br, ELD.PI.4.7.Ex, ELD.PI.4.7.Br, ELD.PI.4.12a.Ex, ELD.PI.4.12a.Br, ELD.PII.4.6.Ex, ELD.PII.4.6.Br

See the California Standards section.

Text Evidence

1 Comprehension

Author's Point of View

Reread the first two sentences in the first paragraph. Underline the words that describe the author's thoughts about genetically modified foods.

2 Specific Vocabulary ACT

Reread the second paragraph. The word *crossbreeding* means "combining one kind of living thing with another living thing to produce a new kind of living thing." Underline the sentence that describes a kind of *crossbreeding*.

3 Sentence Structure ACT

Reread the third and fourth sentences in the fourth paragraph. Combine the sentences into one sentence.

____

____

________________________________.

Text Evidence

1 Sentence Structure ACT

Reread the second paragraph. Circle the words that the pronoun *It* refers to. Underline why it is good for the environment.

2 Comprehension

Author's Point of View

Reread the third paragraph. Underline what GM golden rice can do. How does the author feel about GM golden rice?

____

____________________________.

3 Specific Vocabulary ACT

Reread the Superfoods chart. The word *supersized* has two smaller words. Write a definition for the word *supersized*.

____________________________.

How do GM salmon become supersized? Underline the words that tell you.

Support for Superfoods

Scientists believe the new techniques can create crops with a resistance to pests and disease. Bt corn is a genetically modified corn.

It has an insect-killing gene that comes from a bacterium. Farmers who grow Bt corn can use fewer chemicals while they grow their crops. That is good for the farmer and the **environment**.

Some superfoods are extra nutritious. Golden rice has been genetically modified with three different genes. One gene is a form of bacterium. The other two are from daffodils. The new genes help the rice to make a nutrient that prevents some forms of blindness.

Disease-resistant GM potatoes were introduced in the 1990's.

Superfoods

These foods may seem common. But did you know that the genetically modified versions have special powers?

Rice

Rice contains phytic acid. Too much of this acid can be bad for people. A new type of rice has been bred with a low level of phytic acid.

Salmon

To create **supersized** salmon, scientists changed the gene that controls growth. The genetically altered salmon grow twice as fast as their wild cousins.

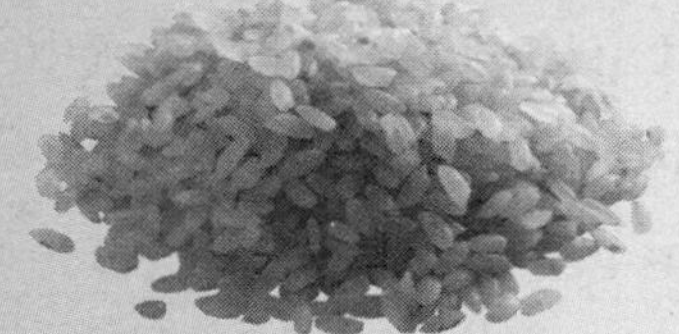

Tomatoes

Genetically engineered tomatoes can be picked when they are ripe and still not bruise when shipped. One food company tried to use an arctic flounder fish gene to create a tomato that could survive frost. The fish-tomato did not succeed.

ELD.PI.4.1.Ex, ELD.PI.4.1.Br, ELD.PI.4.5.Ex, ELD.PI.4.5.Br, ELD.PI.4.6a.Ex, ELD.PI.4.6a.Br, ELD.PI.4.12a.Ex, ELD.PI.4.12a.Br, ELD.PII.4.2a.Ex, ELD.PII.4.2a.Br See the California Standards section.

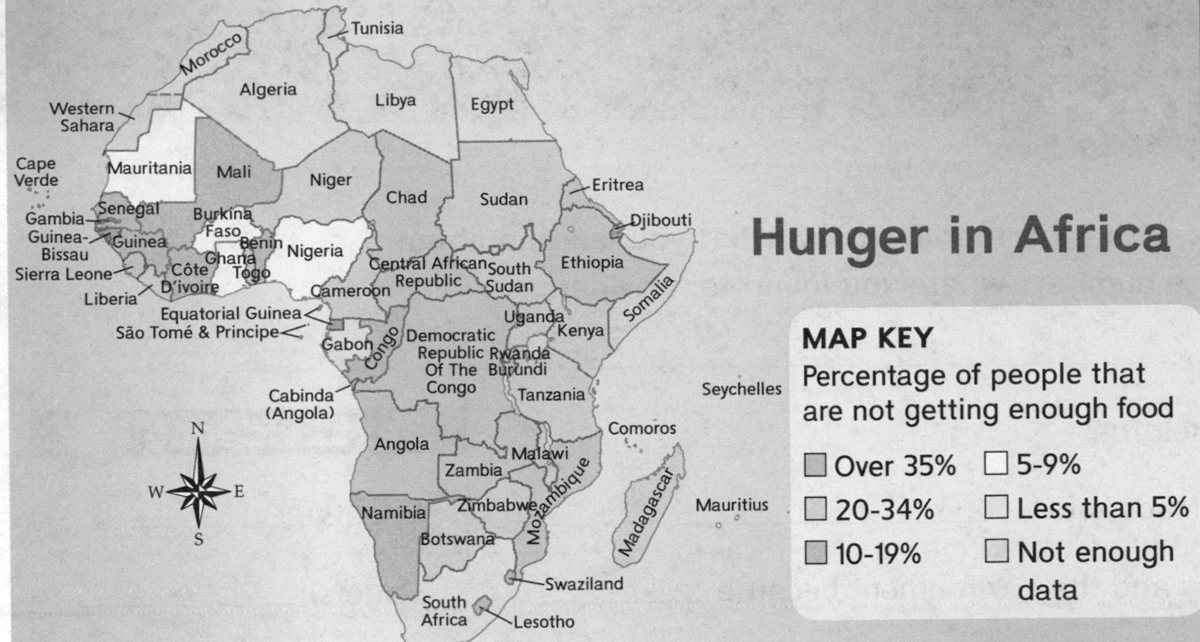

Safety Issues

POINT COUNTERPOINT

Many people have disagreed with the idea that GM foods are a good idea. They worry GM foods will hurt the environment and humans. One concern is that plants with new genes will crossbreed with weeds to make pesticide-resistant weeds. Another concern is that GM foods may **trigger** allergies.

Genetically modified crops are prevalent in the U.S. But some people will not buy them because of health concerns. As a result, many companies avoid GM foods although there is no physical evidence that they are unhealthy.

Time Will Tell

Genetically modified foods have not hurt anyone. Most genetic researchers think that if troubles do crop up, they will be manageable. It is important to keep researching GM foods because these types of foods can better fight the world's chronic hunger problems.

Make Connections

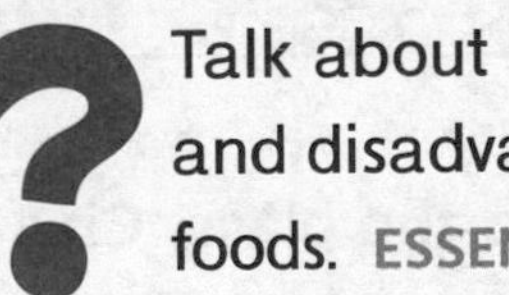

Talk about the advantages and disadvantages of GM foods. ESSENTIAL QUESTION

Would you buy GM foods? TEXT TO SELF

Text Evidence

1 Specific Vocabulary ACT

Reread the first paragraph. *Trigger* means "to cause something to happen." Circle the word that tells what might be triggered by GM foods.

2 Sentence Structure ACT

Reread the last sentence in the second paragraph. Underline the clauses that can stand on their own. Circle the word that connects the two clauses.

3 Talk About It

Discuss the reasons why some people are in favor of using GM foods. Then talk about the reasons why some people are opposed to them. Then write what your opinion is about GM foods.

____

____

______________________________.

ELD.PI.4.1.Ex, ELD.PI.4.1.Br, ELD.PI.4.3.Ex, ELD.PI.4.3.Br, ELD.PI.4.5.Ex, ELD.PI.4.5.Br, ELD.PI.4.6a.Ex, ELD.PI.4.6a.Br, ELD.PI.4.7.Ex, ELD.PI.4.7.Br, ELD.PI.4.11a.Ex, ELD.PI.4.11a.Br, ELD.PI.4.12a.Ex, ELD.PI.4.12a.Br See the California Standards section.

Opposite: (tc) Peter Dazeley/Photographer's Choice/Getty Images; (cr) Stockbyte/Getty Images; (bl) The McGraw-Hill Companies,Inc./Jacques Cornell photographer; (b) Digital Vision/Getty; (tr) Mapping Specialists Images

Respond to the Text

Partner Discussion Work with a partner. Describe what you learned about "Food Fight." Write the page numbers where you found text evidence.

How may GM foods be helpful?	**Text Evidence**
The goal in creating GM foods is to ______.	Page(s): ______
Bt corn is good for farmers and the environment because ______.	Page(s): ______
According to the text, some GM foods are ______.	Page(s): ______
For example, GM golden rice can ______.	Page(s): ______

How may GM foods be harmful?	**Text Evidence**
Some people worry GM foods can ______.	Page(s): ______
One concern is GM foods might ______.	Page(s): ______
According to the text, many people will not buy GM foods, causing ______.	Page(s): ______

Group Discussion Present your answers to the class. Cite text evidence to justify your thinking. Listen to and discuss the group's opinions about your answers.

ELD.PI.4.1.Ex, ELD.PI.4.1.Br, ELD.PI.4.3.Ex, ELD.PI.4.3.Br, ELD.PI.4.5.Ex, ELD.PI.4.5.Br, ELD.PI.4.9.Ex, ELD.PI.4.9.Br, ELD.PI.4.11a.Ex, ELD.PI.4.11a.Br, ELD.PI.4.12a.Ex, ELD.PI.4.12a.Br See the California Standards section.

Write Work with a partner. Look at your notes about "Food Fight." Then write your answer to the essential question. Use text evidence to support your answer. Use vocabulary words from this week's reading in your writing.

In what ways can GM foods be helpful or harmful?

GM foods are helpful because ______________________________

____.

GM foods are harmful because ______________________________

____.

The author thinks GM foods are ______________________________

____.

I think GM foods are ______________ because ______________

____.

COLLABORATE

Share Writing Present your writing to the class. Discuss their opinions. Think about what they have to say. Did they justify their claims? Explain why you agree or disagree with their claims.

I agree with ______________ because ______________.

I disagree with ______________ because ______________.

Write to Sources

Take Notes About the Text **I took notes on this idea web to answer the question:** ***In your opinion, are GM foods safe to eat?***

Shared Read Genre • Persuasive Article

Food Fight

Is it safe to interfere with Mother Nature?

Essential Question

pages 190–193

Are GM foods safe to eat?

- Superfoods like the Bt corn use fewer chemicals, which is good for the environment.
- Golden rice has a nutrient that prevents some blindnesses.
- They may be harmful to the environment and to humans.
- They may cause allergies.

Nick White/ImageSource

Write About the Text **I used my notes from my idea web to write an opinion about how safe GM foods are to eat.**

Student Model: *Opinion*

I think there are some problems with GM foods so they may be unsafe to eat. They may be harmful to the environment and to humans. They could even cause allergies. Some GM foods are helpful. Researchers don't think GM foods will cause problems. I won't buy them until they are sure.

TALK ABOUT IT

Text Evidence

Draw a box around a reason that supports Cristina's opinion from the notes. Did Cristina give a good reason to support her opinion?

Grammar

Circle the words with prefixes and suffixes. How do they change the meaning of the words?

Connect Ideas

Underline the last two sentences. How can you combine them into one detailed sentence?

Your Turn

Does the author present a strong case for growing GM foods? Use text evidence in your writing.

>> *Go Digital*
Write your response online. Use your editing checklist.

ELD.PI.4.1.Ex, ELD.PI.4.1.Br, ELD.PI.4.2.Ex, ELD.PI.4.2.Br, ELD.PI.4.10b.Ex, ELD.PI.4.10b.Br, ELD.PI.4.11a.Ex, ELD.PI.4.11a.Br, ELD.PI.4.12a.Ex, ELD.PI.4.12a.Br, ELD.PII.4.6.Ex, ELD.PII.4.6.Br See the California Standards section.

Unit 4

FACT OR FICTION?

THE BIG IDEA

How do different writers treat the same topic?

Dale O'Dell/Alamy

TALK ABOUT IT

Weekly Concept Our Government

Essential Question

Why do we need government?

>> *Go Digital*

Discuss what you see in the photo. Think about the reasons we have government. Write the words in the chart.

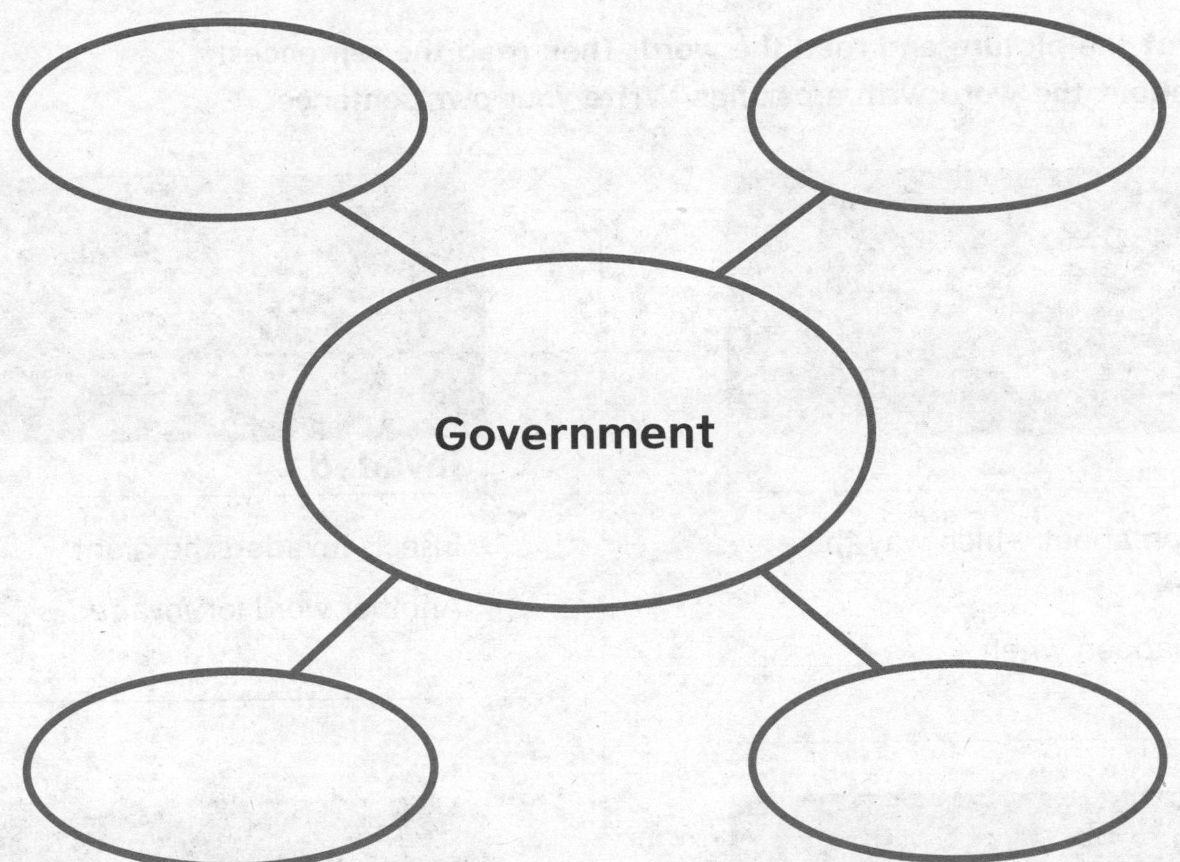

Discuss why government is important for a community. Use the words from the chart. You can say:

Government is important in a community because ______.

People need government because ______________________.

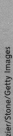

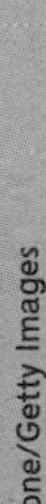

ELD.PI.4.1.Ex, ELD.PI.4.1.Br, ELD.PI.4.5.Ex, ELD.PI.4.5.Br, ELD.PI.4.12a.Ex, ELD.PI.4.12a.Br See the California Standards section.

More Vocabulary

Look at the picture and read the word. Then read the sentences. Talk about the word with a partner. Write your own sentence.

confusion

There is **confusion** about which way the hikers should go.

Confusion may happen when ______________

______________________________.

inspect

The farmer must **inspect** the corn for our safety.

Another word for *inspect* is ______________

______________________________.

invaded

Insects **invaded** the plant.

Another word for *invaded* is ______________

______________________________.

maintain

They **maintain** the garden by weeding and watering.

It is important to *maintain* a garden because

______________________________.

 ELD.PI.4.1.Ex, ELD.PI.4.1.Br, ELD.PI.4.5.Ex, ELD.PI.4.5.Br, ELD.PI.4.12a.Ex, ELD.PI.4.12a.Br See the California Standards section.

sensible

She wears **sensible** clothes for the weather.

Sensible clothes on a rainy day would be ______

____.

services

Garbage collection is one of the **services** a city provides.

Some services in my city are ____________

____.

Words and Phrases

Indefinite Pronouns: *nobody, everyone*

nobody **= no one**

Nobody is home.

everyone **= all people**

Everyone is invited to the party.

Read the sentences below. Write the indefinite pronoun that means the same as the underlined word or words.

No one in my family is tall.

____________ in my family is tall.

All people in my class like peaches.

____________ in my class likes peaches.

» Go Digital **Add these indefinite pronouns to your New Words notebook. Write a sentence to show the meaning of each.**

(t)Martin Mark Soerensen; (b)Yuri_Arcurs/iStock/Getty Images Plus

Text Evidence

COLLABORATE

1 Talk About It

Look at the picture. Read the title. Talk about what you see. Write your ideas.

What does this title tell you?

____

____

____

________________________________.

Describe the playground.

____

____

____

________________________________.

Take notes as you read the text.

Shared Read Genre • Narrative Nonfiction

A WORLD WITHOUT RULES

CLOSED

Essential Question

Why do we need government?

Read how government and laws help to protect us every day.

ELD.PI.4.1.Ex, ELD.PI.4.1.Br, ELD.PI.4.5.Ex, ELD.PI.4.5.Br, ELD.PI.4.6a.Ex, ELD.PI.4.6a.Br
See the California Standards section.

You may sometimes wonder if rules were made to keep you from having fun and to tell you what to do. But what if we had no rules at all? Nobody would tell you what to do ever again! Sounds great, right? Well, let's see what it's like to **inhabit** a world without rules. You just might change your mind!

A Strange Morning

Let's start at home. Your alarm clock goes off. Why hurry? Without rules you don't have to go to school. Eventually you wander downstairs and find your little brother eating cookies in the kitchen. Since there are no rules, you can have cookies for breakfast! But you wonder if you should have something **sensible** like a bowl of cereal. You reach a compromise (KOM•pruh•mighz) and crumble the cookies over your cereal. In this new world, you will not have to brush your teeth anymore. Of course, the next time you see the dentist, you may have a cavity.

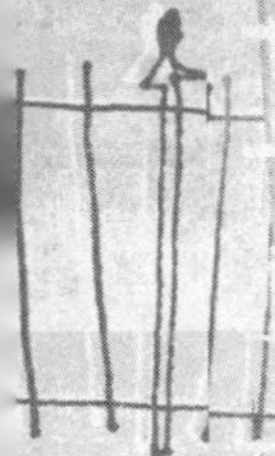

A Community in Confusion

Now, you step outside. You decide to go to the playground because there's no law saying you have to go to school. No crossing guard stands at the corner to help you across the street. Without traffic laws, cars zip by at an alarming speed honking at each other, and there is not a police officer in sight. There is no safe alternate way to cross the street. Besides, once you see the playground, you may decide it is not worth the risk of getting hit by a car. Broken swings dangle from rusty chains. Trash cans overflow with plastic bottles, snack wrappers, and paper bags. A huge tree branch lies across the sliding board. As a result of all state and federal **services** being gone, nobody is in charge of taking care of the playground.

R. G. Roth

ELD.PI.4.1.Ex, ELD.PI.4.1.Br, ELD.PI.4.5.Ex, ELD.PI.4.5.Br, ELD.PI.4.6a.Ex, ELD.PI.4.6a.Br, ELD.PI.4.7.Ex, ELD.PI.4.7.Br, ELD.PI.4.12a.Ex, ELD.PI.4.12a.Br See the California Standards section.

Text Evidence

1 Specific Vocabulary ACT

Reread the fifth sentence in the first paragraph. The word *inhabit* means "to live in." What does the author think it would be like to inhabit a world without rules?

____

______________________________.

2 Sentence Structure ACT

Reread the fourth sentence in the third paragraph. Circle the commas. Underline the dependent clause that tells why cars are speeding by and why there are no police officers.

3 Comprehension

Cause and Effect

Reread the third paragraph. Circle the words that tell what the playground looks like. Underline the words that tell you what caused the playground to look this way.

Text Evidence

1 Specific Vocabulary ACT

Reread the fifth sentence in the first paragraph. The phrase *local governments* means "city and town governments." Underline what local governments help to do.

2 Comprehension

Cause and Effect

Reread the first paragraph. What is the effect of not having lifeguards and governments to maintain parks? Circle the words that tell you.

3 Talk About It

Reread the second paragraph. Explain the relationship between the government and the army. Then write about it.

____

____

________________________________.

Now think about trying to do all the other things you love. Want to go to the beach? The lifeguards will not be there to keep you safe. Want to play soccer in the park? Your state and **local governments** are not around to **maintain** the parks, so you'll never find a place to play. Feel like eating lunch outside? As a result of pollution, the air quality is so bad that you will probably have to wear a gas mask every day.

Have you ever thought about our country being **invaded** by another country? Remember, the government runs the army. Without the government, there is no army to protect us if another country decided to take over our country.

Back to Reality

Thankfully, that version of our world isn't real. We live in a democracy (di•MOK•ruh•see) where we have the privilege (PRIV•uh•lij) of voting for the people that we want to run the country. Our elected government passes legislation (lej•is•LAY•shuhn), or laws, meant to help and protect us. If the country outgrows an old law, then the government can pass amendments to the law. Community workers such as crossing guards, police officers, and lifeguards all work to keep you safe, while government agencies such as the Environmental Protection Agency have made a commitment to **inspect** the air and water for pollution. And don't forget the armed forces, which were created to protect our nation.

Our government and laws were designed to keep you safe and **ensure** you are treated as fairly as everyone else. Without them, the world would be a different place.

ELD.PI.4.1.Ex, ELD.PI.4.1.Br, ELD.PI.4.5.Ex, ELD.PI.4.5.Br, ELD.PI.4.6a.Ex, ELD.PI.4.6a.Br, ELD.PI.4.7.Ex, ELD.PI.4.7.Br, ELD.PI.4.12a.Ex, ELD.PI.4.12a.Br See the California Standards section.

Make Connections

Talk about how government helps us maintain order and helps preserve our freedom. ESSENTIAL QUESTION

What are some ways that the government protects you every day? TEXT TO SELF

R. G. Roth

ELD.PI.4.1.Ex, ELD.PI.4.1.Br, ELD.PI.4.5.Ex, ELD.PI.4.5.Br, ELD.PI.4.6a.Ex, ELD.PI.4.6a.Br, ELD.PI.4.7.Ex, ELD.PI.4.7.Br, ELD.PI.4.12a.Ex, ELD.PI.4.12a.Br See the California Standards section.

Text Evidence

1 Specific Vocabulary ACT

Reread the first sentence in the last paragraph on page 206. The word *ensure* means "to make sure or certain that something will happen." Underline the words that tell you what our government ensures.

2 Sentence Structure ACT

Reread the last sentence in the last paragraph on page 206. Circle the nouns in the paragraph that the pronoun *them* refers to.

3 Talk About It

How does the author try to convince you that we need rules? Does the author succeed? Justify your answer.

____

____

______________________________.

Respond to the Text

Partner Discussion **Work with a partner. Describe what you learned about "A World Without Rules." Write the page numbers where you found text evidence.**

What did you learn about what life would be like without rules?	**Text Evidence**
Without traffic laws, you ______________________.	Page(s): __________
With no state and federal services, a playground would __________.	Page(s): __________
If the government did not run the army, there would be __________.	Page(s): __________

How does government help your community?	**Text Evidence**
Our elected government passes laws to ______________________.	Page(s): __________
The Environmental Protection Agency inspects ______________.	Page(s): __________
Government laws are designed to ______________________.	Page(s): __________

Group Discussion **Present your answers to the class. Cite text evidence to justify your thinking. Listen to and discuss the group's opinions about your answers.**

ELD.PI.4.1.Ex, ELD.PI.4.1.Br, ELD.PI.4.3.Ex, ELD.PI.4.3.Br, ELD.PI.4.5.Ex, ELD.PI.4.5.Br, ELD.PI.4.9.Ex, ELD.PI.4.9.Br, ELD.PI.4.11a.Ex, ELD.PI.4.11a.Br, ELD.PI.4.12a.Ex, ELD.PI.4.12a.Br See the California Standards section.

Write Work with a partner. Look at your notes about "A World Without Rules." Then write your answer to the essential question. Use text evidence to support your answer. Use vocabulary words from this week's reading in your writing.

Why is government needed in a community?

Traffic laws help to ____

____.

Federal and local services help to ____

____.

The Environmental Protection Agency helps to ____

____.

Government laws are meant to ____

____.

COLLABORATE

Share Writing Present your writing to the class. Discuss their opinions. Think about what they have to say. Did they justify their claims? Explain why you agree or disagree with their claims.

I agree with ____________ because ____________.

I disagree with ____________ because ____________.

ELD.PI.4.1.Ex, ELD.PI.4.1.Br, ELD.PI.4.3.Ex, ELD.PI.4.3.Br, ELD.PI.4.5.Ex, ELD.PI.4.5.Br, ELD.PI.4.9.Ex, ELD.PI.4.9.Br, ELD.PI.4.10b.Ex, ELD.PI.4.10b.Br, ELD.PI.4.11a.Ex, ELD.PI.4.11a.Br, ELD.PI.4.12a.Ex, ELD.PI.4.12a.Br See the California Standards section.

Write to Sources

Take Notes About the Text I took notes on an idea web to answer the question: ***Did the author do a good job of proving that we need government and laws?***

pages 204–207

Detail
Maintains playgrounds, parks, and beaches.

Detail
Makes traffic laws to keep us safe.

Main idea
What our government does.

Detail
Runs the army to protect our country.

Detail
The Environmental Protection Agency inspects the air and water for pollution.

 ELD.PI.4.1.Ex, ELD.PI.4.1.Br, ELD.PI.4.5.Ex, ELD.PI.4.5.Br, ELD.PI.4.6a.Ex, ELD.PI.4.6a.Br See the California Standards section.

Write About the Text **I used my notes from my idea web to write my opinion about whether the author did a good job of proving why we need government and laws.**

Student Model: *Opinion*

The author did a good job of showing why we need government and laws. The author explains what would happen if we didn't have them. Our playgrounds wouldn't be taken care of. Our parks wouldn't be taken care of. There would be no one to inspect the air and water for pollution. There would be no army to protect our country. Our government and laws keep us safe. The author showed that government and rules are very important.

TALK ABOUT IT

Text Evidence

Draw a box around a sentence that comes from the notes. Does the sentence provide a detail that supports Malia's opinion?

Grammar

Circle an auxiliary verb in the second sentence. What does the auxiliary verb tell you?

Condense Ideas

Underline the third and fourth sentences. How can you combine the sentences into one detailed sentence?

Your Turn

What was the best example the author gave for why we need laws? Use text evidence.

>> *Go Digital*
Write your response online. Use your editing checklist.

ELD.PI.4.1.Ex, ELD.PI.4.1.Br, ELD.PI.4.5.Ex, ELD.PI.4.5.Br, ELD.PI.4.6a.Ex, ELD.PI.4.6a.Br, ELD.PI.4.10b.Ex, ELD.PI.4.10b.Br,ELD.PI.4.12a.Ex, ELD.PI.4.12a.Br, ELD.PII.4.1.Ex, ELD.PII.4.1.Br, ELD.PII.4.3.Ex, ELD.PII.4.3.Br, ELD.PII.4.7.Ex, ELD.PII.4.7.Br See the California Standards section.

TALK ABOUT IT

Weekly Concept Leadership

Essential Question

Why do people run for public office?

» *Go Digital*

Describe what the people in the photo are doing. Why is it important that they have good leadership? Write the qualities of a good leader in the chart.

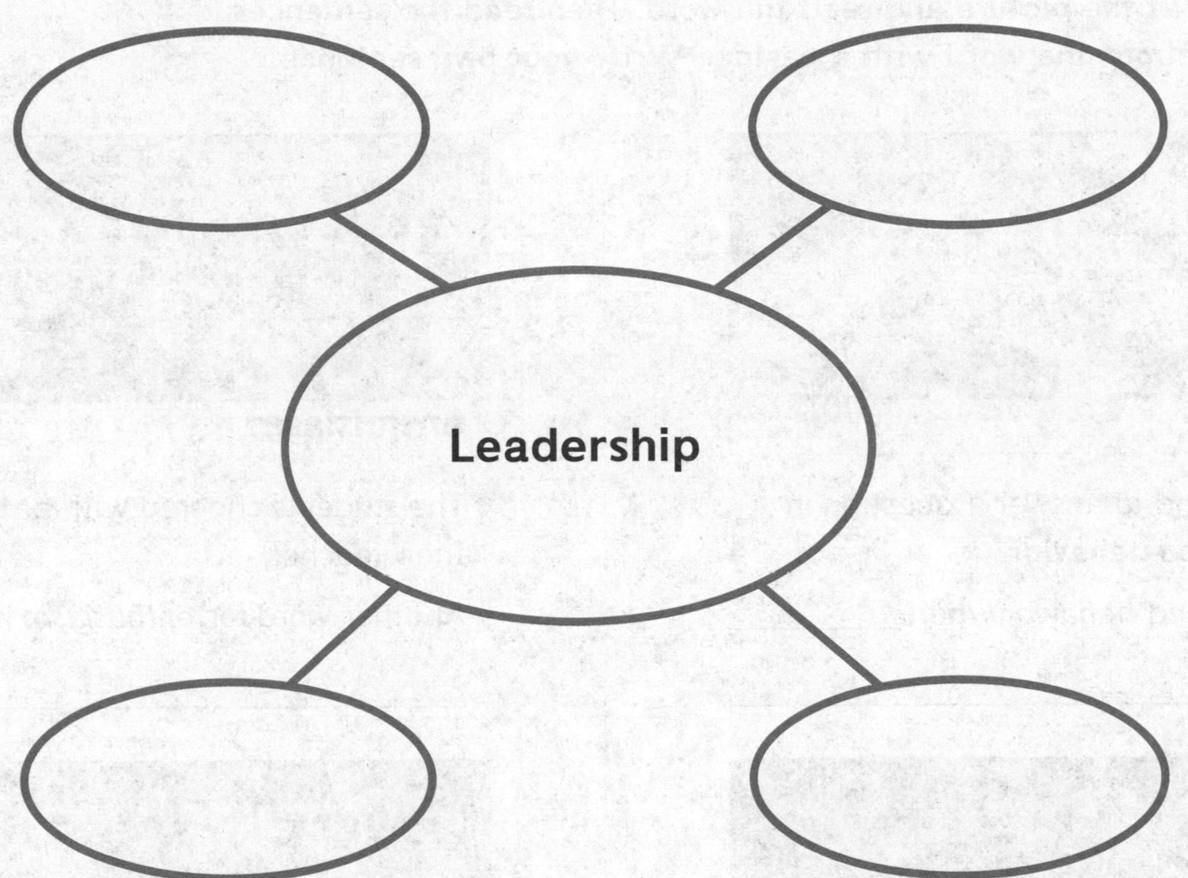

Discuss why good leadership is important for people who want things to change. Why do people become leaders? Use the words from the chart. You can say:

Good leadership is important because ______________.

People become leaders because they ______________.

ELD.PI.4.1.Ex, ELD.PI.4.1.Br, ELD.PI.4.5.Ex, ELD.PI.4.5.Br, ELD.PI.4.12a.Ex, ELD.PI.4.12a.Br See the California Standards section.

More Vocabulary

COLLABORATE

Look at the picture and read the word. Then read the sentences. Talk about the word with a partner. Write your own sentence.

behavior

Raising your hand to answer a question in gym class is good **behavior**.

My class has good *behavior* when ____________

____.

enthusiasm

The students cheered with **enthusiasm** for their teacher.

Another word for *enthusiasm* is ____________

____.

ceremony

They received awards at the **ceremony**.

Another word for *ceremony* is an ____________

____.

guide

A **guide** led the group through the park.

A *guide* shows people ____________________

____.

 ELD.PI.4.1.Ex, ELD.PI.4.1.Br, ELD.PI.4.5.Ex, ELD.PI.4.5.Br, ELD.PI.4.12a.Ex, ELD.PI.4.12a.Br See the California Standards section.

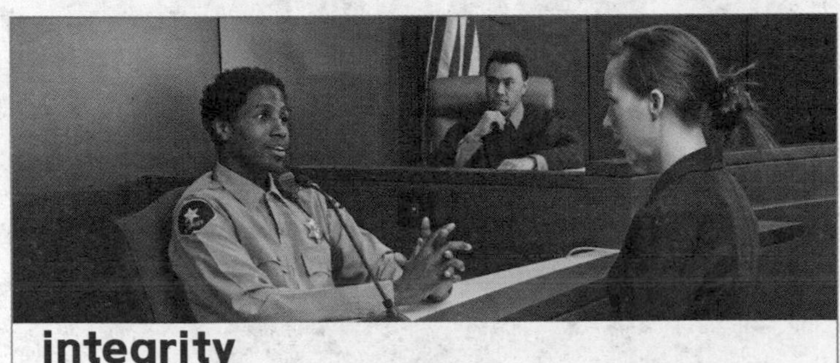

integrity

People must show **integrity** in a courtroom.

Another word for *integrity* is ______________

______________________________.

invention

The space station is an important **invention** for astronauts to learn about space.

Space *inventions* are important because

______________________________.

Words and Phrases

Possessives

A possessive noun is a noun that shows who or what owns or has something. The possessive of a plural noun is formed by adding an -*s* and an apostrophe at the end of the noun.

The classmates' project was a success.

The possessive of a proper noun is formed by adding an apostrophe and an -*s* after the proper noun.

Lincoln's Memorial is in Washington, D.C.

Read the sentences below. Underline the correct possessive noun in the parentheses for each sentence.

(Washingtons'/Washington's) face is on a one dollar bill.

Miguel was unhappy with his two (friends'/friend's) behavior.

» *Go Digital* **Add these possessives to your New Words notebook. Write a sentence to show the meaning of each.**

Text Evidence

COLLABORATE

1 Talk About It

Look at the picture. Read the title. Talk about what you see. Write your ideas.

What does this title tell you?

____

____

______________________________.

What is the boy wearing?

____

____

______________________________.

Take notes as you read the story.

Shared Read | Genre • Fantasy

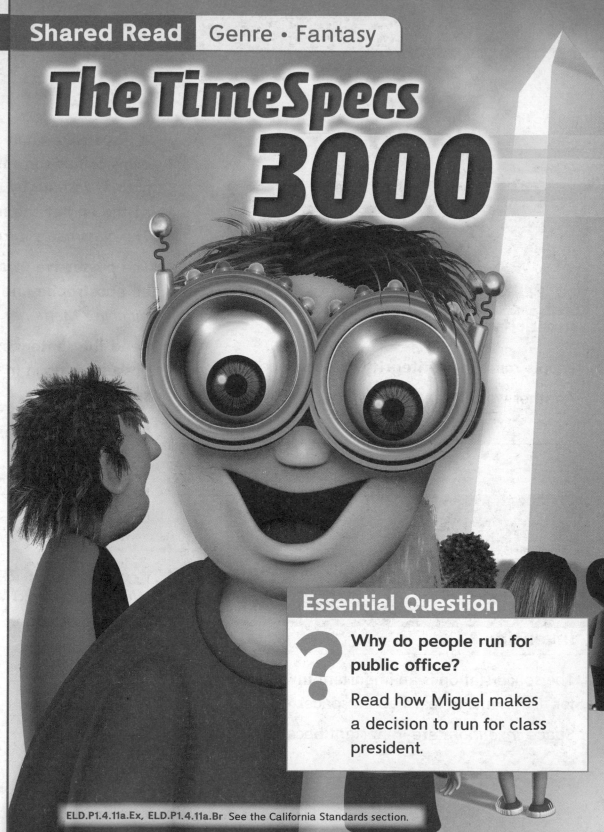

The TimeSpecs 3000

Essential Question

Why do people run for public office?

Read how Miguel makes a decision to run for class president.

ELD.P1.4.11a.Ex, ELD.P1.4.11a.Br See the California Standards section.

« » ⊞

September 15

Dear Grandpa,

I just got back from our class field trip to Washington, D.C., and I have a lot to tell you. Going to Washington helped me decide to run for class president.

I owe it all to your **invention**, the TimeSpecs 3000! **In a nutshell**, it helped me get some helpful advice about my problem. I intend to tell you everything when I visit Saturday, but for now I've pasted my field notes into this e-mail, so you can understand how well your invention worked.

FIELD NOTES: **DAY 1**

I use the TimeSpecs 3000 at the Washington Monument. Our **guide** accompanies us everywhere, and while she's talking I put on the specs. The design needs tweaking because my friend Ken whispered, "Nerdy shades, dude!"

Immediately, I'm seeing the monument in the past. I am watching the **ceremony** when they laid the cornerstone in 1848, and everybody's wearing large hats and funny, old-fashioned clothes. When I take off the TimeSpecs 3000, I realize my class is heading to lunch so I run after them.

Chris Boyd

ELD.PI.4.1.Ex, ELD.PI.4.1.Br, ELD.PI.4.5.Ex, ELD.PI.4.5.Br, ELD.PI.4.6a.Ex, ELD.PI.4.6a.Br, ELD.PI.4.8.Ex, ELD.PI.4.8.Br, ELD.PI.4.12a.Ex, ELD.PI.4.12a.Br See the California Standards section.

Text Evidence

1 Comprehension

Point of View

Reread the second paragraph. What is Miguel's point of view about the TimeSpecs 3000? Underline the sentences that show what he thinks.

2 Specific Vocabulary ACT

Reread the second sentence in the second paragraph. The phrase *in a nutshell* means "to tell about something in a short statement." What did Miguel tell his grandfather in a nutshell?

____

____

3 Sentence Structure ACT

Reread the second sentence in the last paragraph. Circle the word that connects the two parts of the sentence. Underline the parts of the sentence that are independent clauses, or sentences that can stand on their own.

Text Evidence

1 Sentence Structure ACT

Reread the third sentence in the first paragraph. Circle the punctuation mark that separates the sentence into two parts. Underline the part of the sentence that gives an example of the classmates' immature behavior.

2 Specific Vocabulary ACT

Reread the third sentence in the second paragraph. The words *out of the blue* mean "with no warning." Circle the words that tell what came out of the blue.

3 Talk About It

Reread the fourth paragraph. Describe the sequence of advice Lincoln's statue gives Miguel. Then write about it.

____

____

______________________________.

FIELD NOTES: **DAY 2**

We're back on the National Mall, which is nothing like Brookfield's mall with all its stores. This mall is outside and has a long reflecting pool. My teacher is finding it hard to tolerate some of my classmates' immature **behavior**, which includes running around throwing pebbles in the reflecting pool. I'm getting kind of weary of all the noise, and I'd rather learn about history on my own. So I put on the TimeSpecs 3000 and check out the Lincoln Memorial.

I see how dignified Lincoln's statue looks and wonder if I could ever help people like he did. This starts me thinking again about whether I should run for class president. Suddenly, right **out of the blue**, I hear this voice. "Excuse me, young man. You're thinking of running for president?" I look up and realize that Lincoln's statue is talking to me. It's so overwhelming that I stand there speechless for a minute.

Finally, I stammer, "President . . . Lincoln?"

"Maybe you should first run for mayor of your town," the statue says. "Or perhaps for governor? Once you get the hang of being in public office, you could run for president."

"Actually, it's for president of my 4th grade class," I say.

The giant statue nods. "That's an excellent start."

ELD.P1.4.6a.Ex, ELD.P1.4.7.Ex, ELD.P1.4.11a.Ex; ELD.P1.4.6a.Br, ELD.P1.4.7.Br, ELD.P1.4.11a.Br
See the California Standards section.

I **figure** while I have Lincoln's ear, I should get some advice. "I have a problem. I hate writing and giving speeches, and my opponent, Tommy, is great at both things."

"What kind of campaign would you run?" Lincoln asks.

"I have lots of ideas for our school," I tell him. "For instance, I want our school to use fruits and vegetables from the local farmers' market in the cafeteria. I also want to start a book drive for our school library."

"There's your speech," he says. "Tell people your ideas with honesty, **integrity**, and **enthusiasm**, and you can't possibly go wrong."

"Thanks, Mr. President," I say. "I think I can do that!"

Grandpa, I can't wait to see you on Saturday because I have to tell you about our visit to the Natural History Museum.

Your grandson and future class president,

Miguel

P.S. I would advise not wearing the TimeSpecs 3000 while looking at dinosaur bones.

Make Connections

Talk about why Miguel decides to run for class president. ESSENTIAL QUESTION

What would you do for your school if you were class president? TEXT TO SELF

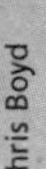

Text Evidence

1 Specific Vocabulary ACT

Reread the first sentence in the first paragraph. The word *figure* in this sentence means "think it is reasonable or makes sense." Underline what Miguel figures he should do.

2 Sentence Structure ACT

Reread the second sentence in the fourth paragraph. Circle the word that connects the two parts of the sentence. Underline the independent clauses, or the parts of the sentence that can stand on their own.

3 Talk About It

Discuss how the TimeSpecs 3000 helped Miguel decide to run for class president. Then write about it.

____

______________________________.

ELD.P1.4.3.Ex, ELD.P1.4.6a.Ex, ELD.P1.4.7.Ex, ELD.P1.4.11a.Ex; ELD.P1.4.3.Br, ELD.P1.4.6a.Br, ELD.P1.4.7.Br, ELD.P1.4.11a.Br See the California Standard.s section.

Respond to the Text

Partner Discussion **Work with a partner. Describe what you learned about "The TimeSpecs 3000." Write the page numbers where you found text evidence.**

	Text Evidence
What does Miguel learn about himself in Washington, D.C?	
Miguel uses TimeSpecs 3000 to ____________________.	Page(s): ________
When Miguel sees Lincoln's statue, he wonders if he could ________.	Page(s): ________
Miguel's problem with running for class president is ____________.	Page(s): ________

	Text Evidence
What advice does Lincoln's statue give Miguel?	
Lincoln tells Miguel he should run first for ________, and then run for ____________________.	Page(s): ________
When Miguel tells Lincoln about his problem, Lincoln asks Miguel about his ____________________.	Page(s): ________
Lincoln tells Miguel to tell his ideas with ____________________.	Page(s): ________

Group Discussion **Present your answers to the class. Cite text evidence to justify your thinking. Listen to and discuss the group's opinions about your answers.**

 ELD.PI.4.1.Ex, ELD.PI.4.1.Br, ELD.PI.4.3.Ex, ELD.PI.4.3.Br, ELD.PI.4.5.Ex, ELD.PI.4.5.Br, ELD.PI.4.9.Ex, ELD.PI.4.9.Br, ELD.PI.4.11a.Ex, ELD.PI.4.11a.Br, ELD.PI.4.12a.Ex, ELD.PI.4.12a.Br See the California Standards section.

Write Work with a partner. Review your notes about "The TimeSpecs 3000." Then write your answer to the essential question. Use text evidence to support your answer. Use vocabulary words from this week's reading in your writing.

Why does Miguel want to run for class president?

At the Lincoln Memorial, Miguel wonders if he can ______________________

____.

Miguel tells Lincoln that he has a problem with ______________________

____.

Miguel tells Lincoln about his campaign ideas of ______________________

____

____.

COLLABORATE

Share Writing Present your writing to the class. Discuss their opinions. Think about what they have to say. Did they justify their claims? Explain why you agree or disagree with their claims.

I agree with ____________ because ______________________.

I disagree with ____________ because ______________________.

ELD.PI.4.1.Ex, ELD.PI.4.1.Br, ELD.PI.4.3.Ex, ELD.PI.4.3.Br, ELD.PI.4.5.Ex, ELD.PI.4.5.Br, ELD.PI.4.9.Ex, ELD.PI.4.9.Br, ELD.PI.4.10b.Ex, ELD.PI.4.10b.Br, ELD.PI.4.11a.Ex, ELD.PI.4.11a.Br, ELD.PI.4.12a.Ex, ELD.PI.4.12a.Br See the California Standards section.

Write to Sources

pages 216–219

Take Notes About the Text **I took notes on the idea web about the story to help me respond to this prompt:** ***Write an email from Miguel to his grandfather. Have Miguel describe what he saw at the dinosaur bones when he put on the TimeSpecs 3000.***

What happened when Miguel wore TimeSpecs 3000 in Washington, D.C.?

- Saw the Washington Monument in 1848 with people wearing old-fashioned clothes.
- Lincoln's statue started talking to him.
- Lincoln gave advice about running for class president.

Mari/iStock/360/Getty Images

Write About the Text I used notes from my idea web to write an email from Miguel to his grandfather, describing what he saw at the dinosaur bones when he put on the TimeSpecs 3000.

Student Model: *Narrative Text*

Dear Grandpa,

Our class visit to the Natural History Museum was amazing! I loved seeing the Washington Monument in 1848. So at the dinosaur bones, I put on the TimeSpecs 3000. Then I saw a giant dinosaur fly down. It was very close to me. I felt its hot breath on my neck. I was afraid. I didn't want to be its dinner. So, I took off the TimeSpecs 3000. I won't put them on when visiting dinosaur bones!

Love,

Miguel

TALK ABOUT IT

Text Evidence

Draw a box around a detail that comes from the notes. Why is it important to include this detail?

Grammar

Circle one subject pronoun and one object pronoun. What does each pronoun refer to?

Connect Ideas

Underline two sentences that tell how Miguel feels when the dinosaur flies down. How can you combine the sentences to connect the ideas?

Your Turn

Write an email from Miguel to President Lincoln. Have Miguel tell the President how he felt while giving his speech for class president.

>> *Go Digital*
Write your response online. Use your editing checklist.

ELD.PI.4.1.Ex, ELD.PI.4.1.Br, ELD.PI.4.2.Ex, ELD.PI.4.2.Br, ELD.PI.4.5.Ex, ELD.PI.4.5.Br, ELD.PI.4.12a.Ex, ELD.PI.4.12a.Br, ELD.PII.4.2a.Ex, ELD.PII.4.2a.Br, ELD.PII.4.6.Ex, ELD.PII.4.6.Br See the California Standards section.

TALK ABOUT IT

Weekly Concept Breakthroughs

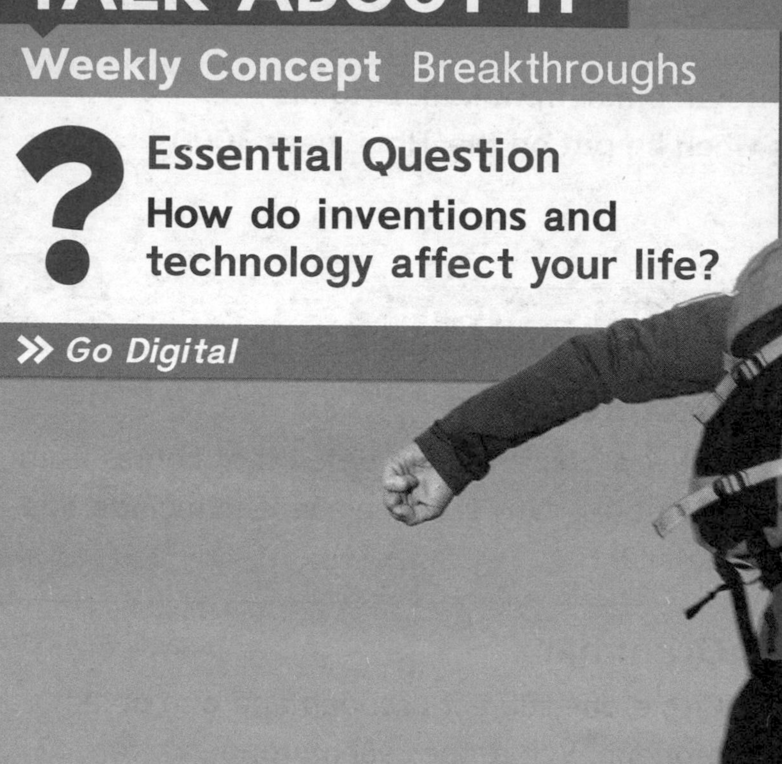

Essential Question

How do inventions and technology affect your life?

» *Go Digital*

Look at the photo of the man. Discuss how technology can change a person's life. How have different technologies affected people? Write the words in the chart.

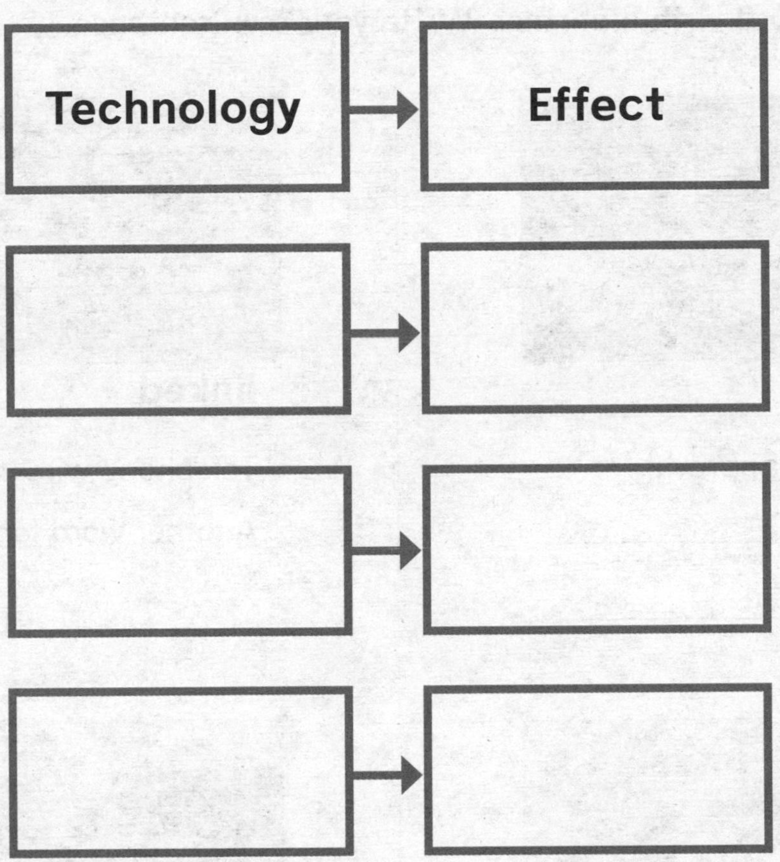

Discuss how technology can affect people's lives. Use the words from the chart. You can say:

The technology of __________ is helpful because __________.

It affects the way people ______________________________.

More Vocabulary

Look at the picture and read the word. Then read the sentences. Talk about the word with a partner. Write your own sentence.

gestured

The students **gestured** their approval.

Another word for *gestured* is ______________

______________________________.

linked

Telephone wires are **linked** by poles.

Another word for *linked* is ______________

______________________________.

installed

The workers **installed** solar panels on the roof.

Things *installed* in our classroom include

______________________________.

marvel

The Grand Canyon is a **marvel**.

The Grand Canyon is a *marvel* because ________

______________________________.

 ELD.PI.4.1.Ex, ELD.PI.4.1.Br, ELD.PI.4.5.Ex, ELD.PI.4.5.Br, ELD.PI.4.12a.Ex, ELD.PI.4.12a.Br See the California Standards section.

miserable

The weather is **miserable** for playing outside.

An antonym for *miserable* is ______________.

progress

Progress has made phones smaller and better.

Progress is important because ____________

______________________________________.

Words and Phrases
Idioms

An idiom is a phrase with a different meaning than the meaning of each word in the phrase.

progress marched on = progress continued

picture all the amazing benefits = imagine or think of all the amazing benefits

Read the sentences below. Underline the sentence with an idiom.

The hike was long but the children marched on.
Time marched on for the hikers.

The picture shows what the future may look like.
Picture what the future will look like.

» *Go Digital* **Add these examples of idioms to your New Words notebook. Write a sentence to show the meaning of each.**

Text Evidence

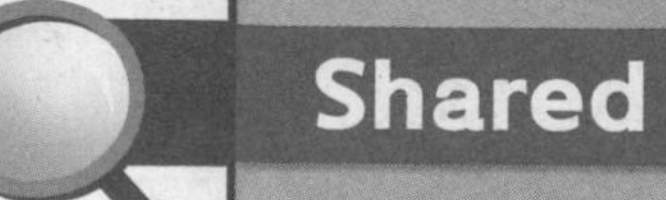

COLLABORATE

1 Talk About It

Look at the picture. Read the title. Talk about what you see. Write your ideas.

What does this title tell you?

____

____

______________________________.

What are the man and girl doing?

____

____

______________________________.

Take notes as you read the story.

Shared Read Genre • Historical Fiction

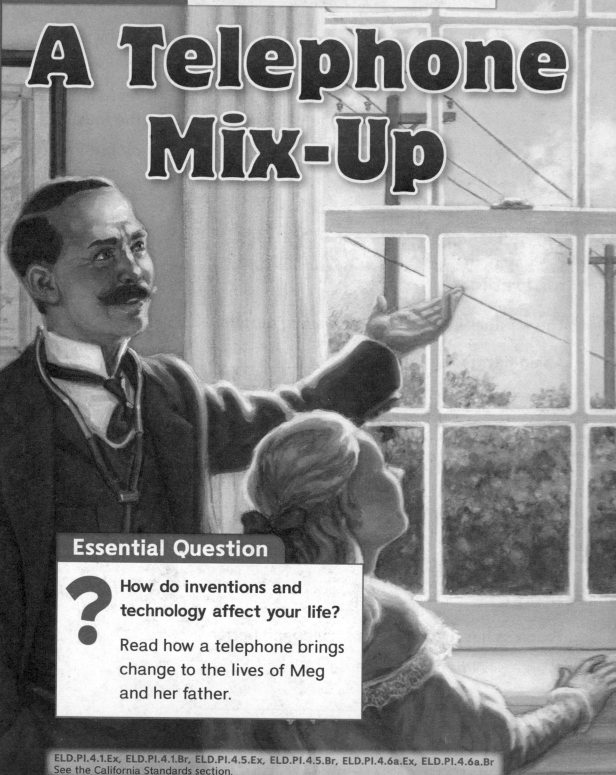

A Telephone Mix-Up

Essential Question

How do inventions and technology affect your life?

Read how a telephone brings change to the lives of Meg and her father.

ELD.PI.4.1.Ex, ELD.PI.4.1.Br, ELD.PI.4.5.Ex, ELD.PI.4.5.Br, ELD.PI.4.6a.Ex, ELD.PI.4.6a.Br
See the California Standards section.

"By tomorrow afternoon there will be eight telephones right here in Centerburg, Ohio, and one of them will be ours!" Dr. Ericksen said to his daughter, Meg. "I predict that before this decade is over, in just another five years, there could be a hundred! That's how fast I **foresee** this technology will spread! When people need help, they'll call me on the telephone. Envision how many lives it will save! Picture all the amazing benefits!"

Meg realized that not everyone thought the telephone was an engineering **marvel**. She had heard people say that telephones were a useless invention. A few others felt the newfangled machine would open up a Pandora's box of troubles, causing people to stop visiting each other and writing letters.

Despite the concerns of some people, **progress** marched on. Just weeks earlier, Centerburg's first telephone had been **installed** in Mr. Kane's general store, another was put in at the hotel, and yet another at the newspaper office. Mrs. Kane was the town's first switchboard operator, directing incoming calls to the correct lines.

The next morning, Meg wrote "October 9, 1905" on the top of her slate with chalk while she squirmed in her seat, wishing that the long school day was over.

Tristan Elwell

ELD.PI.4.1.Ex, ELD.PI.4.1.Br, ELD.PI.4.5.Ex, ELD.PI.4.5.Br, ELD.PI.4.6a.Ex, ELD.PI.4.6a.Br, ELD.PI.4.7.Ex, ELD.PI.4.7.Br, ELD.PI.4.12a.Ex, ELD.PI.4.12a.Br See the California Standards section.

Text Evidence

1 Comprehension

Point of View

Reread the first paragraph. What is the author's point of view about telephones? Underline two sentences that show what the author thinks.

2 Specific Vocabulary ACT

Look at the word *foresee* in the first paragraph. It means "to predict or guess something will happen in the future." Underline the sentence that tells what Dr. Ericksen foresees.

Dr. Ericksen foresees ____________

____

______________________________.

3 Sentence Structure ACT

Reread the second sentence in the third paragraph. Circle the commas. Underline the places where telephones were installed.

Text Evidence 

1 Talk About It

Reread the first paragraph. Describe how Meg imagines the new wires. Then write about it.

____

______________________________.

2 Sentence Structure ACT

Reread the first sentence in the second paragraph. The word *As* shows that two things are happening at the same time. Underline the two things that are happening at the same time.

3 Specific Vocabulary ACT

Reread the second sentence in the fifth paragraph. The word *static* means "electric noise that blocks out other sounds." Underline the sentences that give context clues about the meaning of static.

Walking home that afternoon, Meg scouted the street, looking for the tall wooden poles that were going up weekly. Thick wire **linked** one pole to another, and Meg imagined how each wire would carry the words of friends and neighbors, their conversations zipping over the lines bringing news, birthday wishes, and party invitations.

As Meg hurried into the house, she let the screen door slam shut behind her. There on the wall was the gleaming wooden telephone box with its heavy black receiver on a hook. Her father was smiling broadly while tinkering with the shiny brass bells on top. "Isn't it a beauty?" he asked. "Have you ever seen such magnificence?"

Suddenly the telephone jangled loudly, causing both Ericksens to jump.

Meg laughed as her father picked up the receiver and shouted, "Yes, hello, this is the doctor!"

"Again please, Mrs. Kane! There's too much **static**" Dr. Ericksen shouted. "I didn't get the first part. Bad cough? Turner farm?"

"Can I go, Father?" Meg asked as Dr. Ericksen returned the receiver to the hook.

"Absolutely," he said, grabbing his medical kit and heading outside where his horse and buggy waited.

When they got to the farm, they found Mr. Turner walking toward the barn.

ELD.PI.4.1.Ex, ELD.PI.4.1.Br, ELD.PI.4.5.Ex, ELD.PI.4.5.Br, ELD.PI.4.6a.Ex, ELD.PI.4.6a.Br, ELD.PI.4.7.Ex, ELD.PI.4.7.Br, ELD.PI.4.12a.Ex, ELD.PI.4.12a.Br See the California Standards section.

"Jake, I got here as quick as I could," Dr. Ericksen said. "Is it Mrs. Turner? Little Emma?"

"You?" Jake Turner looked confused, but he **gestured** them toward the barn.

There they found a baby goat curled near its mother. The baby snorted, coughed, and looked **miserable**.

"Jake, I'm no vet!" said Dr. Ericksen. "You need Dr. Kerrigan."

"I was wondering why you showed up instead. I reckon there was a mix-up."

"Apparently so," Dr. Ericksen laughed. "When I get back I'll send Dr. Kerrigan."

As years passed the telephone **proved** to be very useful to the town of Centerburg, but there was always the occasional mix-up. It became common among the Ericksens to refer to a missed communication as "another sick goat."

Make Connections

? How did the invention of the telephone affect the town of Centerburg? ESSENTIAL QUESTION

Think of an invention and tell how it has affected your life. TEXT TO SELF

Tristan Elwell

ELD.PI.4.1.Ex, ELD.PI.4.1.Br, ELD.PI.4.5.Ex, ELD.PI.4.5.Br, ELD.PI.4.6a.Ex, ELD.PI.4.6a.Br, ELD.PI.4.7.Ex, ELD.PI.4.7.Br, ELD.PI.4.11a.Ex, ELD.PI.4.11a.Br, ELD.PI.4.12a.Ex, ELD.PI.4.12a.Br See the California Standards section.

Text Evidence

1 Sentence Structure ACT

Reread the second paragraph. Circle the word that connects Jake's two actions. Underline the actions.

2 Specific Vocabulary ACT

Reread the first sentence in the seventh paragraph. The word *proved* means "showed that something was true with facts." What did the telephone prove to be?

The telephone proved to be ______

______.

3 Talk About It

Discuss whether the telephone was a good or bad invention for the town of Centerburg in this story. Justify your answer.

______

______.

Respond to the Text

Partner Discussion Work with a partner. Describe what you learned about "A Telephone Mix-Up." Write the page numbers where you found text evidence.

What did people think about telephones when they first arrived in Centerburg?	Text Evidence
Some people, like Dr. Ericksen, were excited and thought ______________________________.	Page(s): ________
Other people thought ______________________________.	Page(s): ________
When Meg saw the telephone wires and poles, she imagined ______________________________.	Page(s): ________

What happened on the first afternoon that the Ericksens had a telephone?	Text Evidence
Dr. Ericksen thought the telephone was ______________________________.	Page(s): ________
Then Mrs. Kane called because ______________________________.	Page(s): ________
Dr. Ericksen and Meg went to the Turner farm, only to find out ______________________________.	Page(s): ________

Group Discussion Present your answers to the class. Cite text evidence for your ideas. Listen to and discuss the group's opinions about your answers.

 ELD.PI.4.1.Ex, ELD.PI.4.1.Br, ELD.PI.4.3.Ex, ELD.PI.4.3.Br, ELD.PI.4.5.Ex, ELD.PI.4.5.Br, ELD.PI.4.9.Ex, ELD.PI.4.9.Br, ELD.PI.4.11a.Ex, ELD.PI.4.11a.Br, ELD.PI.4.12a.Ex, ELD.PI.4.12a.Br See the California Standards section.

Write **Work with a partner. Review your notes about "A Telephone Mix-Up." Then write your answer to the essential question. Use text evidence to support your answer. Use vocabulary words from this week's reading in your writing.**

How did the telephone affect the Ericksens?

Dr. Ericksen thought telephones would help to ______________________________

____

______________________________.

When Dr. Ericksen received his first call, he and Meg went ______________

______________________________.

When Meg and Dr. Ericksen arrived at the Turner Farm, they learned that ______

____

______________________________.

COLLABORATE

Share Writing **Present your writing to the class. Discuss their opinions. Think about what they have to say. Did they justify their claims? Explain why you agree or disagree with their claims.**

I agree with ______________ because ______________________________.

I disagree with ______________ because ______________________________.

ELD.PI.4.1.Ex, ELD.PI.4.1.Br, ELD.PI.4.3.Ex, ELD.PI.4.3.Br, ELD.PI.4.5.Ex, ELD.PI.4.5.Br, ELD.PI.4.9.Ex, ELD.PI.4.9.Br, ELD.PI.4.10b.Ex, ELD.PI.4.10b.Br, ELD.PI.4.11a.Ex, ELD.PI.4.11a.Br, ELD.PI.4.12a.Ex, ELD.PI.4.12a.Br See the California Standards section.

Write to Sources

pages 228–231

Take Notes About the Text **I took notes on the sequence chart about the story to help me respond to the prompt:** ***Write a dialogue between Meg and her father. Have them discuss what happened at the Turner farm.***

Meg and her father, Dr. Ericksen, get a new phone.

↓

Dr. Ericksen gets a call. He has a hard time hearing the message. He and Meg go to the Turner farm..

↓

At the Turner farm, the Ericksens discover that the Turners have a sick goat. They need a vet.

↓

Dr. Ericksen tells the vet about the Turner's goat when he gets home. The Ericksens call telephone mix-ups "another sick goat."

 ELD.PI.4.1.Ex, ELD.PI.4.1.Br, ELD.PI.4.5.Ex, ELD.PI.4.5.Br, ELD.PI.4.6a.Ex, ELD.PI.4.6a.Br, ELD.PII.4.1.Ex, ELD.PII.4.1.Br See the California Standards section.

Write About the Text **I used my notes from my sequence chart to write a dialogue between Meg and her father about what happened on the Turner farm.**

Student Model: *Narrative Text*

"That was a big mix up at the Turner's farm today, Father," Meg said. "Do you think the telephone will be helpful?"

Father answered, "Yes, I do. It takes time to get used to new things. Next time I will ask more questions. I will get more details before we leave."

"Good idea. We don't want another 'sick goat!'" Meg said. "But I'm glad we could send the vet to help Mr. Turner's goat."

TALK ABOUT IT

Text Evidence

Draw a box around a detail from the notes. Why is this detail important to the dialogue?

Grammar

Circle an example of the future tense. Why does Patrice use the future tense here?

Condense Ideas

Underline the two sentences that tell about what Meg's father says he will do the next time. How can you condense these sentences into one detailed sentence?

Your Turn

Write a dialogue between Dr. Ericksen and Dr. Kerrigan in which they discuss the telephone mix-up. Use text evidence.

>> ***Go Digital***
Write your response online. Use your editing checklist.

ELD.PI.4.1.Ex, ELD.PI.4.1.Br, ELD.PI.4.2.Ex, ELD.PI.4.2.Br, ELD.PI.4.5.Ex, ELD.PI.4.5.Br, ELD.PI.4.6a.Ex, ELD.PI.4.6a.Br, ELD.PI.4.12a.Ex, ELD.PI.4.12a.Br, ELD.PII.4.1.Ex, ELD.PII.4.1.Br, ELD.PII.4.3.Ex, ELD.PII.4.3.Br, ELD.PII.4.7.Ex, ELD.PII.4.7.Br See the California Standards section.

TALK ABOUT IT

Weekly Concept Wonders in the Sky

Essential Question

How do you explain what you see in the sky?

» Go Digital

Describe what you see in the photo. Write what you can see in the sky at night in the chart.

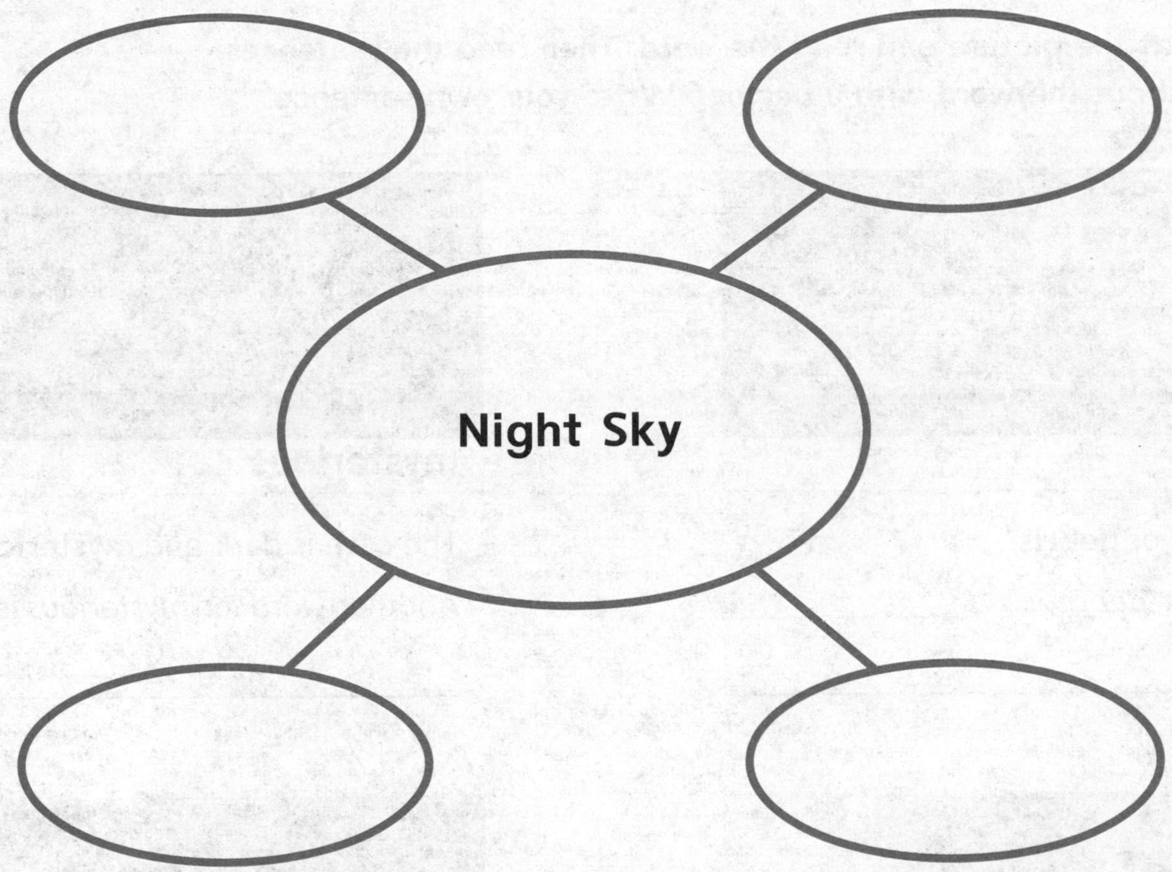

Discuss what you see in the sky at night. Use the words from the chart. You can say:

In the night sky I can see the __________ and __________.

Sometimes I can see ____________ in the night sky.

More Vocabulary

Look at the picture and read the word. Then read the sentences. Talk about the word with a partner. Write your own sentence.

debris

The beach is full of **debris**.

Another word for *debris* is ______________

______________________________________.

mysterious

The cave is dark and **mysterious** inside.

Another word for *mysterious* is ______________

______________________________________.

fragments

The piggy bank broke into **fragments**.

Other things that can break into *fragments* are ______________________________

______________________________________.

patterns

The peacock has colorful **patterns** on its feathers.

Some different kinds of *patterns* are ______________

____

______________________________________.

 ELD.PI.4.1.Ex, ELD.PI.4.1.Br, ELD.PI.4.5.Ex, ELD.PI.4.5.Br, ELD.PI.4.12a.Ex, ELD.PI.4.12a.Br See the California Standards section.

reflecting

The building lights are **reflecting** off the water in the lake.

I have seen light reflecting off of ____________ ____________________________.

revealed

She removed the mask and **revealed** her face.

Another word for *revealed* is ____________ ____________________________.

Words and Phrases

Suffixes: *-ous, -able*

The suffix *-ous* means "full of."
mystery - y + i + *-ous* = mysterious
Comets are mysterious.

The suffix *-able* means "able to."
afford + *-able* = affordable
The price of the book is affordable.

Write the meaning of the underlined word on the line.

Camila is adventurous.

____

My bed is comfortable.

____

Write your own sentences using *adventurous* and *comfortable*.

____

____

» Go Digital **Add these words to your New Words notebook. Include your sentences.**

Text Evidence

Shared Read

Genre • Expository Text

Wonders of the Night Sky

COLLABORATE

1 Talk About It

Look at the photograph. Read the title. Talk about what you see. Write your ideas.

What does this title tell you?

____

____

______________________________.

What does the sky look like?

____

____

______________________________.

Take notes as you read the text.

Essential Question

How do you explain what you see in the sky?

Read about what causes some of the sights you see in the sky.

ELD.PI.4.1.Ex, ELD.PI.4.1.Br, ELD.PI.4.5.Ex, ELD.PI.4.5.Br, ELD.PI.4.6a.Ex, ELD.PI.4.6a.Br
See the California Standards section.

As Earth rotates on its axis, day becomes night. Suddenly, a gallery of lights is **revealed**! You may see a beautiful crescent moon. Maybe you'll see one of the other phases of the moon. You may even see a series of lights spread across the sky like colored ribbons. For thousands of years, people have loved looking at the night sky. For almost as long, scientists have been trying to explain what they see.

Aurora Borealis

Every few years, an amazing light show is seen in the skies near the North Pole. It is known as "the northern lights," or the aurora borealis (uh-RAWR-uh bawr-ee-AL-is). Brilliant bands of green, yellow, red, and blue lights appear in the sky.

People used to believe the lights were caused by sunlight **reflecting** off polar ice caps. The theory was that when the light bounced back from the caps it created **patterns** in the sky. In fact, the lights happen because of **magnetic attraction**.

The sun constantly gives off a stream of electrically charged particles in every direction. These nearly invisible pieces of matter join into a stream called a solar wind. As Earth orbits the sun, solar winds reach Earth's magnetic field. As a result, electric charges occur that are sometimes strong enough to be seen from Earth. These electric charges cause the colorful bands of lights in the sky.

The aurora borealis above Hammerfest, Norway

ELD.PI.4.1.Ex, ELD.PI.4.1.Br, ELD.PI.4.5.Ex, ELD.PI.4.5.Br, ELD.PI.4.6a.Ex, ELD.PI.4.6a.Br, ELD.PI.4.7.Ex, ELD.PI.4.7.Br, ELD.PI.4.12a.Ex, ELD.PI.4.12a.Br See the California Standards section.

Text Evidence

1 Sentence Structure ACT

Reread the first sentence in the second paragraph. Circle the dependent clause, or the part of the sentence that cannot stand on its own. Then underline the independent clause, or the part of the sentence that can stand on its own.

2 Specific Vocabulary ACT

Reread the last sentence in the third paragraph. The words *magnetic attraction* mean "the movement between electrically charged particles." What happens because of magnetic attraction?

____

______________________________.

3 Comprehension Cause and Effect

Reread the fourth paragraph. Circle the words that tell what causes the colorful bands of light.

Text Evidence 

1 Talk About It

Reread the second paragraph. Discuss why long ago people feared comets. Then write about it.

____

____________________________________.

2 Comprehension

Cause and Effect

Reread the third paragraph. What causes the long tail of comets? Draw a box around the sentence that tells you.

3 Sentence Structure ACT

Reread the last paragraph. In the last sentence circle all the pronouns. Then underline the nouns each pronoun refers to.

This diagram shows the parts of a comet. Some comets' tails can be millions of miles long.

Comets

Another kind of light you might see move across the night sky is a comet. The word comet comes from a Greek word that means "wearing long hair." It came from the Greek philosopher Aristotle (AR-uh-stot-uhl), who thought that comets looked like stars with hair.

Long ago, people feared these **mysterious** streaks because they believed that they might bring war or sickness to Earth. Today, comets are less scary and mysterious because we know that they are a mixture of rock, dust, ice, and frozen gases that orbit the sun.

Comets move around the sun in an oval-shaped orbit. When a comet comes closer to the sun, the result is that a "tail" of gas and dust is pushed out behind the comet. This long tail is what people see from Earth.

Scientists think comets are some of the oldest objects in space. They can track specific comets and predict when they can be seen from Earth again.

ELD.PI.4.1.Ex, ELD.PI.4.1.Br, ELD.PI.4.5.Ex, ELD.PI.4.5.Br, ELD.PI.4.6a.Ex, ELD.PI.4.6a.Br, ELD.PI.4.12a.Ex, ELD.PI.4.12a.Br, ELD.PII.4.2a.Ex, ELD.PII.4.2a.Br See the California Standards section.

Meteors

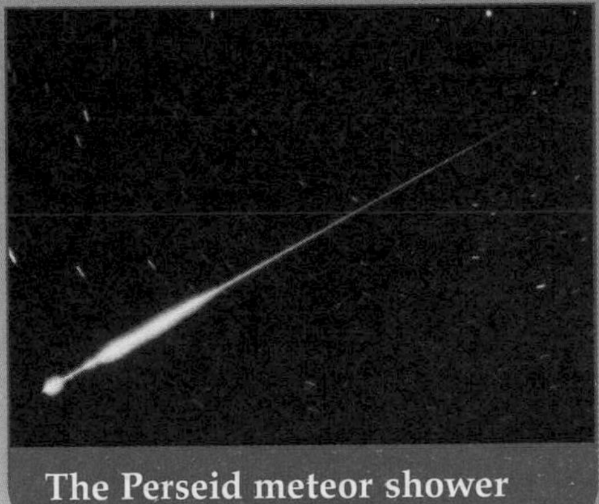
The Perseid meteor shower

Have you ever looked up at the sky and seen a shooting star? Those **streaks** of light are not really stars at all. What we call shooting stars are usually meteors (MEE-tee-erz). Meteors are another name for the rocky **debris** and **fragments** that enter Earth's atmosphere. Sometimes Earth passes through an area in space with a lot of debris. This is when a meteor shower occurs. You may see hundreds of "shooting stars" on the night of a meteor shower.

These days an astronomer or anyone with a portable telescope can raise new questions about space. What do you see when you look up at the night sky? Whether you look at a sliver of the moon or a fantastic light show, you are bound to see something amazing.

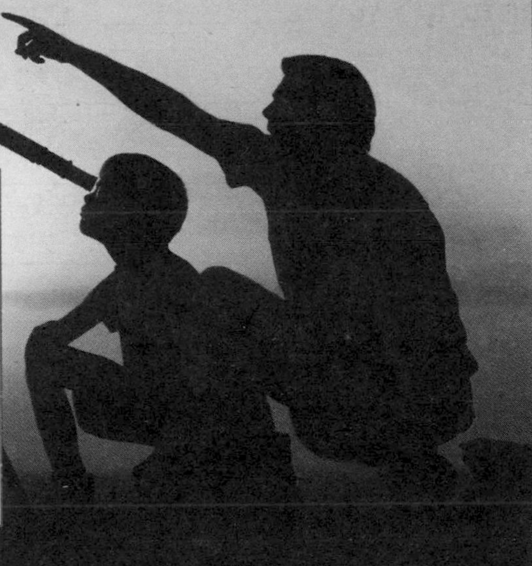

Make Connections

Talk about what causes some of the sights in the night sky. ESSENTIAL QUESTION

What do you wonder about when you look up at the night sky? TEXT TO SELF

ELD.PI.4.1.Ex, ELD.PI.4.1.Br, ELD.PI.4.5.Ex, ELD.PI.4.5.Br, ELD.PI.4.6a.Ex, ELD.PI.4.6a.Br, ELD.PI.4.7.Ex, ELD.PI.4.7.Br See the California Standards section.

Text Evidence

1 Comprehension

Cause and Effect

Reread the first paragraph. What is the cause of a meteor shower? Underline the sentence that tells you.

2 Specific Vocabulary ACT

Reread the second sentence in the first paragraph. The word *streaks* means "colored lines." Circle the words that tell what the streaks of light really are.

3 Sentence Structure ACT

Reread the last sentence in the first paragraph. Underline the prepositional phrase that tells when you may see shooting stars.

Respond to the Text

Partner Discussion **Work with a partner. Describe what you learned about "Wonders of the Night Sky." Write the page numbers where you found text evidence.**

What did you learn about the aurora borealis?	**Text Evidence**
The aurora borealis is also called ____________.	Page(s): ________
It looks like ____________.	
The aurora borealis lights happen because of ____________.	Page(s): ________
Electric charges cause the ____________.	Page(s): ________

What did you learn about comets and meteors?	**Text Evidence**
As a comet moves closer to the sun, a ____________ ____________.	Page(s): ________
Meteors are another name for ____________.	Page(s): ________
Meteor showers occur when ____________.	Page(s): ________

COLLABORATE **Group Discussion** **Present your answers to the class. Cite text evidence to justify your thinking. Listen to and discuss the group's opinions about your answers.**

 ELD.PI.4.1.Ex, ELD.PI.4.1.Br, ELD.PI.4.3.Ex, ELD.PI.4.3.Br, ELD.PI.4.5.Ex, ELD.PI.4.5.Br, ELD.PI.4.9.Ex, ELD.PI.4.9.Br, ELD.PI.4.11a.Ex, ELD.PI.4.11a.Br, ELD.PI.4.12a.Ex, ELD.PI.4.12a.Br See the California Standards section.

Write Work with a partner. Look at your notes about "Wonders of the Night Sky." Then write your answer to the essential question. Use text evidence to support your answer. Use vocabulary words from this week's reading in your writing.

How do astronomers explain what we see in the night sky?

The aurora borealis happens when ____

____.

Comets are caused by ____

____.

Meteors are ____

____.

COLLABORATE

Share Writing Present your writing to the class. Discuss their opinions. Think about what they have to say. Did they justify their claims? Explain why you agree or disagree with their claims.

I agree with ____________ because ______________________________.

I disagree with ____________ because ______________________________.

ELD.PI.4.1.Ex, ELD.PI.4.1.Br, ELD.PI.4.3.Ex, ELD.PI.4.3.Br, ELD.PI.4.5.Ex, ELD.PI.4.5.Br, ELD.PI.4.9.Ex, ELD.PI.4.9.Br, ELD.PI.4.10b.Ex, ELD.PI.4.10b.Br, ELD.PI.4.11a.Ex, ELD.PI.4.11a.Br, ELD.PI.4.12a.Ex, ELD.PI.4.12a.Br See the California Standards section.

Write to Sources

Take Notes About the Text I took notes on the idea web to answer the question: ***What information does the author tell about what causes the aurora borealis?***

pages 240–243

Detail
The aurora borealis happens because of magnetic attraction.

Detail
The sun gives off electric particles that join together and become solar winds.

Main Idea
The author gives information about the aurora borealis.

Detail
When solar winds reach Earth's magnetic field, it causes strong electric charges.

Detail
The electric charges cause the colorful bands of light.

 ELD.PI.4.1.Ex, ELD.PI.4.1.Br, ELD.PI.4.5.Ex, ELD.PI.4.5.Br, ELD.PI.4.6a.Ex, ELD.PI.4.6a.Br See the California Standards section.

Write About the Text **I used my notes from my idea web to write a paragraph about what causes the aurora borealis.**

Student Model: *Informative Text*

The author tells about what causes the aurora borealis. The aurora borealis happens because of magnetic attraction. The sun gives off electric particles that join together and become solar winds. When solar winds reach the Earth's magnetic field, it causes electric charges. The electric charges cause the colorful bands of light of the aurora borealis. It is a spectacular light show!

TALK ABOUT IT

Text Evidence

Draw a box around a detail from the notes that describes the cause of the aurora borealis. Why did Jason use this information as a supporting detail?

Grammar

Draw an arrow from the adjective *solar* to the noun it describes. Why was it important that Jason use the adjective *solar?*

Condense Ideas

Underline the two sentences that tell about the solar wind. How can you combine the sentences into one detailed sentence?

Your Turn

What information does the author tell about comets? Use text evidence.

>> *Go Digital*
Write your response online. Use your editing checklist.

ELD.PI.4.1.Ex, ELD.PI.4.1.Br, ELD.PI.4.2.Ex, ELD.PI.4.2.Br, ELD.PI.4.5.Ex, ELD.PI.4.5.Br, ELD.PI.4.6a.Ex, ELD.PI.4.6a.Br, ELD.PI.4.12a.Ex, ELD.PI.4.12a.Br, ELD.PII.4.7.Ex, ELD.PII.4.7.Br See the California Standards section.

TALK ABOUT IT

Weekly Concept Achievements

Essential Question

How do writers look at success in different ways?

>> *Go Digital*

Describe how the photo of the boy shows success. Discuss how people have different ideas of success. Write the words in the chart.

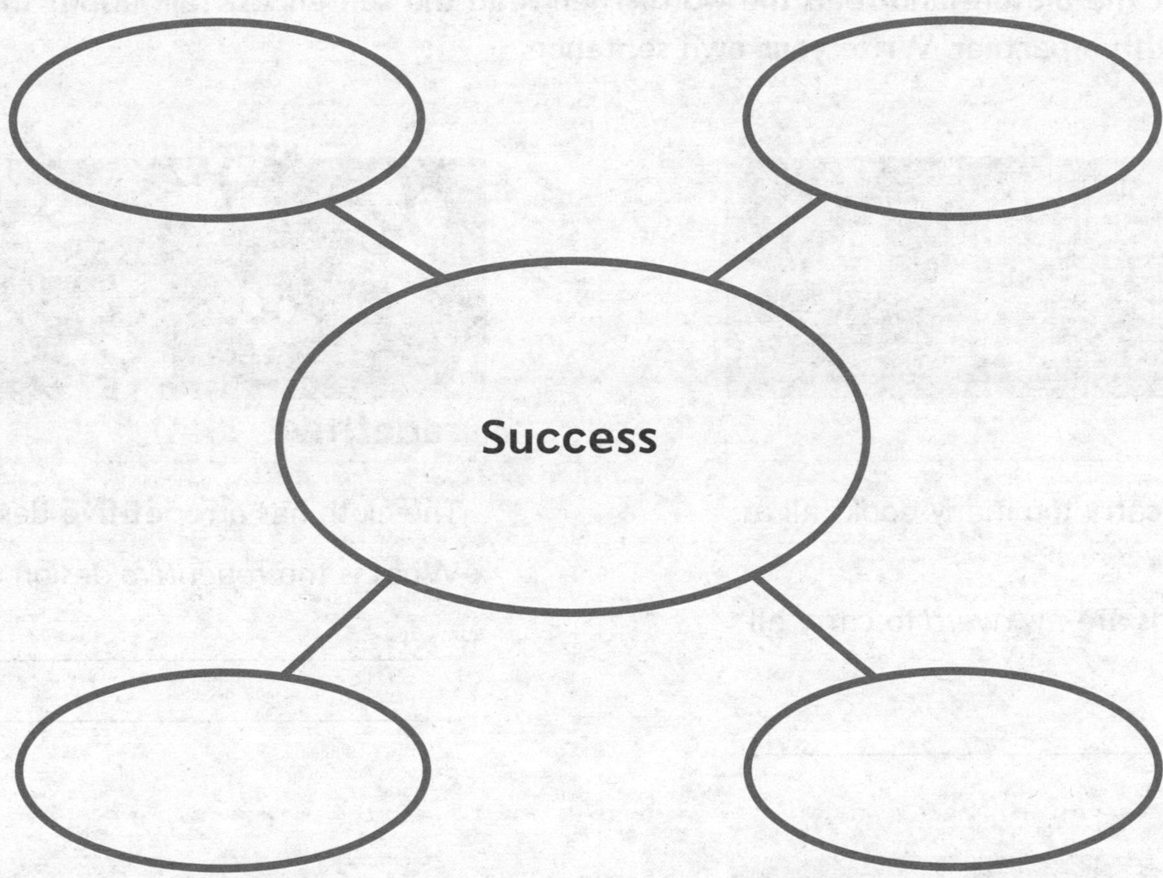

Discuss what you think it means to be successful. Use the words from the chart. You can say:

Success can be ________________________________.

It can also be ________________________________.

Fuse/Corbis/Getty Images

ELD.PI.4.1.Ex, ELD.PI.4.1.Br, ELD.PI.4.5.Ex, ELD.PI.4.5.Br, ELD.PI.4.12a.Ex, ELD.PI.4.12a.Br See the California Standards section.

More Vocabulary

Look at the picture and read the word. Then read the sentences. Talk about the word with a partner. Write your own sentence.

awkward

It is **awkward** to carry too many books all at once.

What other things are *awkward* to carry all at once?

______________________________.

repetitive

The cloth has a **repetitive** design.

What is the *repetitive* design on the cloth?

____

______________________________.

fading

The sunlight is **fading** as the sun sets.

What is another word for *fading?*

______________________________.

slippery

The ice is **slippery**.

What are other things that are *slippery?*

______________________________.

(tl)zgr_pro/iStock/Getty Images Plus; (tr)Cienpies Design/Alamy; (bl)Commander John Bortniak - NOAA Corps - NOAA/Department of Commerc; (br) XiXinXing/Getty Images

 ELD.PI.4.1.Ex, ELD.PI.4.1.Br, ELD.PI.4.5.Ex, ELD.PI.4.5.Br, ELD.PI.4.12a.Ex, ELD.PI.4.12a.Br See the California Standards section.

Poetry Terms

stanza

A **stanza** is a group of two or more lines in a poem.
A stanza does not have to rhyme.

Some enjoy running,

Others like jumping,

I have fun watching.

---

repetition

Repetition is repeating the same words or phrases in a poem.

The striped red and yellow balloon
drifts away,
drifts away.

COLLABORATE

Work with a partner. Write a stanza about something you like to do. Use some or all of the words below.

Make two lines the same to create repetition. Read your stanza aloud to your partner.

laugh	**sing**
play	**dance**

I like to ____________.

I ________________.

I like to ____________.

I ________________.

Text Evidence 

1 Literary Element
Stanza

A *stanza* is a group of lines in a poem. Reread the first stanza. Circle the words in the first stanza that tell you he is playing the piano.

2 Specific Vocabulary ACT

Reread the fourth stanza. The word *tangle* means "something that is in a mess." Underline the words that tell what is making the tangle of noise.

3 Sentence Structure ACT

Reread the fifth stanza. Who does the pronoun *she* refer to? Underline the noun.

Take notes as you read the poems.

Shared Read Genre • Narrative Poetry

Sing to Me

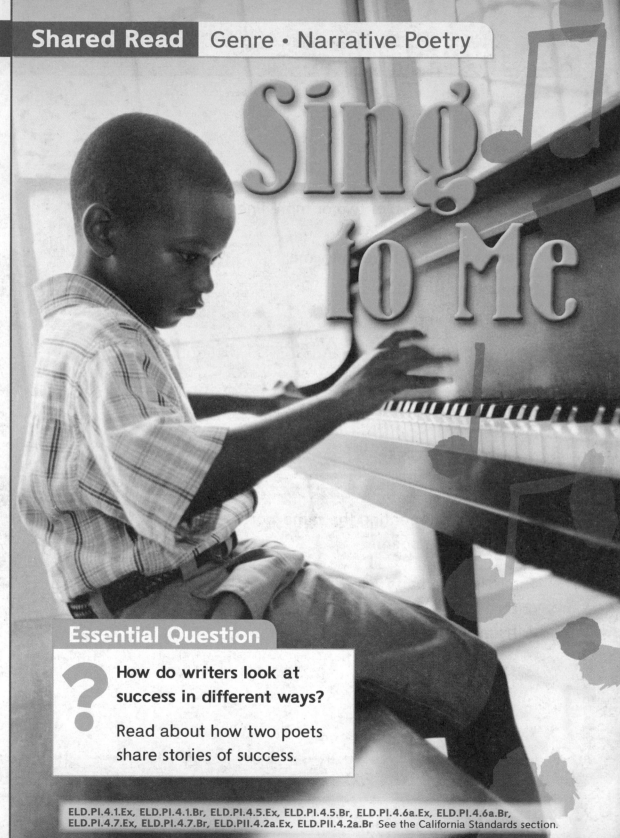

Essential Question

How do writers look at success in different ways?

Read about how two poets share stories of success.

ELD.PI.4.1.Ex, ELD.PI.4.1.Br, ELD.PI.4.5.Ex, ELD.PI.4.5.Br, ELD.PI.4.6a.Ex, ELD.PI.4.6a.Br, ELD.PI.4.7.Ex, ELD.PI.4.7.Br, ELD.PII.4.2a.Ex, ELD.PII.4.2a.Br See the California Standards section.

The cool white keys stretched for miles.
How would my hands pull
and sort through the notes,
blending them into music?

I practiced
and practiced all day.
My fingers reaching for a melody
that hung dangling,
like an apple just out of reach.

I can't do this.
I can't do this.

The day ground on,
notes leaping hopefully into the air,
hovering briefly, only to crash,
an **awkward** jangle, a **tangle** of noise
before slowly **fading** away.

My mom found me, forehead on the keys.
She asked, "Would you like some help?
It took months for my hands to do what I wanted."
She sat down on the bench,
her slender fingers plucking notes
from the air.

I can do this.
I can do this.

She sat with me every night that week,
working my fingers until their efforts
made the keys sing to me, too.

— Will Meyers

ELD.PI.4.1.Ex, ELD.PI.4.1.Br, ELD.PI.4.5.Ex, ELD.PI.4.5.Br, ELD.PI.4.6a.Ex, ELD.PI.4.6a.Br, ELD.PI.4.12a.Ex, ELD.PI.4.12a.Br See the California Standards section.

Text Evidence

1 Literary Element
Repetition

Circle the stanzas that show repetition. Why does the boy feel the way he does in each stanza?

In one stanza, he feels

_______________________.

In the other stanza, he feels

_______________________.

2 Comprehension
Theme

Reread the last stanza. Underline a detail that helps identify the theme.

3 Talk About It

Reread the poem. Discuss how the boy's feelings change from the beginning of the poem to the end of the poem.

Text Evidence

1 Specific Vocabulary A C T

Reread the first two stanzas. The word *mocking* means "teasing." What is the girl's brother mocking her about? Underline the sentence that tells you.

2 Sentence Structure A C T

Reread the third stanza. Circle the commas. What does the girl do first? What does she do next? What is the last thing she does? Underline the verbs. Then write a sentence.

She ______________________________

____

__________________________________.

3 Literary Element
Repetition

Reread the poem. Circle the words the poet repeats in the third, fourth, and fifth stanzas. What is special about that day?

____

__________________________________.

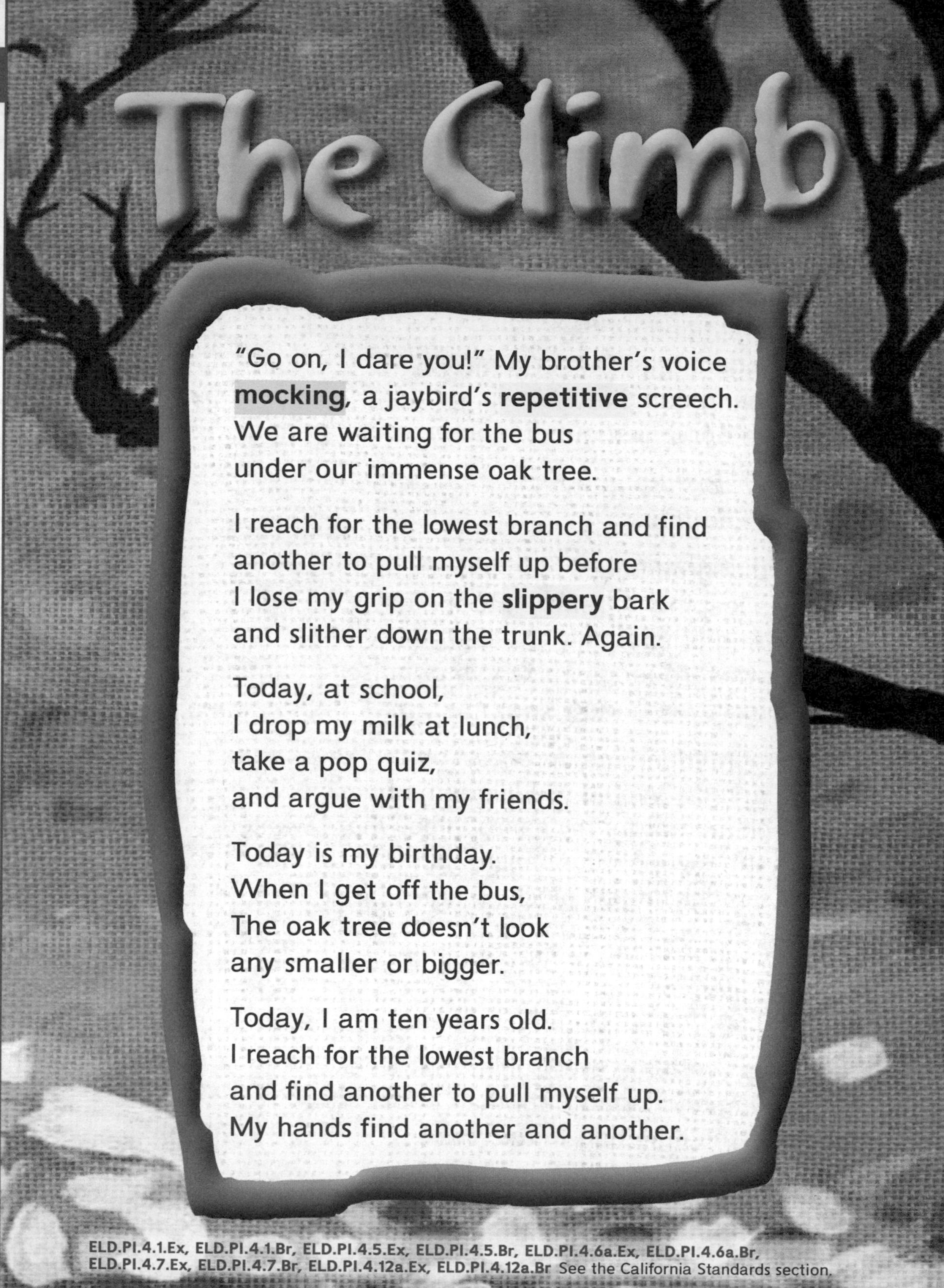

The Climb

"Go on, I dare you!" My brother's voice
mocking, a jaybird's **repetitive** screech.
We are waiting for the bus
under our immense oak tree.

I reach for the lowest branch and find
another to pull myself up before
I lose my grip on the **slippery** bark
and slither down the trunk. Again.

Today, at school,
I drop my milk at lunch,
take a pop quiz,
and argue with my friends.

Today is my birthday.
When I get off the bus,
The oak tree doesn't look
any smaller or bigger.

Today, I am ten years old.
I reach for the lowest branch
and find another to pull myself up.
My hands find another and another.

ELD.PI.4.1.Ex, ELD.PI.4.1.Br, ELD.PI.4.5.Ex, ELD.PI.4.5.Br, ELD.PI.4.6a.Ex, ELD.PI.4.6a.Br, ELD.PI.4.7.Ex, ELD.PI.4.7.Br, ELD.PI.4.12a.Ex, ELD.PI.4.12a.Br See the California Standards section.

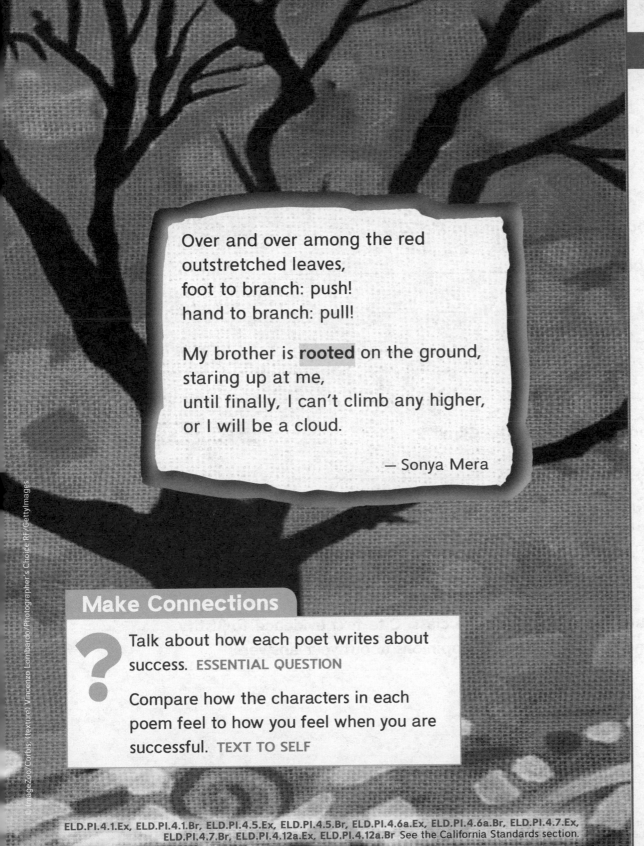

Over and over among the red
outstretched leaves,
foot to branch: push!
hand to branch: pull!

My brother is **rooted** on the ground,
staring up at me,
until finally, I can't climb any higher,
or I will be a cloud.

— Sonya Mera

Make Connections

Talk about how each poet writes about success. ESSENTIAL QUESTION

Compare how the characters in each poem feel to how you feel when you are successful. TEXT TO SELF

ELD.PI.4.1.Ex, ELD.PI.4.1.Br, ELD.PI.4.5.Ex, ELD.PI.4.5.Br, ELD.PI.4.6a.Ex, ELD.PI.4.6a.Br, ELD.PI.4.7.Ex, ELD.PI.4.7.Br, ELD.PI.4.12a.Ex, ELD.PI.4.12a.Br See the California Standards section.

Text Evidence

1 Comprehension
Theme

Reread the last stanza of the poem. Underline a detail that helps to identify the theme of the poem.

2 Specific Vocabulary ACT

Reread the last stanza. The word *rooted* means "standing firmly." What is the girl doing while her brother is rooted on the ground?

____

_______________.

3 Talk About It

Reread the sixth and seventh stanzas of the poem. Discuss what the girl accomplishes at the end of the poem. How do you think this makes her feel? Then write about it.

____

____

_______________.

Respond to the Text

Partner Discussion **Work with a partner. Describe what you learned about "Sing to Me" and "The Climb." Write the line numbers where you found text evidence.**

	Text Evidence
What do you learn about the boy in "Sing to Me"?	
The boy wants to be able to ______________.	Line(s): ________
As the boy tries to play on his own, he ______________.	Line(s): ________
With his mother's help, the boy ______________.	Line(s): ________

	Text Evidence
What do you learn about the girl in "The Climb"?	
After being dared by her brother, the girl ______________.	Line(s): ________
On the girl's birthday, she______________.	Line(s): ________
At the end of the poem, the girl ______________.	Line(s): ________

Group Discussion **Present your answers to the class. Cite text evidence to justify your thinking. Listen to and discuss the group's opinions about your answers.**

 ELD.PI.4.1.Ex, ELD.PI.4.1.Br, ELD.PI.4.3.Ex, ELD.PI.4.3.Br, ELD.PI.4.5.Ex, ELD.PI.4.5.Br, ELD.PI.4.9.Ex, ELD.PI.4.9.Br, ELD.PI.4.11a.Ex, ELD.PI.4.11a.Br, ELD.PI.4.12a.Ex, ELD.PI.4.12a.Br See the California Standards section.

Write Work with a partner. Review your notes about "Sing to Me" and "The Climb." Then write your answer to the essential question. Use text evidence to support your answer. Use vocabulary words from this week's reading in your writing.

How does each writer think of success?

For the writer of "Sing to Me," success means ______________________________

____.

For the writer of "The Climb," success means ______________________________

____.

At the end of the poems, both writers think success is when ____________________

____.

COLLABORATE

Share Writing Present your writing to the class. Discuss their opinions. Think about what they have to say. Did they justify their claims? Explain why you agree or disagree with their claims.

I agree with____________ because ______________________________.

I disagree with ____________ because ______________________________.

Write to Sources

Take Notes About the Text **I took notes on the chart to answer the question:** ***How does the poet of "Sing to Me" use repetition?***

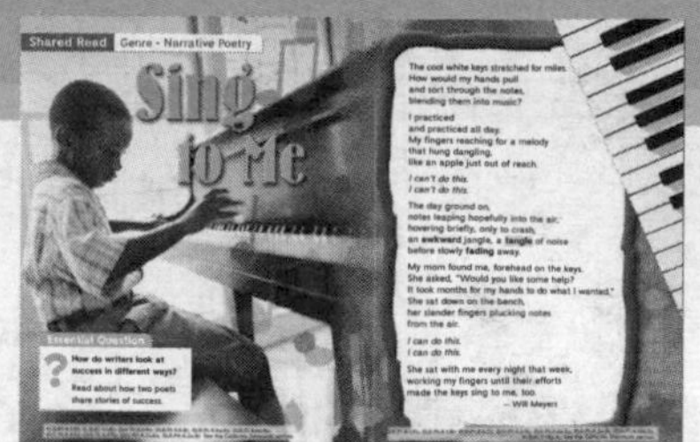

pages 252–253

Repetition

- I practiced and practiced all day.
- I can't do this. I can't do this.
- I can do this. I can do this.

Hill Street Studios/Blend Images/Getty Images

 ELD.PI.4.1.Ex, ELD.PI.4.1.Br, ELD.PI.4.5.Ex, ELD.PI.4.5.Br, ELD.PI.4.6a.Ex, ELD.PI.4.6a.Br See the California Standards section.

Write About the Text **I used my notes from my chart to write a paragraph about how the poet of "Sing to Me" uses repetition.**

Student Model: *Informative Text*

Repetition is when a poet repeats a word or a phrase. The poet says, "I practiced and practiced all day." This shows he is trying to learn how to play. "I can't do this. I can't do this" is an example of repetition. It shows the speaker is upset because he can't play the piano. "I can do this. I can do this" is another example of repetition. It shows that the poet's feelings have changed. His mom helped him make the keys sing. Repetition helps the reader know how the poet feels.

TALK ABOUT IT

Text Evidence

Draw a box around sentences that show repetition that comes from the notes. How does the poet feel?

Grammar

Circle the pronoun *it*. Underline the words that tell what the pronoun refers to. Why does Alex use the pronoun *it?*

Connect Ideas

Circle the seventh and eighth sentences that tell how the poet feels and why he feels this way. How can you connect the sentences into one detailed sentence?

Your Turn

Write about something you felt successful at. Use repetition.

>> *Go Digital*
Write your response online. Use your editing checklist.

Unit 5

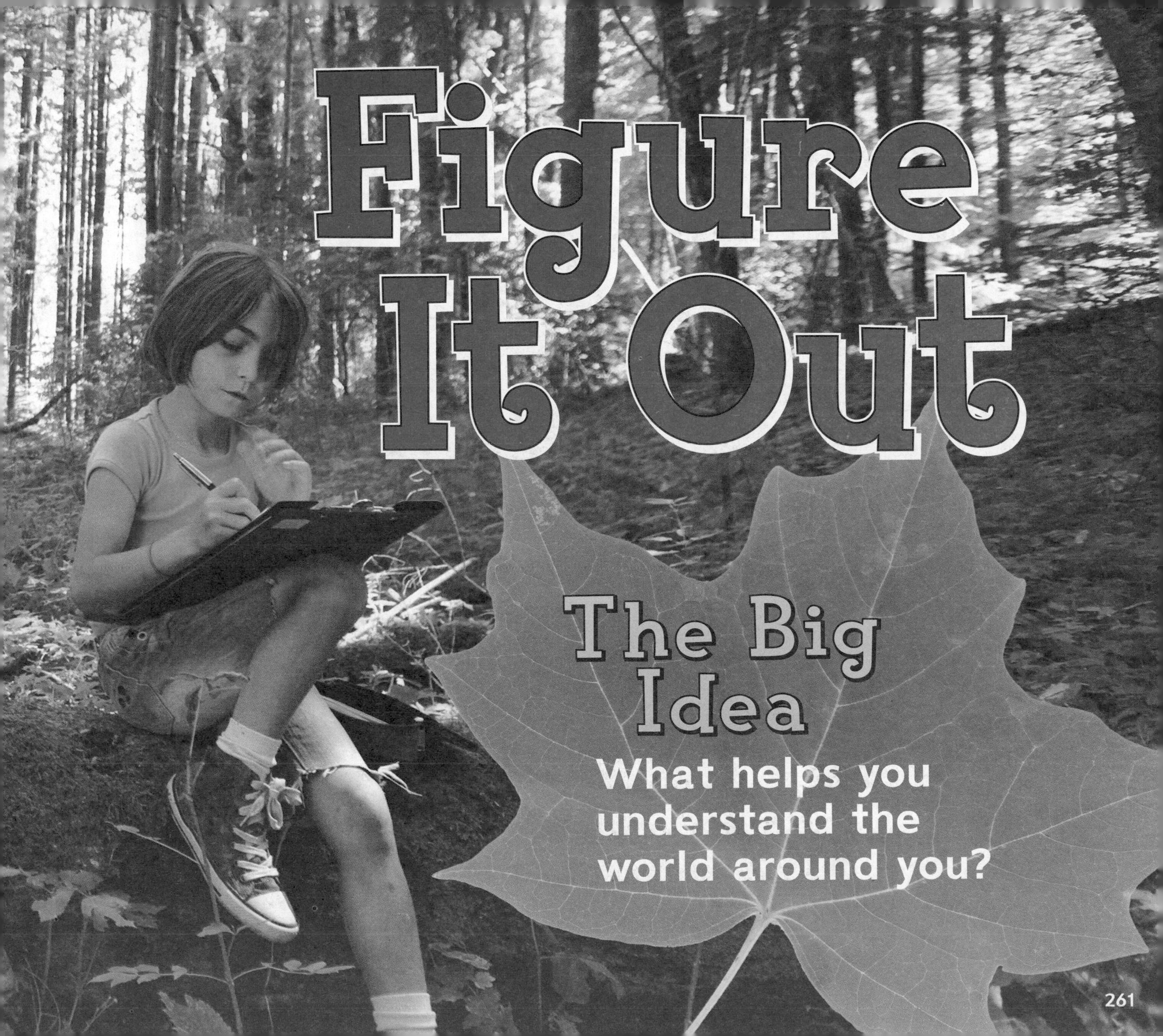

Figure It Out

The Big Idea

What helps you understand the world around you?

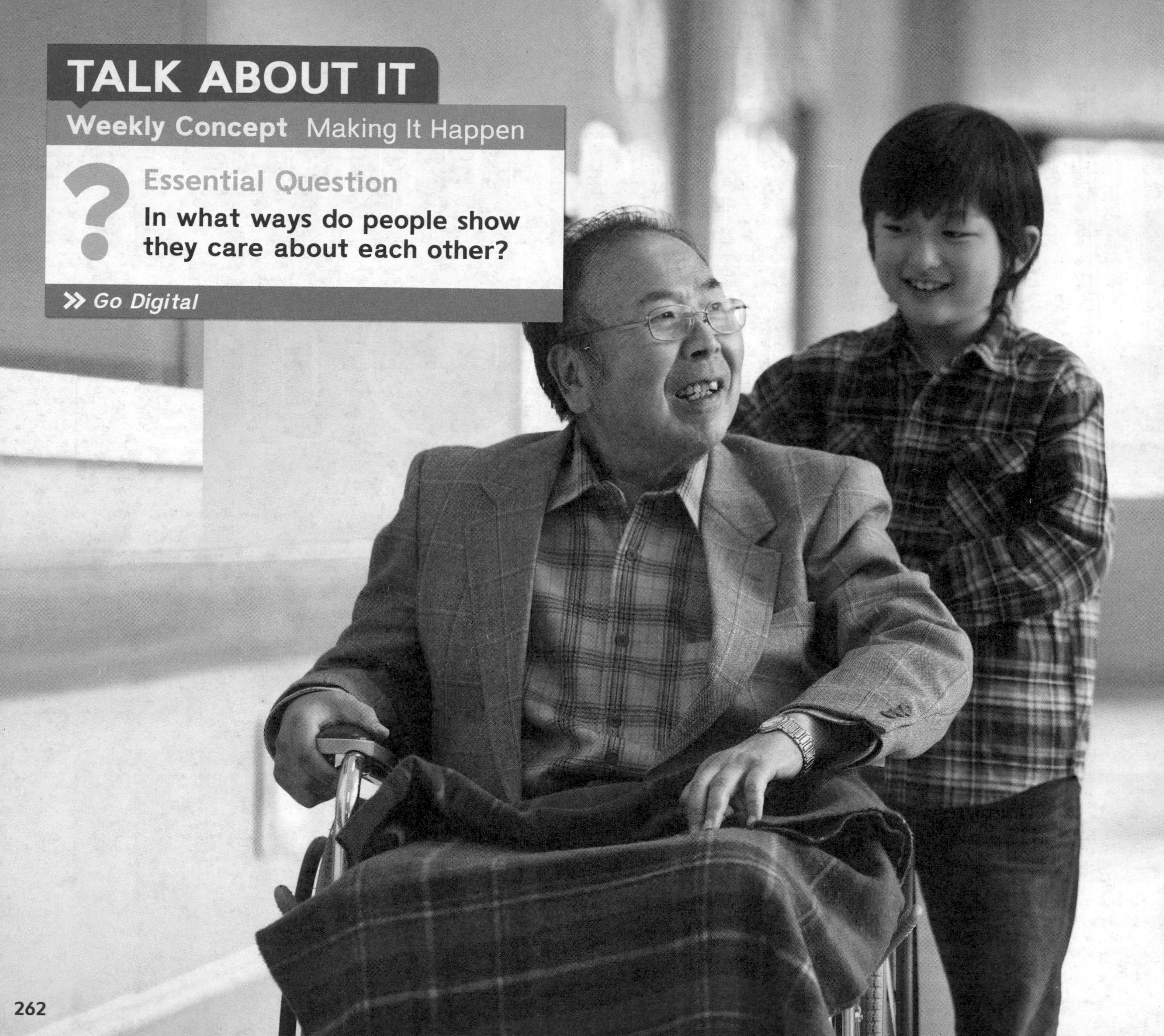
TALK ABOUT IT
Weekly Concept Making It Happen
Essential Question
In what ways do people show they care about each other?
Go Digital

How is the boy in the photo showing he cares about the man? In the chart, write about other ways people show they care about others.

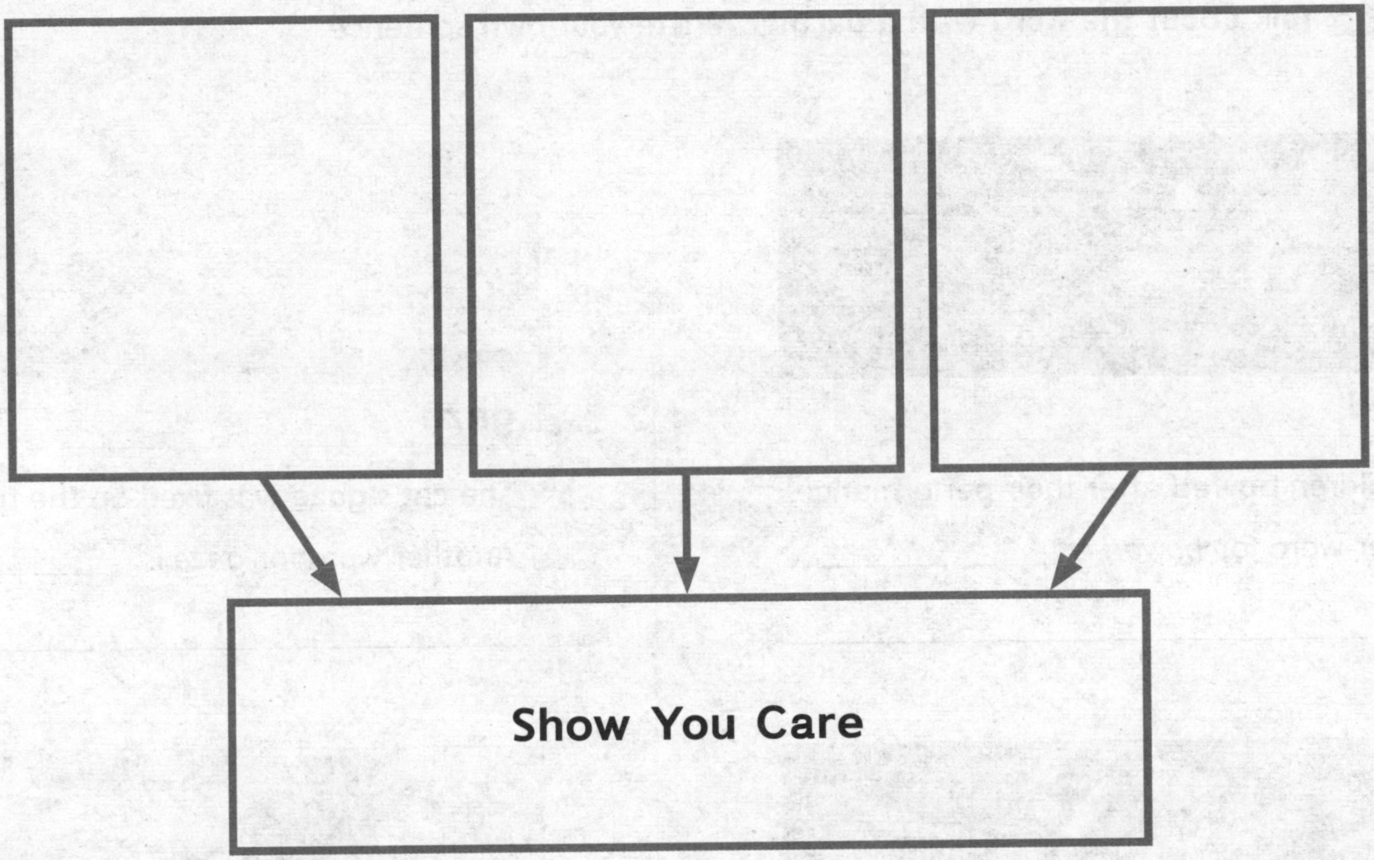

Show You Care

Look at the photo. Discuss how people show others that they care. Use the words from the chart. You can say:

People show they care by ____________________.

Another way people show they care is by ______________.

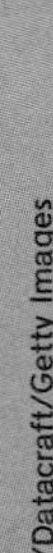

ELD.PI.4.1.Ex, ELD.PI.4.1.Br, ELD.PI.4.5.Ex, ELD.PI.4.5.Br, ELD.PI.4.12a.Ex, ELD.PI.4.12a.Br See the California Standards section.

More Vocabulary

Look at the picture and read the word. Then read the sentences. Talk about the word with a partner. Write your own sentence.

bowed

The children **bowed** after their performance.

Another word for *bowed* is ______________

______________________________.

collided

The wild goats **collided** into each other on the mountain.

The wild goats ***collided*** because they were

______________________________.

gaze

The cat's **gaze** was fixed on the fish.

Another word for *gaze* is ______________

______________________________.

preferred

They **preferred** to buy apples over pears.

I *preferred* to eat __________ for lunch

because ______________________________.

 ELD.PI.4.1.Ex, ELD.PI.4.1.Br, ELD.PI.4.5.Ex, ELD.PI.4.5.Br, ELD.PI.4.12a.Ex, ELD.PI.4.12a.Br See the California Standards section.

signaling

The police officer is **signaling** to the cars.

Another word for *signaling* is ______________

______________________________.

substitution

The girl chose an energy-saving light as a **substitution**.

An energy-saving light is a better *substitution*

because ______________________________.

Words and Phrases

Adverbials

The phrase *all over again* means "to start and finish something another time."

I missed my turn so we had to start the game <u>*all over again*</u>*.*

The phrase *all over the place* means "spread everywhere."

I was excited by the project but my ideas were <u>*all over the place*</u>*.*

Read the sentences below. Write the phrase that means the same as the underlined words.

My dog brought mud into the kitchen so I had to clean <u>another time</u>.

My dog brought mud into the kitchen so I had to clean ______________________________.

In my room clothes were <u>spread</u> <u>everywhere</u>.

In my room clothes were ______________________.

» Go Digital **Add the adverbial phrases to your New Words notebook. Write a sentence to show the meaning of each.**

1 Talk About It

Look at the picture. Read the title. Talk about what you see. Write your ideas.

What does this title tell you?

____

____

What are the girls in the picture doing?

____

____

____

____

Take notes as you read the story.

Sadie's Game

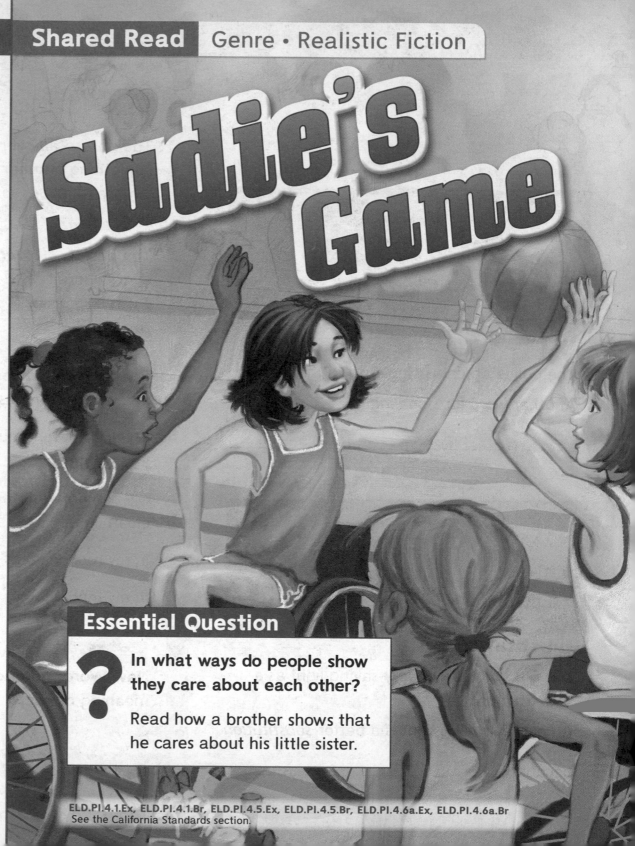

Essential Question

In what ways do people show they care about each other?

Read how a brother shows that he cares about his little sister.

ELD.PI.4.1.Ex, ELD.PI.4.1.Br, ELD.PI.4.5.Ex, ELD.PI.4.5.Br, ELD.PI.4.6a.Ex, ELD.PI.4.6a.Br
See the California Standards section.

The referee's whistle went off like a shrieking bird, **signaling** Sadie's second foul of the game. It was only the first **quarter**, and Sadie had already **collided** twice with another player's wheelchair. Her coach waved her off the court for a **substitution** as the crowd shouted catcalls and jeered behind her. She had never seen a crowd express such disappointment before.

Sadie watched her teammates whirl and spin in front of her. Her emotions were all over the place, and it showed in her basketball playing. If only she and her brother had not argued this morning about the game. "What's so important, Richie, that you can't be at the game? Don't I matter anymore?" Sadie had asked.

James Bernardin

ELD.PI.4.1.Ex, ELD.PI.4.1.Br, ELD.PI.4.5.Ex, ELD.PI.4.5.Br, ELD.PI.4.6a.Ex, ELD.PI.4.6a.Br, ELD.PI.4.7.Ex, ELD.PI.4.7.Br, ELD.PI.4.12a.Ex, ELD.PI.4.12a.Br See the California Standards section.

Text Evidence

1 Specific Vocabulary ACT

Reread the second sentence in the first paragraph. The word *quarter* can mean "an American coin worth 25 cents" or "one of four parts." Underline the word that gives you a clue to the meaning. How many more quarters are there in the game?

____

2 Sentence Structure ACT

Reread the third sentence in the first paragraph. Circle the word that shows that two things are happening at the same time. Underline the two things that are happening at the same time.

3 Comprehension

Problem and Solution

Reread the second paragraph. Underline the words that tell about Sadie's problem.

Text Evidence

1 Comprehension

Problem and Solution

Reread the first paragraph. What was the problem that Sadie faced? Underline the words that tell you. What was Richie's solution to this problem?

____

________________________________.

2 Specific Vocabulary ACT

Reread the fourth sentence in the third paragraph. The word *priorities* means "things that are more important." What are Richie's new priorities?

____

________________________________.

3 Sentence Structure ACT

Reread the last sentence in the fourth paragraph. Circle the subject of the sentence. Underline the actions of the subject in this sentence.

Richie was Sadie's whole world, and they both loved sports, especially basketball. Sadie loved to play before her accident, and it was Richie who had taught her to play again afterward. There had been days when she did not want to get out of bed, and he would coax and bully her until she got up. He even borrowed a wheelchair himself to help her learn to play the game all over again. Together they would roll across the outdoor court, zipping, zooming, passing, and dribbling all day long.

But lately Richie **preferred** to hang out with his new high school friends. Sadie would watch through the window as Richie polished every little nook of his new car. He was as fussy as a mother cat cleaning her kittens. When he drove away, Sadie would keep staring out of the window, tears clouding her eyes.

Mama was her sun. Her arms would reach out and encircle her in a long, warm embrace. "Sadie," she would say, "your brother loves you. Even though he's got new **priorities** now, that doesn't mean he doesn't care." But Sadie felt hurt.

Sadie looked up and saw her coach frowning. She searched sadly for her mother, expecting disappointment in her eyes, but instead she saw a wide smile. It was the same happy face she saw in portraits of her mother at home. Sadie followed her mother's **gaze** to find Richie jogging toward her across the gym, holding a purple and white bouquet of flowers wrapped tightly with a ribbon. Richie's eyes sparkled, and his smile gleamed. He **bowed** to his sister and handed her the flowers as though she were a queen.

ELD.PI.4.1.Ex, ELD.PI.4.1.Br, ELD.PI.4.5.Ex, ELD.PI.4.5.Br, ELD.PI.4.6a.Ex, ELD.PI.4.6a.Br, ELD.PI.4.7.Ex, ELD.PI.4.7.Br, ELD.PI.4.12a.Ex, ELD.PI.4.12a.Br See the California Standards section.

"But we're losing. How do you know we're going to win?" she asked.

"I don't," Richie said. "It's not important. What I know is you're like a whirlwind on the court, and there is no way I am going to miss my little sister's big game!" He put his hand on her shoulder as he said, "It's great to have a lot of new friends, but I **realized** that you're my best friend."

Sadie smiled. Those words meant more to her than "I'm sorry" ever could. She rested the flowers on her lap and went back out onto the court. Right then Sadie decided to play the rest of the game with the bouquet in her lap. With her brother watching from the sidelines, Sadie stole the ball from an opponent and dribbled her way to the net, making the first of what would be many amazing shots for the team.

Make Connections

Talk about how Richie shows he cares about his little sister, Sadie. ESSENTIAL QUESTION

Whom do you care about in the same way that Richie cares about Sadie? Explain how you show you care. TEXT TO SELF

James Bernardin

ELD.PI.4.1.Ex, ELD.PI.4.1.Br, ELD.PI.4.5.Ex, ELD.PI.4.5.Br, ELD.PI.4.6a.Ex, ELD.PI.4.6a.Br, ELD.PI.4.7.Ex, ELD.PI.4.7.Br, ELD.PI.4.12a.Ex, ELD.PI.4.12a.Br See the California Standards section.

Text Evidence

1 Specific Vocabulary ACT

Reread the fourth sentence in the second paragraph. The word *realized* means "began to understand." Underline the words that tell what Richie realized.

2 Sentence Structure ACT

Reread the last sentence in the last paragraph. Circle the parts of the sentence that can stand on their own, or the independent clauses. Underline the parts of the sentence that can't stand on their own, or the dependent clauses.

3 Talk About It

Describe how Richie shows he cares about Sadie throughout the story. How does Richie help Sadie after her accident? What does Richie do to support Sadie during her game?

Respond to the Text

Partner Discussion **Work with a partner. Describe what you learned about "Sadie's Game." Write the page numbers where you found text evidence.**

What did you learn about Richie?	**Text Evidence**
Richie helped Sadie after her accident by ______________________ ______________________.	Page(s): __________
Richie's new priorities are ______________________.	Page(s): __________
In the end, Richie arrived at the game and ______________________ ______________________.	Page(s): __________

What did you learn about Sadie?	**Text Evidence**
After her accident, Sadie ______________________ ______________________.	Page(s): __________
Sadie was upset at the game because ______________________.	Page(s): __________
Sadie gets help from her mother when ______________________.	Page(s): __________

Group Discussion **Present your answers to the class. Cite text evidence to justify your thinking. Listen to and discuss the group's opinions about your answers.**

 ELD.PI.4.1.Ex, ELD.PI.4.1.Br, ELD.PI.4.3.Ex, ELD.PI.4.3.Br, ELD.PI.4.5.Ex, ELD.PI.4.5.Br, ELD.PI.4.9.Ex, ELD.PI.4.9.Br, ELD.PI.4.11a.Ex, ELD.PI.4.11a.Br, ELD.PI.4.12a.Ex, ELD.PI.4.12a.Br See the California Standards section.

Write Work with a partner. Review your notes about "Sadie's Game." Then write your answer to the essential question. Use text evidence to support your answer. Use vocabulary words from this week's reading in your writing.

How do people show they care about each other?

After Sadie's accident, Richie showed he cared about Sadie by ______________________

____.

Sadie's mother showed she cared about Sadie by ______________________

____.

At the game, Richie showed he cared about Sadie by ______________________

____.

COLLABORATE

Share Writing Present your writing to the class. Discuss their opinions. Think about what they have to say. Did they justify their claims? Explain why you agree or disagree with their claims.

I agree with ______________________ because ______________________.

I disagree with ______________________ because ______________________.

ELD.PI.4.1.Ex, ELD.PI.4.1.Br, ELD.PI.4.3.Ex, ELD.PI.4.3.Br, ELD.PI.4.5.Ex, ELD.PI.4.5.Br, ELD.PI.4.9.Ex, ELD.PI.4.9.Br, ELD.PI.4.10b.Ex, ELD.PI.4.10b.Br, ELD.PI.4.11a.Ex, ELD.PI.4.11a.Br, ELD.PI.4.12a.Ex, ELD.PI.4.12a.Br See the California Standards section.

Write to Sources

pages 266–269

Take Notes About the Text I took notes on a chart to respond to the prompt: ***Write a letter from Mama to Richie. Describe how she felt when Richie came to Sadie's game.***

Event	Character's Reaction
Sadie and Richie argued about why he can't go to her game.	Mama tells Sadie that her brother still cares about her.
Sadie is upset at her basketball game.	She plays badly and is taken off the court.
Richie jogs into the gym. He brings flowers for Sadie.	Mama has a big smile.

 ELD.PI.4.1.Ex, ELD.PI.4.1.Br, ELD.PI.4.5.Ex, ELD.PI.4.5.Br, ELD.PI.4.6a.Ex, ELD.PI.4.6a.Br See the California Standards section.

Write About the Text I used notes from my chart to write a letter from Mama to Richie. The letter describes how Mama felt when Richie came to Sadie's game.

Student Model: *Narrative Text*

Dear Richie,

You made me smile today. Thank you for coming to Sadie's game. She felt bad about arguing with you. She wasn't playing well. Then you jogged into the gym. You gave her a bouquet of flowers. She started playing better. You showed her that you still care about her.

Love,

Mama

TALK ABOUT IT

Text Evidence

Draw a box around a detail from the notes that begins the letter. Why is this a strong opening?

Grammar

Circle the pronouns in the last sentence. Identify who each pronoun refers to.

Connect Ideas

Underline the fifth and sixth sentences. How can you connect the sentences into one detailed sentence?

Your Turn

Write a letter from Sadie to her coach. Explain why you were playing badly during the game.

>> *Go Digital*
Write your response online. Use your editing checklist.

ELD.PI.4.1.Ex, ELD.PI.4.1.Br, ELD.PI.4.2.Ex, ELD.PI.4.2.Br, ELD.PI.4.5.Ex, ELD.PI.4.5.Br, ELD.PI.4.6a.Ex, ELD.PI.4.6a.Br, ELD.PI.4.10b.Ex, ELD.PI.4.10b.Br, ELD.PI.4.12a.Ex, ELD.PI.4.12a.Br, ELD.PII.4.2a.Ex, ELD.PII.4.2a.Br, ELD.PII.4.7.Ex, ELD.PII.4.7.Br See the California Standards section.

TALK ABOUT IT

Weekly Concept On the Move

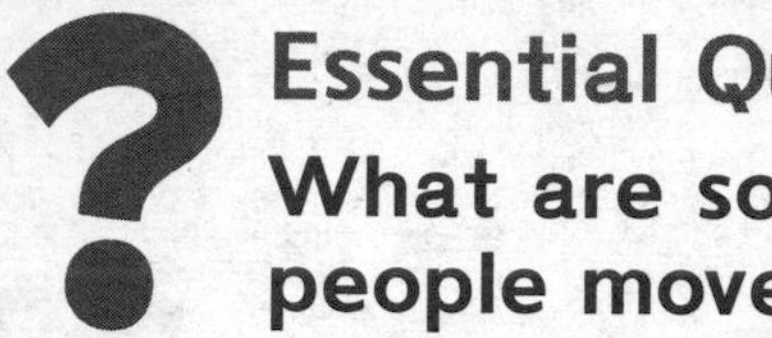

Essential Question

What are some reasons people moved west?

» *Go Digital*

Describe what you see in the photograph. Why would people be moving from that place? Discuss reasons for moving to a new place. Write your ideas in the chart.

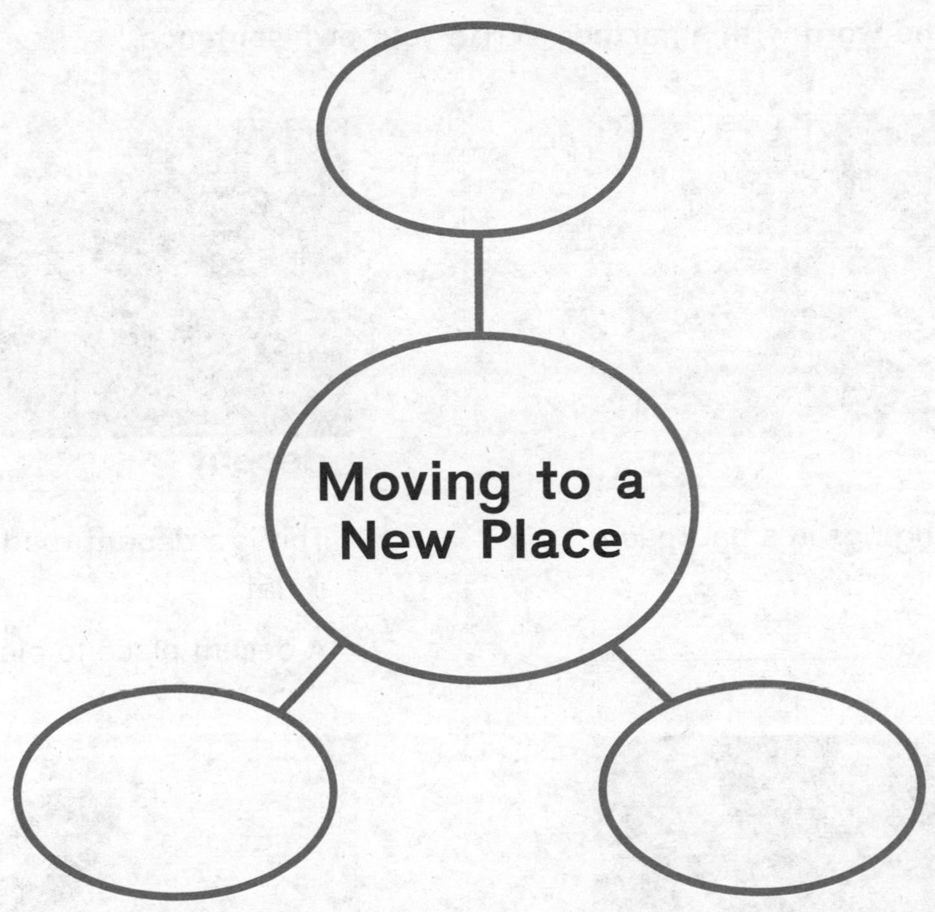

Look at the photo. Discuss why people leave their homes and move to new places. Use the words from the chart. You can say:

Some people move to other places because of ______________.

Others leave in search of ________________________________.

Photo Quest/Getty Images

More Vocabulary

Look at the picture and read the word. Then read the sentences. Talk about the word with a partner. Write your own sentence.

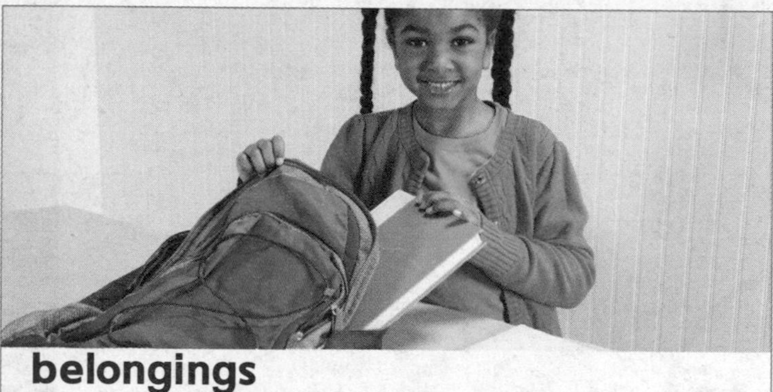

belongings

The girl keeps her **belongings** in a backpack while at school.

I keep my *belongings* in a ________________ at school.

commenced

The race **commenced** at the starting line.

Another word for *commenced* is __________

____.

decent

This is a **decent** road to travel on because it is flat.

A decent place to play is the ______________.

hauled

The man **hauled** the boys to the top of the hill.

Another word for *hauled* is __________________

____.

(ul)Eclipse Studios/McGraw-Hill Education; (ur)George Clerk/E+/Getty Images; (bl)moodboard/SuperStock; (br)Glow Images

 ELD.PI.4.1.Ex, ELD.PI.4.1.Br, ELD.PI.4.5.Ex, ELD.PI.4.5.Br, ELD.PI.4.12a.Ex, ELD.PI.4.12a.Br See the California Standards section.

hollered

The girl **hollered** over the fence.

Another word for *hollered* is ______________

______________________________.

trail

Hikers stay on the **trail** to stay safe.

It is important for hikers to stay on the *trail*

because ______________________________.

Words and Phrases

Figurative Language: Metaphor

Metaphor is a comparison of two unlike things without the use of *like* or *as*.

The rain came down in buckets.

The rain came down hard.

She is a tadpole of a girl.

She is a very small girl.

Read the sentences below. Circle the word that means the same as the underlined metaphor.

It is raining cats and dogs.

hard slow down

I am so hungry I can eat a horse.

eat nothing eat very little eat a lot

» Go Digital **Add the metaphors to your New Words notebook. Write a sentence to show the meaning of each.**

Text Evidence

1 Talk About It

Look at the picture. Read the title. Talk about what you see. Write your ideas.

What does this title tell you?

____

____

____

______________________________.

What does the illustration show?

____

____

____

______________________________.

Take notes as you read the story.

Shared Read Genre • Tall Tale

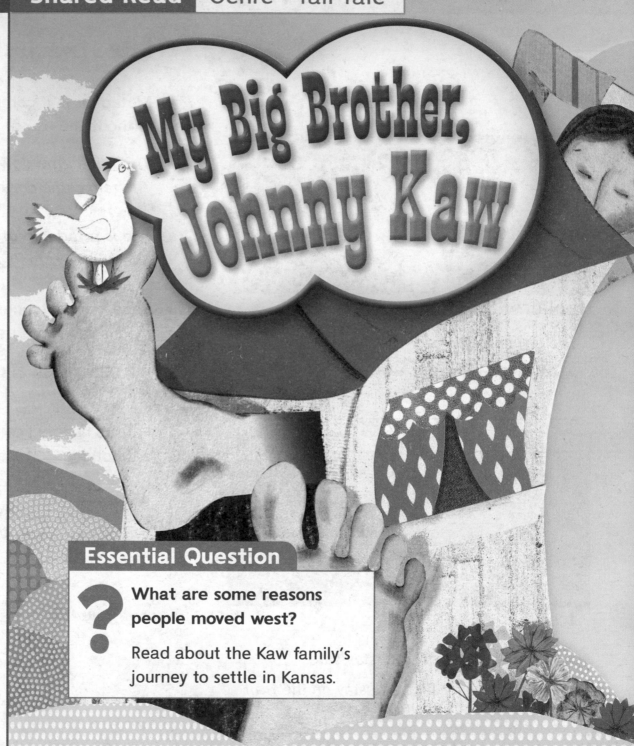

My Big Brother, Johnny Kaw

Essential Question

What are some reasons people moved west?

Read about the Kaw family's journey to settle in Kansas.

ELD.PI.4.1.Ex, ELD.PI.4.1.Br, ELD.PI.4.5.Ex, ELD.PI.4.5.Br, ELD.PI.4.6a.Ex, ELD.PI.4.6a.Br
See the California Standards section.

I was just a **tadpole** of a girl when my family decided to leave the crowded city life behind. My daddy said, "There are territories out west with wide open spaces. The Kaw family needs room to grow!"

He was mostly talking about my big brother. At fifteen, Johnny had grown so tall that when he stretched out in bed at night his head hung out the front door and his feet hung out the back door all the way into the chicken coop where the hens laid eggs between his toes.

Mama loaded up the wagon with our **belongings**, and Daddy hitched up the oxen. We began to head west, but it wasn't long until Johnny **hollered** for everybody to stop.

"We'll never get there with these slowpokes pulling us!" Johnny scoffed. He unhitched the team and put one ox on each shoulder.

"Mind you don't let them topple off!" Daddy hollered.

"Yes, sir!" Johnny said. "Tadpole can keep an eye on 'em!" He picked me up and set me on top of his head where I had to hang on to handfuls of Johnny's red hair to keep from falling off. Then Johnny grabbed hold of the hitch and began pulling the wagon.

Josee Basaillon

ELD.PI.4.1.Ex, ELD.PI.4.1.Br, ELD.PI.4.5.Ex, ELD.PI.4.5.Br, ELD.PI.4.6a.Ex, ELD.PI.4.6a.Br, ELD.P.I.4.12a.Ex, ELD.P.I.4.12a.Br See the California Standards section.

Text Evidence

1 Comprehension

Cause and Effect

Reread the first two paragraphs. Underline the words that tell what caused the Kaw family to move west.

2 Specific Vocabulary ACT

Reread the first sentence in the first paragraph. A *tadpole* is a very small frog or toad. Who is a tadpole of a girl?

____

How does she compare with Johnny? ______________________________

____

3 Sentence Structure ACT

Reread the first sentence in the third paragraph. Circle the word that connects the two parts of the sentence. Underline the subject in each part of the sentence.

Text Evidence

1 Specific Vocabulary ACT

Reread the first paragraph. A *gully* is a "a deep ditch or a small valley." Underline how Johnny made a gully. Circle what the gully became.

2 Comprehension

Cause and Effect

Reread the second and third paragraphs. What caused Johnny to cut down the mountains? Underline the words that tell you. Circle the words that tell you the result of Johnny's actions.

3 Sentence Structure ACT

Reread the first sentence in the fourth paragraph. Circle the word that connects the two parts of the sentence, or clauses. Underline the two clauses.

He never did have much sense of direction. He pulled that wagon one way then the other, faster and faster, digging out the biggest **gully** you ever saw. The next night a big rain came and filled it up. I hear that now they call that crooked gully the Kaw River.

Johnny pulled our wagon to a Kansas settlement where people were trying to figure out how to raise crops. "Problem is these mountains," one settler said. "They are in the way."

Johnny said that was no problem. He saw a big cottonwood tree, used a saw to cut it down, and whittled it into a giant scythe. Next, he whacked the mountains off down near the ground, **hauled** them west, and piled them up in a big row. Today folks call them the Rocky Mountains.

Everybody in Kansas was so happy with the nice flat land that they asked us to stay and homestead with them. We built a sod house and started planting wheat.

Now one summer it was mighty dry. All of the wheat had started to shrivel up in the field. Our neighbors came and asked for Johnny's assistance. "My crop has about withered away to nothing," said one neighbor. "Without rain we're done for!"

"I have got an idea," said Johnny, looking up at some puffy clouds. He grabbed hold of his big hoe and **commenced** poking holes in the clouds. Down came the rain in buckets, and the wheat was saved!

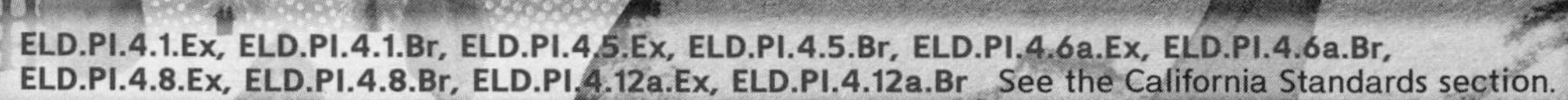
ELD.PI.4.1.Ex, ELD.PI.4.1.Br, ELD.PI.4.5.Ex, ELD.PI.4.5.Br, ELD.PI.4.6a.Ex, ELD.PI.4.6a.Br, ELD.PI.4.8.Ex, ELD.PI.4.8.Br, ELD.PI.4.12a.Ex, ELD.PI.4.12a.Br See the California Standards section.

One morning at the riverbank, Mama was plunging our dirty clothes in the water to get them clean when a prospector rode up. He said he was headed to California to find gold. "Trouble is," he said, "there's not one **decent trail** between here and there."

Mama said, "Let me talk to my son."

Johnny was happy to help. For a week he hiked back and forth to all kinds of places dragging his giant bags of wheat everywhere, clearing trails of trees, **brush**, and boulders. The gold rush folks were tickled to find good clear paths that they named the Oregon Trail, the Santa Fe Trail, and the Chisholm Trail.

I'm sure glad our family ended up in Kansas. Our neighbors tell us that this is a bad place for twisters, but so far we haven't seen one. I can't wait, though! Johnny plans to lasso that twister and ride it like a bucking bronco–and he's promised his little sister a ride!

Make Connections

Talk about why the Kaw family moved to Kansas. ESSENTIAL QUESTION

If you could move somewhere new, where would you go? Why? TEXT TO SELF

Josee Basaillon

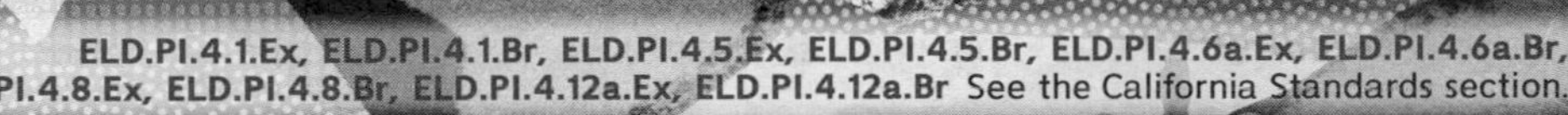

Text Evidence

1 Comprehension Cause and Effect

Reread the third paragraph. What was the effect of Johnny clearing paths with bags of wheat?

____

____

2 Specific Vocabulary ACT

Reread the third paragraph. The word *brush* can mean "a tool used to paint" or "a small, low bush." Circle the words that give you a clue about the meaning of brush. What is the meaning of brush in the second sentence?

____

3 Sentence Structure ACT

Reread the last sentence in the last paragraph. Circle the independent clauses that can stand on their own. Underline the dependent clauses that cannot stand on their own.

Respond to the Text

Partner Discussion **Work with a partner. Describe what you learned about "My Big Brother, Johnny Kaw." Write the page numbers where you found text evidence.**

What did you learn about the Kaw family?	Text Evidence
Johnny helped his family move west by ______________________ ______________________________________.	Page(s): ________
When the Kaws arrived in Kansas, Johnny helped the people in the settlement by ______________________.	Page(s): ________
Johnny helped the prospectors by ______________________.	Page(s): ________

What did you learn about families moving west?	Text Evidence
I read that the Kaws moved west because ______________________.	Page(s): ________
People settled in Kansas so they could ______________________.	Page(s): ________
Prospectors went west because they wanted to ________________.	Page(s): ________

Group Discussion **Present your answers to the class. Cite text evidence to justify your thinking. Listen to and discuss the group's opinions about your answers.**

 ELD.PI.4.1.Ex, ELD.PI.4.1.Br, ELD.PI.4.3.Ex, ELD.PI.4.3.Br, ELD.PI.4.5.Ex, ELD.PI.4.5.Br, ELD.PI.4.9.Ex, ELD.PI.4.9.Br, ELD.PI.4.11a.Ex, ELD.PI.4.11a.Br, ELD.PI.4.12a.Ex, ELD.PI.4.12a.Br See the California Standards section.

Write Work with a partner. Review your notes about "My Big Brother, Johnny Kaw." Then write your answer to the essential question. Use text evidence to support your answer. Use vocabulary words from this week's reading in your writing.

Why did people move west?

The Kaw family moved west because ____

____

____.

People settled in Kansas so they could ______________________________________

____.

Prospectors went west because ____

____

____.

COLLABORATE

Share Writing Present your writing to the class. Discuss their opinions. Think about what they have to say. Did they justify their claims? Explain why you agree or disagree with their claims.

I agree with ______________________________ because ___________________________.

I disagree with ____________________________ because ___________________________.

Write to Sources

Take Notes About the Text **I took notes on a sequence chart to respond to the prompt:** ***Add an event to the end of the story. Use exaggeration and details from the story.***

pages 278–281

Johnny Kaw is very tall. His family moves west because Johnny needs room to grow.

↓

Johnny moves the mountains so people can farm.

↓

Johnny pokes holes in the clouds so it will rain. He clears trails for prospectors heading to California.

↓

He wants to lasso a twister and ride it like a bucking bronco. He promises Tadpole a ride.

Write About the Text **I used notes from my sequence chart to add an event to the story. I used exaggeration and details from the story.**

Student Model: *Narrative Text*

Soon, a twister came to town. It was a huge, black cloud that covered the whole sky.

"Tadpole," Johnny called. "Let's go for a ride." Then he took some rope, and he lassoed the twister.

Johnny held me tight. He rode the twister without any hands. The twister bucked like an angry bronco. Soon it got tired. Everyone thanked Johnny for saving the town from the twister.

TALK ABOUT IT

Text Evidence

Draw a box around a sentence that comes from the sequence chart about what Johnny does when he sees the twister. Why is this an example of exaggeration?

Grammar

Circle the last sentence in the second paragraph. Underline the independent clauses. Why is this a compound sentence?

Connect Ideas

Underline the two sentences in the third paragraph that tell what the twister does. How can you combine these sentences?

Your Turn

Add an event to the story. Describe how Johnny helps his family build a house. Use exaggeration in your story.

>> *Go Digital*
Write your response online. Use your editing checklist.

ELD.PI.4.1.Ex, ELD.PI.4.1.Br, ELD.PI.4.5.Ex, ELD.PI.4.5.Br, ELD.PI.4.6a.Ex, ELD.PI.4.6a.Br, ELD.PI.4.10b.Ex, ELD.PI.4.10b.Br, ELD.PI.4.12a.Ex,ELD.PI.4.12a.Br, ELD.PII.4.1.Ex, ELD.PII.4.1.Br, ELD.PII.4.6.Ex ELD.PII.4.6.Br See the California Standards section.

TALK ABOUT IT
Weekly Concept Inventions
Essential Question
How can inventions solve problems?
Go Digital

Describe how the compact car in the photo helps to solve problems. In the chart, write about other new inventions that help to solve problems.

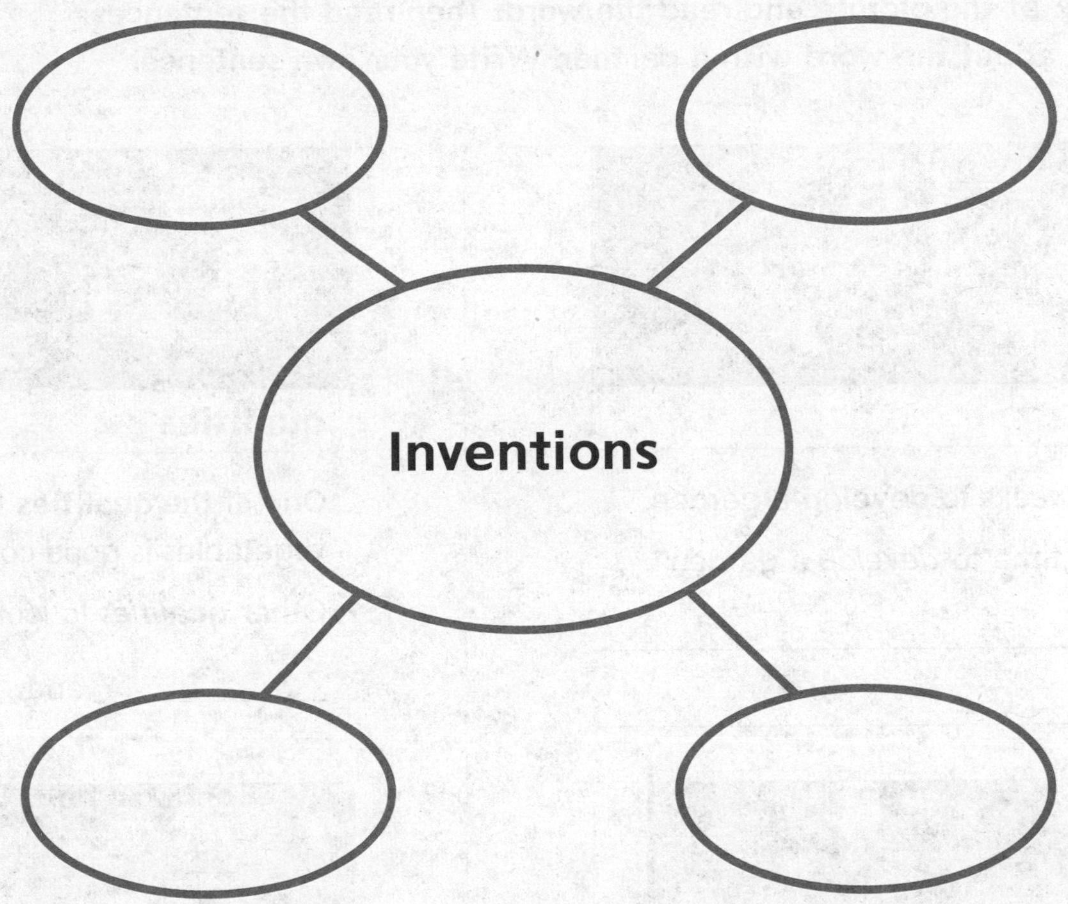

Discuss the problems some new inventions have solved. Use the words from the chart. You can say:

The ___________ has helped solve the problem of ________________

____.

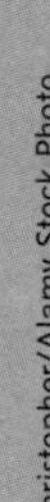

ELD.PI.4.1.Ex, ELD.PI.4.1.Br, ELD.PI.4.5.Ex, ELD.PI.4.5.Br, ELD.PI.4.12a.Ex, ELD.PI.4.12a.Br See the California Standards section.

More Vocabulary

Look at the picture and read the word. Then read the sentences. Talk about the word with a partner. Write your own sentence.

develop

It takes many weeks to **develop** a garden.

It takes a long time to *develop* a garden

because ______________________________

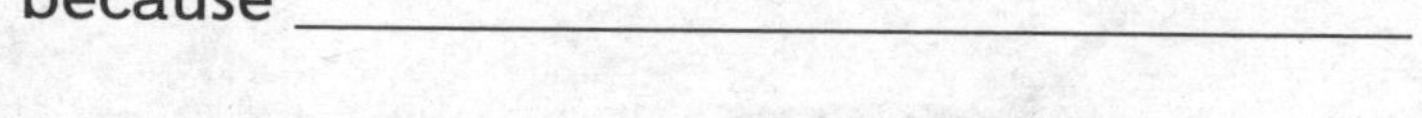

______________________________________.

fireproof

The firefighters wear **fireproof** clothes.

The clothes are *fireproof* because __________

______________________________________.

qualities

One of the **qualities** to look for in choosing vegetables is good color.

Other *qualities* to look for in vegetables are

______________ and ____________________.

reinforce

They use poles to **reinforce** the tent.

Another word for *reinforce* is ________________

______________________________________.

(ul)Hero Images/Getty Images; (ur)Bear Dancer Studios/Mark Dierker; (bl)image 100/Alamy; (br)ZenShui/Odilon Dimier/PhotoAlto Agency RF Collections/Getty Images

 ELD.PI.4.1.Ex, ELD.PI.4.1.Br, ELD.PI.4.5.Ex, ELD.PI.4.5.Br, ELD.PI.4.12a.Ex, ELD.PI.4.12a.Br See the California Standards section.

stiff

The egg carton is made from **stiff** cardboard because it will not bend.

Another word for *stiff* is ____________________

____________________.

urging

The coach is **urging** the team to play their best.

Another word for *urging* is ____________________

____________________.

Words and Phrases
consequently and *however*

Connecting words can link two sentences.

***consequently* = as a result**

I do my homework. Consequently, I have good grades.

***however* = but**

I ate my lunch. However, I am still hungry.

Read the sentences below. Write the connecting word that means the same as the underlined word.

It is raining. As a result, the game is canceled.

It is raining. ____________________ the game is canceled.

It is bedtime. But I am not tired.

It is bedtime. __________, I am not tired.

» Go Digital **Add the connecting words to your New Words notebook. Write a sentence to show the meaning of each.**

Text Evidence

COLLABORATE

1 Talk About It

Look at the photographs. Read the title. Talk about what you see. Write your ideas.

What does this title tell you?

____

____

What do you see in the photographs?

____

____

Take notes as you read the text.

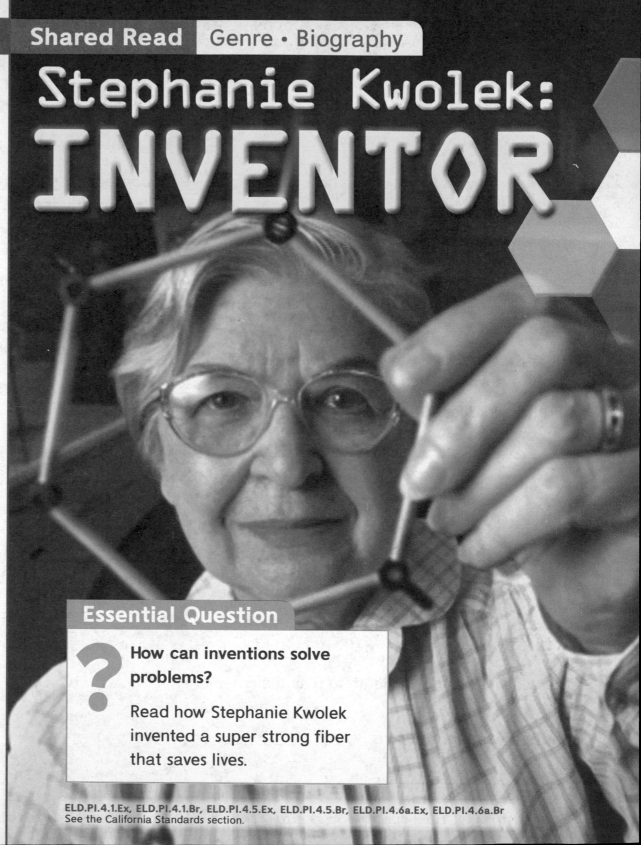

Shared Read Genre • Biography

Stephanie Kwolek: INVENTOR

Essential Question

How can inventions solve problems?

Read how Stephanie Kwolek invented a super strong fiber that saves lives.

ELD.PI.4.1.Ex, ELD.PI.4.1.Br, ELD.PI.4.5.Ex, ELD.PI.4.5.Br, ELD.PI.4.6a.Ex, ELD.PI.4.6a.Br
See the California Standards section.

Kevlar® is used in vests for police and police dogs.

If you could invent a material for a superhero, what would it be like? It would have to be light, strong, bullet-resistant, and **fireproof**, right? Chemist Stephanie Kwolek actually invented a material just like this. It's called Kevlar®. Superheroes don't wear it, but everyday heroes like police officers and firefighters do.

Becoming a Chemist

From the time she was young, Stephanie was interested in math and science. She was not the kind of student who caused mischief, and she worked hard in school. Stephanie's teachers spotted her talent and talked to her about careers in science. With their encouragement, Stephanie studied chemistry in college. She had hoped to go on to medical school but could not afford it.

Consequently, Stephanie took a job working at a textile lab. She planned to save up enough money from her job so that she could pay for medical school. At the lab, she discovered that she had a genuine love of chemistry. She learned how to make chain-like **molecules** called polymers that could be spun into fabrics and plastics.

Stephanie enjoyed doing experiments so much that she decided not to go to medical school.

(l) Michael Branscom, courtesy of the Lemelson-MIT Program; (tl) Tom Vickers/Newscom; (tr) Science & Society Picture Library/Getty Images

ELD.PI.4.1.Ex, ELD.PI.4.1.Br, ELD.PI.4.5.Ex, ELD.PI.4.5.Br, ELD.PI.4.6a.Ex, ELD.PI.4.6a.Br, ELD.PI.4.7.Ex, ELD.PI.4.7.Br, ELD.PI.4.12a.Ex, ELD.PI.4.12a.Br See the California Standards section.

Text Evidence

1 Sentence Structure ACT

Reread the second sentence in the second paragraph. Underline the word that connects the two parts of the sentence. Circle the independent clauses in the sentence, or the parts of the sentence that can stand on their own.

2 Comprehension Problem and Solution

Reread the second and third paragraphs. Underline the problem Stephanie faced when she got out of college. Circle what she did to solve her problem.

3 Specific Vocabulary ACT

Reread the third paragraph. A *molecule* is formed when atoms are joined together. Circle what Stephanie called her chain-like molecules. Underline the words that tell you what could be done with the molecules.

Text Evidence

1 Comprehension

Problem and Solution

Reread the first paragraph. In 1964 what was the problem scientists wanted to solve? Underline the words that tell you. Circle the words that tell what the solution was.

2 Sentence Structure ACT

Reread the third sentence in the first paragraph. Circle the noun the pronoun *They* refers to. In this sentence, the prepositional phrase *rather than* means "instead of." Underline what the scientists wanted instead of heavy steel wires.

3 Specific Vocabulary ACT

Reread the fourth sentence in the last paragraph. The word *clog* means "to block or stop from flowing out." What did the worker think might clog the spinning machine?

____

____

A Strange Liquid

In 1964, Stephanie's lab supervisor asked her to work on making a strong, **stiff** fiber. The United States was facing a possible gas shortage, and scientists wanted to help. They believed that if you could **reinforce** tires with a lightweight fiber rather than heavy steel wire, cars and airplanes would use less gasoline. Stephanie began experimenting by mixing polymers. One day, she made an unusual solution, or mixture. Polymer solutions are often thick like molasses. However, this solution was cloudy and watery.

Stephanie brought her strange liquid to the worker in charge of spinning liquids into fibers. He looked at Stephanie's solution and laughed. He thought it was hilarious that she believed it could be made into fiber. It looked too much like water and might even **clog** the spinning machine. But Stephanie kept **urging** him to spin it until he finally agreed. When he followed the procedure, a strong fiber began to form. Stephanie's head spun, and she felt dizzy with excitement.

A TIMELINE OF ACHIEVEMENTS

1923	1946	1964	1971	1995
Born in New Kensington, Pennsylvania	Earned a degree in chemistry from Carnegie Mellon University	Discovered the fibers for Kevlar®	Kevlar® first marketed	Inducted into the Inventor's Hall of Fame

Kevlar® is used in cars, such as this solar racing car.

ELD.PI.4.1.Ex, ELD.PI.4.1.Br, ELD.PI.4.5.Ex, ELD.PI.4.5.Br, ELD.PI.4.6a.Ex, ELD.PI.4.6a.Br, ELD.PI.4.7.Ex, ELD.PI.4.7.Br, ELD.PI.4.12a.Ex, ELD.PI.4.12a.Br, ELD.PII.4.2a.Ex, ELD.PII.4.2a.Br See the California Standards section.

Stronger than Steel

Firefighters wear suits made from Kevlar®.

Stephanie tested the fiber in the lab and found that it was fireproof. It was stronger and lighter than steel, too. With these **qualities**, she believed that the fiber could be turned into a useful material. She was right. The material became known as Kevlar®.

After Stephanie's discovery, it took almost a decade of teamwork to **develop** Kevlar®. Some people spent hours on the telephone with the patent office. Others had to think of ways to use and sell it. Nowadays, Kevlar® is used by almost everyone. The President and other politicians wear protective clothing made from it. So do lumberjacks, firefighters, and police officers. Kevlar® is also used in tires, bicycles, spacecraft, and skis. By developing Kevlar®, Stephanie had found a way to make protective clothing and equipment that is both light and strong.

Stephanie's invention has saved many lives over the years. She was inducted into the National Inventors Hall of Fame for her work, and her photograph has appeared on a book cover and in advertisements for Kevlar®. She says that she never expected to be an inventor but is delighted that her work has helped so many people.

Make Connections

What problems did Stephanie's invention solve? ESSENTIAL QUESTION

What would you make out of Kevlar®? Explain why. TEXT TO SELF

Text Evidence

1 Comprehension
Problem and Solution

Reread the second paragraph. What problem did Kevlar® solve? Underline the words that tell you.

2 Sentence Structure ACT

Reread the first sentence in the third paragraph. Circle the prepositional phrase in the sentence that tells about when something happened. Underline what happened during that time.

3 Talk About It

Reread the second paragraph. Explain the effect that Kevlar® has had on people's lives. Then write about it.

____

____

____

_______________________________.

(bl) CB2/ZOB/WENN.com/Newscom; (tr) Stocktrek Images/Getty Images

ELD.PI.4.1.Ex, ELD.PI.4.1.Br, ELD.PI.4.5.Ex, ELD.PI.4.5.Br, ELD.PI.4.6a.Ex, ELD.PI.4.6a.Br, ELD.PI.4.12a.Ex, ELD.PI.4.12a.Br See the California Standards section.

Respond to the Text

Partner Discussion **Work with a partner. Describe what you learned about "Stephanie Kwolek: Inventor." Write the page numbers where you found text evidence.**

What did you learn about Stephanie Kwolek?	**Text Evidence**
I read that Stephanie Kwolek discovered her love for chemistry when she ______________________.	Page(s): ______
Stephanie learned how to make __________ that could be spun into ______________________.	Page(s): ______
Stephanie made a solution that was __________ and __________.	Page(s): ______

What did you learn about Kevlar® in the text?	**Text Evidence**
Stephanie tested the fiber and discovered that it was __________.	Page(s): ______
Kevlar® is used by ______________________ ______________________.	Page(s): ______
It is also used to make equipment, such as ______________________ ______________________.	Page(s): ______

Group Discussion **Present your answers to the class. Cite text evidence to justify your thinking. Listen to and discuss the group's opinions about your answers.**

 ELD.PI.4.1.Ex, ELD.PI.4.1.Br, ELD.PI.4.3.Ex, ELD.PI.4.3.Br, ELD. PI.4.5.Ex, ELD.PI.4.5.Br, ELD.PI.4.9.Ex, ELD.PI.4.9.Br, ELD.PI.4.11a.Ex, ELD.PI.4.11a.Br, ELD.PI.4.12a.Ex, ELD.PI.4.12a.Br See the California Standards section.

Write **Work with a partner. Review your notes about "Stephanie Kwolek: Inventor." Then write your answer to the essential question. Use text evidence to support your answer. Use vocabulary words from this week's reading in your writing.**

What problems did Stephanie Kwolek's invention help to solve?

While working at the lab in 1964, Stephanie was asked to make ______________________________.

Scientists wanted to strengthen tires, so ______________________________
____.

Kevlar® has helped firefighters and police officers because ______________________________
____.

COLLABORATE

Share Writing **Present your writing to the class. Discuss their opinions. Think about what they have to say. Did they justify their claims? Explain why you agree or disagree with their claims.**

I agree with ______________________ because ______________________.

I disagree with ______________________ because ______________________.

Write to Sources

Take Notes About the Text **I took notes on an idea web to answer the question: *What information does the author tell us about polymer solutions?***

pages 290–293

Polymer Solutions

- Polymers are chain-like molecules. They can be spun into plastics and fabrics.
- They are usually thick like molasses. But Stephanie made a cloudy, watery solution.
- It was spun into a strong fiber that is fireproof.
- The fiber is used to make protective clothing.

 ELD.PI.4.1.Ex, ELD.PI.4.1.Br, ELD.PI.4.5.Ex, ELD.PI.4.5.Br, ELD.PI.4.6a.Ex, ELD.PI.4.6a.Br, ELD.PII.4.1.Ex, ELD.PII.4.1.Br See the California Standards section.

Write About the Text **I used my notes from my idea web to write a paragraph about polymer solutions.**

Student Model: *Informative Text*

The author describes polymer solutions in "Stephanie Kwolek: Inventor." First, the author explains what polymers are. Polymers are made from chain-like molecules.

Then the author tells what polymer solutions are like. They are thick, like molasses. But Stephanie made a cloudy, watery solution.

Finally, the author says that Stephanie's polymer solution was spun into a strong, fireproof fiber. It is used to make protective clothing.

TALK ABOUT IT

Text Evidence

Draw a box around a sentence that comes from the notes. Does the sentence provide a supporting detail?

Grammar

Circle a present-tense verb. Why did Brady use the present tense?

Condense Ideas

Underline the second and third sentences in the first paragraph. How can the sentences be condensed into one detailed sentence?

Your Turn

What are the problems that were solved by Kevlar®? Use text evidence.

>> *Go Digital*
Write your response online. Use your editing checklist.

ELD.PI.4.1.Ex, ELD.PI.4.1.Br, ELD.PI.4.5.Ex, ELD.PI.4.5.Br, ELD.PI.4.6a.Ex, ELD.PI.4.6a.Br, ELD.PI.4.10b.Ex, ELD.PI.4.10b.Br, ELD.PI.4.12a.Ex, ELD.PI.4.12a.Br See the California Standards section.

TALK ABOUT IT

Weekly Concept Zoom In

Essential Question

What can you discover when you look closely at something?

» *Go Digital*

Look closely at the photograph of the peacock. In the chart, write about all the details of the peacock you can see.

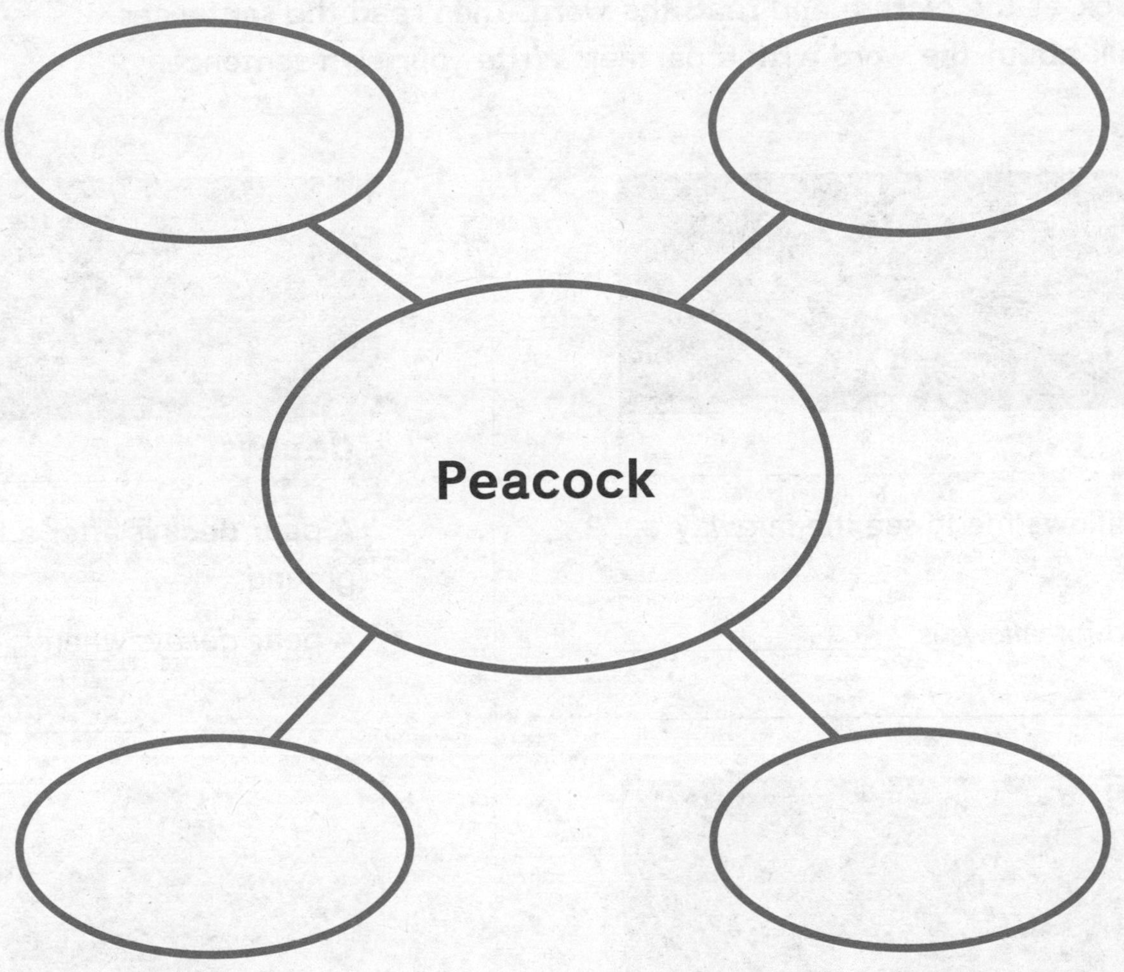

Discuss what you can see when you look closely at the peacock's feathers. Use the words from the chart. You can say:

I can see that the peacock's feathers are ______________________

____.

ELD.PI.4.1.Ex, ELD.PI.4.1.Br, ELD.PI.4.5.Ex, ELD.PI.4.5.Br, ELD.PI.4.12a.Ex, ELD.PI.4.12a.Br See the California Standards section.

More Vocabulary

Look at the picture and read the word. Then read the sentences. Talk about the word with a partner. Write your own sentence.

allows

A telescope **allows** me to see the faraway stars up close.

Another word for *allows* is ______________

______________________________.

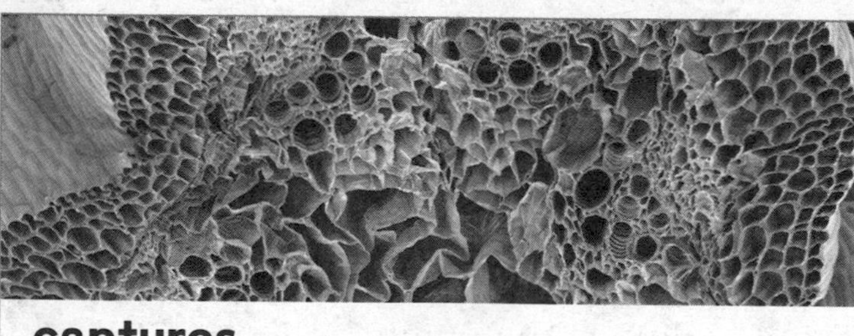

captures

This photograph **captures** a close up of the cells in a plant leaf.

Another word for *captures* is ______________

______________________________.

decays

A pear **decays** after a few days on the ground.

A pear *decays* when ______________

______________________________.

extreme

People need to wear warm clothes in places with **extreme** temperatures.

What is *extreme* about this weather? ________

______________________________.

 ELD.PI.4.1.Ex, ELD.PI.4.1.Br, ELD.PI.4.5.Ex, ELD.PI.4.5.Br, ELD.PI.4.12a.Ex, ELD.PI.4.12a.Br See the California Standards section.

fresh

The boy picks a **fresh** tomato from the plant.

The tomato is *fresh* because ______________

______________________________.

images

The boy likes to take **images** of flowers with his camera.

I would like to take *images* of ______________

______________________________.

Words and Phrases

Root Words

micro **= small** ***scope*** **= to watch or see**

We looked at insects under a <u>microscope</u>.

photo **= light** ***graph*** **= writing**

He took a <u>photograph</u> of the tree.

tele **= far away**

I talk to my friend in Mexico on the <u>telephone</u>.

Read the sentences below. Circle the word in each sentence that includes any of the roots used above.

I used a telescope to look at the planets.

I made a photocopy of my paper.

We used a microwave oven to heat our food.

A photographer took a picture of me.

» *Go Digital* **Add the root words to your New Words notebook. Write a sentence to show the meaning of each.**

COLLABORATE

1 Talk About It

Look at the photographs. Read the title. Talk about what you see. Write your ideas.

What does this title tell you?

___

___

___

___.

What do the photographs show?

___

___

___

___.

Take notes as you read the text.

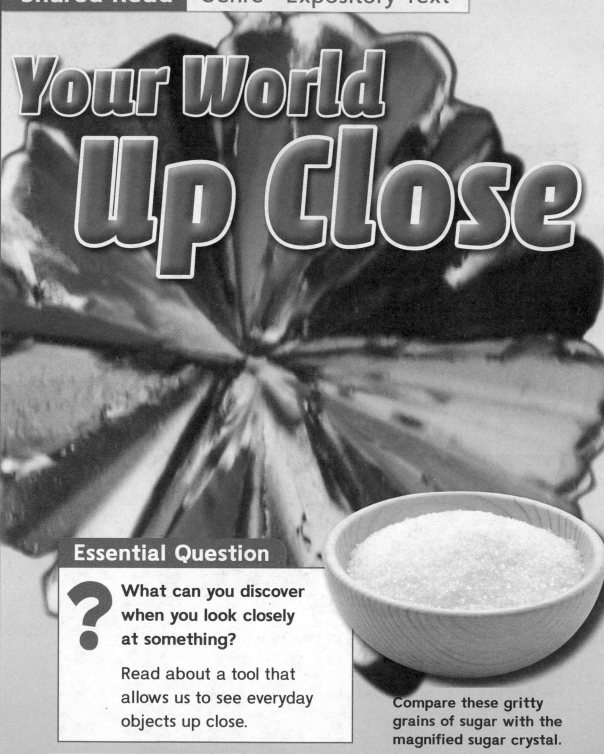

Your World Up Close

Essential Question

What can you discover when you look closely at something?

Read about a tool that allows us to see everyday objects up close.

Compare these gritty grains of sugar with the magnified sugar crystal.

ELD.PI.4.1.Ex, ELD.PI.4.1.Br, ELD.PI.4.5.Ex, ELD.PI.4.5.Br, ELD.PI.4.6a.Ex, ELD.PI.4.6a.Br
See the California Standards section.

Does the picture on the left show a diamond or a glass prism? Look closer. Take a step back. You are *too* close.

It is a picture of a sugar crystal. This **extreme** close-up was taken by an **electron** microscope, a tool that can magnify an item to thousands of times its actual size.

Pictures taken with a high-tech electron microscope are called photomicrographs. The sugar crystal on the left may look huge, but the word *micro* means small. We are seeing a small part of the sugar crystal up close.

Photomicrography dates back to 1840 when a scientist named Alfred Donné first photographed **images** through a microscope. Around 1852, a German pharmacist made the first version of a camera that took photomicrographs. In 1882, Wilson "Snowflake" Bentley of Vermont became the first person to use a camera with a built-in microscope to take pictures of snowflakes. His photographs showed that there is no such thing as a typical snowflake. Each is unique. Nowadays, we have electron micrographs.

These electron micrographs show that snowflakes are shaped like hexagons.

ELD.PI.4.1.Ex, ELD.PI.4.1.Br, ELD.PI.4.5.Ex, ELD.PI.4.5.Br, ELD.PI.4.6a.Ex, ELD.PI.4.6a.Br, ELD.PI.4.7.Ex, ELD.PI.4.7.Br, ELD.PI.4.12a.Ex, ELD.PI.4.12a.Br, ELD.PII.4.1.Ex, ELD.PII.4.1.Br, ELD.PII.4.2a.Ex, ELD.PII.4.2a.Br See the California Standards section.

Text Evidence

1 Specific Vocabulary ACT

Reread the second sentence in the second paragraph. An *electron* is "a very small piece of matter that is a part of an atom; it has a negative charge." Circle the words that describe what an electron microscope can do.

2 Sentence Structure ACT

Reread the fourth sentence in the last paragraph. Underline who the pronoun *His* refers to. Circle what his photographs showed.

3 Comprehension

Sequence

Reread the last paragraph. What event happened in 1840? Underline the words that tell you. Circle the event that happened right after that.

Text Evidence

1 Specific Vocabulary

Reread the first paragraph. The word *weak* means "not strong." Underline what is being described as weak. A homophone is a word that sounds the same as another word but has a different spelling and meaning. What is a homophone for *weak?*

A homophone for *weak* is _______.

2 Sentence Structure

Reread the second sentence in the last paragraph. Circle the prepositional phrase that describes the time something happened. Underline what happened during this time.

3 Talk About It

Discuss how the two photographs of human skin are alike and how they are different.

The light microscopes you use in school are **weak** and do not show much detail. An electron microscope is a much more powerful tool, and it **allows** scientists to see things we can't see with our own eyes such as skin cells or dust mites.

The picture below is a close-up of human skin and shows the detail an electron microscope can **capture**. The more an image is magnified, the more detail you will see in the photograph. The most magnification that a photomicrograph can capture is about 2 million times the original image size.

Magnified images have helped scientists to see what causes diseases. Over the years, scientists have learned how these diseases behave. Looking through microscopes, we have even learned what is inside a cell or how a snowflake dissolves into a drop of water.

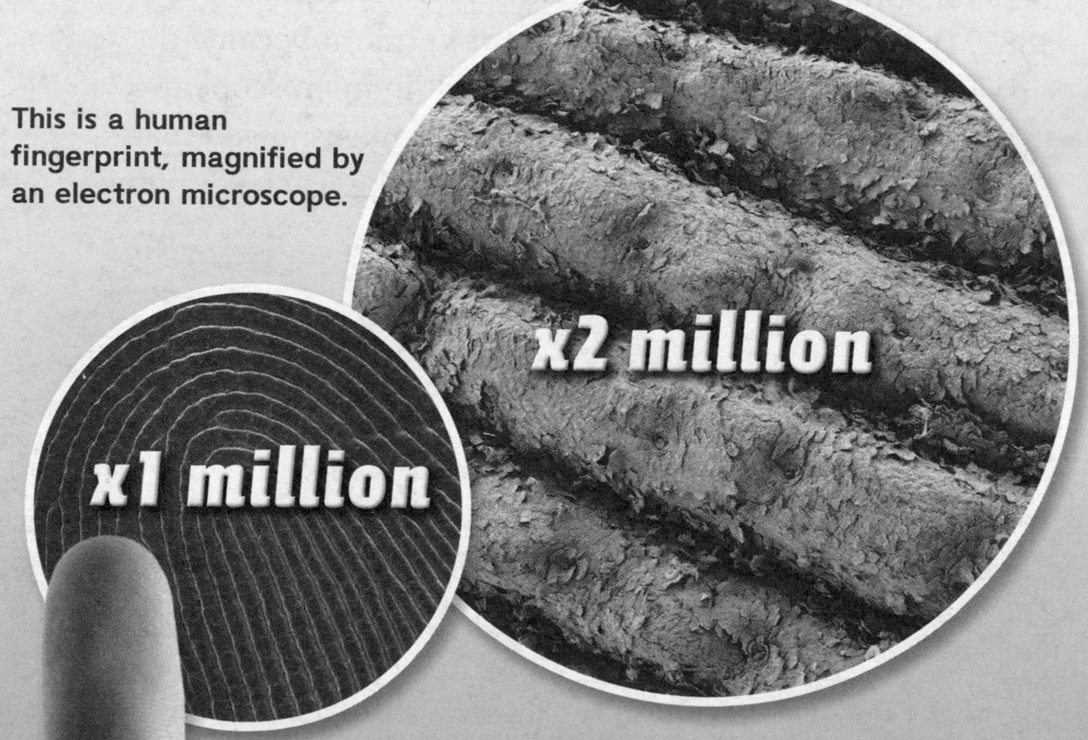

This is a human fingerprint, magnified by an electron microscope.

ELD.PI.4.1.Ex, ELD.PI.4.1.Br, ELD.PI.4.5.Ex, ELD.PI.4.5.Br, ELD.PI.4.6a.Ex, ELD.PI.4.6a.Br, ELD.PI.4.7.Ex, ELD.PI.4.7.Br, ELD.PI.4.12a.Ex, ELD.PI.4.12a.Br See the California Standards section.

When the mold on a strawberry is looked at under an electron microscope, it resembles grapes.

Scientists use electron micrographs to see how objects change over time. For example, we can look at a piece of fruit to see how it **decays**. First the fruit looks **fresh**. After a few days it begins to soften. Then **specks** of mold appear and cling to it. Days pass and eventually the fruit is covered in mold. We can see these changes under the microscope far earlier than we can see them with just our eyes.

Suppose you mingle outside on a humid day with friends. What would the sweat on your skin look like magnified? The possibilities are endless if you examine your world up close.

Make Connections

How do electron microscopes help scientists? ESSENTIAL QUESTION

What objects in your classroom would you like to see under a microscope? TEXT TO SELF

ELD.PI.4.1.Ex, ELD.PI.4.1.Br, ELD.PI.4.5.Ex, ELD.PI.4.5.Br, ELD.PI.4.6a.Ex, ELD.PI.4.6a.Br, ELD.PI.4.7.Ex, ELD.PI.4.7.Br, ELD.PI.4.12a.Ex, ELD.PI.4.12a.Br, ELD.PII.4.1.Ex, ELD.PII.4.1.Br
See the California Standards section.

Text Evidence

1 Comprehension
Sequence

Reread the first paragraph. When does fresh fruit begin to soften? Underline the words that tell you. Circle the words that tell you the last event in the sequence.

2 Specific Vocabulary ACT

Reread the fifth sentence in the first paragraph. The word *specks* means "very small spots or marks." Underline the kind of specks that appear.

3 Talk About It

Describe how electron microscopes have helped scientists. Then write about it.

____

____

____

______________________.

Respond to the Text

Partner Discussion Work with a partner. Describe what you learned about "Your World Up Close." Write the page numbers where you found text evidence.

What did you learn about electron microscopes?	Text Evidence
An electron microscope is a tool that can ____________.	Page(s): ________
Pictures taken with electron microscopes are called ____________.	Page(s): ________
In 1882, Wilson Bentley was the first person to use ____________ ________________________.	Page(s): ________

What can scientists learn using electron microscopes?	Text Evidence
Scientists can learn what causes ____________.	Page(s): ________
Scientists also study how things change over time, such as ____________ ________________________.	Page(s): ________

Group Discussion Present your answers to the class. Cite text evidence to justify your thinking. Listen to and discuss the group's opinions about your answers.

 ELD.PI.4.1.Ex, ELD.PI.4.1.Br, ELD.PI.4.3.Ex, ELD.PI.4.3.Br, ELD.PI.4.5.Ex, ELD.PI.4.5.Br, ELD.PI.4.9.Ex, ELD.PI.4.9.Br, ELD.PI.4.11a.Ex, ELD.PI.4.11a.Br, ELD.PI.4.12a.Ex, ELD.PI.4.12a.Br See the California Standards section.

Write Work with a partner. Look at your notes about "Your World Up Close." Then write your answer to the essential question. Use text evidence to support your answer. Use vocabulary words from this week's reading in your writing.

What have scientists discovered using electron microscopes?

Scientists can learn what causes diseases because ______________________.

Scientists have studied how fruit changes over time:

First the fruit is ______________________

After a few days, ______________________.

Then ______________________.

Eventually, ______________________.

COLLABORATE

Share Writing Present your writing to the class. Discuss their opinions. Think about what they have to say. Did they justify their claims? Explain why you agree or disagree with their claims.

I agree with ______________ because ______________________.

I disagree with ______________ because ______________________.

ELD.PI.4.1.Ex, ELD.PI.4.1.Br, ELD.PI.4.3.Ex, ELD.PI.4.3.Br, ELD.PI.4.5.Ex, ELD.PI.4.5.Br, ELD.PI.4.9.Ex, ELD.PI.4.9.Br, ELD.PI.4.11a.Ex, ELD.PI.4.11a.Br, ELD.PI.4.12a.Ex, ELD.PI.4.12a.Br, ELD.PII.4.1.Ex, ELD.PII.4.1.Br See the California Standards section.

Write to Sources

Take Notes About the Text **I took notes on a chart to answer the question:** ***Does the author do a good job of describing why the electron microscope is an important tool?***

pages 302–305

They are very powerful.

They can take photographs that magnify an object thousands of times its size.

Why the electron microscope is an important tool.

Magnified images have helped scientists see what causes some diseases.

Scientists are able to study how objects change over time, such as fruit spoiling.

 ELD.PI.4.1.Ex, ELD.PI.4.1.Br, ELD.PI.4.5.Ex, ELD.PI.4.5.Br, ELD.PI.4.6a.Ex, ELD.PI.4.6a.Br, ELD.PII.4.1.Ex, ELD.PII.4.1.Br See the California Standards section.

Write About the Text **I used my notes from my chart to write an opinion about the electron microscope.**

Student Model: *Opinion*

I think the author does a good job of showing that the electron microscope is an important tool. Electron microscopes are very powerful. They can take photographs that magnify an object thousands of times its actual size. Those images have helped scientists see the cause of some diseases. Scientists are also able to study how objects change over time. They have looked at fruit spoiling. I think electron microscopes give us a closer look at our world.

TALK ABOUT IT

Text Evidence

Draw a box around a sentence that comes from the notes. Does the sentence give a supporting detail of Delia's opinion?

Grammar

Underline the adjective in the second sentence. Circle the noun the adjective is describing.

Connect Ideas

Underline the fifth and sixth sentences. How can you combine the sentences into one sentence?

Your Turn

What is the most useful thing about electron microscopes? Use text evidence.

>> *Go Digital*
Write your response online. Use your editing checklist.

ELD.PI.4.1.Ex, ELD.PI.4.1.Br, ELD.PI.4.2.Ex, ELD.PI.4.2.Br, ELD.PI.4.10b.Ex, ELD.PI.4.10b.Br, ELD.PI.4.11a.Ex, ELD.PI.4.11a.Br, ELD.PI.4.12a.Ex, ELD.PI.4.12a.Br, ELD.PII.4.1.Ex, ELD.PII.4.1.Br, ELD.PII.4.6.Ex ELD.PII.4.6.Br See the California Standards section.

TALK ABOUT IT

Weekly Concept Digging Up the Past

Essential Question

How can learning about the past help you understand the present?

>> *Go Digital*

Describe what the diver in the photo is looking at. In the chart, write why studying things from the past is important.

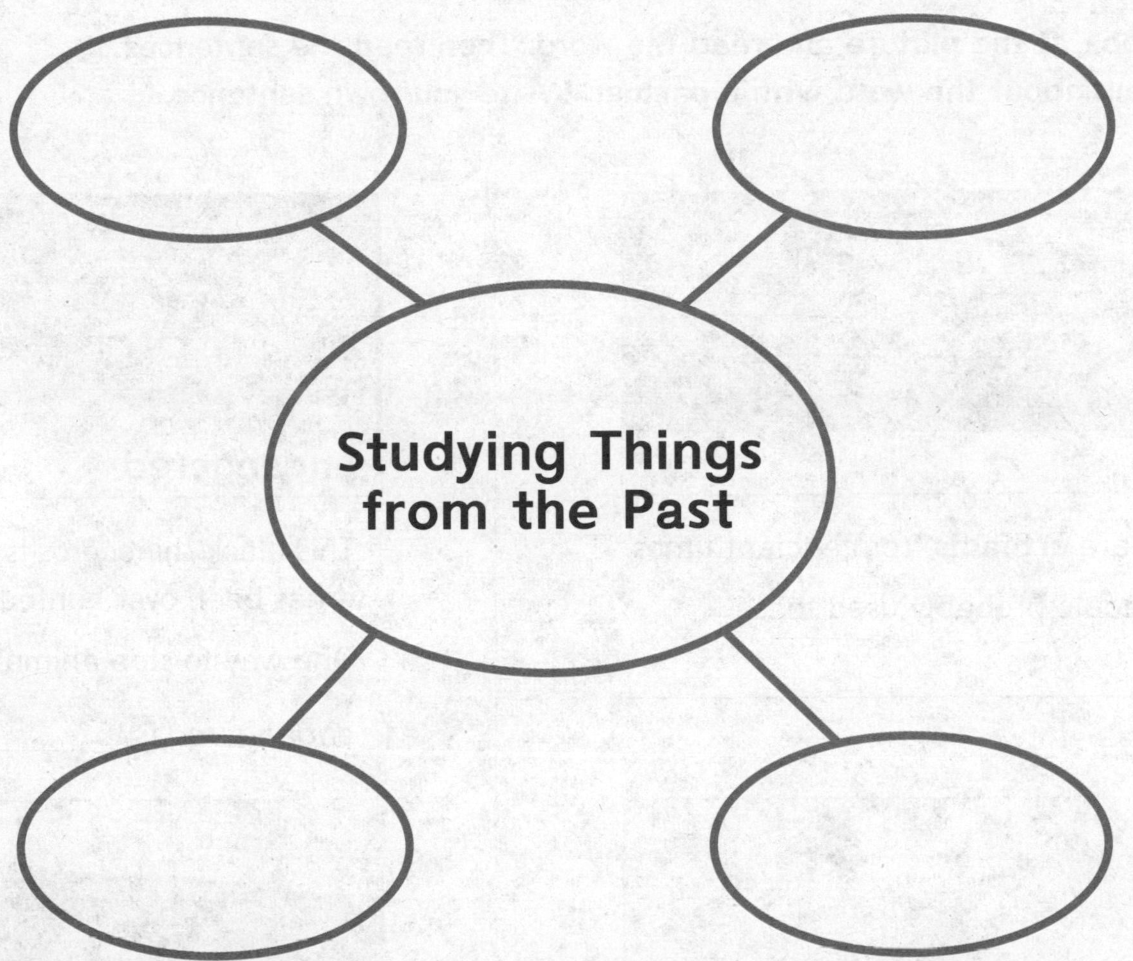

Discuss why learning about the past helps us to understand the present. Use the words from the chart. You can say:

By studying things from the past, we can learn ______________________

____.

Jeffrey Rotman/Corbis Documentary/Getty Images

ELD.PI.4.1.Ex, ELD.PI.4.1.Br, ELD.PI.4.5.Ex, ELD.PI.4.5.Br, ELD.PI.4.12a.Ex, ELD.PI.4.12a.Br See the California Standards section.

More Vocabulary

Look at the picture and read the word. Then read the sentences. Talk about the word with a partner. Write your own sentence.

artifacts

The pottery are **artifacts** from ancient times.

Long ago people probably used these *artifacts* to ______________________.

challenges

The mountain climbers face many **challenges**.

Another word for *challenges* is __________.

endangered

This black rhinoceros is **endangered** because it has been over hunted.

One way to stop animals from becoming *endangered* is to ______________________.

experienced

An **experienced** pilot will fly the plane.

Another word for *experienced* is __________.

 ELD.PI.4.1.Ex, ELD.PI.4.1.Br, ELD.PI.4.5.Ex, ELD.PI.4.5.Br, ELD.PI.4.12a.Ex, ELD.PI.4.12a.Br See the California Standards section.

expert

The teacher is an **expert** in math.

The teacher is an *expert* because she ________

______________________________________.

scarce

Water is **scarce** in the desert.

Another word for *scarce* is ________________.

Words and Phrases

Phrasal Verbs

bound for **= going to a certain place**

I am *<u>bound for</u>* *the library.*

to swap for **= trade one thing for another thing**

I am going *<u>to swap an apple for</u>* *a banana.*

Read the sentences below. Write the phrasal verb that means the same as the underlined words.

I am going <u>to trade grapes for</u> cherries.

I am going ________________ cherries.

We are <u>going to</u> the store.

We are ________________ the store.

» *Go Digital* **Add the phrasal verbs to your New Words notebook. Write a sentence to show the meaning of each.**

Text Evidence

1 Talk About It

Look at the pictures. Read the title. Talk about what you see. Write your ideas.

What does this title tell you?

____

____

______________________________.

What does the photograph show?

____

____

______________________________.

What does the illustration show?

____

____

______________________________.

Take notes as you read the story.

Shared Read Genre • Informational Article

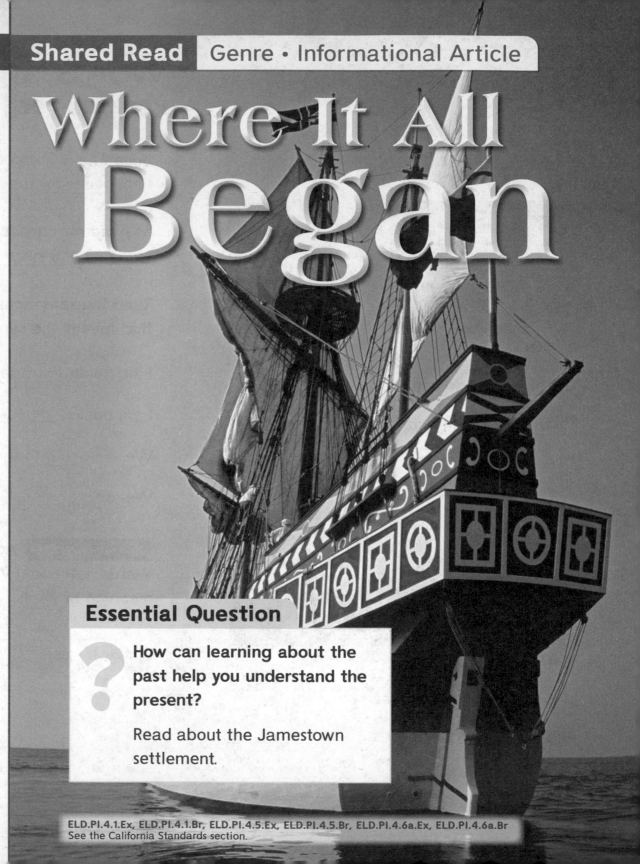

Where It All Began

Essential Question

How can learning about the past help you understand the present?

Read about the Jamestown settlement.

ELD.PI.4.1.Ex, ELD.PI.4.1.Br, ELD.PI.4.5.Ex, ELD.PI.4.5.Br, ELD.PI.4.6a.Ex, ELD.PI.4.6a.Br
See the California Standards section.

The building of the Jamestown settlement in 1607.

Take a tour of Jamestown, Virginia, the birthplace of America.

They thought they were lost. The *Susan Constant*, the *Godspeed*, and the *Discovery* had sailed from London, England, on December 20, 1606. The expedition was bound for Virginia, carrying 144 people.

Finally, on April 26, 1607, the ships sailed into Chesapeake Bay. In the words of one **voyager**, they found "fair meadows and goodly tall trees." On an island in a river, they built a fort and named it after their king, James. Jamestown would become the first successful, permanent English settlement in the New World.

The Struggle to Survive

There is a proverb that says, "Ignorance is bliss." In the case of the 104 men and boys who came ashore, this was true. They were faced with tremendous **challenges**. The water from the James River was not safe to drink, and food was **scarce**. Two weeks after the settlers arrived, 200 Indians attacked them.

Northwind Picture Archives

ELD.PI.4.1.Ex, ELD.PI.4.1.Br, ELD.PI.4.5.Ex, ELD.PI.4.5.Br, ELD.PI.4.6a.Ex, ELD.PI.4.6a.Br, ELD.PI.4.7.Ex, ELD.PI.4.7.Br, ELD.PII.4.1.Ex, ELD.PII.4.1.Br, ELD.PII.4.2a.Ex, ELD.PII.4.2a.Br

See the California Standards section.

Text Evidence

1 Sentence Structure ACT

Reread the first sentence in the first paragraph. Circle the words in the paragraph that tell who the pronoun *They* refers to. Underline the words that tell you where they were going.

2 Specific Vocabulary ACT

Reread the second paragraph. The word *voyager* means "someone who makes a long trip by ship." Circle the words that give you clues to the meaning of *voyager*. Underline what the voyagers did when they arrived.

3 Comprehension

Sequence

Reread the paragraphs. How long did it take the settlers to sail from England to Chesapeake Bay?

____

Circle the words that tell you what happened two weeks after the settlers arrived.

Text Evidence

1 Specific Vocabulary ACT

Reread the last two sentences in the first paragraph. The word *attitude* means "an opinion or feeling someone has about something." Circle the words that tell the kind of attitude John Smith thought would be dangerous for the colony.

2 Comprehension
Sequence

Reread "The Real-Life Pocahontas." Underline what happened to Pocahontas after she married John Rolfe. Circle why Pocahontas never returned home.

3 Talk About It

Discuss how Pocahontas's life was different from other Native American women of her time.

____

____

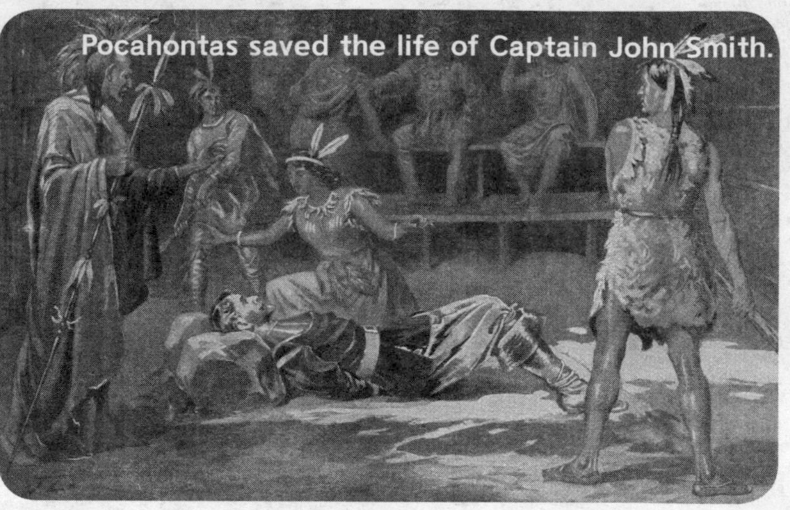

Pocahontas saved the life of Captain John Smith.

John Smith, an **experienced** military man, became head of the colony in 1608. He had been in charge of finding local tribes willing to swap food for English copper and beads. Smith was tough with both the Indians and Englishmen. "He that will not work, shall not eat," he told the colonists. Smith knew that an **attitude** of every man for himself would **endanger** the colony.

The western Chesapeake area was ruled by Chief Powhatan, who governed an empire of 14,000 Algonquian-speaking peoples. His daughter Pocahontas became a useful friend and ally to John Smith.

The Real-Life Pocahontas

Princess Matoaka was born around 1595. Her father, Chief Powhatan, called her Pocahontas. She saved John Smith's life twice, and he wrote that Pocahontas's "wit and spirit" were unequaled.

Pocahontas married a planter named John Rolfe, the first marriage in that era between an Englishman and a Native American woman. Rolfe, Pocahontas, and their son visited London. She never returned home–she fell ill aboard a ship bound for Jamestown in March 1617 and died.

ELD.PI.4.1.Ex, ELD.PI.4.1.Br, ELD.PI.4.5.Ex, ELD.PI.4.5.Br, ELD.PI.4.6a.Ex, ELD.PI.4.6a.Br, ELD.PI.4.7.Ex, ELD.PI.4.7.Br, ELD.PII.4.1.Ex, ELD.PII.4.1.Br See the California Standards section.

Ohio

Pennsylvania

New Jersey

Maryland

Delaware

West Virginia

Virginia

Jamestown

Kentucky

North Carolina

N S E W

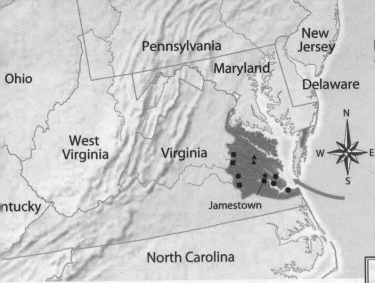

Map of Settlement of Virginia 1607–1700

MAP KEY

- Immigration (English, French, Italians, Poles, and Africans)
- Extent of European Settlement, 1700
- ● Village
- ■ Fort
- ▲ Indian Reservation
- ★ Capital

Taking a Closer Look

Archaeologists digging in Jamestown have discovered Indian **artifacts** along with English ones, evidence that Indians lived in the fort for some time. "It must have been a very close relationship," says William Kelso, an **expert** in colonial American archaeology.

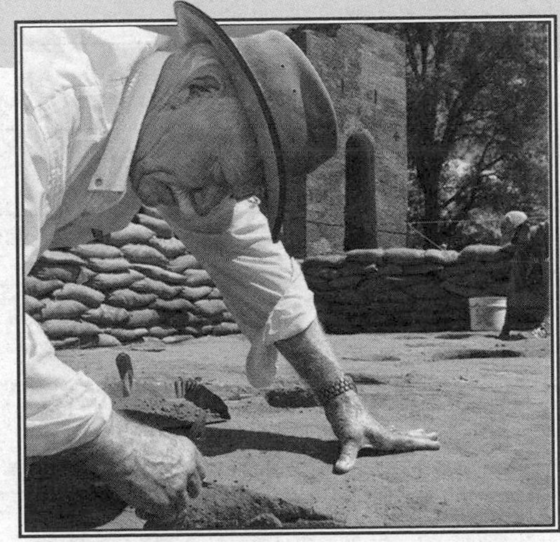

Dr. William Kelso working on the archaeological dig in Jamestown

Kelso has worked for 10 years to document this site. His team has managed to uncover more than 1 million artifacts and has mapped out the fort's shape, its foundations, and a burial ground.

Jamestown left a record of greed and war, but it was also the start of **representative** government. The settlers gave America a solid foundation to build upon.

Make Connections

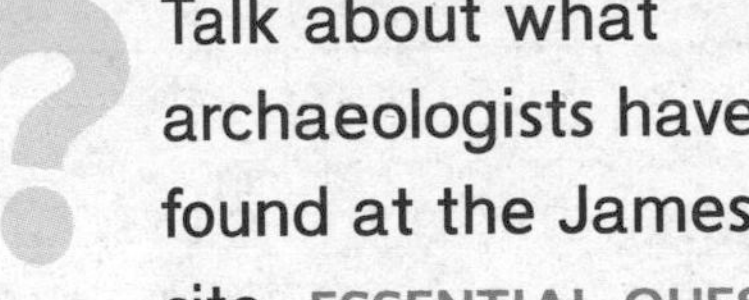

Talk about what archaeologists have found at the Jamestown site. ESSENTIAL QUESTION

What would you have liked to ask John Smith about Jamestown? TEXT TO SELF

Text Evidence

1 Sentence Structure ACT

Reread the first sentence in the first paragraph. Circle the part of the sentence that can stand on its own, or the independent clause. Circle the part of the sentence that cannot stand on its own, or the dependent clause.

2 Specific Vocabulary ACT

Reread the first sentence in the last paragraph. The word *representative* means "chosen to act or speak for others." What was representative in Jamestown? Circle the word that tells you. What did the settlers of Jamestown do for America? Underline the words that tell you.

3 Talk About It

Discuss how learning about Jamestown helps you understand the present.

ELD.PI.4.1.Ex, ELD.PI.4.1.Br, ELD.PI.4.5.Ex, ELD.PI.4.5.Br, ELD.PI.4.6a.Ex, ELD.PI.4.6a.Br, ELD.PI.4.7.Ex, ELD.PI.4.7.Br, ELD.PI.4.12a.Ex, ELD.PI.4.12a.Br See the California Standards section.

Respond to the Text

Partner Discussion **Work with a partner. Describe what you learned about "Where It All Began." Write the page numbers where you found text evidence.**

What did you learn about Jamestown's past?	**Text Evidence**
I learned that in 1607 ______________________.	Page(s): ________
The settlers built ______________________.	Page(s): ________
John Smith was ______________________.	Page(s): ________

What have archaeologists discovered about Jamestown?	**Text Evidence**
Archaeologists have found ______________, which is evidence that ______________________.	Page(s): ________
According to the text, although Jamestown left a record of ______________, it was the start of ______________________.	Page(s): ________

Group Discussion **Present your answers to the class. Cite text evidence to justify your thinking. Listen to and discuss the group's opinions about your answers.**

 ELD.PI.4.1.Ex, ELD.PI.4.1.Br, ELD.PI.4.3.Ex, ELD.PI.4.3.Br, ELD.PI.4.5.Ex, ELD.PI.4.5.Br, ELD.PI.4.9.Ex, ELD.PI.4.9.Br, ELD.PI.4.11a.Ex, ELD.PI.4.11a.Br, ELD.PI.4.12a.Ex, ELD.PI.4.12a.Br See the California Standards section.

Write **Work with a partner. Review your notes about "Where It All Began." Then write your answer to the essential question. Use text evidence to support your answer. Use vocabulary words from this week's reading in your writing.**

How does learning about Jamestown in the past help you understand the present?

Jamestown was the first ______________________________

____.

Archaeologists have uncovered artifacts that shows that ______________

____.

Jamestown had greed and war, but it was the start of ______________

______________________________________.

COLLABORATE

Share Writing **Present your writing to the class. Discuss their opinions. Think about what they have to say. Did they justify their claims? Explain why you agree or disagree with their claims.**

I agree with ____________ because ______________________________.

I disagree with ____________ because ______________________________.

ELD.PI.4.1.Ex, ELD.PI.4.1.Br, ELD.PI.4.3.Ex, ELD.PI.4.3.Br, ELD.PI.4.5.Ex, ELD.PI.4.5.Br, ELD.PI.4.9.Ex, ELD.PI.4.9.Br, ELD.PI.4.12a.Ex, ELD.PI.4.12a.Br See the California Standards section.

Write to Sources

Take Notes About the Text **I took notes on this idea web to respond to the prompt:** ***Explain the importance of John Smith to Jamestown.***

pages 314–317

Why John Smith was important to Jamestown.

- He was an experienced military man, who became the leader of the colony in 1608.
- He found tribes that would trade food for copper and beads.
- He was tough with both Indians and Englishmen.
- He made everyone work together.

Jamie Grill/Getty Images

Write About the Text I used my notes from my idea web to write a paragraph explaining the importance of John Smith to Jamestown.

Student Model: *Informative Text*

John Smith was important to the colony of Jamestown. He was an experienced military man. He became the leader of the colony in 1608. He found tribes that would trade food for copper and beads. He was tough with the Indians. He was tough with the Englishmen. He made everyone work together. He was a strong leader for the new colony.

TALK ABOUT IT

Text Evidence

Draw a box around sentence that comes from the notes. Does the sentence give a supporting detail to Byron's conclusion?

Grammar

Circle the prepositional phrase in the last sentence. What does the phrase explain?

Condense Ideas

Underline the sentences that tell who John Smith was tough with. How can you condense the two sentences into one detailed sentence?

Your Turn

COLLABORATE

Explain why Jamestown is an important archaeological site to learn about American history. Use text evidence.

>> *Go Digital*
Write your response online. Use your editing checklist.

ELD.PI.4.1.Ex, ELD.PI.4.1.Br, ELD.PI.4.2.Ex, ELD.PI.4.2.Br, ELD.PI.4.10b.Ex, ELD.PI.4.10b.Br, ELD.PI.4.12a.Ex, ELD.PI.4.12a.Br, ELD.PII.4.7.Ex ELD.PII.4.7.Br See the California Standards section.

Unit 6

Past, Present, and Future

THE BIG IDEA

How can you build on what came before?

Sean Gallup/Getty Images News/Getty Images

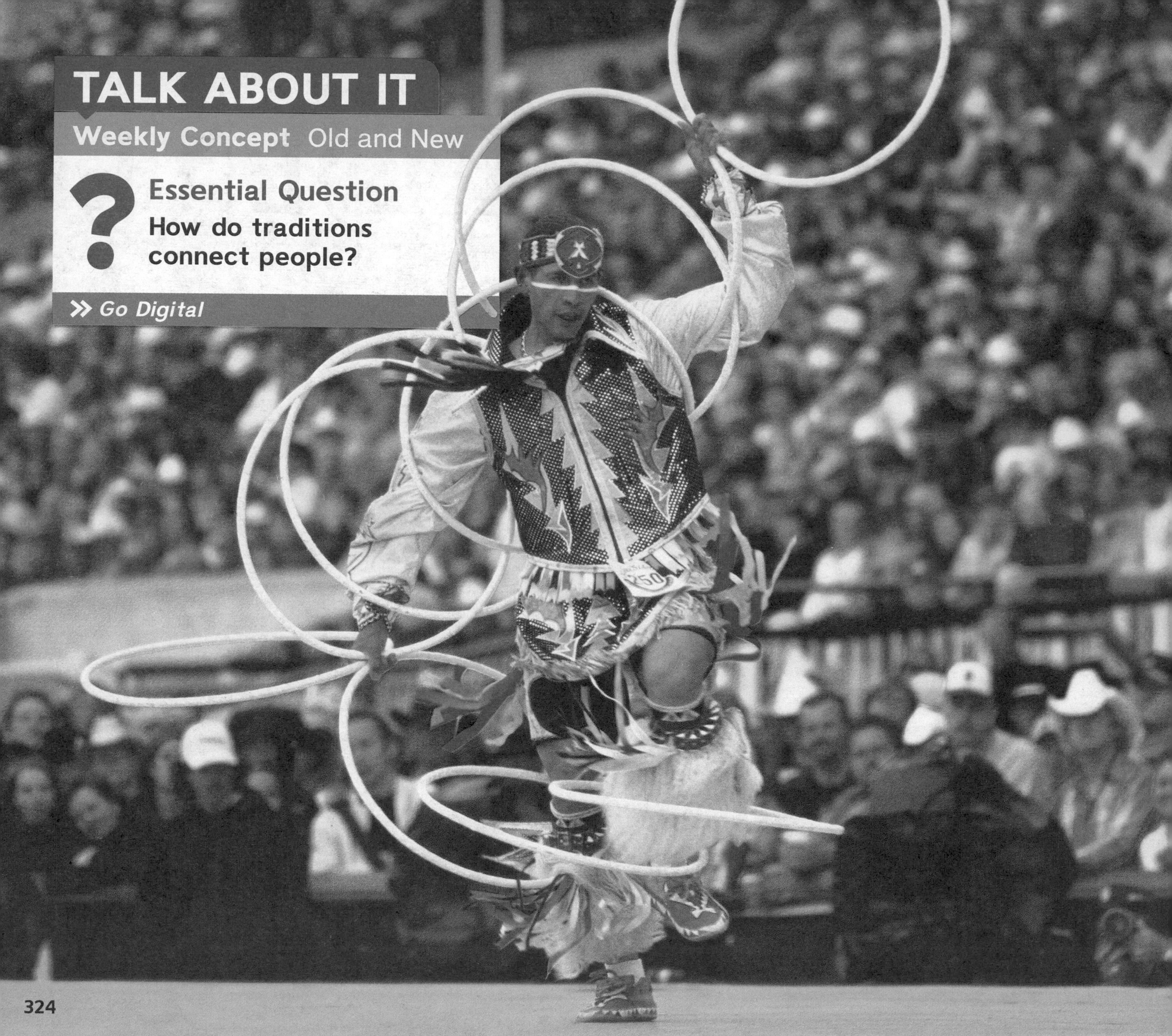

TALK ABOUT IT

Weekly Concept Old and New

Essential Question

How do traditions connect people?

» *Go Digital*

Describe the tradition the man in the photo is sharing with others. What other kinds of traditions do people share? Write the words in the chart.

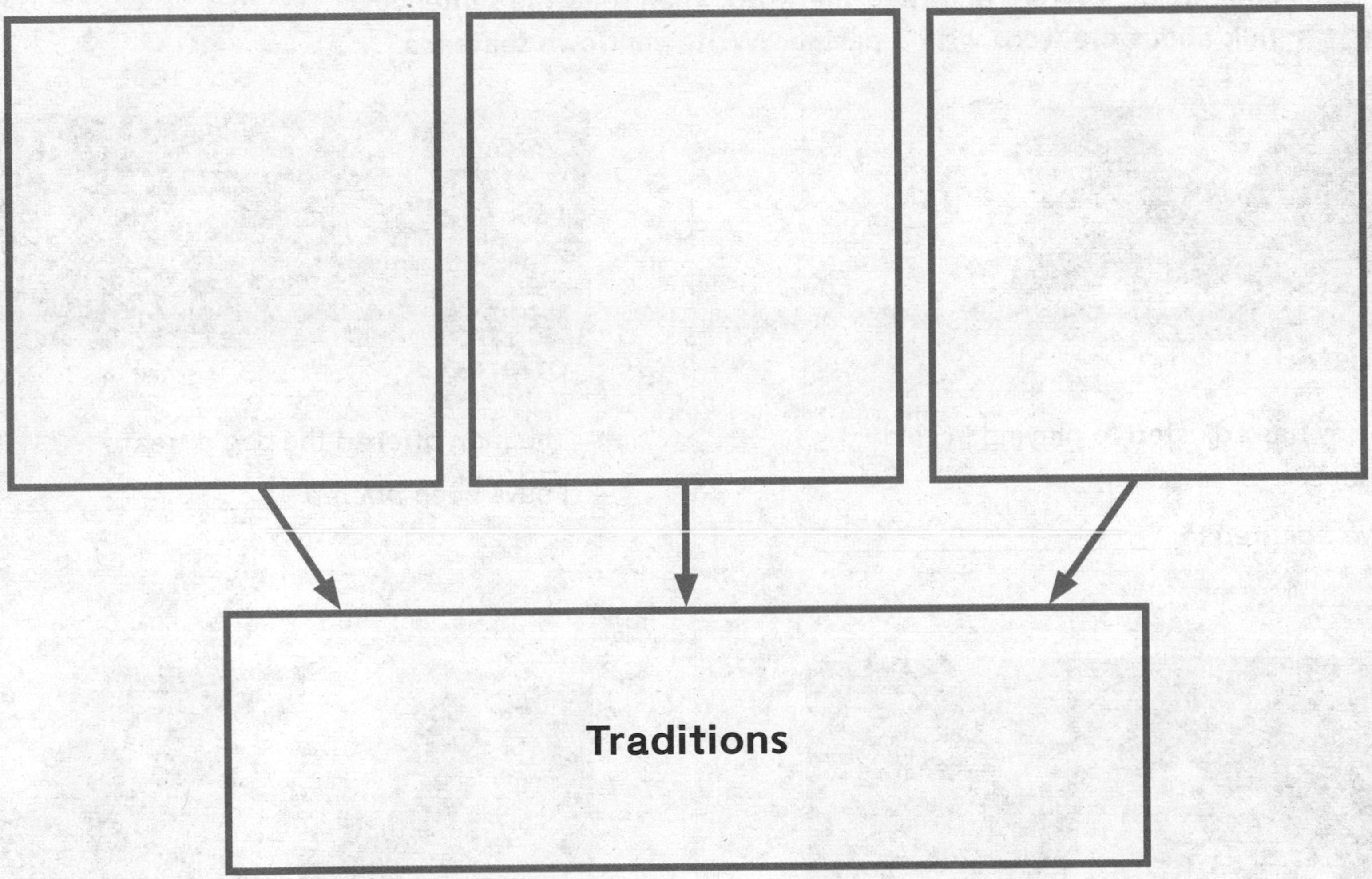

Traditions

Discuss how traditions connect people. Use the words from the chart. You can say:

Traditions such as ______________ and ___________ help to connect people because ______________________________.

Gunter Marx/Alamy Stock Photo

ELD.PI.4.1.Ex, ELD.PI.4.1.Br, ELD.PI.4.5.Ex, ELD.PI.4.5.Br, ELD.PI.4.12a.Ex, ELD.PI.4.12a.Br See the California Standards section.

More Vocabulary

Look at the picture and read the word. Then read the sentences. Talk about the word with a partner. Write your own sentence.

adjusted

The boy has **adjusted** to playing in cold weather.

I have *adjusted* to ______________________.

offered

The man **offered** the dog a treat.

I have been *offered* ____________________.

assertive

Kim is **assertive** and shares her ideas with the class.

Another word for *assertive* is ____________.

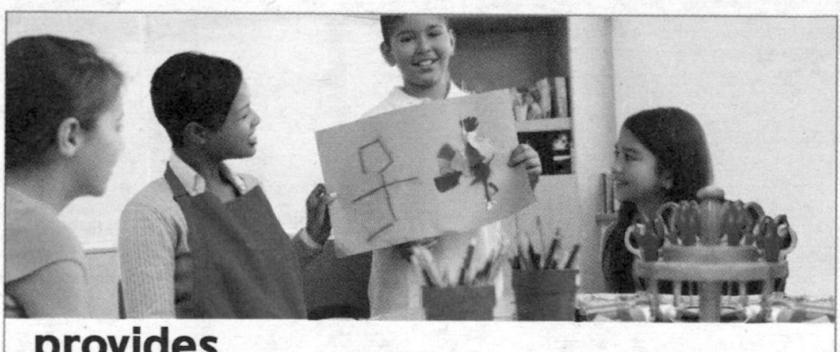

provides

The teacher **provides** paper and crayons for class projects.

Another word for *provides* is ________________.

(ul)Ariel Skelley/Blend Images/Getty Images; (ur)Huntstock/Getty Images; (bl)Tetra Images/Getty Images; (br)Monkey Business/Design Pics

 ELD.PI.4.1.Ex, ELD.PI.4.1.Br, ELD.PI.4.5.Ex, ELD.PI.4.5.Br, ELD.PI.4.12a.Ex, ELD.PI.4.12a.Br See the California Standards section.

strength

The athlete has a lot of **strength**.

You need *strength* to ________________.

transport

School buses **transport** students to school.

Another word for *transport* is ____________.

Words and Phrases
Subordinate Conjunctions: *as, that*

The subordinate conjunctions *as* and *that* connect two ideas.

The word *as* can mean "when or while."
My friend waved as she walked by.

The word *that* can be used to show a reason or a cause.
I am sorry that you lost your dog.

Read the sentences below. Write the conjunction *as* or *that* in each sentence.

I am happy ____________ we are friends.

Gina sang ____________ she washed the dishes.

It was a game he played ____________ a child.

The student had a math problem ____________ was hard to solve.

» Go Digital **Add these subordinate conjunctions to your New Words notebook. Write a sentence to show the meaning of each.**

Text Evidence

COLLABORATE

1 Talk About It

Look at the picture. Read the title. Talk about what you see. Write your ideas.

What does this title tell you?

____

____

____

______________________________.

Describe what you see in the picture.

____

____

____

______________________________.

Take notes as you read the story.

Shared Read Genre • Historical Fiction

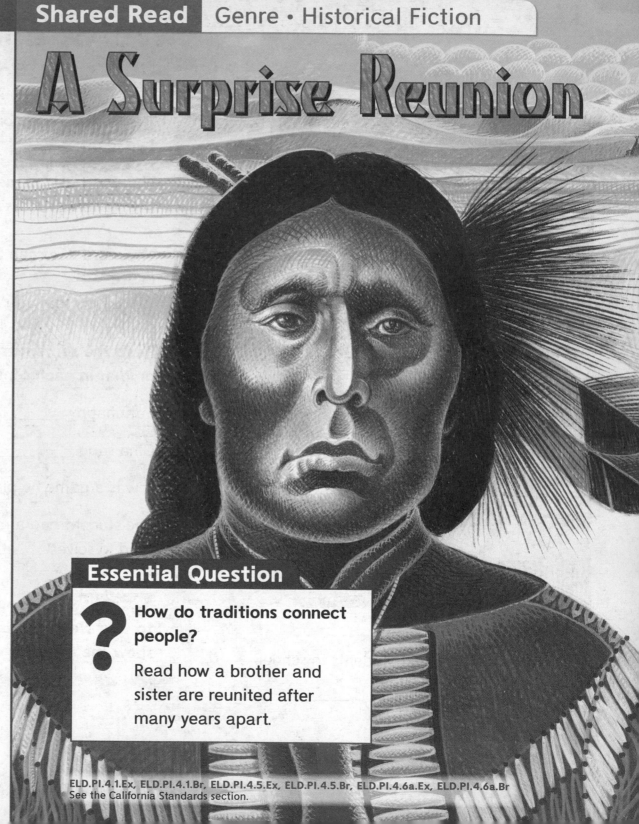

A Surprise Reunion

Essential Question

How do traditions connect people?

Read how a brother and sister are reunited after many years apart.

ELD.PI.4.1.Ex, ELD.PI.4.1.Br, ELD.PI.4.5.Ex, ELD.PI.4.5.Br, ELD.PI.4.6a.Ex, ELD.PI.4.6a.Br
See the California Standards section.

Chief Cameahwait looked with intensity across the Shoshone camp. The tribe prepared for the Rabbit Dance as warriors oiled their leather costumes. The dance was done to honor the rabbit as an important food source. The Shoshone had used traditions such as this dance since the beginning of time to mark special occasions and remember their ancestors.

In the distance laughing children were playing with a ball made from rawhide. They rolled the ball into a circle drawn in the dust. If the ball rolled outside the circle, the child must forfeit his or her turn. Cameahwait smiled as he remembered the games he had played as a child.

But Cameahwait grimaced beneath his smile. He felt a dull pain in his stomach for his little sister. She had been **snatched** from the camp during a raid long ago. He despised those who had taken her. He closed his eyes and pictured the games they had played together. She had been scrawny and demanding and had an irritating habit of following him everywhere, he remembered. He missed her **assertive** manner and her constant questions. What had become of her?

David McCall Johnston

ELD.PI.4.1.Ex, ELD.PI.4.1.Br, ELD.PI.4.5.Ex, ELD.PI.4.5.Br, ELD.PI.4.6a.Ex, ELD.PI.4.6a.Br, ELD.PI.4.7.Ex, ELD.PI.4.7.Br, ELD.PI.4.12a.Ex, ELD.PI.4.12a.Br See the California Standards section.

Text Evidence

1 Sentence Structure ACT

Reread the first sentence in the first paragraph. Circle the prepositional phrase in the sentence that tells where Cameahwait looked.

2 Comprehension Theme

Reread the first paragraph. Circle the words that tell you what the tribe is doing. Why do the Shoshone follow certain traditions?

____

____

______________________________.

3 Specific Vocabulary ACT

Reread the third sentence in the last paragraph. The word *snatched* in this sentence means "taken by force." Circle the words that help tell the meaning of *snatched*. Underline who was snatched from the camp long ago.

Text Evidence

1 Specific Vocabulary ACT

Reread the second sentence in the first paragraph. The phrase *came back to reality* means "thinking about something from the past and then returning your thoughts to the present." What was Cameahwait thinking about from the past?

____

______________________________.

2 Sentence Structure ACT

Reread the sixth sentence in the second paragraph. Who does the pronoun *He* refer to? Find the name of the person in the paragraph and circle it.

3 Talk About It

Reread the second paragraph. Circle the favor Captain Lewis asked Cameahwait for. Then underline how Lewis returned the favor.

"It is time to ride," Hawk-That-Soars said, interrupting his thoughts. Cameahwait **came back to reality**, turned, and mounted his horse.

A man named Captain Lewis had approached the Shoshone days before. Cameahwait knew that Lewis had come in peace, and so he welcomed him and his party. Lewis told the Shoshone his story. He explained that he was part of a company with a mission: he was to explore the land that stretched from the Missouri River to the great ocean. He then asked the chief for a favor. He explained that the rest of his party was waiting at the river with a supply boat. Lewis needed the **strength** and endurance of the Shoshone horses to help **transport** the supplies across the difficult land. In return Lewis **offered** the Shoshone food and other goods.

Cameahwait's party arrived at Lewis's camp. There he met Captain Clark.

"Let's sit and discuss how we may help each other," said Clark. He led the men inside a large tent. Buffalo blankets were spread all around. As they settled inside, Lewis addressed the chief. "We travel with a woman who knows your language."

A slender woman with long, dark braids entered the tent. Her eyes **adjusted** to the dim light filtered through the thick cloth. She nodded to the chief. "I am Sacagawea," she said.

ELD.PI.4.1.Ex, ELD.PI.4.1.Br, ELD.PI.4.5.Ex, ELD.PI.4.5.Br, ELD.PI.4.6a.Ex, ELD.PI.4.6a.Br, ELD.PI.4.8.Ex, ELD.PI.4.8.Br, ELD.PI.4.12a.Ex, ELD.PI.4.12a.Br, ELD.PII.4.2a.Ex, ELD.PII.4.2a.Br, See the California Standards section.

David McCall Johnston

Cameahwait could not believe his eyes! He examined the features of her face. He watched as her **expression** slowly changed. He immediately knew this was the same sweet face of his lost sister.

Sacagawea quickly ran to him. Tears filled her dark eyes. The pain and sadness that Cameahwait had carried over the years retreated to a forgotten place.

"My brother!" she cried. "Is it really you? How long has it been?"

Lewis and Clark were happy to have been unwitting partners in this reunion. Chief Cameahwait promised them he would **provide** whatever help and resources they needed.

"You have given me a great gift," Cameahwait told them. "You have reunited me with my beloved sister. Our people will sing and tell stories so that all may remember and honor this day for generations to come."

Make Connections

? How do traditions and the past connect the chief and his sister? ESSENTIAL QUESTION

What traditions do you honor in your family? TEXT TO SELF

ELD.PI.4.1.Ex, ELD.PI.4.1.Br, ELD.PI.4.5.Ex, ELD.PI.4.5.Br, ELD.PI.4.6a.Ex, ELD.PI.4.6a.Br, ELD.PI.4.7.Ex, ELD.PI.4.7.Br, ELD.PI.4.12a.Ex, ELD.PI.4.12a.Br, ELD.PII.4.2a.Ex, ELD.PII.4.2a.Br, See the California Standards section.

Text Evidence

1 Specific Vocabulary ACT

Reread the first paragraph. The word *expression* means "the look on a person's face that shows how she or he is thinking or feeling." Circle the word that tells you how Sacagawea's expression changed. Underline the words that tell what Cameahwait learned while looking at Sacagawea's expression.

2 Sentence Structure ACT

Reread the fourth paragraph. Who does the pronoun *them* refer to? Find the nouns in the paragraph and draw a box around them.

3 Comprehension Theme

Reread the last paragraph. Underline the words that tell you why the Shoshone will honor that day in the future. Circle the words that tell what the Shoshone will do to honor that day.

Respond to the Text

Partner Discussion **Work with a partner. Describe what you learned about "A Surprise Reunion." Write the page numbers where you found text evidence.**

	Text Evidence
What did you learn about the Shoshone?	
The Shoshone honored the rabbit because ______________.	Page(s): ________
The Shoshone traditions mark ______________ and ______________.	Page(s): ________
Cameahwait had not seen his sister in a long time because ______________.	Page(s): ________

	Text Evidence
What happened when the Shoshone visited Lewis and Clark's camp?	
The Shoshone went to the camp because ______________ ______________.	Page(s): ________
Cameahwait knew immediately that Sacagawea was ______________.	Page(s): ________

Group Discussion **Present your answers to the class. Cite text evidence to justify your thinking. Listen to and discuss the group's opinions about your answers.**

 ELD.PI.4.1.Ex, ELD.PI.4.1.Br, ELD.PI.4.3.Ex, ELD.PI.4.3.Br, ELD.PI.4.5.Ex, ELD.PI.4.5.Br, ELD.PI.4.9.Ex, ELD.PI.4.9.Br, ELD.PI.4.11a.Ex, ELD.PI.4.11a.Br, ELD.PI.4.12a.Ex, ELD.PI.4.12a.Br See the California Standards section.

Write **Work with a partner. Review your notes about "A Surprise Reunion." Then write your answer to the essential question. Use text evidence to support your answer. Use vocabulary words from this week's reading in your writing.**

Why did the Shoshone want to make a tradition of the day Sacagawea and Chief Cameahwait reunited?

Chief Cameahwait and Sacagawea are ____________________ and ____________________________________.

They have not seen each other for ____________________.

The Shoshone will celebrate that day for many generations by ____________ ____________________________________.

COLLABORATE

Share Writing **Present your writing to the class. Discuss their opinions. Think about what they have to say. Did they justify their claims? Explain why you agree or disagree with their claims.**

I agree with ______________ because ______________.

I disagree with______________ because ______________.

ELD.PI.4.1.Ex, ELD.PI.4.1.Br, ELD.PI.4.3.Ex, ELD.PI.4.3.Br, ELD.PI.4.5.Ex, ELD.PI.4.5.Br, ELD.PI.4.9.Ex, ELD.PI.4.9.Br, ELD.PI.4.11a.Ex, ELD.PI.4.11a.Br, ELD.PI.4.12a.Ex, ELD.PI.4.12a.Br See the California Standards section.

Write to Sources

pages 328–331

Take Notes About the Text I took notes on a chart about the story to help me respond to the prompt: ***Write a dialogue between Cameahwait and his sister, Sacagawea, when they were children.***

Cameahwait watches the children play a ball game.

↓

He painfully remembers his little sister being snatched from the camp.

↓

He pictures them playing games.

↓

He misses her constant questions and assertive manner.

 ELD.PI.4.1.Ex, ELD.PI.4.1.Br, ELD.PI.4.5.Ex, ELD.PI.4.5.Br, ELD.PI.4.6a.Ex, ELD.PI.4.6a.Br, ELD.PII.4.1.Ex, ELD.PII.4.1.Br See the California Standards section.

Write About the Text **I used notes from my chart to write a dialogue between Cameahwait and Sacagawea when they were children.**

Student Model: *Narrative Text*

"Cameahwait! Wait for me!" Sacagawea shouted at her brother.

"I'm playing ball with my friends right now," Cameahwait said.

"Can I play, too?" Sacagawea asked. "Will you show me how to play?"

Cameahwait sighed loudly. He smiled. "Okay, let me show you how to play. But you must watch carefully."

"Thanks, big brother!" Sacagawea said. "You're the best!"

TALK ABOUT IT

Text Evidence

Draw a box around a sentence that comes from the notes. How is the dialogue different than the sentence in the notes?

Grammar

Circle the adverbs in the fourth paragraph. Underline the verb that each adverb modifies.

Connect Ideas

Underline the dialogue in the fourth paragraph. How can you combine the two sentences into one sentence?

Your Turn

Write a dialogue between Chief Cameahwait and Sacagawea after their reunion.

>> *Go Digital*
Write your response online. Use your editing checklist.

ELD.PI.4.1.Ex, ELD.PI.4.1.Br, ELD.PI.4.2.Ex, ELD.PI.4.2.Br, ELD.PI.4.5.Ex, ELD.PI.4.5.Br, ELD.PI.4.6a.Ex, ELD.PI.4.6a.Br, ELD.PI.4.12a.Ex, ELD.PI.4.12a.Br, ELD.PII.4.6.Ex, ELD.PII.4.6.Br See the California Standards section.

TALK ABOUT IT

Weekly Concept Notes from the Past

Essential Question

Why is it important to keep a record of the past?

>> *Go Digital*

Describe the photo of the family. Why is the photo an important record of this family's past? Write your ideas in the web.

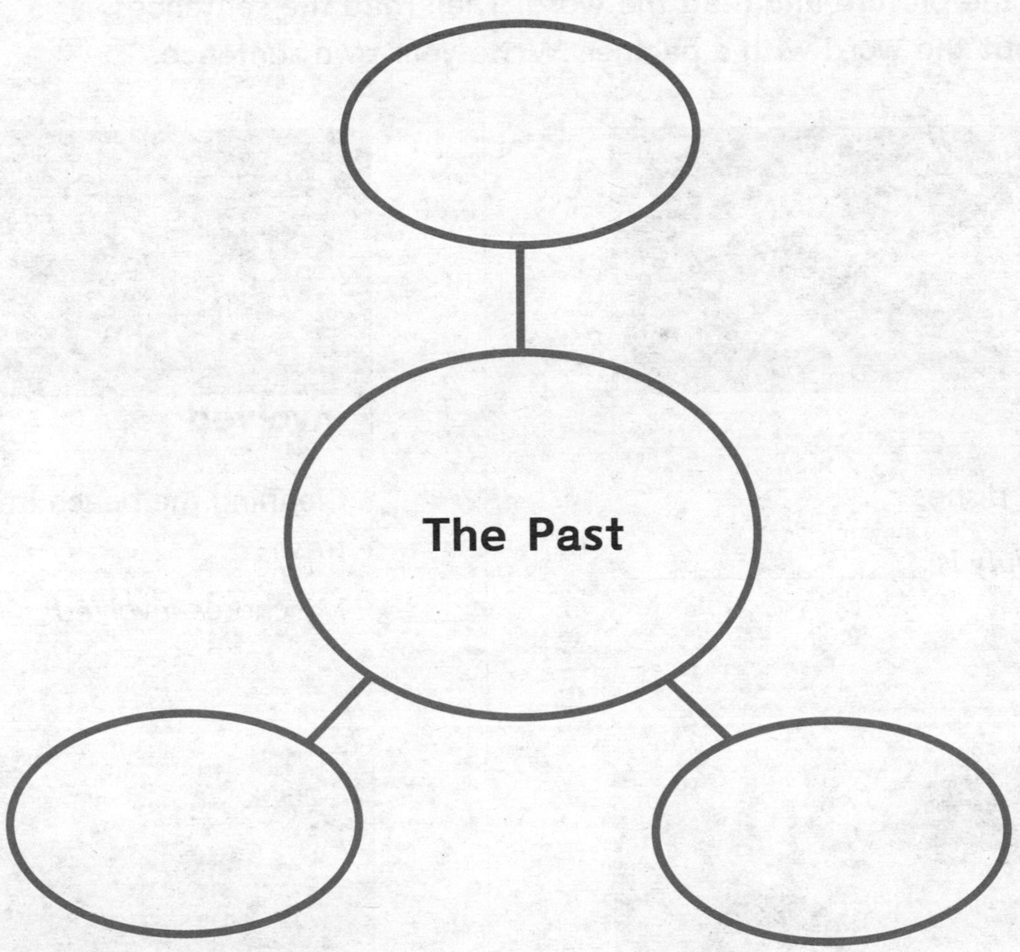

Discuss why it is important to keep a record of the past. Use the words from the web. You can say:

By keeping a record of the past you can ________________.

It is important to keep a record of the past because ____________.

ELD.PI.4.1.Ex, ELD.PI.4.1.Br, ELD.PI.4.5.Ex, ELD.PI.4.5.Br, ELD.PI.4.12a.Ex, ELD.PI.4.12a.Br See the California Standards section.

More Vocabulary

Look at the picture and read the word. Then read the sentences. Talk about the word with a partner. Write your own sentence.

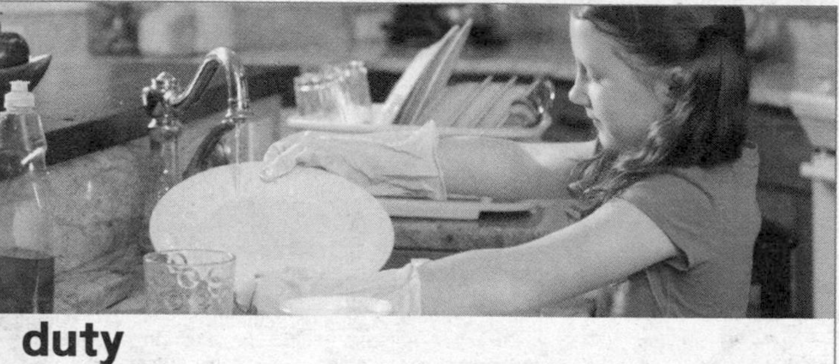

duty

My **duty** is to wash dishes.

Another word for *duty* is ________________.

escape

The penguin runs fast to **escape** its predator.

Another word for *escape* is ______________.

involved

Cleaning the beach **involved** picking up trash.

My chores *involved* ____________________.

journey

The ship made a **journey** across the ocean.

Another word for *journey* is ________________.

(ul)David Sucsy/E+/Getty Images; (ur)Chris Sattlberger/Getty Images; (bl)Rosemary Calvert/Photographer's Choice RF/Getty Images; (br)Ian Coles

plantation

Farmers grow crops on the **plantation**.

Another word for a *plantation* is a ________.

seek

They **seek** a friendly pet to bring home.

People *seek* pets that are ____________.

Words and Phrases

Prepositional Phrases

Prepositional phrases can show location

at **= in a place or a position**
We did our homework at the library.

through **= to go in one side and go out the other side**
I walked through the door.

Read the sentences below. Write the correct preposition for each sentence.

I was ____________ the beach.

I ran ____________ the field.

We walked ____________ the woods.

We ate our lunch ____________ the park.

» Go Digital **Add the words *at* and *through* to your New Words notebook. Write a sentence to show the meaning of each.**

(t)Gail Shumway/Getty Images; (b)kali9/E+/Getty Images

Text Evidence

1 Talk About It

Look at the picture. Read the title. Talk about what you see. Write your ideas.

What does this title tell you?

____

____

____

______________________________.

What is the boy in the picture writing about in his diary?

____

____

____

______________________________.

Take notes as you read the story.

Shared Read Genre • Historical Fiction

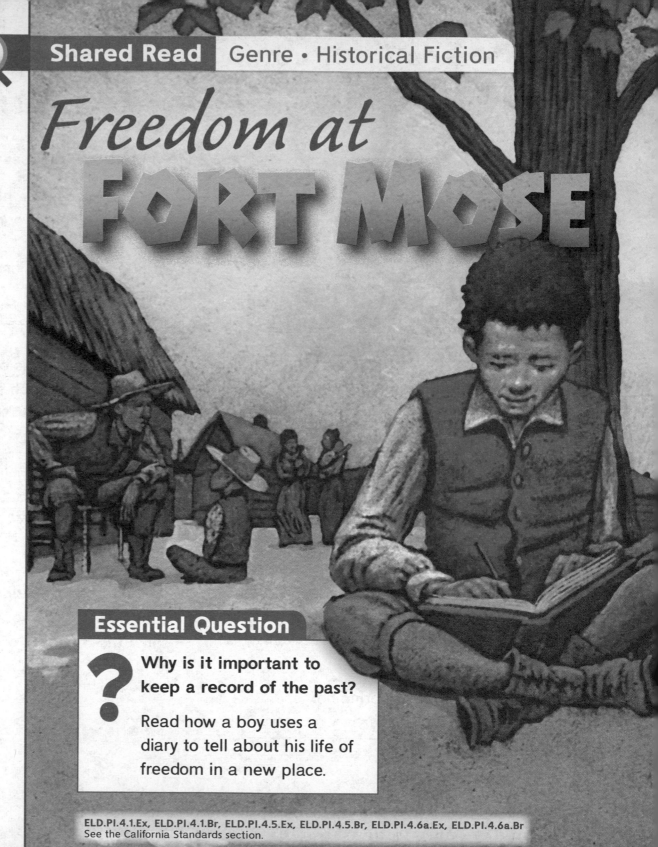

Freedom at FORT MOSE

Essential Question

Why is it important to keep a record of the past?

Read how a boy uses a diary to tell about his life of freedom in a new place.

ELD.PI.4.1.Ex, ELD.PI.4.1.Br, ELD.PI.4.5.Ex, ELD.PI.4.5.Br, ELD.PI.4.6a.Ex, ELD.PI.4.6a.Br
See the California Standards section.

By September of 1754, twelve-year-old Lucius Jackson and his family had been living at Fort Mose in St. Augustine, Florida, for a year. They were part of a group who had **escaped** from a **plantation** in South Carolina. They had heard that Fort Mose was a place of refuge for runaways. Over the years many people were willing to **endure** the treacherous **journey** there in return for the promise of freedom. During his time at Fort Mose, Lucius kept a diary to record what happened there.

17th September 1754

It has been raining for more than a week now. This weather reminds me of my days learning to read and write back in Charleston. When the rains came we couldn't work in the fields, and we were forced to stay in the cabins. We knew that Mr. Slocum, the landowner, detested getting his boots wet so he rarely came to check on us. He thought that all we knew were work and obedience. Miss Celia took a great risk writing letters and words on the dirt floor of the cabin for us children to learn. She said that, as the eldest member in our cabin, it was a risk she was willing to take. Learning to read was easy for me because I was so happy to learn how to turn letters into words and words into ideas. I believe that reading is a gift that cannot be measured. Mr. Samuel Canter believes this, too. He is a farmer who lives near us and who gave me this fine diary. He said, "You are doing a good thing, Lucius. In years to come people can read about this place and understand what we have risked to gain our freedom."

Neil Shigley

ELD.PI.4.1.Ex, ELD.PI.4.1.Br, ELD.PI.4.5.Ex, ELD.PI.4.5.Br, ELD.PI.4.6a.Ex, ELD.PI.4.6a.Br, ELD.PI.4.7.Ex, ELD.PI.4.7.Br, ELD.PI.4.12a.Ex, ELD.PI.4.12a.Br See the California Standards section.

Text Evidence

1 Specific Vocabulary ACT

Reread the first paragraph. The word *endure* means "to be in a difficult situation for a long time and not complain about it." Underline why people were willing to endure a treacherous journey.

2 Sentence Structure ACT

Reread the third sentence in the second paragraph. Underline the independent clauses. Circle the word that connects the two clauses.

3 Comprehension

Theme

Reread the last sentence in the last paragraph. Why did Mr. Canter say it was important for Lucius to write about his experiences?

____

____

____

Text Evidence

1 Specific Vocabulary ACT

Reread the third sentence in the first paragraph. The phrase *cannot let down our guard* means "to be aware of everything around them to prevent any danger." Underline why the people at Fort Mose cannot let down their guard.

2 Sentence Structure ACT

Reread the second sentence in the third paragraph. What does the pronoun *they* refer to? Underline the noun.

COLLABORATE

3 Talk About It

Reread the diary entry for October 8, 1754. Describe the sequence of events that Lucius writes about. Then number the paragraphs in the order the events happened.

8th October 1754

Last night I got to go on patrol with my father! My **duty involved** walking along the wall of the fort with him looking and listening for anything unusual. It has been a while since we came under attack, but we **cannot let down our guard.** We also listen for any people who may be coming here to **seek** freedom, as we did about one year ago.

While on patrol I thought about the night my family came to Fort Mose and how scared but hopeful all of us felt as we entered through the big heavy gates.

I must stop writing now as it is my turn today to help gather palm fronds, which we lay out in the sun to dry. Once they are dried, they can be used to repair older huts and to build new ones. Each week more people come to the fort. Our priest, Father de Las Casas, keeps the records, and he tells us that there are almost a hundred people now.

ELD.PI.4.1.Ex, ELD.PI.4.1.Br, ELD.PI.4.5.Ex, ELD.PI.4.5.Br, ELD.PI.4.6a.Ex, ELD.PI.4.6a.Br, ELD.PI.4.8.Ex, ELD.PI.4.8.Br, ELD.PI.4.12a.Ex, ELD.PI.4.12a.Br, ELD.PII.4.1.Ex, ELD.PII.4.1.Br
See the California Standards section.

26th October 1754

Last week a new family arrived all the way from Virginia and, like everyone else, they arrived almost starved and weak beyond belief. My mother helped the family by giving them clean clothes to replace the ones they had been wearing, and their old ones were quickly discarded. The day after they arrived, I tried to talk to the boy who is about my age, but he ignored me.

The next day, I tried again to speak to the boy whose name is Will. I showed him this diary and explained that it depicts as **accurately** as possible our life at Fort Mose and the people who come here. He seemed surprised and asked, "You know how to read and write?"

"Yes," I told him. He looked at me without speaking, but I could see a question in his eyes. "Do you want to learn?" I asked him.

"Is it not dangerous?" he asked quietly, looking around to see if anyone could hear us.

I smiled, remembering how long it took me to understand freedom and what it meant.

"Will," I said to my new friend, "here at Fort Mose, you are free to learn, and I am free to teach you."

We began our lessons right away.

Make Connections

? Talk about why diaries like Lucius Jackson's represent an important record of the past. ESSENTIAL QUESTION

If you could read a diary from any era in the past, what time period would you choose? Why? TEXT TO SELF

Neil Shigley

ELD.PI.4.1.Ex, ELD.PI.4.1.Br, ELD.PI.4.5.Ex, ELD.PI.4.5.Br, ELD.PI.4.6a.Ex, ELD.PI.4.6a.Br, ELD.PI.4.7.Ex, ELD.PI.4.7.Br, ELD.PI.4.12a.Ex, ELD.PI.4.12a.Br See the California Standards section.

Text Evidence

1 Sentence Structure ACT

Reread the first sentence in the first paragraph. Underline the independent clauses. Circle the dependent clause that cannot stand on its own.

2 Specific Vocabulary ACT

Reread the second sentence in the second paragraph. The word *accurately* in this sentence means "in a way that shows what is true." Underline what Lucius has done as accurately as possible.

3 Comprehension

Theme

Reread the last three paragraphs. What is Lucius's understanding of freedom in these paragraphs?

____

____

____

______________________________.

Respond to the Text

Partner Discussion **Work with a partner. Describe what you learned about "Freedom at Fort Mose." Write the page numbers where you found text evidence.**

What did you learn about Lucius's life in South Carolina?	**Text Evidence**
I read Lucius and his family escaped the plantation because ______________________.	Page(s): ________
Miss Celia took a risk in teaching people how to read and write because ______________.	Page(s): ________
Mr. Samuel Canter gave Lucius the diary because ______________________.	Page(s): ________

What did you learn about Lucius's life at Fort Mose in Florida?	**Text Evidence**
Fort Mose was a refuge for runaways because ______________.	Page(s): ________
Lucius and his father patrol the fort because ______________.	Page(s): ________
People at Fort Mose use palm fronds to ______________.	Page(s): ________
Lucius learned what freedom meant at Fort Mose so he ________.	Page(s): ________

Group Discussion **Present your answers to the class. Cite text evidence to justify your thinking. Listen to and discuss the group's opinions about your answers.**

ELD.PI.4.1.Ex, ELD.PI.4.1.Br, ELD.PI.4.3.Ex, ELD.PI.4.3.Br, ELD.PI.4.5.Ex, ELD.PI.4.5.Br, ELD.PI.4.9.Ex, ELD.PI.4.9.Br, ELD.PI.4.11a.Ex, ELD.PI.4.11a.Br, ELD.PI.4.12a.Ex, ELD.PI.4.12a.Br See the California Standards section.

Write Work with a partner. Review your notes about "Freedom at Fort Mose." Then write your answer to the essential question. Use text evidence to support your answer. Use vocabulary words from this week's reading in your writing.

Why is Lucius's diary an important record of the past?

Based on the story, Lucius wrote about life on the plantation in South Carolina

because ____

____

____.

The things Lucius wrote about his life at Fort Mose will help people understand

that ____

____

____.

COLLABORATE

Share Writing Present your writing to the class. Discuss their opinions. Think about what they have to say. Did they justify their claims? Explain why you agree or disagree with their claims.

I agree with ______________ because ______________________________.

I disagree with ______________ because ______________________________.

ELD.PI.4.1.Ex, ELD.PI.4.1.Br, ELD.PI.4.3.Ex, ELD.PI.4.3.Br, ELD.PI.4.5.Ex, ELD.PI.4.5.Br, ELD.PI.4.9.Ex, ELD.PI.4.9.Br, ELD.PI.4.10b.Ex, ELD.PI.4.10b.Br, ELD.PI.4.11a.Ex, ELD.PI.4.11a.Br, ELD.PI.4.12a.Ex, ELD.PI.4.12a.Br See the California Standards section.

Write to Sources

Take Notes About the Text I took notes about the story on a chart to respond to the prompt: ***Write a diary entry from Will's point of view. Describe how he felt about meeting Lucius.***

pages 340–343

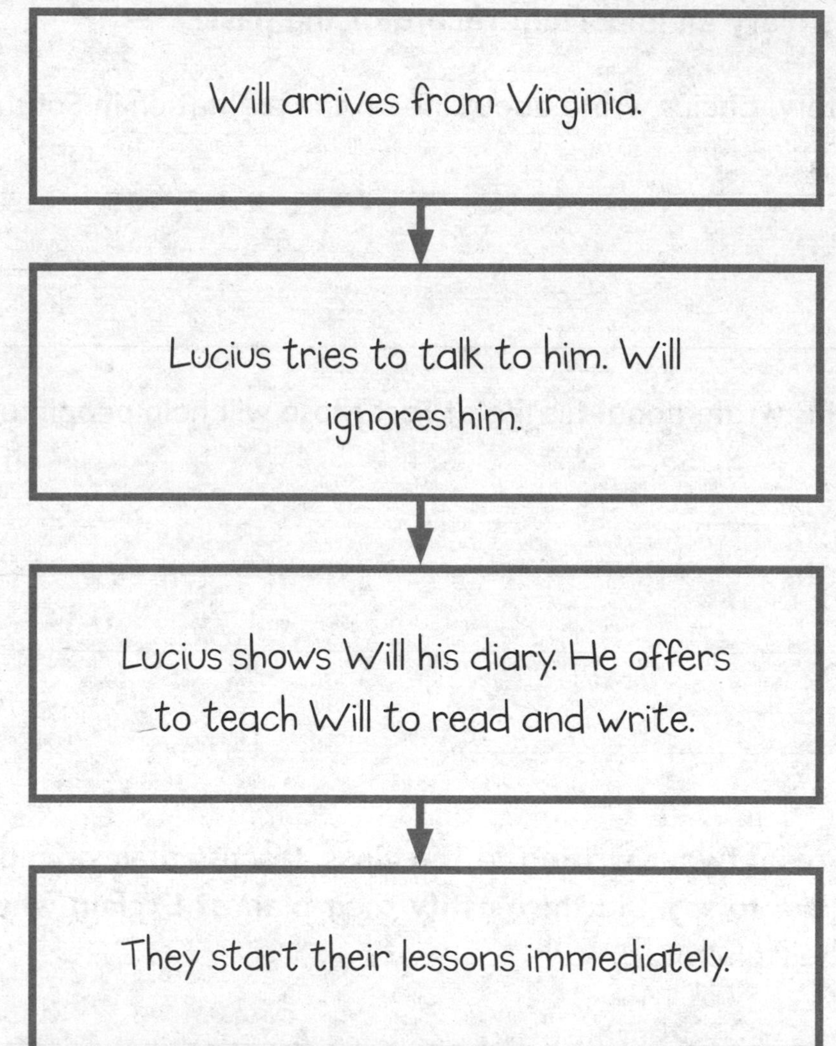

lafIor/iStock/360/Getty Images

 ELD.PI.4.1.Ex, ELD.PI.4.1.Br, ELD.PI.4.5.Ex, ELD.PI.4.5.Br, ELD.PI.4.6a.Ex, ELD.PI.4.6a.Br, ELD.PII.4.1.Ex, ELD.PII.4.1.Br See the California Standards section.

Will arrives from Virginia.
Lucius tries to talk to him. Will ignores him.
Lucius shows Will his diary. He offers to teach Will to read and write.
They start their lessons immediately.

Write About the Text **I used notes from my chart to write a diary entry describing how Will felt about meeting Lucius.**

Student Model: *Narrative Text*

19th December 1754

When we arrived at Fort Mose from Virginia, I felt nervous and scared. Then I met a boy named Lucius. At first, I ignored him. I was shy. Then he showed me his diary. I couldn't believe he knew how to read and write! He said he could teach me. We started our lessons right away. Now I can read and write, too!

TALK ABOUT IT

Text Evidence

Draw a box around a sentence that comes from the notes. Does the sentence provide a supporting detail?

Grammar

Circle a possessive pronoun. Underline the name of the person the object belongs to.

Connect Ideas

Underline the two sentences that tell how Will acted when he first met Lucius. How can you connect the sentences into one sentence?

Your Turn

Write a diary entry from Lucius's point of view. Tell how you felt teaching Will how to read and write.

>> *Go Digital*
Write your response online. Use your editing checklist.

ELD.PI.4.1.Ex, ELD.PI.4.1.Br, ELD.PI.4.5.Ex, ELD.PI.4.5.Br, ELD.PI.4.6a.Ex, ELD.PI.4.6a.Br, ELD.PI.4.10b.Ex, ELD.PI.10b.Br, ELD.PI.4.12a.Ex, ELD.PI.4.12a.Br, ELD.PII.4.2a.Ex, ELD.PII.4.2a.Br, ELD.PII.4.6.Ex, ELD.PII.4.6.Br See the California Standards section.

TALK ABOUT IT

Weekly Concept Resources

Essential Question

How have our energy resources changed over the years?

» *Go Digital*

What sources of energy do you see in the photograph? What are some other sources of energy? Write your ideas in the chart.

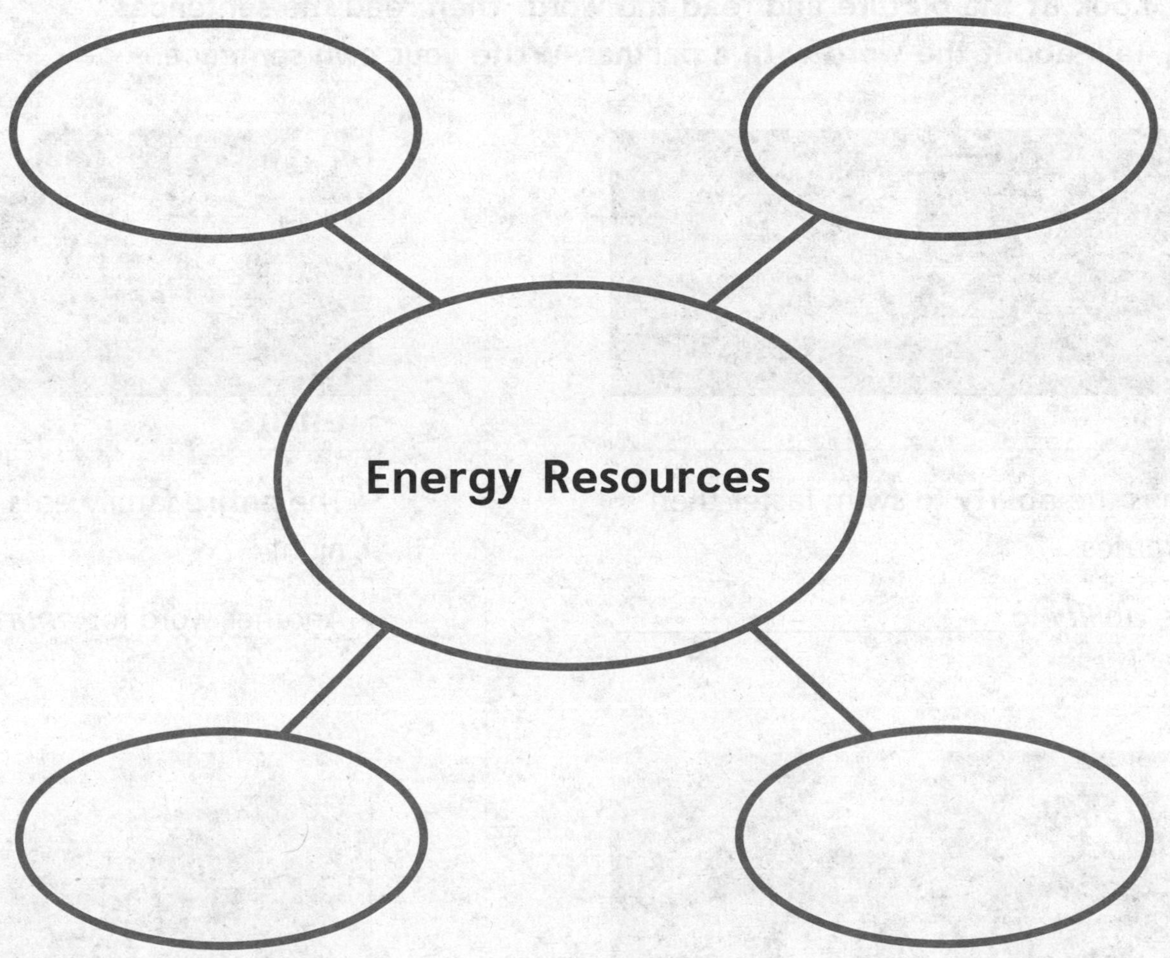

Discuss the energy resources we use today. Then talk about how energy sources have changed over time. Use the words from the chart. You can say:

Some sources of energy are ______________ and ____________.

Some ways energy sources have changed over time are ___________.

ELD.PI.4.1.Ex, ELD.PI.4.1.Br, ELD.PI.4.5.Ex, ELD.PI.4.5.Br, ELD.PI.4.12a.Ex, ELD.PI.4.12a.Br See the California Standards section.

More Vocabulary

Look at the picture and read the word. Then read the sentences. Talk about the word with a partner. Write your own sentence.

ability

The girl has the **ability** to swim faster than her classmates.

I have the *ability* to ________________.

entire

The **entire** family eats dinner together every night.

Another word for *entire* is ______________.

ancient

We visited the **ancient** ruins in Mexico.

Another word for *ancient* is ____________.

percent

Half of an orange is the same as 50 **percent**.

Another word for *percent* is ______________.

 ELD.PI.4.1.Ex, ELD.PI.4.1.Br, ELD.PI.4.5.Ex, ELD.PI.4.5.Br, ELD.PI.4.12a.Ex, ELD.PI.4.12a.Br See the California Standards section.

population

The town has a small **population**.

I live in a place with a ________________

population because ________________.

related

Making good grades is **related** to doing homework.

Another word for *related* is ______________.

Words and Phrases

Connecting Words

as well as **= in addition to**

I ate eggs as well as toast.

therefore **= as a result**

It is raining, therefore, I need an umbrella.

Read the sentences below. Write the connecting word(s) that best completes each sentence.

It is cold, ______________, I will wear a coat.

There are snacks ______________ drinks.

The park has swings ______________ a slide.

I am tired, ______________, I need to rest.

» Go Digital **Add *as well as* and *therefore* to your New Words notebook. Write a sentence to show the meaning of each.**

Text Evidence

1 Talk About It

Look at the photographs. Read the title. Talk about what you see. Write your ideas.

What does this title tell you?

____

____

____

______________________________.

Where are the people and what are they doing?

____

____

____

______________________________.

Take notes as you read the text.

Shared Read Genre • Narrative Nonfiction

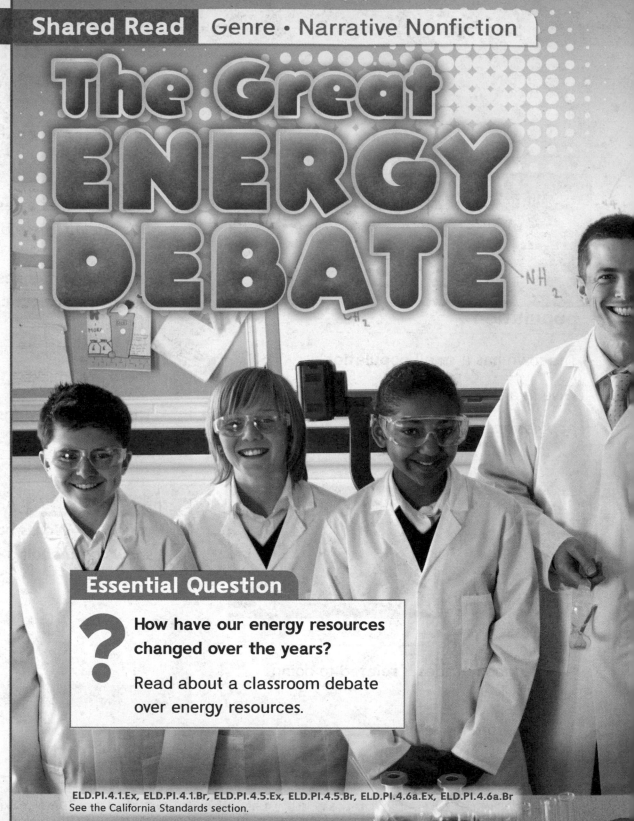

The Great ENERGY DEBATE

Essential Question

How have our energy resources changed over the years?

Read about a classroom debate over energy resources.

ELD.PI.4.1.Ex, ELD.PI.4.1.Br, ELD.PI.4.5.Ex, ELD.PI.4.5.Br, ELD.PI.4.6a.Ex, ELD.PI.4.6a.Br
See the California Standards section.

Our energy debate will be an incredible event, but I need to study. Our teacher won't tell us which side of the debate we'll be on until the day before it happens, which means we'll have to preplan arguments for both sides.

The debate will be next Tuesday and will include a discussion about different energy sources. Each team will have a microphone. One team will talk about the benefits of an energy source, and the other team will talk about its **drawbacks**. We'll have to learn about the environmental consequences **related** to each resource, as well as the costs.

(bkgd) Echo/Cultura/Getty Images; (t) Reggie Casagrande/Photographer's Choice RF/Getty Images; (b) Erik Isakson/Blend Images/Getty Images

ELD.PI.4.1.Ex, ELD.PI.4.1.Br, ELD.PI.4.5.Ex, ELD.PI.4.5.Br, ELD.PI.4.6a.Ex, ELD.PI.4.6a.Br, ELD.PI.4.7.Ex, ELD.PI.4.7.Br, ELD.PI.4.12a.Ex, ELD.PI.4.12a.Br See the California Standards section.

Text Evidence

1 Sentence Structure ACT

Reread the first sentence in the first paragraph. Underline the independent clauses. Circle the subject and verb in each clause.

2 Specific Vocabulary ACT

Reread the second paragraph. The word *drawbacks* means "things that are not good or problems." What word in the sentence is an antonym for *drawbacks?* Circle the word.

3 Comprehension

Main Idea and Key Details

Reread the last paragraph. Draw a box around two key details about the debate. What is the main idea of the paragraph? Underline the words that tell you.

Text Evidence

1 Comprehension

Main Idea and Key Details

Reread the first paragraph. Underline two key details about fossil fuels. Underline the words that tell you what will happen to fossil fuels in the future.

2 Specific Vocabulary ACT

Reread the second paragraph. The word *hypercritical* means "quick to give your opinion about something that you do not like." Circle the sentences in the first paragraph that tell why some people would be hypercritical of fossil fuels.

COLLABORATE

3 Talk About It

Reread the sidebar "What Is Energy?" Compare energy sources. In your opinion, which energy source would be better for the environment? Justify your answer.

What Is Energy?

Energy is the **ability** to do work or make a change. It also is a source of power for making electricity or doing mechanical work. We use the wind, the sun, fossil fuels, and biofuels to produce energy. Burning coal produces heat energy that is converted into electrical energy. We use that energy to light our houses. Solar energy comes from the sun. Solar panels convert sunlight into electrical energy.

We may be asked to debate the future of gasoline as an energy source. If so, I would say that gasoline is made from oil, a fossil fuel. According to geologists, fossil fuels formed over hundreds of millions of years from **ancient** plant and animal remains. But here's the problem: we use these fuels far faster than it takes them to form. Because fossil fuels are nonrenewable resources, if we keep using them eventually there will be none left. Plus burning these fuels pollutes the air!

It is easy to be **hypercritical** of fossil fuels. However, most of our cars and factories use this type of fuel, and therefore changing everything would be a huge undertaking.

ELD.PI.4.1.Ex, ELD.PI.4.1.Br, ELD.PI.4.3.Ex, ELD.PI.4.3.Br, ELD.PI.4.5.Ex, ELD.PI.4.5.Br, ELD.PI.4.6a.Ex, ELD.PI.4.6a.Br, ELD.PI.4.7.Ex, ELD.PI.4.7.Br, ELD.PI.4.12a.Ex, ELD.PI.4.12a.Br
See the California Standards section.

(bkgd) Echo/Cultura/Getty Images; (br) Hal Bergman/Photodisc/Getty Images; (bl) Livio Sinibaldi/Digital Vision/Getty Image

If we are asked to debate the use of wind energy, we would have to know that this is a renewable energy source. For example, unlike fossil fuels, wind will never run out. One large wind turbine could produce enough energy for a whole city! In addition, this method doesn't damage the environment. Turbines can be placed all over the world to capture wind energy. Then the energy from the turbines is converted into electrical energy. But there is a drawback. Wind may not be as efficient as other energy sources. Only about 30 or 40 percent of all wind energy is changed into electricity. It would be very expensive to have wind turbines installed all over the world.

This debate is important for people in the United States. Our country makes up only about 5 percent of the **entire** world's **population**. Yet we consume about 30 **percent** of the world's energy. It is not a coincidence that students are asked to take part in these debates. We will probably have to make these decisions when we are adults. The debate will be difficult, but I will be ready!

Make Connections

How might our dependence on fossil fuels change in the future? ESSENTIAL QUESTION

What can you do to help save energy resources? TEXT TO SELF

ELD.PI.4.1.Ex, ELD.PI.4.1.Br, ELD.PI.4.5.Ex, ELD.PI.4.5.Br, ELD.PI.4.6a.Ex, ELD.PI.4.6a.Br, ELD.PI.4.10b.Ex, ELD.PI.4.10b.Br, ELD.PI.4.12a.Ex, ELD.PI.4.12a.Br
See the California Standards section.

Text Evidence

1 Comprehension
Main Idea and Key Details

Reread the first paragraph. Underline two key details about wind energy.

2 Sentence Structure ACT

Reread the second sentence in the first paragraph. Circle the two energy sources that are being compared. Underline how one energy source is different from the other.

3 Talk About It

Discuss how energy sources may change in the future. Predict what you think will be the main source of energy. Then write about it.

____

____

____

______________________________.

Respond to the Text

Partner Discussion **Work with a partner. Describe what you learned about "The Great Energy Debate." Write the page numbers where you found text evidence.**

What did you learn about fossil fuels in the text?	**Text Evidence**
I read fossil fuels are a ______.	Page(s): ______
Based on the text, fossil fuels were formed ______ ______.	Page(s): ______
According to the author, the drawbacks of fossil fuels are ______ ______.	Page(s): ______

What did you learn about the wind and the sun as energy sources?	**Text Evidence**
I read solar panels convert ______.	Page(s): ______
Unlike fossil fuels, wind will ______.	Page(s): ______
According to the author, the drawbacks of wind energy are ______ ______.	Page(s): ______

Group Discussion **Present your answers to the class. Cite text evidence to justify your thinking. Listen to and discuss the group's opinions about your answers.**

 ELD.PI.4.1.Ex, ELD.PI.4.1.Br, ELD.PI.4.3.Ex, ELD.PI.4.3.Br, ELD.PI.4.5.Ex, ELD.PI.4.5.Br, ELD.PI.4.9.Ex, ELD.PI.4.9.Br, ELD.PI.4.11a.Ex, ELD.PI.4.11a.Br, ELD.PI.4.12a.Ex, ELD.PI.4.12a.Br See the California Standards section.

Write **Work with a partner. Review your notes about "The Great Energy Debate." Then write your answer to the essential question. Use text evidence to support your answer. Use vocabulary words from this week's reading in your writing.**

How have energy resources changed over time?

In the United States, most of the cars and factories use ______________________.

To change from fossil fuels, it would be ______________________________.

Solar panels convert ____.

Wind energy is good because __________________________________.

The problem with wind energy is ______________________________

____.

COLLABORATE

Share Writing **Present your writing to the class. Discuss their opinions. Think about what they have to say. Did they justify their claims? Explain why you agree or disagree with their claims.**

I agree with ______________ because ____________________________.

I disagree with ______________ because ___________________________.

Write to Sources

pages 352–355

Take Notes About the Text I took notes on an idea web to ***answer this question: Do you agree with the author that the energy debate is important for people in the United States?***

Our country makes up 5 percent of the world's population.

We use 30 percent of the world's energy.

Why the energy debate is important for people in the United States.

Fossil fuels formed over hundreds of millions of years.

We use fossil fuels much faster than they can form.

Kali Nine LLC/iStock/360/Getty Images

 ELD.PI.4.1.Ex, ELD.PI.4.1.Br, ELD.PI.4.5.Ex, ELD.PI.4.5.Br, ELD.PI.4.6a.Ex, ELD.PI.4.6a.Br, ELD.PII.4.1.Ex, ELD.PII.4.1.Br See the California Standards section.

Write About the Text **I used notes from my idea web to write an opinion about whether I agree that the energy debate is important.**

Student Model: *Opinion*

I agree with the author that the energy debate is important. Our country makes up only 5 percent of the world's population. We use 30 percent of the world's energy. We use a lot more energy than other countries do. In addition, fossil fuels take millions of years to form. We're using them much faster than they can form. I think the energy debate will help us think about other energy sources. We never want to run out of energy!

TALK ABOUT IT

Text Evidence

Draw a box around a sentence that comes from the notes. What key words did Kisha use to connect her ideas and details?

Grammar

Circle the words with apostrophes. Underline the words that are possessive nouns.

Connect Ideas

Underline the two sentences that tell about percents. How can you combine these sentences into one detailed sentence?

Your Turn

Do you think it is better to use fossil fuel or solar energy? Use text evidence.

>> *Go Digital*
Write your response online. Use your editing checklist.

ELD.PI.4.1.Ex, ELD.PI.4.1.Br, ELD.PI.4.5.Ex, ELD.PI.4.5.Br, ELD.PI.4.6a.Ex, ELD.PI.4.6a.Br, ELD.PI.4.10b.Ex, ELD.PI.4.10b.Br, ELD.PI.4.12a.Ex, ELD.PI.4.12a.Br, ELD.PII.4.6.Ex, ELD.PII.4.6.Br See the California Standards section.

TALK ABOUT IT

Weekly Concept Money Matters

Essential Question

What has been the role of money over time?

» *Go Digital*

Describe what the children in the photo are doing. What are some ways people use money? Write your ideas in the chart.

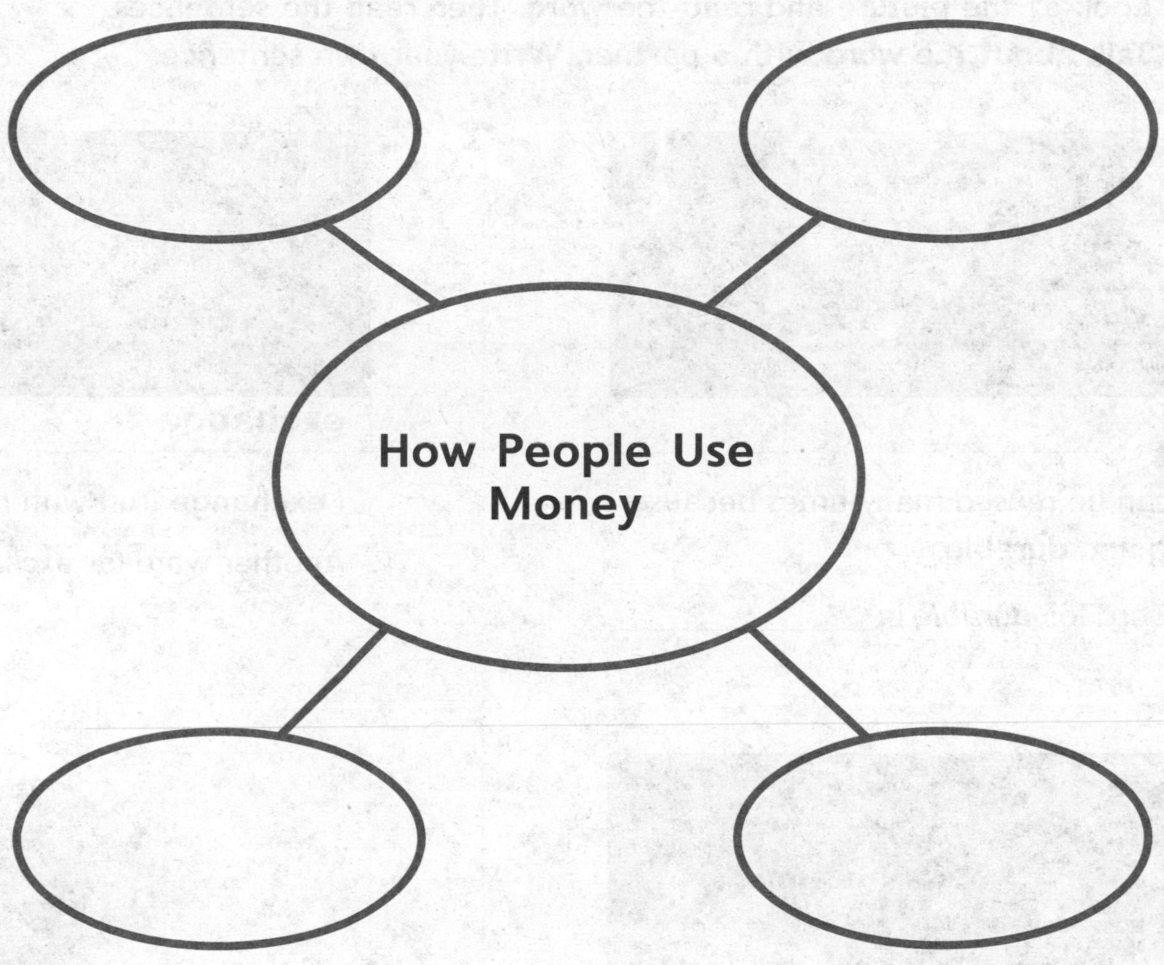

Discuss the ways people use money. Use the words from the chart. You can say:

People use money to ______________________________.

They also use money to ____________________________.

Stephen Mallon/Taxi/Getty

ELD.PI.4.1.Ex, ELD.PI.4.1.Br, ELD.PI.4.5.Ex, ELD.PI.4.5.Br, ELD.PI.4.12a.Ex, ELD.PI.4.12a.Br See the California Standards section.

More Vocabulary

COLLABORATE

Look at the picture and read the word. Then read the sentences. Talk about the word with a partner. Write your own sentence.

durable

The bag can be reused many times because it is strong and **durable**.

Another word for *durable* is ______________.

exchange

I **exchange** fruit with my friend.

Another word for *exchange* is ____________.

emerged

Many cars that use less gas have **emerged** in cities across the country.

Something new that has *emerged* recently is ________________________________.

precious

The ring has a **precious** jewel.

Another word for *precious* is ______________.

 ELD.PI.4.1.Ex, ELD.PI.4.1.Br, ELD.PI.4.5.Ex, ELD.PI.4.5.Br, ELD.PI.4.12a.Ex, ELD.PI.4.12a.Br See the California Standards section.

range

The school supplies **range** from books to crayons.

My hobbies *range* from ____________________

to ____________________________________.

system

Buses are a **system** of transportation used by many people.

Another *system* of transportation is ________.

Words and Phrases
catching on and *pay off*

catching on **= becoming popular**
The new game is <u>catching on</u>.

pay off **= bring good results**
Tony's hard work will <u>pay off</u>.

Read the sentences below. Write the phrasal verb that means the same as the underlined words.

The new song is <u>becoming popular</u>.

The new song is ______________________________.

Studying will <u>bring good results</u> when you take the test.

Studying will _________________ when you take the test.

» Go Digital **Add these phrasal verbs to your New Words notebook. Write a sentence to show the meaning of each.**

Text Evidence

COLLABORATE

1 Talk About It

Look at the picture. Read the title. Talk about what you see. Write your ideas.

What does this title tell you?

____

____

____

______________________________.

Describe what you see in the picture.

____

____

____

______________________________.

Take notes as you read the text.

Shared Read Genre • Expository Text

THE HISTORY of MONEY

Essential Question

What has been the role of money over time?

Read about the history of money.

A painting of a commercial center in Beijing, China, in 1840

ELD.PI.4.1.Ex, ELD.PI.4.1.Br, ELD.PI.4.5.Ex, ELD.PI.4.5.Br, ELD.PI.4.6a.Ex, ELD.PI.4.6a.Br
See the California Standards section.

What makes money valuable? If you think about it, a dollar bill is only a piece of paper. You cannot eat, wear, or live in a dollar bill. So why do people want it? Think about the proverb, "Money doesn't grow on trees." Money is considered valuable because it is hard to get.

Bartering

Imagine you're a goat herder visiting a marketplace in China in 1200 B.C. The merchandise being sold around you **ranges** from cattle to tools. Suppose you need to purchase a piece of rope. How will you pay for it? The goats you own are your sole source of **income** so you would not want to trade a goat for the rope. The goat is too valuable! Instead, you might trade goat milk for the rope. This **system** of economics is called bartering. But what if the rope merchant does not want goat milk?

Early Currency

No need to cry over spilt milk. Luckily, you sold some goat milk earlier in the day in **exchange** for ten cowrie shells, the first system of currency in China. You hand two cowrie shells to the rope merchant and put the rest in your pocket. This is a much easier way to buy and sell things. Cowrie shells are lightweight, **durable**, and easier to take with you than a goat. The idea of currency is catching on around the world in Thailand, India, and Africa.

You decide to save your extra shells until you have enough to invest in another goat. You will be spending cowries with the expectation that another goat will pay off later since you can drink or sell the milk it produces. Taking this type of business risk makes you an entrepreneur.

ELD.PI.4.1.Ex, ELD.PI.4.1.Br, ELD.PI.4.5.Ex, ELD.PI.4.5.Br, ELD.PI.4.6a.Ex, ELD.PI.4.6a.Br, ELD.PI.4.7.Ex, ELD.PI.4.7.Br, ELD.PI.4.12a.Ex, ELD.PI.4.12a.Br, ELD.PII.4.7.Ex, ELD.PII.4.7.Br
See the California Standards section.

Text Evidence

1 Specific Vocabulary ACT

Reread the second paragraph. The word *income* means "money that is earned from work." What is a goat herder's source of income? Underline the words that tell you.

2 Sentence Structure ACT

Reread the last two sentences in the second paragraph. How can you connect the two sentences into one sentence? Write the sentence.

___

___

___

___

3 Comprehension
Main Idea and Key Details

Reread the last paragraph. Underline a key detail that supports the idea of being an entrepreneur.

Text Evidence

1 Sentence Structure ACT

Reread the third sentence in the second paragraph. Underline the independent clause. Draw a box around the dependent clause that tells about time.

2 Specific Vocabulary ACT

Reread the last sentence in the second paragraph. The word *stamped* means "to make a mark or pattern on something using a special tool." Circle the word that tells you what was being stamped. Underline the words that tell you what the design stated.

COLLABORATE

3 Talk About It

Explain how currency and a marketplace relate to each other. Then write about it.

____

____

____

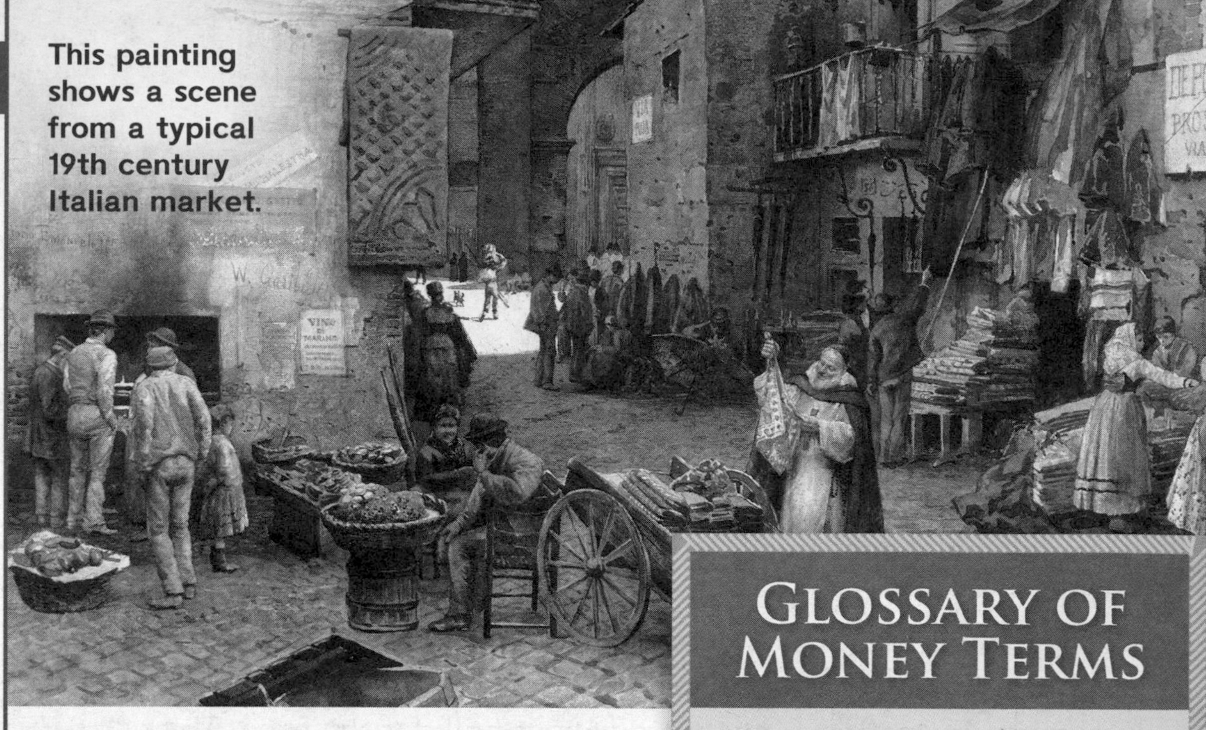

This painting shows a scene from a typical 19th century Italian market.

New Kinds of Currency

If you were at a marketplace in Rome around 900 B.C., you might have used salt as a form of currency. The idiom "to be worth one's salt" is still used today.

Another form of currency, metal coins, first **emerged** in China around 1000 B.C. Coins varied in shape, size, and worth. By the 7th century B.C., coins made of **precious** metals such as silver and gold became popular in Europe and the Middle East. These coins were usually round. After being weighed on a scale to determine their value, coins were **stamped** with designs that stated their worth.

Glossary of Money Terms

BARTERING (BAR-tur-ing) Trading by exchanging food, services, or goods instead of using money.

CURRENCY (KUR-uhn-see) Any form of money that is used in a country.

ECONOMY (ee-KON-uh-mee) A system or method of managing the production and distribution of money, goods, and services.

MARKETPLACE (MAR-kit-plays) A place where food and goods are bought and sold, or the world of business, trade, and economics.

ELD.PI.4.1.Ex, ELD.PI.4.1.Br, ELD.PI.4.5.Ex, ELD.PI.4.5.Br, ELD.PI.4.6a.Ex, ELD.PI.4.6a.Br, ELD.PI.4.7.Ex, ELD.PI.4.7.Br, ELD.PI.4.12a.Ex, ELD.PI.4.12a.Br See the California Standards section.

Paper Money

Carrying a bag of coins can be heavy. The weight of coins and a metal shortage are two reasons the use of paper money developed in China in the 10th century. The earliest European paper money appeared in Sweden at the beginning of the 17th century. Italy started to use paper money about 90 years later. Paper money originally represented the gold or silver a person had in the bank. Today, we can tell the value of paper money by reading the numbers printed on it.

Modern Money

In today's global economy, exchanging money electronically is common. Many people use a credit or debit card to make a digital transaction. Numbers on a computer screen represent dollars and cents, but no actual paper money is exchanged.

As easy as it is to spend money today, saving money is important. When considering spending money, think of the famous proverb, "A penny saved is a penny earned."

Make Connections

? Why did using currency replace bartering? ESSENTIAL QUESTION

How does money affect your daily life? TEXT TO SELF

Text Evidence

1 Sentence Structure ACT

Reread the second sentence in the first paragraph. Circle the prepositional phrase in the sentence that tells about time. Underline what was being developed at that time.

2 Comprehension

Main Idea and Key Details

Reread the first paragraph. Underline two details that supports the main idea of why people began using paper money.

3 Talk About It

Describe how modern money is different than paper money. Then write about it.

____

____

____

______________________________.

ELD.PI.4.1.Ex, ELD.PI.4.1.Br, ELD.PI.4.5.Ex, ELD.PI.4.5.Br, ELD.PI.4.6a.Ex, ELD.PI.4.6a.Br, ELD.PI.4.12a.Ex, ELD.PI.4.12a.Br See the California Standards section.

Respond to the Text

Partner Discussion **Work with a partner. Describe what you learned about "The History of Money." Write the page numbers where you found text evidence.**

What did you learn about money used in the past?	**Text Evidence**
I read people used to trade or ________________.	Page(s): ______
Cowrie shells were the first system of currency because ________ ________________________.	Page(s): ______
In ancient Rome a form of currency was ________________.	Page(s): ______
People stamped metal coins to ________________.	Page(s): ______

What did you learn about the forms of money used today?	**Text Evidence**
I learned paper money developed because ________________.	Page(s): ______
Paper money originally represented ________________.	Page(s): ______
Today many people make __________ transactions using ________________________.	Page(s): ______

COLLABORATE

Group Discussion **Present your answers to the class. Cite text evidence to justify your thinking. Listen to and discuss the group's opinions about your answers.**

ELD.PI.4.1.Ex, ELD.PI.4.1.Br, ELD.PI.4.3.Ex, ELD.PI.4.3.Br, ELD.PI.4.5.Ex, ELD.PI.4.5.Br, ELD.PI.4.9.Ex, ELD.PI.4.9.Br, ELD.PI.4.11a.Ex, ELD.PI.4.11a.Br, ELD.PI.4.12a.Ex, ELD.PI.4.12a.Br See the California Standards section.

COLLABORATE

Write **Work with a partner. Look at your notes about "The History of Money." Then write your answer to the essential question. Use text evidence to support your answer. Use vocabulary words from this week's reading in your writing.**

How has money changed over time?

Cowrie shells were a good currency at the time because ______________________

____.

Coins made from precious metals were stamped with ______________________

____.

Paper money was developed because ______________________.

Today, money is commonly exchanged ______________________.

COLLABORATE

Share Writing **Present your writing to the class. Discuss their opinions. Think about what they have to say. Did they justify their claims? Explain why you agree or disagree with their claims.**

I agree with ____________ because ______________________.

I disagree with ____________ because ______________________.

ELD.PI.4.1.Ex, ELD.PI.4.1.Br, ELD.PI.4.3.Ex, ELD.PI.4.3.Br, ELD.PI.4.5.Ex, ELD.PI.4.5.Br, ELD.PI.4.9.Ex, ELD.PI.4.9.Br, ELD.PI.4.11a.Ex, ELD.PI.4.11a.Br, ELD.PI.4.12a.Ex, ELD.PI.4.12a.Br See the California Standards section.

Write to Sources

Take Notes About the Text **I took notes on the sequence chart to answer the question:** ***How does the author use sequence to tell about the history of money?***

pages 364–367

In 1200 B.C. in China, people bartered or used cowrie shells to get what they needed.

↓

Around 1000 B.C., metal coins were used in China. In 7th century B.C. silver and gold coins were used in Europe and the Middle East.

↓

Paper money developed in China in the 10th century partly because coins were heavy.

↓

Today we use paper money and credit or debit cards.

Write About the Text **I used notes from my sequence chart to write a paragraph to tell about the history of money.**

Student Model: *Informative Text*

The author uses dates to tell about the sequence of events in the history of money. In 1200 B.C., people in China could barter to get what they needed. They could also use cowrie shells. Around 1000 B.C., the Chinese began using metal coins instead of shells. In the 7th century B.C., silver and gold coins were used in Europe and the Middle East. Then in the 10th century, paper money was developed in China. Today, people pay for things in stores using paper money and credit cards or debit cards. Money has changed a lot over time!

TALK ABOUT IT

Text Evidence

Draw a box around a sentence that comes from the notes. Did Hassan use the correct sequence of events?

Grammar

Circle the prepositional phrases that describe the sequence of events. Are the phrases in the correct sequence?

Condense Ideas

Underline the two sentences that tell about the events in 1200 B.C. How can you condense these sentences into one sentence?

Your Turn

How does the Glossary of Money Terms help you understand what you read? Use text evidence.

>> *Go Digital*
Write your response online. Use your editing checklist.

ELD.PI.4.1.Ex, ELD.PI.4.1.Br, ELD.PI.4.2.Ex, ELD.PI.4.2.Br, ELD.PI.4.5.Ex, ELD.PI.4.5.Br, ELD.PI.4.6a.Ex, ELD.PI.4.6a.Br, ELD.PI.4.10b.Ex, ELD.PI.4.10b.Br, ELD.PI.4.12a.Ex, ELD.PI.4.12a.Br, ELD.PII.4.1.Ex, ELD.PII.4.1.Br, ELD.PII.4.6.Ex, ELD.PII.4.6.Br See the California Standards section.

TALK ABOUT IT

Weekly Concept Finding My Place

Essential Question

What shapes a person's identity?

» *Go Digital*

Look at the photo of the boys. How does the food they are eating shape their identity? What other things help to shape a person's identity? Write your ideas in the chart.

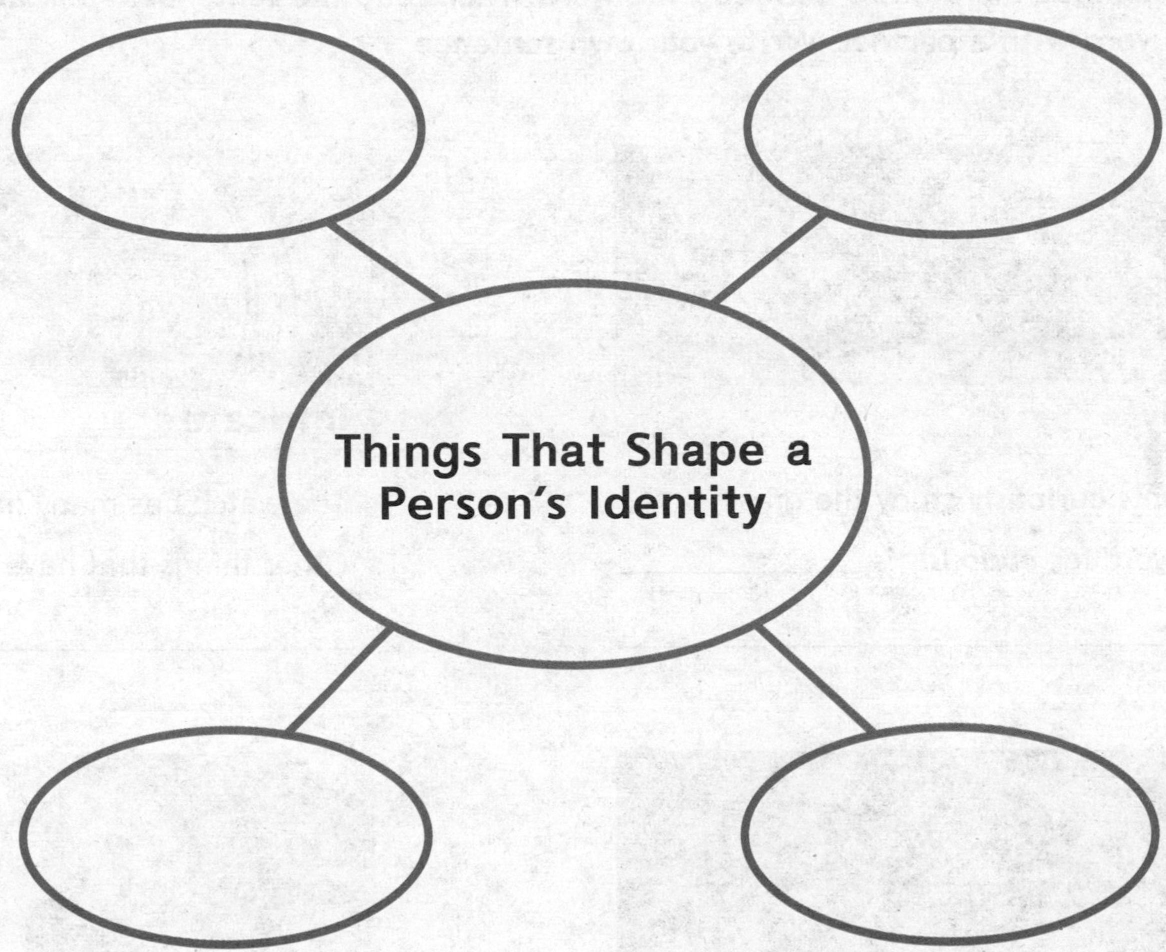

Discuss the things that shape a person's identity. Use the words from the chart. You can say:

Things like ______________ and ___________ help to shape a person's identity because ______________________________.

Simon Marcus Taplin/Corbis/Getty Images

ELD.PI.4.1.Ex, ELD.PI.4.1.Br, ELD.PI.4.5.Ex, ELD.PI.4.5.Br, ELD.PI.4.12a.Ex, ELD.PI.4.12a.Br See the California Standards section.

More Vocabulary

Look at the picture and read the word. Then read the sentences. Talk about the word with a partner. Write your own sentence.

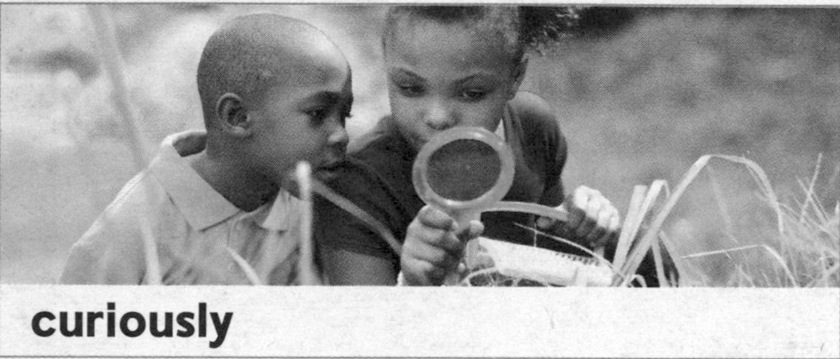

curiously

The students **curiously** study the grass.

Another word for *curiously* is ______________

______________________________________.

intricate

The watch has many **intricate** parts.

Other things that have *intricate* parts are

______________________________________.

glimmer

The stars **glimmer** brightly in the night sky.

Other things that *glimmer* are ______________

______________________________________.

scoffs

The boy **scoffs** at the bad joke.

I *scoff* when ______________________________

______________________________________.

(ul)Agnieszka Kirinicjanow/Getty Images; (ur)Photolibrary/Alamy; (bl)Jill Fromer/Getty Images; (br)Chris Ryan/OJO Images/Getty Images

 ELD.PI.4.1.Ex, ELD.PI.4.1.Br, ELD.PI.4.5.Ex, ELD.PI.4.5.Br, ELD.PI.4.12a.Ex, ELD.PI.4.12a.Br See the California Standards section.

Poetry Terms

metaphor

A **metaphor** compares two unlike things without using the words *like* or *as*.

Snow is a blanket.

imagery

Imagery is the use of words to create a picture in your mind.

The yellow leaves glimmer against the green ones.

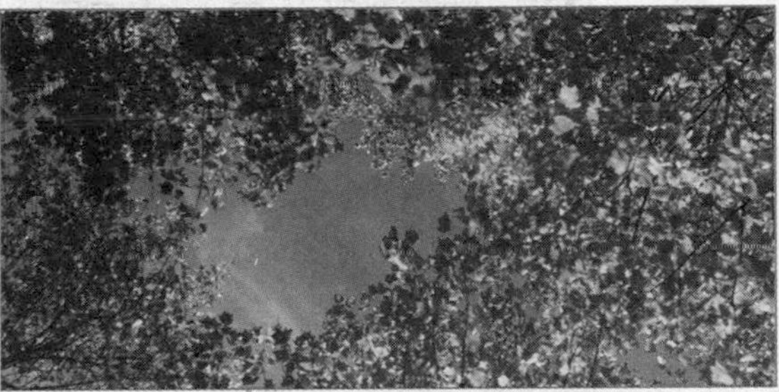

personification

Personification gives human qualities to something that is not human.

Lightning danced in the night sky.

COLLABORATE

Work with a partner. Choose a word for each personification sentence. Then choose two words for each metaphor sentence.

Personification:

dance **smile** **whistles**

The wind ___.

The flowers ___ at the sun.

The leaves ___ in the wind.

Metaphor:

trees **clouds** **cotton** **umbrellas**

The ___ are ___.

The ___ are ___.

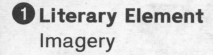

Text Evidence

1 Literary Element

Imagery

Imagery is using specific words to create a picture in the reader's mind. Reread the first stanza. Circle an example of imagery. Discuss what you can tell about the poem based on the imagery.

2 Comprehension

Theme

Reread the second and third stanzas. Underline the words that tell you the boys have hiked with their grandfather before. How does the poet feel about his grandfather?

____

____

3 Sentence Structure ACT

Reread the second line in the second stanza. Circle the subject in this line. Draw a box around the verb.

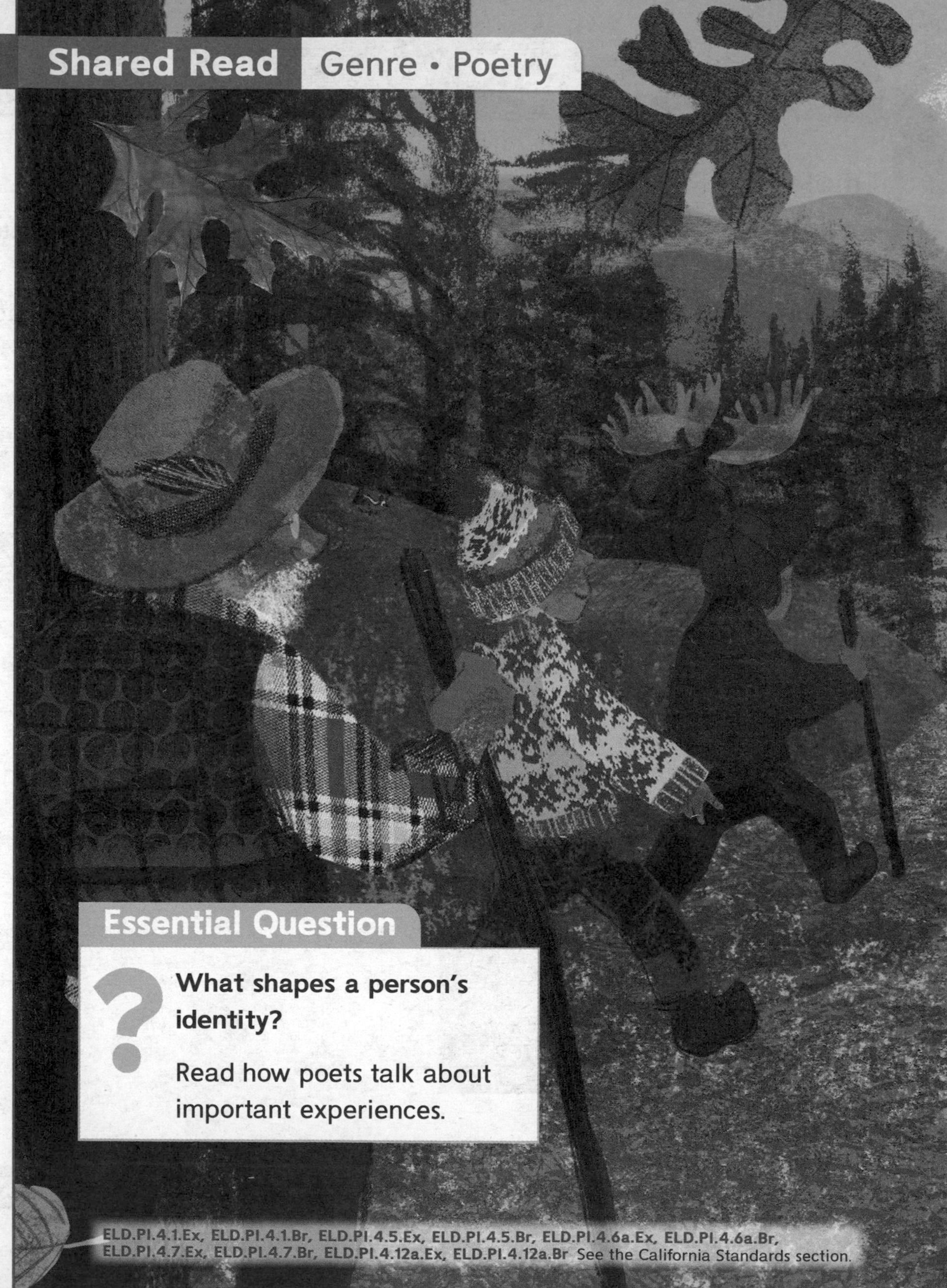

Essential Question

What shapes a person's identity?

Read how poets talk about important experiences.

ELD.PI.4.1.Ex, ELD.PI.4.1.Br, ELD.PI.4.5.Ex, ELD.PI.4.5.Br, ELD.PI.4.6a.Ex, ELD.PI.4.6a.Br, ELD.PI.4.7.Ex, ELD.PI.4.7.Br, ELD.PI.4.12a.Ex, ELD.PI.4.12a.Br See the California Standards section.

CLIMBING BLUE HILL

When the yellow leaves begin to
glimmer among the green ones,
we hike up Blue Hill
through an early morning mist.

"It's not much farther, boys!"
My grandfather bellows happily,
his words an echo of all the other times
he's had to **urge** us up a steep trail.

I hear the comforting squeak of his boots
as the ground's chill breath whispers
against our ankles and the overgrown
branches tug **curiously** at my hair.

Abruptly, the trail spits us out,
onto gray rock, into blue sky and sunlight.
My brother shouts, shoves me aside,
races to the low bushes huddled against the wind.

His fingers tug at the tiny leaves.
"Look! Blueberries!" He yells.
And we gobble the blue sweetness up,
my brother, my grandfather, and me.

— Andrew Feher

ELD.PI.4.1.Ex, ELD.PI.4.1.Br, ELD.PI.4.5.Ex, ELD.PI.4.5.Br, ELD.PI.4.6a.Ex, ELD.PI.4.6a.Br, ELD.PI.4.7.Ex, ELD.PI.4.7.Br, ELD.PI.4.12a.Ex, ELD.PI.4.12a.Br See the California Standards section.

Text Evidence

1 Specific Vocabulary ACT

Reread the second stanza. The word *urge* means "to try to get someone to do something." Underline the words that tell you who is urging someone. What is the person being urged to do? Circle the words that tell you.

2 Literary Element Personification

Personification is giving human qualities to something that is not human. Reread the fourth stanza. Draw a box around an example of personification. Circle what is being personified.

3 Talk About It

Discuss how the poet feels about hiking with his grandfather. Underline the words that give you clues about how he feels.

1 Sentence Structure ACT

Reread the first line. Who does the pronoun *I* refer to? Underline the noun in the second stanza.

2 Literary Element

Imagery

Reread lines 2 to 5. Circle an example of imagery. What is the poet describing with this imagery?

____

____

______________________________.

3 Comprehension

Theme

Reread the poem. Underline the words that describe what ivy does. What is the theme of this poem?

____

____

______________________________.

My Name Is Ivy

"Why did I name you after a plant?

Look, this is ivy," my mother explains,
pointing at an **intricate** fan

of glossy green heart-shaped leaves
decorating the side
of our house.

"Ivy will grip onto anything,
will grow where it wants to go.
Will use its long skinny fingers
to find a way over

brick walls, up stone walls,
will climb a roof and keep on
going until it touches
the stars."

—Bryce Neale

ELD.PI.4.1.Ex, ELD.PI.4.1.Br, ELD.PI.4.5.Ex, ELD.PI.4.5.Br, ELD.PI.4.6a.Ex, ELD.PI.4.6a.Br, ELD.PI.4.12a.Ex, ELD.PI.4.12a.Br, ELD.PII.4.2a.Ex, ELD.PII.4.2a.Br See the California Standards section.

Collage

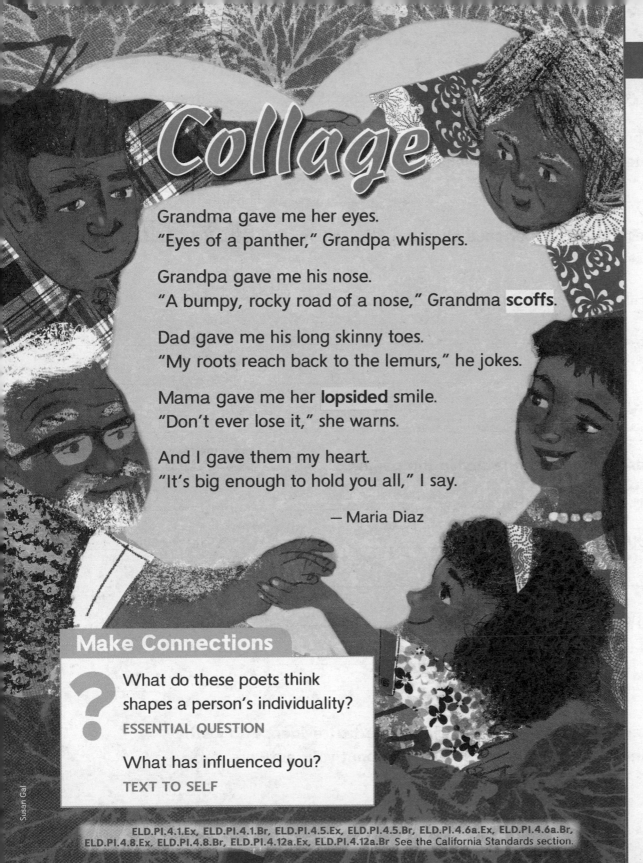

Grandma gave me her eyes.
"Eyes of a panther," Grandpa whispers.

Grandpa gave me his nose.
"A bumpy, rocky road of a nose," Grandma **scoffs**.

Dad gave me his long skinny toes.
"My roots reach back to the lemurs," he jokes.

Mama gave me her **lopsided** smile.
"Don't ever lose it," she warns.

And I gave them my heart.
"It's big enough to hold you all," I say.

— Maria Diaz

Make Connections

What do these poets think shapes a person's individuality?
ESSENTIAL QUESTION

What has influenced you?
TEXT TO SELF

Susan Gal

ELD.PI.4.1.Ex, ELD.PI.4.1.Br, ELD.PI.4.5.Ex, ELD.PI.4.5.Br, ELD.PI.4.6a.Ex, ELD.PI.4.6a.Br, ELD.PI.4.8.Ex, ELD.PI.4.8.Br, ELD.PI.4.12a.Ex, ELD.PI.4.12a.Br See the California Standards section.

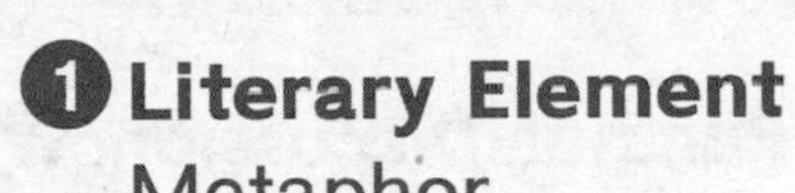

Text Evidence

1 Literary Element
Metaphor

A metaphor compares two unlike things without using the word *like* or *as*. Reread the second stanza. Draw a box around the metaphor. Circle the two things that are being compared.

2 Specific Vocabulary ACT

Reread the fourth stanza. The word *lopsided* means "one side is lower than the other side." What is being described as lopsided? Circle the noun.

3 Talk About It

Describe how the people in your family have shaped who you are. Then write about it.

____

____

______________________________.

Respond to the Text

Partner Discussion **Work with a partner. Describe what you learned about "Climbing Blue Hill." Write the page numbers where you found text evidence.**

	Text Evidence
How does the poet describe his experience climbing Blue Hill in the poem?	
The poet climbs Blue Hill when ______________________.	Page(s): __________
The poet hikes with ______________________.	Page(s): __________
In the last stanza, they reach ______________________.	Page(s): __________

	Text Evidence
How does the poet describe his grandfather in the poem?	
The poet tells about how his grandfather acts ______________________.	Page(s): __________
The poet remembers other times when ______________________ ______________________.	Page(s): __________
In the last stanza, the poet feels ______________________ ______________________.	Page(s): __________

Group Discussion **Present your answers to the class. Cite text evidence to justify your thinking. Listen to and discuss the group's opinions about your answers.**

 ELD.PI.4.1.Ex, ELD.PI.4.1.Br, ELD.PI.4.3.Ex, ELD.PI.4.3.Br, ELD.PI.4.5.Ex, ELD.PI.4.5.Br, ELD.PI.4.9.Ex, ELD.PI.4.9.Br, ELD.PI.4.11a.Ex, ELD.PI.4.11a.Br, ELD.PI.4.12a.Ex, ELD.PI.4.12a.Br See the California Standards section.

Write **Work with a partner. Look at your notes about "Climbing Blue Hill." Then write your answer to the essential question. Use text evidence to support your answer. Use vocabulary words from this week's reading in your writing.**

How is the poet's life shaped by his grandfather?

In the poem, the poet describes hiking by telling about ______________________

____.

The poet is comforted by his grandfather because ______________________

____

____.

When they reach the top of the hill, the poet feels ______________________

____

____.

COLLABORATE

Share Writing **Present your writing to the class. Discuss their opinions. Think about what they have to say. Did they justify their claims? Explain why you agree or disagree with their claims.**

I agree with ____________ because ______________________.

I disagree with ____________ because ______________________.

ELD.PI.4.1.Ex, ELD.PI.4.1.Br, ELD.PI.4.3.Ex, ELD.PI.4.3.Br, ELD.PI.4.5.Ex, ELD.PI.4.5.Br, ELD.PI.4.9.Ex, ELD.PI.4.9.Br, ELD.PI.4.10b.Ex, ELD.PI.4.10b.Br, ELD.PI.4.11a.Ex, ELD.PI.4.11a.Br, ELD.PI.4.12a.Ex, ELD.PI.4.12a.Br See the California Standards section.

Write to Sources

pages 376–379

Take Notes About the Text **I took notes on the idea web to answer the question:** ***In your opinion, does the poet of "Climbing Blue Hill" do a good job of using imagery?***

The yellow leaves glimmer among the green ones.

They hike through an early morning mist.

Imagery is the use of words to create a picture in the reader's mind.

The boy hears the comforting squeak of his grandfather's boots.

They gobble up the blue sweetness of blueberries.

 ELD.PI.4.1.Ex, ELD.PI.4.1.Br, ELD.PI.4.2.Ex, ELD.PI.4.2.Br, ELD.PI.4.10b.Ex, ELD.PI.4.10b.Br, ELD.PI.4.11a.Ex, ELD.PI.4.11a.Br, ELD.PI.4.12a.Ex, ELD.PI.4.12a.Br, ELD.PII.4.1.Ex, ELD.PII.4.1.Br See the California Standards section.

Write About the Text **I used my notes from my idea web to write an opinion about the poet's use of imagery in "Climbing Blue Hill."**

Student Model: *Opinion*

In my opinion, I think the poet of "Climbing Blue Hill" does a good job of using imagery. He uses words that help me picture the hike up Blue Hill. I can see the yellow leaves glimmering among the green leaves. I can see and feel the early morning mist. I can hear the comforting squeak of his grandfather's boots. I can taste the blue sweetness of the blueberries. The poet's words make me feel like I was there, too.

TALK ABOUT IT

Text Evidence

Draw a box around a sentence that comes from the notes. Why did Grace use this example as a supporting detail?

Grammar

Circle the adjectives that describe the mist. What other adjectives could you use to describe mist?

Connect Ideas

Underline the sentences about what Grace can hear and taste. How can you combine these sentences into a compound sentence?

Your Turn

Does the poet of "Climbing Blue Hill" do a good job of using personification? Use text evidence.

>> Go Digital
Write your response online. Use your editing checklist.

ELD.PI.4.1.Ex, ELD.PI.4.1.Br, ELD.PI.4.2.Ex, ELD.PI.4.2.Br, ELD.PI.4.3.Ex, ELD.PI.4.3.Br, ELD.PI.4.10b.Ex, ELD.PI.4.10b.Br, ELD.PI.4.11a.Ex, ELD.PI.4.11a.Br, ELD.PI.4.12a.Ex, ELD.PI.4.12a.Br, ELD.PII.4.1.Ex, ELD.PII.4.1.Br, ELD.PII.4.4.Ex, ELD.PII.4.4.Br, ELD.PII.4.6.Ex, ELD.PII.4.6.Br See the California Standards section.

California English Language Development Standards

At the bottom of some of the pages in this book, you will see letters and numbers. What do these numbers and letters mean? In **ELD.PI.4.1.Ex, ELD** stands for English Language Development. The **PI** stands for **Part I**. The number **4** stands for Grade 4. The number **1** is the standard number. The **Ex** stands for the language level **Expanding**.

Part	Grade Level	Standard Number	Proficiency Level
I	4	1	Expanding

This standard is about speaking in class, small groups, or with a partner to discuss the topic you are learning about during a lesson.

1. Exchanging information/ideas

This means that you will follow turn-taking rules, ask and answer questions, and add new information to the discussion.

The California English Language Development Standards are divided into three parts:

Part I – Interacting in Meaningful Ways

These standards are about how well you listen and understand spoken English, how you develop and expand your vocabulary, and how well you share your ideas and information by speaking and writing.

Part II – Learning About How English Works

This part of the standards focuses on how well you read, understand, and write different types of texts. This includes: understanding how a text is organized, the grammar used in the text, and most importantly, how you use English to write your own texts to share your stories, ideas, and opinions.

Part III – Using Foundational Literacy Skills

These standards are about how well you understand the letters used to form sounds, words, and sentences in English. It is also about how well you use your understanding of letters and sounds to listen, speak, read, and write.

Every standard is presented in three language levels. As you progress through the lessons, you will also progress through each of the language levels. The three language levels are:

Em – Emerging **Ex** – Expanding **Br** – Bridging

There may be some standards that you are performing at the third level; there may be other standards where you are performing the basic skills, but most of the standards you may be performing somewhere in the middle.

Your Standards for all three parts and language levels follow. **Take a look!**

Grade 4 California English Language Development Standards

PART I: INTERACTING IN MEANINGFUL WAYS	
A. Collaborative	
1. Exchanging information and ideas	
PI.4.1.Em	Contribute to conversations and express ideas by asking and answering *yes-no* and *wh-* questions and responding using short phrases.
PI.4.1.Ex	Contribute to class, group, and partner discussions, including sustained dialogue, by following turn-taking rules, asking relevant questions, affirming others, and adding relevant information.
PI.4.1.Br	Contribute to class, group, and partner discussions, including sustained dialogue, by following turn-taking rules, asking relevant questions, affirming others, adding relevant information, building on responses, and providing useful feedback.
2. Interacting via written English	
PI.4.2.Em	Collaborate with peers on joint writing projects of short informational and literary texts, using technology where appropriate for publishing, graphics, etc.
PI.4.2.Ex	Collaborate with peers on joint writing projects of longer informational and literary texts, using technology where appropriate for publishing, graphics, etc.
PI.4.2.Br	Collaborate with peers on joint writing projects of a variety of longer informational and literary texts, using technology where appropriate for publishing, graphics, etc.
3. Offering opinions	
PI.4.3.Em	Negotiate with or persuade others in conversations using basic learned phrases (e.g., *I think . . .*), as well as open responses, in order to gain and/or hold the floor.
PI.4.3.Ex	Negotiate with or persuade others in conversations using an expanded set of learned phrases (e.g., *I agree with X, but . . .*), as well as open responses, in order to gain and/or hold the floor, provide counter-arguments, etc.
PI.4.3.Br	Negotiate with or persuade others in conversations using a variety of learned phrases (e.g., *That's a good idea. However . . .*), as well as open responses, in order to gain and/or hold the floor, provide counter-arguments, elaborate on an idea, etc.

Grade 4 California English Language Development Standards

4. Adapting language choices	
PI.4.4.Em	Adjust language choices according to social setting (e.g., playground, classroom) and audience (e.g., peers, teacher) with substantial support.
PI.4.4.Ex	Adjust language choices according to purpose (e.g., persuading, entertaining), task (e.g., telling a story versus explaining a science experiment), and audience with moderate support.
PI.4.4.Br	Adjust language choices according to purpose, task (e.g., facilitating a science experiment), and audience with light support.
B. Interpretive	
5. Listening actively	
PI.4.5.Em	Demonstrate active listening of read-alouds and oral presentations by asking and answering basic questions with prompting and substantial support.
PI.4.5.Ex	Demonstrate active listening of read-alouds and oral presentations by asking and answering detailed questions with occasional prompting and moderate support.
PI.4.5.Br	Demonstrate active listening of read-alouds and oral presentations by asking and answering detailed questions with minimal prompting and light support.
6. Reading/viewing closely	
PI.4.6.Em	a) Describe ideas, phenomena (e.g., volcanic eruptions), and text elements (main idea, characters, events, etc.) based on close reading of a select set of grade-level texts with substantial support. b) Use knowledge of frequently-used affixes (e.g., *un-*, *mis-*) and linguistic context, reference materials, and visual cues to determine the meaning of unknown words on familiar topics.
PI.4.6.Ex	a) Describe ideas, phenomena (e.g., animal migration), and text elements (main idea, central message, etc.) in greater detail based on close reading of a variety of grade-level texts with moderate support. b) Use knowledge of morphology (e.g., affixes, roots, and base words), linguistic context, and reference materials to determine the meaning of unknown words on familiar topics.
PI.4.6.Br	a) Describe ideas, phenomena (e.g., pollination), and text elements (main idea, character traits, event sequence, etc.) in detail based on close reading of a variety of grade-level texts with light support. b) Use knowledge of morphology (e.g., affixes, roots, and base words) and linguistic context to determine the meaning of unknown and multiple-meaning words on familiar and new topics.

Grade 4 California English Language Development Standards

7. Evaluating language choices	
PI.4.7.Em	Describe the specific language writers or speakers use to present or support an idea (e.g., the specific vocabulary or phrasing used to provide evidence) with prompting and substantial support.
PI.4.7.Ex	Describe how well writers or speakers use specific language resources to support an opinion or present an idea (e.g., whether the vocabulary or phrasing used to provide evidence is strong enough) with prompting and moderate support.
PI.4.7.Br	Describe how well writers and speakers use specific language resources to support an opinion or present an idea (e.g., the clarity or appealing nature of language used to present evidence) with prompting and light support.
8. Analyzing language choices	
PI.4.8.Em	Distinguish how different words with similar meaning produce different effects on the audience (e.g., describing a character's actions as *whined* versus *said*).
PI.4.8.Ex	Distinguish how different words with similar meanings (e.g., describing a character as *smart* versus *an expert*) and figurative language (e.g., *as big as a whale*) produce shades of meaning and different effects on the audience.
PI.4.8.Br	Distinguish how different words with related meanings (e.g., *fun* versus *entertaining* versus *thrilling, possibly* versus *certainly*) and figurative language produce shades of meaning and different effects on the audience.
C. Productive	
9. Presenting	
PI.4.9.Em	Plan and deliver brief oral presentations on a variety of topics and content areas (e.g., retelling a story, explaining a science process, reporting on a current event, recounting a memorable experience, etc.) with substantial support.
PI.4.9.Ex	Plan and deliver longer oral presentations on a variety of topics and content areas (e.g., retelling a story, explaining a science process, reporting on a current event, recounting a memorable experience, etc.) with moderate support.
PI.4.9.Br	Plan and deliver oral presentations on a variety of topics in a variety of content areas (e.g., retelling a story, explaining a science process, reporting on a current event, recounting a memorable experience, etc.) with light support.

Grade 4 California English Language Development Standards

10. Writing	
PI.4.10.Em	a) Write short literary and informational texts (e.g., a description of a flashlight) collaboratively (e.g., joint construction of texts with an adult or with peers) and sometimes independently. b) Write brief summaries of texts and experiences using complete sentences and key words (e.g., from notes or graphic organizers).
PI.4.10.Ex	a) Write longer literary and informational texts (e.g., an explanatory text on how flashlights work) collaboratively (e.g., joint construction of texts with an adult or with peers) and with increasing independence using appropriate text organization. b) Write increasingly concise summaries of texts and experiences using complete sentences and key words (e.g., from notes or graphic organizers).
PI.4.10.Br	a) Write longer and more detailed literary and informational texts (e.g., an explanatory text on how flashlights work) collaboratively (e.g., joint construction of texts with an adult or with peers) and independently using appropriate text organization and growing understanding of register. b) Write clear and coherent summaries of texts and experiences using complete and concise sentences and key words (e.g., from notes or graphic organizers).
11. Supporting opinions	
PI.4.11.Em	a) Support opinions by expressing appropriate/accurate reasons using textual evidence (e.g., referring to text) or relevant background knowledge about content with substantial support. b) Express ideas and opinions or temper statements using basic modal expressions (e.g., *can, will, maybe*).
PI.4.11.Ex	a) Support opinions or persuade others by expressing appropriate/accurate reasons using some textual evidence (e.g., paraphrasing facts) or relevant background knowledge about content with moderate support. b) Express attitude and opinions or temper statements with familiar modal expressions (e.g., *maybe/probably, can/must*).
PI.4.11.Br	a) Support opinions or persuade others by expressing appropriate/accurate reasons using detailed textual evidence (e.g., quotations or specific events from text) or relevant background knowledge about content with light support. b) Express attitude and opinions or temper statements with nuanced modal expressions (e.g., *probably/certainly, should/would*) and phrasing (e.g., *In my opinion . . .*).
12. Selecting language resources	
PI.4.12.Em	a) Use a select number of general academic and domain-specific words to create precision while speaking and writing. b) Select a few frequently used affixes for accuracy and precision (e.g., She walk*s*, I'm *un*happy.).

Grade 4 California English Language Development Standards

PI.4.12.Ex	a) Use a growing number of general academic and domain-specific words, synonyms, and antonyms to create precision and shades of meaning while speaking and writing. b) Select a growing number of frequently used affixes for accuracy and precision (e.g., She walk*ed*. He like*s* . . . , I'm *un*happy.).
PI.4.12.Br	a) Use a wide variety of general academic and domain-specific words, synonyms, antonyms, and figurative language to create precision and shades of meaning while speaking and writing. b) Select a variety of appropriate affixes for accuracy and precision (e.g., She's walk*ing*. I'm *un*comfortable. They left reluctant*ly*.).
PART II: LEARNING ABOUT HOW ENGLISH WORKS	
A. Structuring Cohesive Texts	
1. Understanding text structure	
PII.4.1.Em	Apply understanding of how different text types are organized to express ideas (e.g., how a narrative is organized sequentially) to comprehending texts and writing basic texts.
PII.4.1.Ex	Apply increasing understanding of how different text types are organized to express ideas (e.g., how a narrative is organized sequentially with predictable stages versus how an explanation is organized around ideas) to comprehending texts and writing texts with increasing cohesion.
PII.4.1.Br	Apply understanding of how different text types are organized to express ideas (e.g., how a narrative is organized sequentially with predictable stages versus how opinions/arguments are structured logically, grouping related ideas) to comprehending texts and writing cohesive texts.
2. Understanding cohesion	
PII.4.2.Em	a) Apply basic understanding of language resources for referring the reader back or forward in text (e.g., how pronouns refer back to nouns in text) to comprehending texts and writing basic texts. b) Apply basic understanding of how ideas, events, or reasons are linked throughout a text using everyday connecting words or phrases (e.g., *first, yesterday*) to comprehending texts and writing basic texts.
PII.4.2.Ex	a) Apply growing understanding of language resources for referring the reader back or forward in text (e.g., how pronouns or synonyms refer back to nouns in text) to comprehending texts and writing texts with increasing cohesion. b) Apply growing understanding of how ideas, events, or reasons are linked throughout a text using a variety of connecting words or phrases (e.g., *since, next, for example*) to comprehending texts and writing texts with increasing cohesion.

Grade 4 California English Language Development Standards

PII.4.2.Br	a) Apply increasing understanding of language resources for referring the reader back or forward in text (e.g., how pronouns, synonyms, or nominalizations refer back to nouns in text) to comprehending texts and writing cohesive texts. b) Apply increasing understanding of how ideas, events, or reasons are linked throughout a text using an increasing variety of academic connecting and transitional words or phrases (e.g., *for instance, in addition, at the end*) to comprehending texts and writing cohesive texts.
B. Expanding and Enriching Ideas	
3. Using verbs and verb phrases	
PII.4.3.Em	Use various verbs/verb types (e.g., *doing, saying, being/having, thinking/feeling*) and tenses appropriate for the text type and discipline (e.g., simple past for recounting an experience) for familiar topics.
PII.4.3.Ex	Use various verbs/verb types (e.g., *doing, saying, being/having, thinking/feeling*) and tenses appropriate for the task, text type, and discipline (e.g., simple past for retelling, timeless present for science explanation) for an increasing variety of familiar and new topics.
PII.4.3.Br	Use various verbs/verb types (e.g., *doing, saying, being/having, thinking/feeling*) and tenses appropriate for the task and text type (e.g., timeless present for science explanation, mixture of past and present for historical information report) for a variety of familiar and new topics.
4. Using nouns and noun phrases	
PII.4.4.Em	Expand noun phrases in simple ways (e.g., adding an adjective) in order to enrich the meaning of sentences and add details about ideas, people, things, etc.
PII.4.4.Ex	Expand noun phrases in a variety of ways (e.g., adding adjectives to noun phrases or simple clause embedding) in order to enrich the meaning of sentences and add details about ideas, people, things, etc.
PII.4.4.Br	Expand noun phrases in an increasing variety of ways (e.g., adding general academic adjectives and adverbs to noun phrases or more complex clause embedding) in order to enrich the meaning of sentences and add details about ideas, people, things, etc.
5. Modifying to add details	
PII.4.5.Em	Expand sentences with familiar adverbials (e.g., basic prepositional phrases) to provide details (e.g., time, manner, place, cause, etc.) about a familiar activity or process (e.g., They walked *to the soccer field.*).
PII.4.5.Ex	Expand sentences with a growing variety of adverbials (e.g., adverbs, prepositional phrases) to provide details (e.g., time, manner, place, cause, etc.) about a familiar or new activity or process (e.g., They worked *quietly*. They ran *across the soccer field.*).
PII.4.5.Br	Expand sentences with a variety of adverbials (e.g., adverbs, adverb phrases, prepositional phrases) to provide details (e.g., time, manner, place, cause, etc.) about a variety of familiar and new activities and processes (e.g., They worked *quietly all night in their room.*).

Grade 4 California English Language Development Standards

C. Connecting and Condensing Ideas	
6. Connecting ideas	
PII.4.6.Em	Combine clauses in a few basic ways to make connections between and join ideas in sentences (e.g., creating compound sentences using coordinate conjunctions, such as *and, but, so*).
PII.4.6.Ex	Combine clauses in an increasing variety of ways (e.g., creating complex sentences using familiar subordinate conjunctions) to make connections between and join ideas in sentences, for example, to express cause/effect (e.g., *The deer ran because the mountain lion came.*) or to make a concession (e.g., She studied all night *even though* she wasn't feeling well.).
PII.4.6.Br	Combine clauses in a wide variety of ways (e.g., creating complex sentences using a variety of subordinate conjunctions) to make connections between and join ideas, for example, to express cause/effect (e.g., *Since the lion was at the waterhole, the deer ran away.*), to make a concession, or to link two ideas that happen at the same time (e.g., *The cubs played while their mother hunted.*).
7. Condensing ideas	
PII.4.7.Em	Condense clauses in simple ways (e.g., through simple embedded clauses as in, The woman is a doctor. She helps children. → The woman is a doctor *who helps children.*) to create precise and detailed sentences.
PII.4.7.Ex	Condense clauses in an increasing variety of ways (e.g., through a growing number of embedded clauses and other condensing as in, The dog ate quickly. The dog choked. → The dog ate so quickly *that it choked.*) to create precise and detailed sentences.
PII.4.7.Br	Condense clauses in a variety of ways (e.g., through various types of embedded clauses and other ways of condensing as in, There was a Gold Rush. It began in the 1850s. It brought a lot of people to California. → The Gold Rush *that began in the 1850s* brought a lot of people to California.) to create precise and detailed sentences.
Part III: Using Foundational Literacy Skills	
Foundational Literacy Skills (See Appendix A-Grade Four):	
	Literacy in an Alphabetic Writing System • Print concepts • Phonological awareness • Phonics & word recognition • Fluency